THIRD EDITION

Reader's Choice

E. Margaret Baudoin
Ellen S. Bober
Mark A. Clarke
Barbara K. Dobson
Sandra Silberstein

*Developed under the auspices
of the English Language Institute
at The University of Michigan*

Revised by

Mark A. Clarke
University of Colorado at Denver

Barbara K. Dobson
University of Michigan

Sandra Silberstein
University of Washington

Ann Arbor

THE UNIVERSITY OF MICHIGAN PRESS

Copyright © by the University of Michigan 1977, 1988, 1994
All rights reserved
ISBN 0-472-08265-5
Library of Congress Catalog Card No. 94-60411
Published in the United States of America by
The University of Michigan Press
Manufactured in the United States of America

2001   2000   1999   1998   7   6   5   4

Reader's Choice

Acknowledgments

As we enter our third decade of collaboration, we would like to thank spouses and children who have endured countless hours of conference calls and overnight-mail runs. Thanks are also due Sue Hodes and Sharon Tsutsui for thoughtful comments on this edition. And we are especially fortunate to have had the skilled and enthusiastic support of the University of Michigan Press: Associate Editor Chris Milton has been correcting us for as long as we can remember; Executive Editor LeAnn Fields first persuaded us that our sanity could withstand revision; Assistant Director Mary Erwin erased our memories of the first revision; and Director Colin Day has paid the bills.

Ann Arbor, Denver, Seattle, February 1994

We thank the many teachers who, over the years, have provided insights and suggestions for revision. To the roll call from the previous edition, we add the following names and apologize for any omissions: Sally Alexander, Kathryn Allahyari, Carol Deselams, Patricia A. Carrell, Joan Eisterhold, Pat Grogan, Liz Hamp-Lyons, Linda Hillman, Sara Klinghammer, Cherie Lenz-Hackett, Ellen Lipp, Daphne Mackey, Sharon Myers, Marnie Ramker, Sam Shepherd, Jerry Stanfield, Marianne Wieferich, Kay Winfield. We are grateful to our colleagues and to the dynamic context of TESOL reading pedagogy and research. Similarly, we continue to benefit from the contributions of our coauthors on the first edition, Margaret Baudoin Metzinger and Ellen Bober.

Special thanks to research assistants Elisabeth Mitchell, University of Washington, and Kathy Riley, University of Colorado at Denver, and to our colleagues at the University of Michigan Press.

Finally, we once again thank our families for continued support and patience toward a task that, no doubt, they hoped they had seen the last of.

Denver, Detroit, Seattle, June 1987

The successful completion of *Reader's Choice* is the result of the cooperation, confidence, and endurance of many people. The authors greatly appreciate the contributions of the individuals listed below. It is impossible to overestimate the importance of their efforts in helping us meet deadlines, their insights during classroom testing, and their encouragement through critique and rewrite sessions.

Heartfelt thanks, therefore to:

H. Douglas Brown, director of the English Language Institute (ELI), University of Michigan, whose assistance ranged from personal and professional advice to administrative and financial support. Professor Brown has consistently encouraged creativity and innovation at the ELI. His continued support of *Readers' Choice* ensured its successful completion.

Eleanor Foster, ELI administrative assistant and her capable secretarial and production staff: Elaine Allen, Ginny Barnett, Shelly Cole, Gail Curtis, Lynne Davis, Sue Feldstein, Martha Graham, Donna Head, Barbara Kerwin, Debbie Milly, Lisa Neff, Cathy Pappas, and Louisa Plyler.

George E. Luther and Roderick D. Fraser, ELI administrators, whose efforts made possible financial support and the classroom testing of *Reader's Choice*.

David P. Harris, director of the American Language Institute, Georgetown University; ELI authors Joan Morley and Mary Lawrence; Betsy Soden, ELI lecturer and reading coordinator; Carlos A. Yorio, professor of Linguistics, Toronto University—colleagues in English as a second language (ESL) whose critiques of early drafts proved invaluable.

ESL teachers whose patient and skillful use of the materials through numerous stages of development made detailed revisions and improvements possible—Honor Griffith and Lynne Kurylo of the University of Toronto; Betsy Berriman, Cristin Carpenter, Eve Daniels, Susan Dycus, Adelaide Heyde, Wayne Lord, Michele McCullough, Nancy Morrison, Syd Rand, and John Schafer of the English Language Institute.

And finally, thank you to Mario, Patricia, Tom, and Doug, friends and family for their patience and support; our parents and children, for whose pride and enthusiasm we are grateful; our students, whose insightful suggestions made revisions possible; and all the teachers and staff of the English Language Institute for providing an atmosphere which nurtures innovative teaching and creative materials development.

The authors wish to gratefully acknowledge grants from the English Language Institute and *Language Learning*, which provided funds for released time for several of the authors, and for secretarial and production assistance.

Ann Arbor, June 1977

Grateful acknowledgment is made to the following for permission to reprint previously published material.

Aldine de Gruyter for "The Changing Family," an adaptation of "Historical Perspectives on the Development of the Family and Parent-Child Interactions" by Maris Vinovskis. Reprinted with permission, from: Jane B. Lancaster, Jeanne Altmann, Alice S. Rossi, and Lonnie R. Sherrod, Editors, *Parenting Across the Life Span* (New York: Aldine de Gruyter). Copyright © 1987 by the Social Science Research Council. "The Changing Family" first appeared in *LSA* magazine.

American Automobile Association for Nashville map and for portions of Kentucky/Tennessee map and accompanying index, legend, and Driving Distances Chart. © AAA—Reproduced by permission.

Ann Arbor News for "Pockety Women Unite?" by Jane Myers, Staff Reporter, *Ann Arbor News*, September 22, 1974.

Associated Press for "Parents Seeking Cool Classroom for Son."

Beacon Press for adapted excerpts from *Deception Detection* by Jeffrey Schrank. Copyright © 1975 by Jeffrey Schrank. Reprinted by permission of Beacon Press.

Christian Science Publishing Society for "Unfolding Bud" by Naoshi Koriyama, © 1957 The Christian Science Publishing Society. Reprinted by permission from *The Christian Science Monitor.* All rights reserved.

William Collins and World Publishing Company, Inc., for material from *Webster's New World Dictionary,* College Edition, copyright © 1966 by The World Publishing Company. With permission.

Detroit Free Press for material from "The Calendar," *Detroit Free Press,* April 4, 1976.

Encyclopaedia Britannica for material adapted from "Jenner, Edward" in *Encyclopaedia Britannica,* 15th edition (1986), 6:530.

Farrar, Straus and Giroux, Inc., and Brandt and Brandt for "The Lottery" from *The Lottery* by Shirley Jackson. Copyright © 1948, 1949 by Shirley Jackson. Copyright renewed © 1976, 1977 by Laurence Hyman, Barry Hyman, Mrs. Sarah Webster, and Mrs. Joanne Schnurer. "The Lottery" originally appeared in the *New Yorker.* Reprinted by permission of Farrar, Straus and Giroux, Inc.

Features and News Service for adaptation of "How Do You Handle Everyday Stress?" by Dr. Syvil Marquit and Marilyn Lane.

The Futurist, for "World Population Growth Rate Slows," May-June 1990. Reproduced with permission from *The Futurist,* published by the World Future Society, 7910 Woodmont Avenue, Suite 450, Bethesda, Maryland 20814.

Grolier for "Addams, Jane," Austen, Jane," "Dionne Quintuplets," "Curie, Pierre and Marie," and "Eddy, Mary Baker." Reprinted with permission of *The Encyclopedia Americana,* © 1983, by Grolier Inc.

Harcourt Brace & Company for "Fueled" from *Serve Me a Slice of Moon,* copyright © 1965 by Marcie Hans and renewed 1993 by Ernestine Hans; and for "American Values in Education" excerpted from *American Civics,* Second Edition, by William H. Hartley & Company © 1974 by Harcourt Brace & Company. Reprinted by permission of the publisher.

Harper and Row for material adapted from *Cheaper by the Dozen,* copyright 1948, © 1963 by Frank B. Gilbreth, Jr., and Ernestine Gilbreth Carey; for "The Milgram Experiment," adapted from "Blind Obedience to Authority" from *Psychology: The Frontiers of Behavior* by Ronald E. Smith, Irwin G. Sarason, and Barbara R. Sarason, copyright © 1978 by Ronald E. Smith; and for table, figure, and excerpt from *Obedience to Authority* by Stanley Milgram, copyright © 1974 by Stanley Milgram. Reprinted by permission of Harper and Row, Publishers, Inc.

Harper's Magazine Company for "The Odds for Long Life" by Robert Collins. Copyright © 1973 by *Harper's* Magazine. Reprinted from the May, 1973, issue by special permission.

Houghton Mifflin Company for material from *The American Heritage Dictionary of the English Language.* Copyright © 1969, 1970, 1971, 1973, 1975, 1976, Houghton Mifflin Company. Reprinted by permission from *The American Heritage Dictionary of the English Language.*

Houghton Mifflin Company and William Collins Sons and Company for an adapted excerpt from *In the Shadow of Man* by Jane van Lawick-Goodall. Copyright © 1971 by Hugo and Jane van Lawick-Goodall. Reprinted by permission of Houghton Mifflin Company.

King Features for two "Sally Forth" cartoons. Reprinted with special permission of King Features Syndicate, Inc.

Ladies' Home Journal for "Why We Laugh" by Janet Spencer, *Ladies' Home Journal,* November, 1974.

Liveright Publishing Corporation and W. W. Norton for "in Just-" which is reprinted from *Tulips & Chimneys* by E. E. Cummings by permission of Liveright Publishing Corporation. Copyright 1923, 1925 and renewed 1951, 1953 by E. E. Cummings. Copyright © 1973, 1976 by The Trustees for the E. E. Cummings Trust. Copyright © 1973, 1976 by George James Firmage.

Harold Matson Company for "The Chaser" by John Collier. Copyright 1940, © renewed 1968 by John Collier. Reprinted by permission of Harold Matson Company, Inc.

Merriam-Webster, Inc., for dictionary entries for "book," "draw," "skirt," "spot" from *Merriam-Webster's Collegiate Dictionary,* Springfield, Mass.

Michigan Daily for selected advertisements from the classified section, *Michigan Daily,* November 19, 1976.

Harry Miles Muheim for "The Dusty Drawer" by Harry Miles Muheim. Copyright © 1969 by Harry Miles Muheim. Published in *Alfred Hitchcock Presents a Month of Mystery,* copyright © 1969 by Random House, Inc. Reprinted by permission of the author.

New Directions Publishing Corporation and Carcanet New Press Ltd. for "This is Just to Say" by William Carlos Williams, from *Collected Poems, Volume I: 1909–1939.* Copyright 1938 by New Directions Publishing Corporation.

Newspaper Enterprise Association for "Quick Reference Index," "Waterfalls," and "Years of Life Expectancy" from *The World Almanac and Book of Facts,* 1987 edition, copyright © Newspaper Enterprise Association, Inc. 1986, New York, NY 10166.

Newsweek for adaptations of the following articles: "A Burning Issue on the Job and Off" by Ian M. Rolland and Bernard J. Dushman, copyright 1986, Newsweek, Inc.; "Sonar for the Blind" by Matt Clark and Susan Agrest, copyright © 1975 by Newsweek, Inc.; "Graveyard of the Atlantic," copyright © 1974 by Newsweek, Inc.; and "Conjugal Prep," copyright © 1975 by Newsweek, Inc. All rights reserved. Reprinted by permission.

New York Times for "Major Personality Study Finds That Traits Are Mostly Inherited" by Daniel Goleman, *New York Times,* December 2, 1986, copyright © 1986 by The New York Times Company; and for "Japanese Style in Decision-Making" by Yoshio Terasawa, *New York Times,* May 12, 1974, copyright © 1974 by The New York Times Company. Reprinted by permission.

W. W. Norton and The Bodley Head for material reprinted from *The City* by John V. Lindsay by permission of W. W. Norton & Company, Inc. Copyright © 1969, 1970 by W. W. Norton & Company, Inc.

Opera Mundi, Inc., for "Class Day," "Ruth's Birthday," "The Ex-Wife Murder," "Case 463," "Murder on Board," "Death in the Mountains," "Case #194," and "The Break" from *Minute Mysteries* by Austin Ripley.

Overseas Development Council for material from "The Sacred Rac" by Patricia Hughes, in *Focusing on Global Poverty and Development* by Jayne C. Millar (Washington, D.C.: Overseas Development Council, 1974), pp. 357-58. Reprinted by permission.

Random House for an adaptation of "The Midnight Visitor." Copyright 1939 and renewed 1967 by Robert Arthur. Reprinted from *Mystery and More Mystery* by Robert Arthur, by permission of Random House, Inc.

Random House and William Morris Agency for adapted excerpts from *Iberia* by James Michener. Copyright © 1968 by Random House, Inc. Reprinted by permission of Random House, Inc., and by permission of William Morris Agency, Inc., on behalf of the author.

Reader's Digest for "America's New Merchants of Death," by William Ecenberger, Reprinted with permission from the April 1993 *Reader's Digest.* Copyright © 1993 by The Reader's Digest Assn., Inc.

Marian Reiner for "How to Eat a Poem" from *Jamboree: Rhymes for All Times* by Eve Merriam. Copyright © 1962, 1964, 1966, 1973, 1984 by Eve Merriam. All rights reserved. Reprinted by permission of Marian Reiner for the author.

Robert Ritter for "Graveyard of the Atlantic" illustration.

Melvin Schnapper for "Your Actions Speak Louder . . . ," *Peace Corps: The Volunteer,* June, 1969.

Science News for the following articles: "The Trouble State of Calculus," April 5, 1986; "People in Americas before Last Ice Age?" June 28, 1986; and "Babies Sound Off: The Power of Babble," June 21, 1986. Reprinted with permission from *Science News,* the weekly newsmagazine of science, copyright 1986 by Science Service, Inc.

Smithsonian for "Summits of Yore: Promises, Promises, and a Deal or Two," *Smithsonian,* September 1986.

May Swenson for the following poems: "By Morning," "Living Tenderly," and "Southbound on the Freeway," by May Swenson. Used by permission of the author from *Poems to Solve,* copyright © 1966 by May Swenson.

Two Trees Press for "Oregon," in *Admission Requirements for International Students* by Virginia M. Packwood and William T. Packwood, Fargo, N.D.

Universal Press Syndicate for "Love Handles" and "Doonesbury" cartoons. Love Handles copyright 1987 Universal Press Syndicate. Doonesbury copyright 1987 G. B. Trudeau. Reprinted with permission of Universal Press Syndicate. All rights reserved.

U.S. News and World Report for "Crowded Earth—Billions More Coming," for copyright 1974 U.S. News & World Report, reprinted from issue of October 21, 1974.

Viking Penguin and Granada Publishing for adapted excerpts from *My Family and Other Animals* by Gerald Durrell. Copyright © 1956 by Gerald M. Durrell. All rights reserved. Reprinted by permission of Viking Penguin Inc. and Granada Publishing Ltd.

Washington Post Syndicate for "Happy Customers Matter of Honor among Japanese," © The Washington Post.

Wesleyan University Press for "Looking in the Album" by Vern Rutsala. Copyright © 1961 by Vern Rutsala. Reprinted from *The Window* by permission of Wesleyan University Press.

World Monitor for "Smoke Alert: Who's Puffing 5 Trillion Cigarettes," *World Monitor,* 8 October 1991, "The Map."

Every effort has been made to trace the ownership of all copyrighted material in this book and to obtain permission for its use.

Contents

        Composition Foci: Arguing a Point of View / Presenting an Opinion
        "In the Shadow of Man," Jane van Lawick-Goodall   310

        Appendix   321

        Answer Key   323

Introduction

To Students and Teachers

Reader's Choice is a reading textbook for students of English as a second or foreign language. The authors of *Reader's Choice* believe that reading is an active, problem-solving process. This book is based on the theory that proficient reading requires the coordination of a number of skills. Proficient reading depends on the reader's ability to select the proper skills or strategies to solve each reading problem. Efficient readers determine beforehand why they are reading a particular selection and they decide which strategies and skills they will use to achieve their goals. They develop expectations about the kinds of information they will find in a passage and read to determine if their expectations are correct. The exercises and readings in *Reader's Choice* will help students to become independent, efficient readers.

When you look at the Contents page you will notice that there are three kinds of units in *Reader's Choice*. The odd-numbered units (1 through 11) contain skills exercises. These exercises give students intensive practice in developing their ability to obtain the maximum amount of information from a reading selection using the minimum number of language clues. The even-numbered units (2 through 12) contain reading selections that give students the opportunity to use the skills they have learned, to interact with and evaluate the ideas of texts. Finally, Units 13, 14, and 15 consist of longer, more complex reading selections.

Basic language and reading skills are introduced in early units and reinforced throughout the book. The large number of exercises presented gives students repeated practice. Students should not be discouraged if they do not finish each exercise, if they have trouble answering specific questions, or if they do not understand everything in a particular reading. The purpose of the tasks in *Reader's Choice* is to help students improve their problem-solving skills. For this reason, the process of attempting to answer a question is often as important as the answer itself.

Reader's Choice contains exercises that give students practice in both language and reading skills. In this Introduction we will first provide a description of language skills exercises followed by a description of the reading skills work contained in the book.

Language Skills Exercises

Word Study Exercises

Upon encountering an unfamiliar vocabulary item in a passage there are several strategies readers can use to determine the message of the author. First, they can continue reading, realizing that often a single word will not prevent understanding of the general meaning of a selection. If further reading does not solve the problem, readers can use one or more of three basic skills to arrive at an understanding of the unfamiliar word. They can use context clues to see if surrounding words and grammatical structures provide information about the unknown word. They can use word analysis to see if understanding the parts of the word leads to an understanding of the word. Or, they can use a dictionary to find an appropriate definition. *Reader's Choice* contains numerous exercises that provide practice in these three skills.

Word Study: Vocabulary from Context
Guessing the meaning of an unfamiliar word from context clues involves using the following kinds of information:
  a) knowledge of the topic about which you are reading
  b) knowledge of the meanings of the other words in the sentence (or paragraph) in which the word occurs
  c) knowledge of the grammatical structure of the sentences in which the word occurs
Exercises that provide practice in this skill are called Vocabulary from Context exercises.

When these exercises appear in skills units, their purpose is to provide students with practice in guessing the meaning of unfamiliar words using context clues. Students should not necessarily try to learn the meanings of the vocabulary items in these exercises. The Vocabulary from Context exercises that appear with reading selections have a different purpose. Generally these exercises should be done before a reading selection is begun and used as an introduction to the reading. The vocabulary items have been chosen for three reasons:

   a) because they are fairly common, and therefore useful for students to learn
   b) because they are important for an understanding of the passage
   c) because their meanings are not easily available from the context in the selection

Word Study: Stems and Affixes

Another way to discover the meanings of unfamiliar vocabulary items is to use word analysis, that is, to use knowledge of the meanings of the parts of a word. Many English words have been formed by combining parts of older English, Greek, and Latin words. For instance, the word bicycle is formed from the parts *bi*, meaning two, and *cycle*, meaning round or wheel. Often knowledge of the meanings of these word parts can help the reader to guess the meaning of an unfamiliar word. Exercises providing practice in this skill occur at regular intervals throughout the book. The Appendix lists all of the stems and affixes that appear in these exercises.

Word Study: Dictionary Use

Sometimes the meaning of a single word is essential to an understanding of the total meaning of a selection. If context clues and word analysis do not provide enough information, it will be necessary to use a dictionary. We believe that advanced students should use an English/English dictionary. The Word Study: Dictionary Use exercises in the skills units provide students with a review of the information available from dictionaries and practice in using a dictionary to obtain that information. The Dictionary Study exercises that accompany some of the reading selections require students to use the context of an unfamiliar vocabulary item to find an appropriate definition of these items from the dictionary entries provided.

Sentence Study Exercises

Sometimes comprehension of an entire passage requires the understanding of a single sentence. Sentence Study exercises give students practice in analyzing the structure of sentences to determine the relationships of ideas within a sentence. Students are presented with a complicated sentence followed by tasks that require them to analyze the sentence for its meaning. Often the student is required to use the available information to draw inferences about the author's message.

Paragraph Reading and Paragraph Analysis Exercises

These exercises give students practice in understanding how the arrangement of ideas affects the overall meaning of a passage. Some of the paragraph exercises are designed to provide practice in discovering the general message. Students are required to determine the main idea of a passage: that is, the idea which is the most important, around which the paragraph is organized. Other paragraph exercises are meant to provide practice in careful, detailed reading. Students are required not only to find the main idea of a passage, but also to guess vocabulary meanings of words from context, to answer questions about specific details in the paragraph, and to draw conclusions based on their understanding of the passage.

Discourse Focus

Effective reading requires the ability to select skills and strategies appropriate to a specific reading task. The reading process involves using information from the full text and information from the world in order to interpret a passage. Readers use this information to make predictions about what they will find in a text, and to decide how they will read. Sometimes we need to read quickly to obtain only a general idea of a text; at other times we read carefully, drawing inferences about the intent of the author. Discourse-level exercises introduce these various approaches to reading, which are then reinforced throughout the book. These reading skills are described in more detail in the discussion that follows.

Nonprose Reading

Throughout *Reader's Choice* students are presented with nonprose selections (such as a menu, bus schedule, road map, etc.) so that they can practice using their skills to read material that is not arranged in sentences and paragraphs. It is important to remember that the same problem-solving skills are used to read both prose and nonprose material.

Reading Skills Exercises

Students will need to use all of their language skills in order to understand the reading selections in *Reader's Choice*. The book contains many types of selections on a wide variety of topics. These selections provide practice in using different reading strategies to comprehend texts. They also give students practice in four basic reading skills: skimming, scanning, reading for thorough comprehension, and critical reading.

Skimming

Skimming is quick reading for the general idea(s) of a passage. This kind of rapid reading is appropriate when trying to decide if careful reading would be desirable or when there is not time to read something carefully.

Scanning

Like skimming, scanning is also quick reading. However, in this case the search is more focused. To scan is to read quickly in order to locate specific information. When you read to find a particular date, name, or number, you are scanning.

Reading for Thorough Comprehension

Reading for thorough comprehension is careful reading in order to understand the total meaning of the passage. At this level of comprehension the reader is able to summarize the author's ideas but has not yet made a critical evaluation of those ideas.

Critical Reading

Critical reading demands that readers make judgments about what they read. This kind of reading requires posing and answering questions such as *Does my own experience support that of the author? Do I share the author's point of view? Am I convinced by the author's arguments and evidence?*

Systematic use of the exercises and readings in *Reader's Choice* will give students practice in the basic language and reading skills necessary to become proficient readers. Additional suggestions for the use of *Reader's Choice* in a classroom setting are included in the section To the Teacher.

To the Teacher

It is impossible to outline one best way to use a textbook; there are as many ways to use *Reader's Choice* as there are creative teachers. However, based on the experiences of teachers and students who have worked with *Reader's Choice*, we provide the following suggestions to facilitate classroom use. First, we outline general guidelines for the teaching of reading; second, we provide hints for teaching specific exercises and readings in the book; and finally, we suggest a sample lesson plan.

General Guidelines

The ultimate goal of *Reader's Choice* is to produce independent readers who are able to determine their own goals for a reading task, then use the appropriate skills and strategies to reach those goals. For this reason, we believe the best learning environment is one in which all individuals—students and teachers—participate in the process of setting and achieving goals. A certain portion of class time is therefore profitably spent in discussing reading tasks before they are begun. If the topic is a new one for the students, teachers are encouraged to provide and/or access background information for the students, adapting the activities under Before You Begin to specific teaching contexts. When confronted with a specific passage, students should become accustomed to the practice of skimming it quickly, taking note of titles and subheadings, pictures, graphs, etc., in an attempt to determine the most efficient approach to the task. In the process, they should develop expectations about the content of the passage and the amount of time and effort needed to accomplish their goals. In this type of setting students are encouraged to offer their opinions and ask for advice, to teach each other and to learn from their errors.

Reader's Choice was written to encourage maximum flexibility in classroom use. Because of the large variety of exercises and reading selections, the teacher can plan several tasks for each class and hold in reserve a number of appropriate exercises to use as the situation demands. In addition, the exercises have been developed to make possible variety in classroom dynamics. The teacher should encourage the independence of students by providing opportunities for work in small groups, pairs, or individually. Small group work in which students self-correct homework assignments has also been successful.

Exercises do not have to be done in the order in which they are presented. In fact, we suggest interspersing skills work with reading selections. One way to vary reading tasks is to plan lessons around pairs of units, alternating skills exercises with the reading selections. In the process, the teacher can show students how focused skills work transfers to the reading of longer passages. For example, Sentence Study exercises provide intensive practice in analyzing grammatical structures to understand sentences; this same skill should be used by students in working through reading selections. When communication breaks down, the teacher can pull sentences from readings for intensive classroom analysis, thereby demonstrating the value of this skill.

It is important to *teach, then test*. Tasks should be thoroughly introduced, modeled, and practiced before students are expected to perform on their own. Although we advocate rapid-paced, demanding class sessions, we believe it is extremely important to provide students with a thorough introduction to each new exercise. At least for the first example of each type of exercise, some oral work is necessary. The teacher can demonstrate the skill using the example item, and work through the first few items with the class as a whole. Students can then work individually or in small groups.

Specific Suggestions

Reader's Choice has been organized so that specific skills can be practiced before students use those skills to attack reading selections. Although exercises and readings are generally graded according to difficulty, it is not necessary to use the material in the order in which it is presented. Teachers are encouraged:

   a) to intersperse skills work with reading selections
   b) to skip exercises that are too easy or irrelevant to students' interests
   c) to do several exercises of a specific type at one time if students require intensive practice in that skill
   d) to jump from unit to unit, selecting reading passages that satisfy students' interests and needs
   e) to sequence longer readings as appropriate for their students either by interspersing them among other readings and skills work, or by presenting them at the end of the course

Language Skills Exercises

Nonprose Reading

For students who expect to read only prose material, teachers can point out that nonprose reading provides more than an enjoyable change of pace. These exercises provide legitimate reading practice. The same problem-solving skills can be used for both prose and nonprose material. Just as one can skim a textbook for general ideas, it is possible to skim a menu for a general idea of the type of food offered, the price range of the restaurant, etc. Students may claim that they can't skim or scan; working with nonprose items shows them that they can.

Nonprose exercises are good for breaking the ice with new students, for beginning or ending class sessions, for role playing, or for those Monday blues and Friday blahs. Because they are short, rapid-paced exercises, they can be kept in reserve to provide variety, or to fill a time gap at the end of class.

The Menu, Newspaper Advertisements, Bus Schedule, and Road Map exercises present students with realistic language problems they might encounter in an English-speaking environment. The teacher can set up simulations to achieve a realistic atmosphere. The Questionnaire exercise is intended to provide practice in filling out forms. Since the focus is on following directions, students usually work individually.

With poetry, students' problem-solving skills are challenged by the economy of poetic writing. Poetry is especially good for reinforcing vocabulary from context skills, for comprehending through syntax clues, and for drawing inferences.

Word Study

These exercises can be profitably done in class either in rapid-paced group work or by alternating individual work with class discussion. Like nonprose work, Word Study exercises can be used to fill unexpected time gaps.

Context Clues exercises appear frequently throughout the book, both in skills units and with reading selections. Students should learn to be content with a general meaning of a word and to recognize situations in which it is not necessary to know a word's meaning. In skills units, these exercises should be done in class to ensure that students do not look for exact definitions in the dictionary. When Vocabulary from Context exercises appear with reading selections, they are intended as tools for learning new vocabulary items and often for introducing ideas to be encountered in the reading. In this case they can be done at home as well as in class.

Stems and Affixes exercises appear in five units and must be done in the order in which they are presented. The exercises are cumulative: each exercise makes use of word parts presented in previous units. All stems and affixes taught in *Reader's Choice* are listed in the Appendix with their definitions. These exercises serve as an important foundation in vocabulary skills work for students whose native language does not contain a large number of words derived from Latin or Greek. Students should focus on improving their ability to analyze word parts as they work with the words presented in the exercises. During the introduction to each exercise students should be encouraged to volunteer other examples of words containing the stems and affixes presented. Exercises 1 and 2 can be done as homework; the matching exercise can be used as a quiz.

Dictionary Study exercises provide review of information available in English/English dictionaries. Dictionary Use exercise 1 in Unit 1 requires a substantial amount of class discussion to introduce information necessary for dictionary work. Students should view the dictionary as the last resort when attempting to understand an unfamiliar word.

Sentence Study

Students should not be concerned about unfamiliar vocabulary in these exercises; grammatical clues should provide enough information to allow them to complete the tasks. In addition, questions are syntax based; errors indicate structures that students have trouble reading, thus providing the teacher with a diagnostic tool for grammar instruction.

Paragraph Reading and Paragraph Analysis

If Main Idea paragraphs are read in class, they may be timed. If the exercises are done at home, students can be asked to come to class prepared to defend their answers in group discussion. One way to stimulate discussion is to ask students to identify incorrect responses as too broad, too narrow, or false.

Restatement and Inference and Paragraph Analysis exercises are short enough to allow sentence-by-sentence analysis. These exercises provide intensive practice in syntax and vocabulary work. In the Paragraph Analysis exercises the lines are numbered to facilitate discussion.

Discourse Focus

Skimming and scanning activities should be done quickly in order to demonstrate to students the utility of these approaches for some tasks. The short mysteries can profit from group work, as students use specific elements of the text to defend their inferences. Prediction activities are designed to have students focus on the discourse signals that allow them to predict and sample texts. The diversity of student responses that emerges during group work can reinforce the notion that there is not a single correct answer, that all predictions are, by definition, only working hypotheses to be constantly revised.

Reading Selections

Teachers have found it valuable to introduce readings in terms of ideas, vocabulary, and syntax before students are asked to work on their own. The newly added section, Before You Begin, introduces the concepts and issues encountered in reading selections. Several types of classroom dynamics have been successful with reading selections after an introduction to the passage.

1. In class—teacher reads entire selection orally; or teacher reads part, students finish selection individually; or students read selection individually (perhaps under time constraint).
2. In class and at home—part of selection is read in class, followed by discussion; students finish reading at home.
3. At home—students read entire selection at home.

Comprehension questions are usually discussed in class with the class as a whole, in small groups, or in pairs. The paragraphs in the selections are numbered to facilitate discussion.

The teacher can pull out difficult vocabulary and/or sentences for intensive analysis and discussion.

Readings represent a variety of topics and styles. The exercises have been written to focus on the most obvious characteristics of each reading.

a) Fiction and personal experience narratives are to be read for enjoyment. Teachers often find it useful to read these to students, emphasizing humorous parts.

b) Well-organized readings with many facts and figures are appropriate for scanning and skimming. This type of reading can also be used in composition work as a model of organizational techniques.

c) If the reading is an editorial, essay, or other form of personal opinion, students should read critically to determine if they agree with the author. Students are encouraged to identify excerpts that reveal the author's bias or that can be used to challenge the validity of the author's argument.

d) Satire should be read both for enjoyment and for analysis of the author's comment on human affairs.

Longer Readings

These readings can be presented in basically the same manner as other selections in the book. Longer readings can be read either at the end of the course or at different points throughout the term. The schedule for working with longer readings is roughly as follows:

a) Readings are introduced by vocabulary exercises, discussion of the topic, reading and discussion of selected paragraphs.

b) Students read the selection at home and answer the comprehension questions. Students are allowed at least two days to complete the assignment.

c) In-class discussion of comprehension questions proceeds with students referring to the passage to support their answers.

d) The vocabulary review can be done either at home or in class.

e) Vocabulary questions raised on the off day between the assignment and the due day may be resolved with items from Vocabulary from Context exercises and Figurative Language and Idioms exercises.

"The Milgram Experiment" requires students to confront their own attitudes toward authority. The unit begins with a questionnaire that asks students to predict their behavior in particular situations and to compare their behavior with that of fellow natives of their culture and of Americans. Psychologist Stanley Milgram was concerned with the extent to which people would follow commands even when they thought they were hurting someone else. Because the results of the study are surprising and because most people have strong feelings about their own allegiance to authority and their commitment to independence, small group discussions and debriefing from the teacher will be important in this lesson.

"The Dusty Drawer" is a suspense story whose success as a teaching tool depends on students understanding the conflict between the two main characters. Teachers have found that a preliminary reading and discussion of the first eleven paragraphs serves as an introduction to the most important elements of the story. The discussion questions can be integrated into the discussion of comprehension questions.

"In the Shadow of Man" is well organized and may, therefore, be skimmed. Teachers can ask students to read the first and last sentences of the paragraphs, then paraphrase the general position of the author. Discussion of some Discussion/Composition items can serve as an effective introduction to the reading. In addition, some questions lead discussion away from the passage and might, therefore, lead to further reading on the topic. Some teachers may want to show the film *Miss Jane Goodall and the Wild Chimpanzees* (National Geographic Society; Encyclopedia Britannica Educational Films) in conjunction with this reading. Teachers should be aware that this selection raises the subject of evolution, a sensitive topic for students whose religious or personal beliefs deny evolutionary theory.

Answer Key

Because the exercises in *Reader's Choice* are designed to provide students with the opportunity to practice and improve their reading skills, the processes involved in arriving at an answer are often more important than the answer itself. It is expected that students will not use the Answer Key until they have completed the exercises and are prepared to defend their answers. If a student's answer does not agree with the Key, it is important for the student to return to the exercise to discover the source of the error. In a classroom setting, students should view the Answer Key as a last resort, to be used only when they cannot agree on an answer. The Answer Key also makes it possible for students engaged in independent study to use *Reader's Choice*.

Sample Lesson Plan

The following lesson plan is meant only as an example of how goals might be translated into practice. We do not imply that a particular presentation is the only one possible for a given reading activity, nor that the exercises presented here are the only activities possible to achieve our goals. The lesson plan demonstrates how skills work can be interspersed with reading selections.

It is assumed that the lessons described here would be presented after students have worked together for several weeks. This is important for two reasons. First, we hope that a nonthreatening atmosphere has been established in which people feel free to volunteer opinions and make guesses. Second, we assume that by now students recognize the importance of a problem-solving approach to reading and that they are working to improve skills and strategies using a variety of readings and exercises.

Although these lessons are planned for fifty-minute, daily classes, slight modification would make them appropriate for a number of other situations. Approximate time limits for each activity are indicated. The exercises and readings are taken from Units 7, 8, and 12.

Monday
Nonprose Reading: Poetry (20 minutes)
- *a*) The teacher points out that each poem is a puzzle; that students will have to use their reading skills to solve each one.
- *b*) The teacher reads the first poem aloud; students follow in their books.
- *c*) Discussion focuses on obtaining information from vocabulary and syntax clues and drawing inferences.
- *d*) If the students can't guess the subject of the poem, the class should do the Comprehension Clues exercise.
- *e*) The last two poems can be handled in the same manner or students can work individually with discussion following.

Reading Selection: Magazine Article ("Why We Laugh") (30 minutes)
Introduction:
- *a*) Discussion: Why do we laugh? Is laughter culturally conditioned? Do students think English jokes are funny?
- *b*) Vocabulary: Vocabulary from Context exercises 1 and 2; students work as a class or individually, with discussion following.
- *c*) Skimming: the teacher skims the article aloud, reading first (and sometimes second and last) sentences of each paragraph.
- *d*) Discussion: What is the main idea? What type of article is it? Is the author an expert? Who are the experts she quotes?
- *e*) As a group, students review main ideas by answering questions in Comprehension exercise 1.

Homework: Read "Why We Laugh"; do Comprehension exercise 2.

Tuesday
"Why We Laugh" (35 minutes)
  a) Work through Comprehension and Critical Reading exercises as a class, in small groups, or in pairs. Students should defend answers with portions of the text; emphasis is on convincing others or being convinced on the basis of the reading.
  b) Pull out, analyze, and discuss structure problems, difficult vocabulary.
  c) Wrap-up discussion proceeds from Critical Reading and Discussion questions.
Homework: Can include composition work based on Discussion/Composition topics.
Stems and Affixes (15 minutes)
  a) Introduction: students volunteer examples of words containing stems and affixes presented in the exercise.
  b) Class does exercise 1 orally as a group, if time permits.
Homework: Finish Stems and Affixes exercises.

Wednesday
Stems and Affixes (15 minutes)
  a) Go over as a class; students volunteer and defend answers.
  b) The Appendix can be used if a dispute arises concerning one of the stems or affixes presented in previous units.
  c) Work is fast paced and skills focused. Students concentrate on learning word parts.
Sentence Study: Restatement and Inference (35 minutes)
  a) The first one or two items are done orally. The teacher reads the sentence and the choices aloud and students mark answers in the book.
  b) Discussion follows. Students must defend answers using grammatical analysis of sentences.
  c) Students complete the exercise individually after which answers are discussed.
Word Study: Context Clues (if time permits)
  a) Group or individual work.
  b) Students arrive at a definition, synonym, or description of each word, then defend their answers by referring to the syntax and other vocabulary items in the sentence.

Thursday
Reading Selection: Narrative ("An Attack on the Family") (40 minutes)
  a) Discussion: What is it like to be the youngest child in the family?
  b) Vocabulary from Context: students work as a class or individually with discussion following.
  c) The teacher reads story aloud, students follow in their books.
  d) Students take ten minutes to answer Comprehension questions individually.
  e) Discussion follows. Students will have to examine the text carefully to answer the questions.
Paragraph Analysis: Reading for Full Understanding (10 minutes)
  a) The teacher reads the Example paragraph aloud. Students mark answers in their books.
  b) The class discusses the answers using the Explanation on pages 139–40.
Homework: Finish Paragraph Analysis exercise.

Friday
Paragraph Analysis (25 minutes)
  a) Discussion of the homework: students must use excerpts from the paragraphs to defend their answers or to refute the choices of other students.
  b) Grammatical analysis can be used to develop convincing arguments supporting the correct answers. Context clues often furnish the definition of unfamiliar words.

Reading Selection: Narrative ("The Lottery") (25 minutes)
    Introduction:
    a) Discussion of lotteries in general, lotteries in the students' countries.
    b) Vocabulary from Context exercise 1: students work as a class or individually with
        discussion following.
    c) The teacher reads the first nine paragraphs, discusses content, vocabulary, syntax with
        students. Most of Vocabulary from Context exercises 2 and 3 can be covered during this
        discussion.
Homework: Read "The Lottery"; do Comprehension exercises for Monday.

    This lesson plan represents an active, problem-solving approach to the teaching of ESL
reading. Students are required to do more than merely read passages and answer questions.
The type of reading that the students are asked to do varies from task to task. They skim
"Why We Laugh" to determine the main idea, then scan to find the answers to some of the
Comprehension questions. Sentence Study exercises require close grammatical analysis, just as
Stems and Affixes exercises require analysis of word parts. "Why We Laugh" and "The
Lottery" both require critical reading. The vocabulary and syntax work is presented as a tool
for comprehension, appropriate for helping students solve persistent reading problems.
    Within a single week, a great variety of activities is presented. In the course of any single lesson,
the tempo and tasks change several times. In the course of the week, virtually all language and
reading skills are reinforced in a variety of contexts and with a variety of materials. This variety has
important implications for the nature of the class and for the role of the teacher.
    The classroom dynamics change to fit the task. The poetry and the discussion sessions are
class activities, with students debating answers and opinions. The vocabulary and structure
exercises on Tuesday and Wednesday, as well as the paragraph work on Thursday and Friday,
might be organized as workshop sessions, giving students the chance to work at their own pace
and providing the teacher the opportunity to circulate and provide assistance as needed. By
selectively using individual, small-group, and class activities, the teacher hopes to give all
students the opportunity to work at a pace that suits them as individuals, while also assuring that
they get the opportunity to use language to communicate with each other.
    The role of the teacher also changes from activity to activity. During vocabulary and
structure work, the teacher teaches, providing help and encouragement as students work to
solve language problems. The teacher is a facilitator during the poetry and short passage
readings, intervening only in the event that linguistic expertise is needed to keep the discussion
going. In discussions of how readings relate to the "real world," the teacher is primarily a
participant on equal terms with the students in exploring mutually interesting topics. Of course,
the role and behavior of the teacher can change a number of times in the course of a class
session to suit the situation. It is hoped, however, that as the semester progresses, the teacher
as teacher will gradually be replaced by the teacher as facilitator and participant.
    Another important feature of this lesson plan is the opportunity provided to encourage
students to choose their own reading strategies and to apply the skills dictated by the strategy
chosen. It should be noted that "Why We Laugh" and "The Lottery" are introduced by the
teacher through vocabulary work and discussion, followed by skimming and scanning. This type
of introduction gives students the opportunity to develop expectations about the selection and,
guided by their expectations, to read more effectively. It is hoped that this procedure will be
repeated when students encounter similar readings in the future. Often the teacher will want to
simulate a "real life" situation by giving the students a task and asking them how they would
approach it. The approach to a newspaper editorial, for example, might be quite different
depending on whether the selection is read for pleasure or for a university political science
course.
    Throughout the semester, students are taught to shift gears, to vary their reading strategies
according to their goals for the selection at hand. As they become more proficient readers, we
expect them to determine for themselves what they read, why they read it, and how they read it.

FOR YOUR LATE
BREAKFAST PLEASURE . . .

TWO FRESH EGGS, Any Style
  With Toast & Jelly 3.50
  With Fried Ham, Bacon
  or Sausage 4.50
FLUFFY PANCAKES,
  With Syrup & Butter . . . 3.75
  With Fried Ham, Bacon
  or Sausage 4.75
ONE EGG 2.35
No Price Reduction on Orders
without Toast & Jelly

Cocktails

BEFORE DINNER COCKTAILS

Manhattan 2.50
Martini 2.50
Martini, Extra Dry 2.60
Old Fashioned 2.50
Whiskey Sour 2.50
Gimlet 2.50
Bacardi 2.50
Tom Collins 2.50
Gibson 2.50
Bloody Mary 2.50
Screwdriver 2.50

AFTER DINNER COCKTAILS

Stinger 2.75
Grasshopper 2.75
B & B 2.75
Alexander 2.75
Kahlua & Cream 2.75
Black Russian 2.75
Side Car 2.75
Galiano 2.75
Tia Maria 2.75
Special Brands — extra charge

Omelettes

HAM 4.95
HAM AND CHEESE 4.95
MUSHROOM AND CHEESE 4.95
WESTERN 4.95
PLAIN CHEESE 4.75
Served With Toast And Jelly
extra item .35 extra

Special Sandwiches

CHEESEBURGER 5.75
CLUBHOUSE, 3 Decker on Toast 6.50
SIRLOIN BURGER ON TOASTED BUN 5.60
REUBEN SANDWICH 6.50
FRENCH DIP 6.50
HAM AND CHEESE DELIGHT 6.50
Served With Cole Slaw And Potato Chips
May Substitute French Fries For Chips
Tossed Salad with the Above 50¢ Extra.

Hot Sandwiches

HOT BEEF 6.00
HOT TURKEY 6.00
HOT MEAT LOAF 5.85
Served With Mashed Potatoes And Gravy

Beverages

Pot of Hot Tea 80
Milk 80
Hot Chocolate 80
Iced Tea 90
Pot of Sanka 80
Chocolate Milk 80
Soft Drinks 80
Drink to go . . . . 5¢ extra
Large 1.00

WEIGHT WATCHERS' SPECIAL, Hamburger Pat-
tie, Sliced Tomato, Cottage Cheese, and Fruit 5.95

ITALIAN SPAGHETTI 5.95
With Meat Balls, Extra 1.00
Tasty Meat Sauce, Roma Cheese And Tossed Salad

Steaks & Chops

N.Y. STRIP SIRLOIN STEAK 10.50

CHOICE GROUND BEEF STEAK, Fried Onions . . . 7.95
TWO PORK CHOPS, Applesauce 7.95

Seafood

GOLDEN FRIED DEEP SEA SCALLOPS . . . 7.95
GOLDEN FRIED FRESH SHRIMP 8.50

ASSORTED SEAFOOD PLATTER 8.50
BREADED OCEAN PERCH 7.25
FISH & CHIPS 6.95
Above Served With Salad and Potatoes

Special Daily Dinners

ROAST CHOICE ROUND BEEF, Au Jus 7.95
VEAL PARMESAN, with Sauce 7.95
SALISBURY STEAK, with Mushrooms 7.95
BREADED VEAL STEAK, with Spaghetti 7.75
GRILLED BABY BEEF LIVER, with Onions or Bacon 7.65
HOME-BAKED MEAT LOAF, with Mushroom Sauce . 7.00
GOLDEN FRIED CHICKEN 7.00
STEAK SANDWICH 7.95
PORK CHOP SANDWICH 6.25
Above Served With Salad And Potatoes
Side of Mashed Potatoes . . . . 1.00   Vegetable 75

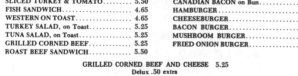

Plain Sandwiches

GRILLED BACON & CHEESE 5.25
CRISP BACON, LETTUCE, TOMATO . . . 5.25
SLICED TURKEY & TOMATO 5.50
FISH SANDWICH 4.65
WESTERN ON TOAST 4.65
TURKEY SALAD, on Toast 5.25
TUNA SALAD, on Toast 5.25
GRILLED CORNED BEEF 5.25
ROAST BEEF SANDWICH 5.50

GRILLED HAM & CHEESE 5.25
GRILLED CHEESE 4.30
CANADIAN BACON on Bun 4.75
HAMBURGER 4.85
CHEESEBURGER 5.00
BACON BURGER 5.50
MUSHROOM BURGER 5.50
FRIED ONION BURGER 5.50

GRILLED CORNED BEEF AND CHEESE 5.25
Delux .50 extra

Salads

GREEK SALAD BOWL,
  Our Special Dressing 6.40
JULIENNE SALAD BOWL 6.40
TURKEY SALAD BOWL 6.40
COTTAGE CHEESE AND FRUIT 4.95
COMBINATION SALAD 4.95
Choice Of Dressing

Side Orders

TOSSED SALAD 1.50
COLE SLAW 1.25
COTTAGE CHEESE 1.25
SMALL GREEK SALAD . . 3.50
APPLESAUCE 1.25
FRUIT CUP 1.25
FRENCH FRIES 1.25
ONION RINGS 1.50
SMALL JULIENNE 3.50

Desserts

Pecan Pie 1.75
Homemade Pie 1.50
Pie a La Mode 2.25
Ice Cream 1.25
Rice Pudding 1.25
Sundae 1.50

Nonprose Reading

Menu

Nonprose writing consists of disconnected words and numbers instead of the sentences and paragraphs you usually learn to read. Each time you need information from a train schedule, a graph, a menu, or the like, you must read nonprose material. This exercise and similar exercises that begin subsequent units will help you practice the problem-solving skills you will need in order to read nonprose material.

On the opposite page is a menu such as you might find in a restaurant in the U.S. or Canada.

Before You Begin   1. What are your first impressions of this restaurant? Is it similar to or different from restaurants with which you are familiar?

2. Do you think you would like to eat at this restaurant? Why or why not?

The questions below are designed to help you quickly become more acquainted with this menu so that you would be able to order a meal. Scan the menu to answer the questions in exercise 1. Do not go on to exercise 2 until you have checked your answers to exercise 1.

Exercise 1

1. If you wanted something alcoholic to drink before dinner, in which section would you find

   it? _____

2. In which section would you find something nonalcoholic to drink? _____

3. In which section would you find something sweet to eat after dinner? _____

4. Which special meal is provided for people who are trying to lose weight? _____

5. If you didn't want to eat pork, list some entries you would avoid. _____

   _____

6. Do we know if this restaurant serves Coca-Cola? _____

7. How much does a Reuben sandwich with french fries and a tossed salad cost? _____

8. Under which section would you find a small salad to eat with a N.Y. strip steak? _____

9. If you wanted eggs, under which sections would you look? _____

10. How much does two eggs with bacon cost? _____

11. Is tipping permitted in this restaurant? _____

Stop! Do not go on without discussing your answers.

Exercise 2

Indicate if each statement is true (T) or false (F).

1. _____ The cheapest item on the menu containing fish is fish and chips.

2. _____ The grilled baby beef liver dinner is always served with bacon.

3. _____ Potatoes are served with the assorted seafood platter.

4. _____ When you order from the Special Daily Dinners, you may choose any item from the Salad section.

5. _____ None of the salads served in this restaurant contains meat or poultry.

6. _____ Pancakes with bacon costs $8.50.

7. _____ If you had $9.00, you could afford a Special Daily Dinner and dessert plus tip.

Word Study

Context Clues

Efficient reading requires the use of various problem-solving skills. For example, it is impossible for you to know the exact meaning of every word you read, but by developing your guessing ability, you will often be able to understand enough to arrive at the total meaning of a sentence, paragraph, or essay. Context Clues exercises are designed to help you improve your ability to guess the meaning of unfamiliar words by using context clues. (Context refers to the sentence and paragraph in which a word occurs.) In using the context to decide the meaning of a word you have to use your knowledge of grammar and your understanding of the author's ideas. Although there is no formula that you can memorize to improve your ability to guess the meaning of unfamiliar words, you should keep the following points in mind:

1. Use the meanings of the other words in the sentence (or paragraph) and the meaning of the sentence as a whole to reduce the number of possible meanings.
2. Use grammar and punctuation clues that point to the relationships among the various parts of the sentence.
3. Be content with a general idea about the unfamiliar word; the exact definition or synonym is not always necessary.
4. Learn to recognize situations in which it is not necessary to know the meaning of the word.

Example

Each of the sentences in this exercise contains a blank in order to encourage you to look only at the context provided as you attempt to determine the possible meanings of the missing word. Read each sentence quickly and supply a word for each blank. There is no single correct answer. You are to use context clues to help you provide a word that is appropriate in terms of grammar and meaning.

1. I removed the _____ from the shelf and began to read.

2. Harvey is a thief; he would _____ the gold from his grandmother's teeth and not feel guilty.

3. Our uncle was a _____, an incurable wanderer who never could stay in one place.

4. Unlike his brother, who is truly a handsome person, Hogartty is quite _____.

5. The Asian _____, like other apes, is specially adapted for life in trees.

6. But surely everyone knows that if you step on an egg, it will _____.

7. Tom got a new _____ for his birthday. It is a sports model, red, with white interior and bucket seats.

Explanation

1. I removed the _____ from the shelf and began to read.	*book* *magazine* *paper* *newspaper*	The number of things that can be taken from a shelf and read is so few that the word *book* probably jumped into your mind at once. Here, the association between the object and the purpose for which it is used is so close that you have very little difficulty guessing the right word.
2. Harvey is a thief; he would _____ the gold from his grandmother's teeth and not feel guilty.	*steal* *take* *rob*	Harvey is a thief. A thief steals. The semicolon (;) indicates that the sentence that follows contains an explanation of the first statement. Further, you know that the definition of *thief* is: a person who steals.
3. Our uncle was a _____, an incurable wanderer who never could stay in one place.	*nomad* *roamer* *traveler* *drifter*	The comma (,) following the blank indicates a phrase in apposition, that is, a word or group of words that could be used as a synonym of the unfamiliar word. The words at the left are all synonyms of *wanderer*.
4. Unlike his brother, who is truly a handsome person, Hogartty is quite _____.	*ugly* *homely* *plain*	Hogartty is the opposite of his brother, and since his brother is handsome, Hogartty must be ugly. The word *unlike* signals the relationship between Hogartty and his brother.
5. The Asian _____, like other apes, is specially adapted for life in trees.	*gibbon* *monkey* *chimp* *ape*	You probably didn't write *gibbon,* which is the word the author used. Most native speakers wouldn't be familiar with this word either. But since you know that the word is the name of a type of ape, you don't need to know anything else. This is an example of how context can teach you the meaning of unfamiliar words.
6. But surely everyone knows that if you step on an egg, it will _____.	*break*	You recognized the cause and effect relationship in this sentence. There is only one thing that can happen to an egg when it is stepped on.
7. Tom got a new _____ for his birthday. It is a sports model, red, with white interior and bucket seats.	*car*	The description in the second sentence gave you all the information you needed to guess the word *car.*

Exercise 1

In the following exercise, do NOT try to learn the italicized words. Concentrate on developing your ability to guess the meaning of unfamiliar words using context clues. Read each sentence carefully, and write a definition, synonym, or description of the italicized word on the line provided.

1. _____ We watched as the cat came quietly through the grass toward the bird. When it was just a few feet from the victim, it gathered its legs under itself, and *pounced*.

2. _____ Some people have no difficulty making the necessary changes in their way of life when they move to a foreign country; others are not able to *adapt* as easily to a new environment.

3. _____ In spite of the fact that the beautiful *egret* is in danger of dying out completely, many clothing manufacturers still offer handsome prices for their long, elegant tail feathers, which are used as decorations on ladies' hats.

4. _____ When he learned that the club was planning to admit women, the colonel began to *inveigh against* all forms of liberalism; his shouting attack began with universal voting and ended with a protest against divorce.

5. _____ The snake *slithered* through the grass.

6. _____ The man thought that the children were defenseless, so he walked boldly up to the oldest and demanded money. Imagine his surprise when they began to *pelt* him with rocks.

7. _____ Experts in *kinesics,* in their study of body motion as related to speech, hope to discover new methods of communication.

8. _____ Unlike her *gregarious* sister, Jane is a shy, unsociable person who does not like to go to parties or to make new friends.

9. _____ After a day of hunting, Harold is *ravenous*. Yesterday, for example, he ate two bowls of soup, salad, a large chicken, and a piece of chocolate cake before he was finally satisfied.

10. _____ After the accident, the ship went down so fast that we weren't able to *salvage* any of our personal belongings.

Word Study

Dictionary Use

The dictionary is a source of many kinds of information about words. Look at this sample entry carefully; notice how much information the dictionary presents under the word *prefix*.

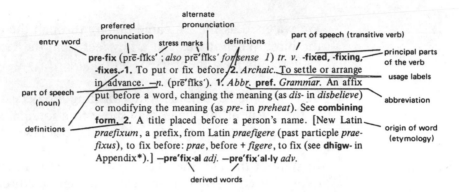

Your dictionary may use a different system of abbreviations or different pronunciation symbols. It is important for you to become familiar with your English dictionary and with the symbols that it uses. Look up *prefix* in your dictionary, and compare the entry to the sample entry. Discuss the differences that you find.

Exercise 1

Use the sample entry above, the dictionary page (opposite), and your own dictionary to discuss this exercise. Your teacher may want you to work alone, in pairs, or in small groups.

1. When a dictionary gives more than one spelling or pronunciation of a word, is the first one always preferred?

2. Look at the sample entry. How many syllables are in *prefix?* What symbol does this dictionary use to separate the syllables? Which syllable is accented in the preferred pronunciation of the verb *prefix?*

3. Why would you need to know where a word is divided into syllables?

4. Where is the pronunciation guide on page 7? Where is it in your dictionary? What is the key word in the pronunciation guide on page 7 that shows you how to pronounce the *e* in the preferred pronunciation of *prefix?*

5. What are *derived words?*

6. What is the meaning of the Latin root from which *pre* has developed?

7. Dictionary entries sometimes include usage labels such as *archaic, obsolete, slang, colloquial, poetic, regional,* and *informal.* Why are these labels useful?

From *The American Heritage Dictionary of the English Language* (Boston: Houghton Mifflin).

in the margin or between lines of a text or manuscript. **2.** An expanded version of such notes; a glossary. **3.** A purposefully misleading interpretation or explanation. **4.** An extensive commentary, often accompanying a text or publication. —*v.* **glossed, glossing, glosses.** —*tr.* **1.** To provide (a text) with glosses. **2.** To give a false interpretation to. —*intr.* To make glosses. [Middle English *glose,* from Old French, from Medieval Latin *glōsa,* from Latin *glōssa,* word that needs explanation, from Greek *glōssa,* tongue, language. See **glōgh-** in Appendix.*] —**gloss'er** *n.*

gloss. glossary.

glos·sal (glôs'əl, glŏs'-) *adj.* Of or pertaining to the tongue. [From Greek *glōssa,* tongue. See **gloss** (explanation).]

glos·sa·ry (glôs'ə-rē, glŏs'-) *n., pl.* **-ries.** *Abbr.* **gloss.** A collection of glosses, such as a vocabulary of specialized terms with accompanying definitions. [Latin *glossārium,* from *glōssa,* GLOSS (explanation).] —**glos·sar'i·al** (glô-sâr'ē-əl, glŏ-) *adj.* —**glos·sar'i·al·ly** *adv.* —**glos'sa·rist** *n.*

glos·sog·ra·phy (glô-sŏg'rə-fē, glŏ-) *n.* The writing and compilation of glosses or glossaries. [Greek *glōssa,* tongue, language, GLOSS (explanation) + -GRAPHY.] —**glos·sog'ra·pher** *n.*

glos·so·la·li·a (glôs'ō-lā'lē-ə, glŏs'-) *n.* **1.** Fabricated nonmeaningful speech, especially as associated with certain schizophrenic syndromes. **2.** The **gift of tongues** *(see).* [New Latin *glossolalia,* from (New Testament) Greek *glōssais lalein,* "to speak with tongues" : *glossa,* tongue (see **glōgh-** in Appendix*) + *lalein,* to talk, babble (see **la-** in Appendix*).]

glos·sol·o·gy (glô-sŏl'ə-jē, glŏ-) *n. Obsolete.* Linguistics. [Greek *glōssa,* tongue, language, GLOSS (explanation) + -LOGY.] —**glos·sol'o·gist** *n.*

gloss·y (glôs'ē, glŏs'ē) *adj.* **-ier, -iest.** **1.** Having a smooth, shiny, lustrous surface. **2.** Superficially attractive; specious. —*n., pl.* **glossies.** *Photography.* A print on smooth, shiny paper. Also called "glossy print." —**gloss'i·ly** *adv.* —**gloss'i·ness** *n.*

glost (glôst, glŏst) *n.* **1.** A lead glaze used for pottery. **2.** Glazed pottery. [Variation of GLOSS (sheen).]

glot·tal (glŏt'l) *adj.* **1.** Of or relating to the glottis. **2.** *Phonetics.* Articulated in the glottis. [From GLOTTIS.]

glottal stop. *Phonetics.* A speech sound produced by a momentary complete closure of the glottis, followed by an explosive release.

glot·tis (glŏt'ĭs) *n., pl.* **-tises** or **glottides** (glŏt'ə-dēz') **1.** The space between the vocal cords at the upper part of the larynx. **2.** The vocal structures of the larynx. [New Latin, from Greek *glōttis,* from *glōtta, glōssa,* tongue, language. See **glōgh-** in Appendix.*]

Glouces·ter (glôs'tər, glŏs'-). **1.** Also **Glouces·ter·shire** (-shîr, -shər). *Abbr.* **Glos.** A county of south-central England, 1,257 square miles in area. Population, 1,034,000. **2.** The county seat of this county. Population, 72,000. **3.** A city, resort center, and fishing port of Massachusetts, 27 miles northeast of Boston. Population, 26,000.

glove (glŭv) *n.* **1. a.** A fitted covering for the hand, usually made of leather, wool, or cloth, having a separate sheath for each finger and the thumb. **b.** A gauntlet. **2. a.** *Baseball.* An oversized padded leather covering for the hand, used in catching balls; especially, one with more finger sheathes than the catcher's or first baseman's mitt. **b.** A **boxing glove** *(see).* —**hand in glove.** In a close or harmonious relationship. —*tr.v.* **gloved, gloving, gloves.** **1.** To furnish with gloves. **2.** To cover with or as if with a glove. [Middle English *glove,* Old English *glōf.* See **lep-²** in Appendix.*]

glove
Pair of 17th-century English leather gloves with embroidered cuffs

glove compartment. A small storage container in the dashboard of an automobile.

glov·er (glŭv'ər) *n.* One who makes or sells gloves.

glow (glō) *intr.v.* **glowed, glowing, glows.** **1.** To shine brightly and steadily, especially without a flame: *"a red bed of embers glowing in the furnace"* (Richard Wright). **2.** To have a bright, warm color, usually reddish. **3. a.** To have a healthful, ruddy coloration. **b.** To flush; to blush. **4.** To be exuberant or radiant, as with pride. —*n.* **1.** A light produced by a body heated to luminosity; incandescence. **2.** Brilliance or warmth of color, especially redness: *"the evening glow of the city streets when the sun has gone behind the tallest houses"* (Sean O'Faolain). **3.** A sensation of physical warmth. **4.** A warm feeling of passion or emotion; ardor. —See Synonyms at **blaze.** [Middle English *glowen,* Old English *glōwan.* See **ghel-²** in Appendix.*]

glow·er (glou'ər) *intr.v.* **-ered, -ering, -ers.** To look or stare angrily or sullenly; to frown. —*n.* An angry, sullen, or threatening stare. [Middle English *glo(u)ren,* to shine, stare, probably from Scandinavian, akin to Norwegian dialectal *glora.* See **ghel-²** in Appendix.*] —**glow'er·ing·ly** *adv.*

glow·ing (glō'ĭng) *adj.* **1.** Incandescent; luminous. **2.** Characterized by rich, warm coloration; especially, having a ruddy, healthy complexion. **3.** Ardently enthusiastic or favorable.

glow plug. A small heating element in a diesel engine cylinder used to facilitate starting.

glow·worm (glō'wûrm') *n.* A firefly; especially, the luminous larva or wingless, grublike female of a firefly.

glox·in·i·a (glŏk-sĭn'ē-ə) *n.* Any of several tropical South American plants of the genus *Sinningia;* especially, *S. speciosa,* cultivated as a house plant for its showy, variously colored flowers. [New Latin, after Benjamin Peter *Gloxin,* 18th-century German botanist and physician.]

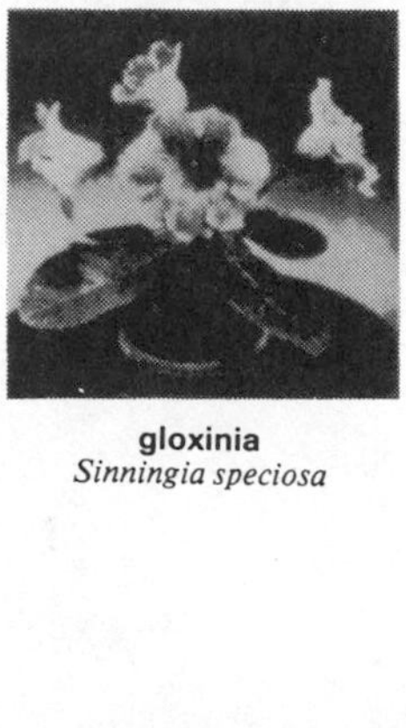

gloxinia
Sinningia speciosa

gloze (glōz) *v.* **glozed, glozing, glozes.** —*tr.* To minimize or underplay; to gloss. Used with *over.* —*intr. Archaic.* To use flattery or cajolery. [Middle English *glosen,* to gloss, falsify, flatter, from Old French *glosser,* from *glose,* GLOSS (explanation).]

Gluck (glo͝ok), **Christoph Willibald.** 1714–1787. German composer of operas.

glu·cose (glo͞o'kōs') *n.* **1.** A sugar, **dextrose** *(see).* **2.** A colorless to yellowish syrupy mixture of dextrose, maltose, and dextrins with about 20 per cent water, used in confectionery, alcoholic fermentation, tanning, and treating tobacco. [French, from Greek *gleukos,* sweet new wine, must. See **dḷku-** in Appendix.*]

glu·co·side (glo͞o'kə-sīd') *n.* A **glycoside** *(see),* the sugar component of which is glucose. —**glu'co·sid'ic** (-sĭd'ĭk) *adj.*

glue (glo͞o) *n.* **1.** An adhesive substance or solution; a viscous substance used to join or bond. **2.** An adhesive obtained by boiling animal **collagen** *(see)* and drying the residue. In this sense, also called "animal glue." —*tr.v.* **glued, gluing, glues.** To stick or fasten together with or as if with glue. [Middle English *gleu,* glue, birdlime, gum, from Old French *glu,* from Late Latin *glūs* (stem *glūt-*), from Latin *glūten.* See **gel-¹** in Appendix.*]

glum (glŭm) *adj.* **glummer, glummest.** **1.** In low spirits; dejected. **2.** Gloomy; dismal. [From Middle English *glomen, gloumen,* to look sullen, GLOOM.] —**glum'ly** *adv.* —**glum'ness** *n.*

Synonyms: *glum, gloomy, morose, dour, saturnine.* These adjectives mean having a cheerless or repugnant aspect or disposition. *Glum* implies dejection and silence, and more often than the other terms refers to a mood or temporary condition rather than to a person's characteristic state. *Gloomy* differs little except in being more applicable to a person given to somberness or depression by nature. *Morose* implies sourness of temper and a tendency to be uncommunicative. *Dour* especially suggests a grim or humorless exterior and sometimes an unyielding nature. *Saturnine* suggests severity of aspect, extreme gravity of nature, and often a tendency to be bitter or sardonic.

glu·ma·ceous (glo͞o-mā'shəs) *adj.* Having or resembling a glume or glumes.

glume (glo͞om) *n. Botany.* A chaffy basal bract on the spikelet of a grass. [New Latin *gluma,* from Latin *glūma,* husk. See **gleubh-** in Appendix.*]

glut (glŭt) *v.* **glutted, glutting, gluts.** —*tr.* **1.** To fill beyond capacity; satiate. **2.** To flood (a market) with an excess of goods so that supply exceeds demand. —*intr.* To eat excessively. —See Synonyms at **satiate.** —*n.* **1.** An oversupply. **2.** The act or process of glutting. [Middle English *glotten, glouten,* probably from Old French *gloutir,* to swallow, from Latin *gluttīre.* See **gwel-⁵** in Appendix.*]

glu·tam·ic acid (glo͞o-tăm'ĭk) *n.* An amino acid present in all complete proteins, found widely in plant and animal tissue, and having a salt, sodium glutamate, that is used as a flavor-intensifying seasoning. [GLUT(EN) + AM(IDE) + -IC.]

glu·ta·mine (glo͞o'tə-mēn', -mĭn) *n.* A white crystalline amino acid, $C_5H_{10}N_2O_3$, occurring in plant and animal tissue and produced commercially for use in medicine and biochemical research. [GLUT(EN) + AMINE.]

glu·ten (glo͞ot'n) *n.* A mixture of plant proteins occurring in cereal grains, chiefly corn and wheat, and used as an adhesive and as a flour substitute. [Latin *glūten,* glue. See **gel-¹** in Appendix.*] —**glu'te·nous** *adj.*

gluten bread. Bread made from flour with a high gluten content and low starch content.

glu·te·us (glo͞o'tē-əs, glo͞o-tē'-) *n., pl.* **-tei** (-tē-ī', -tē'ī'). Any of three large muscles of the buttocks: **a.** *gluteus maximus,* which extends the thigh; **b.** *gluteus medius,* which rotates and abducts the thigh; **c.** *gluteus minimus,* which abducts the thigh. [New Latin, from Greek *gloutos,* buttock. See **gel-¹** in Appendix.*] —**glu'te·al** *adj.*

glu·ti·nous (glo͞ot'n-əs) *adj.* Resembling or of the nature of glue; sticky; adhesive. [Latin *glūtinōsus,* from *glūten,* glue. See **gel-¹** in Appendix.*] —**glu'ti·nous·ly** *adv.* —**glu'ti·nous·ness, glu'ti·nos'i·ty** (-ŏs'ə-tē) *n.*

glut·ton¹ (glŭt'n) *n.* **1.** One that eats or consumes immoderately. **2.** One that has inordinate capacity to receive or withstand something: *a glutton for punishment.* [Middle English *glotoun,* from Old French *gluton, gloton,* from Latin *gluttō.* See **gwel-⁵** in Appendix.*] —**glut'ton·ous** *adj.* —**glut'ton·ous·ly** *adv.*

glut·ton² (glŭt'n) *n.* A mammal, the **wolverine** *(see).* [From GLUTTON (eater), translation of German *Vielfrass,* "great eater."]

glut·ton·y (glŭt'n-ē) *n.* Excess in eating or drinking.

glyc·er·ic acid (glĭ-sĕr'ĭk, glĭs'ər-). A syrupy, colorless compound, $C_3H_6O_4$. [From GLYCERIN.]

glyc·er·ide (glĭs'ə-rīd') *n.* An ester of glycerol and fatty acids. [GLYCER(IN) + -IDE.]

glyc·er·in (glĭs'ər-ĭn) *n.* Glycerol. [French, from Greek *glukeros,* sweet. See **dḷku-** in Appendix.*]

glyc·er·ol (glĭs'ə-rōl', -rôl', -rŏl') *n.* A syrupy, sweet, colorless or yellowish liquid, $C_3H_8O_3$, obtained from fats and oils as a by-product of the manufacture of soaps and fatty acids, and used as a solvent, antifreeze and antifrost fluid, plasticizer, and sweetener, and in the manufacture of dynamite, cosmetics, liquid soaps, inks, and lubricants. [GLYCER(IN) + -OL.]

glyc·er·yl (glĭs'ər-əl) *n.* The trivalent glycerol radical CH_2CHCH_2. [GLYCER(IN) + -YL.]

gly·cin (glī'sĭn) *n.* Also **gly·cine** (-sēn', -sĭn). A poisonous compound, $C_8H_9NO_3$, used as a photographic developer. [From GLYCINE.]

gly·cine (glī'sēn', -sən) *n.* **1.** A white, very sweet crystalline amino acid, $C_2H_5NO_2$, the principal amino acid occurring in sugar cane, derived by alkaline hydrolysis of gelatin, and used in biochemical research and medicine. **2.** Variant of **glycin.** [GLYC(O)- + -INE.]

ă pat/ā pay/âr care/ä father/b bib/ch church/d deed/ĕ pet/ē be/f fife/g gag/h hat/hw which/ĭ pit/ī pie/îr pier/j judge/k kick/l lid, needle/m mum/n no, sudden/ng thing/ŏ pot/ō toe/ô paw, for/oi noise/ou out/o͝o took/o͞o boot/p pop/r roar/s sauce/sh ship, dish/

Exercise 2

In this exercise you will scan a page of a dictionary (on page 7) to find answers to specific questions. Read each question, find the answer as quickly as possible, then write it in the space provided. These questions will introduce you to several kinds of information to be found in a dictionary.

1. Would you find the word *glory* on this page? _____

2. How many syllables are there in *glossolalia*? _____

3. Which syllable is stressed in the word *glutamic*? _____

4. What are the key words that tell you how to pronounce the *o* in the preferred pronunciation

   of *glycerol*? _____

5. What is the preferred spelling of the plural of *glottis*? _____

6. What is the past tense of *to glue*? _____

7. What is the adverb derived from *glower*? _____

8. What word must you look up to find *glossographer*? _____

9. For whom was *gloxinia* named? _____

10. From what two languages has *glucose* developed? _____

11. Is the intransitive verb *gloze* commonly used today? _____

12. How many synonyms are listed for the word *glum*? Why are these words defined here?

    _____

13. When was Christoph Willibald Gluck born? _____

14. What is the population of Gloucester, Massachusetts? _____

15. List the different kinds of information you can find in a dictionary. _____

    _____

    _____

    _____

Word Study

Stems and Affixes

Using context clues is one way to discover the meaning of an unfamiliar word. Another way is word analysis, that is, looking at the meanings of parts of words. Many English words have been formed by combining parts of older English, Greek, and Latin words. If you know the meanings of some of these word parts, you can often guess the meaning of an unfamiliar English word, particularly in context.

For example, *report* is formed from *re,* which means back, and *port,* which means carry. *Scientist* is derived from *sci,* which means know, and *ist,* which means one who. *Port* and *sci* are called stems. A stem is the basic part on which groups of related words are built. *Re* and *ist* are called affixes, that is, word parts that are attached to stems. Affixes like *re,* which are attached to the beginning of stems, are called prefixes. Affixes attached to the end, like *ist,* are called suffixes. Generally, prefixes change the meaning of a word and suffixes change its part of speech. Here is an example:

Stem	pay (verb)	honest (adjective)
Prefix	*re*pay (verb)	*dis*honest (adjective)
Suffix	repay*ment* (noun)	dishonest*ly* (adverb)

Word analysis is not always enough to give you the precise definition of a word you encounter in a reading passage, but often along with context it will help you to understand the general meaning of the word so that you can continue reading without stopping to use a dictionary.

Below is a list of some commonly occurring stems and affixes. Study their meanings. Your teacher may ask you to give examples of other words you know that are derived from these stems and affixes. Then do the exercises that follow.

Prefixes

com-, con-, col-, cor-, co-	together, with	cooperate, connect
in-, im-, il-, ir-	in, into, on	invade, insert
in-, im-, il-, ir-	not	impolite, illegal
micro-	small	microscope, microcomputer
pre-	before	prepare, prehistoric
re-, retro-	back, again	return, retrorocket

Stems

-audi-, -audit-	hear	auditorium, auditor
-chron-	time	chronology, chronological
-dic-, -dict-	say, speak	dictator, dictation
-graph-, -gram-	write, writing	telegraph, telegram
-log-, -ology-	speech, word, study	biology
-phon-	sound	telephone
-scrib-, -script-	write	describe, script
-spect-	look at	inspect, spectator
-vid-, -vis-	see	video, vision

Suffixes

-er, -or	one who	worker, spectator
-ist	one who	typist, biologist
-tion, -ation	condition, the act of	action, celebration

Exercise 1

1. In each item, select the best definition of the italicized word.

   a. He lost his *spectacles*.

   _____ 1. glasses   _____ 3. pants
   _____ 2. gloves   _____ 4. shoes

   b. He drew *concentric* circles.

   _____ 1. OO   _____ 3. OO
   _____ 2. ◉   _____ 4. OD

   c. He *inspected* their work.

   _____ 1. spoke highly of   _____ 3. examined closely
   _____ 2. did not examine   _____ 4. did not like

2. Circle the words where *in-* means *not*. Watch out; there are false negatives in this list.

   inject   inside   insane   inspect

   invaluable   inflammable   inactive   invisible

3. In current usage, the prefix *co-* is frequently used to form new words (for example, *co-* + editors becomes coeditors). Give another example of a word that uses *co* in this way.

   _____

4. The prefix *re-* (meaning *again*) often combines with simple verbs to create new verbs (for example, *re-* + *do* becomes *redo*). List three words familiar to you that use *re-* in this way.

   _____

The teaching of math in U.S is very different from in my country. In this composition I want to show two differences; the books and calculus.

Math books in U.S are very easy. I can understand when I read one because this book showed every problem and how to solves it. The book in my country is very hard to understand and students need to memorize a lot of theory. Then students don't easy to practice any problem. The book doesn't show how to solves step by step. Then students need to pay more to

In U.S has graph calculus. Students can put question and calculus shows picture to students. Students is easy to check out answer. But in My country doesn't have graph calculus, beside student can't use calculus any time. Students are very hard to find out the answer. When they have a test, but they lose more time because they don't have calculus.

In my opinion, Students in U.S is more easy to understant than my country When They absent in class. In my opinion The books and calculus in us are very interesting to students. I like math in this country because it is very easy to Jom.

Exercise 2

Word analysis can help you to guess the meaning of unfamiliar words. Using context clues and what you know about word parts, write a synonym, description, or definition of the italicized words.

1. _____ The doctor asked Martin to *inhale* deeply and hold his breath for 10 seconds.

2. _____ Many countries *import* most of the oil they use.

3. _____ Three newspaper reporters *collaborated* in writing this series of articles.

4. _____ Calling my professor by her first name seems too *informal* to me.

5. _____ It is Joe's *prediction* that by the year 2000 there will be a female president of the United States.

6. _____ Historians use the *inscriptions* on the walls of ancient temples to guide them in their studies.

7. _____ You cannot sign up for a class the first day it meets in September; you must *preregister* in August.

8. _____ After his long illness, he didn't recognize his own *reflection* in the mirror.

9. _____ I *dictated* the letter to my secretary over the phone.

10. _____ I'm sending a sample of my handwriting to a *graphologist* who says he can use it to analyze my personality.

11. _____ That university has a very good *microbiology* department.

12. _____ *Phonograph recordings* of early jazz musicians are very valuable now.

13. _____ At the drug store, the pharmacist refused to give me my medicine because she could not read the doctor's *prescription*.

14. _____ He should see a doctor about his *chronic* cough.

15. _____ Maureen was not admitted to graduate school this year, but she *reapplied* and was admitted for next year.

16. _____ I recognize his face, but I can't *recall* his name.

17. _____   Ten years ago, I decided not to complete high school; *in retrospect,* I believe that was a bad decision.

18. _____   She uses *audiovisual* aids to make her speeches more interesting.

19. _____   Some people believe it is *immoral* to fight in any war.

20. _____   Babies are born healthier when their mothers have good *prenatal* care.

Exercise 3

Following is a list of words containing some of the stems and affixes introduced in this unit. Definitions of these words appear on the right. Put the letter of the appropriate definition next to each word.

1. ____ microbe

2. ____ phonology

3. ____ audience

4. ____ chronicler

5. ____ chronology

6. ____ irregular

7. ____ microphone

8. ____ invisible

a. an instrument used to make soft sounds louder

b. not able to be seen

c. a group of listeners

d. the study of speech sounds

e. not normal

f. a historian; one who records events in the order in which they occur

g. an organism too small to be seen with the naked eye

h. a listing of events arranged in order of their occurrence

Paragraph Reading

Main Idea

In this exercise, you will practice finding the main idea of a paragraph. Being able to determine the main idea of a passage is one of the most useful reading skills you can develop. It is a skill you can apply to any kind of reading. For example, when you read for enjoyment or to obtain general information, it is probably not important to remember all the details of a selection. Instead, you want to quickly discover the general message—the main idea of the passage. For other kinds of reading, such as reading textbooks or articles in your own field, you need both to determine the main ideas and to understand the way in which these are developed.

The main idea of a passage is the thought that is present from the beginning to the end. In a well-written paragraph, most of the sentences support, describe, or explain the main idea. It is sometimes stated in the first or last sentence of the paragraph. Sometimes the main idea is only implied. In a poem, the main idea is often implied rather than stated explicitly.

In order to determine the main idea of a piece of writing, you should ask yourself what idea is common to most of the text. What is the idea that relates the parts to the whole? What opinion do all the parts support? What idea do they all explain or describe?

Read the following paragraphs and poem quickly. Concentrate on discovering the main idea. Remember, don't worry about the details in the selections. You only want to determine the general message.

After each of the first five paragraphs, select the statement that best expresses the main idea. After paragraphs 6 and 7 and the poem, you will not see the multiple choice format. Instead, you will write a sentence that expresses the main idea in your own words.

When you have finished, your teacher may want to divide the class into small groups for discussion. Study the example paragraph carefully before you begin.

Example

By the time the first European travelers on the American continent began to record some of their observations about Indians, the Cherokee people had developed an advanced culture that probably was exceeded only by the civilized tribes of the Southwest: Mayan and Aztec groups. The social structures of the Cherokee people consisted of a form of clan kinship in which there were seven recognized clans. All members of a clan were considered blood brothers and sisters and were bound by honor to defend any member of that clan from wrong. Each clan, the Bird, Paint, Deer, Wolf, Blue, Long Hair, and Wild Potato, was represented in the civil council by a councillor or councillors. The chief of the tribe was selected from one of these clans and did not inherit his office from his kinsmen. Actually, there were two chiefs, a Peace chief and War chief. The Peace chief served when the tribe was at peace, but the minute war was declared, the War chief was in command.

From Tim B. Underwood, *The Story of the Cherokee People* (S. B. Newman Printing Co.).

Select the statement that best expresses the main idea of the paragraph.

_____ a. The Cherokee chief was different in war time than in peace time.

_____ b. Before the arrival of the Europeans the Cherokees had developed a well-organized society.

_____ c. The Mayans and the Aztecs were part of the Cherokee tribe.

_____ d. Several Indian cultures had developed advanced civilizations before Europeans arrived.

Explanation

_____ a. This is not the main idea. Rather, it is one of several examples the author uses to support his statement that the Cherokee people had developed an advanced culture.

✓ b. This statement expresses the main idea of the paragraph. All other sentences in the paragraph are examples supporting the idea that the Cherokees had developed an advanced culture by the time Europeans arrived on the continent.

_____ c. This statement is false, so it cannot be the main idea.

_____ d. This statement is too general. The paragraph describes the social structure of the Cherokee people only. Although the author names other advanced Indian cultures, he does this only to strengthen his argument that the Cherokees had developed an advanced culture.

Paragraph 1
The first invention of human beings was the wheel. Although no wheel forms are found in nature, undoubtedly the earliest "wheels" were smooth logs which were used for moving weights over the earth's surface. No one recorded who he or she was or when it happened, but when the "first inventor" placed a wheel on an axle, people began to roll from one place to another. Records of this type of wheel have been found among Egyptian relics dating back to 2,000 B.C. and earlier Chinese civilizations are credited with independent invention of the same mechanism. The wheel so fascinated the human mind that people have spent centuries building machines around it; yet in over 4,000 years its basic design has remained unchanged. All about us we see the spinning shafts, gears, flywheels, pulleys, and rotors which are the descendents of the first wheel. The roaring propeller of an aircraft engine, the whirling wheel of a giant steam turbine, and the hairspring of a tiny watch are examples of the rotary motion which characterizes our mechanical world. It is hard to conceive of continuous motion without the wheel.

Select the statement that best expresses the main idea of the paragraph.

_____ a. The wheel is used today in industry and transportation.

_____ b. One of human beings' first inventions, the wheel, has remained important for 4,000 years.

_____ c. The basic design of the wheel has been changed to meet the needs of industrial society.

_____ d. Although we don't know exactly who invented the wheel, it is evident that the Egyptians and Chinese used it about 4,000 years ago.

Adapted from William P. Brotherton, *The Evolution of Speed* (Ryan Aeronautical Co.).

Paragraph 2   At the University of Kansas art museum, investigators tested the effects of different colored walls on two groups of visitors to an exhibit of paintings. For the first group the room was painted white; for the second, dark brown. Movement of each group was followed by an electrical system under the carpet. The experiment revealed that those who entered the dark brown room walked more quickly, covered more area, and spent less time in the room than the people in the white environment. Dark brown stimulated more activity, but the activity ended sooner. Not only the choice of colors but also the general appearance of a room communicates and influences those inside. Another experiment presented subjects with photographs of faces that were to be rated in terms of energy and well-being. Three groups of subjects were used; each was shown the same photos, but each group was in a different kind of room. One group was in an "ugly" room that resembled a messy storeroom. Another group was in an average room—a nice office. The third group was in a tastefully designed living room with carpeting and drapes. Results showed that the subjects in the beautiful room tended to give higher ratings to the faces than did those in the ugly room. Other studies suggest that students do better on tests taken in comfortable, attractive rooms than in ordinary-looking or ugly rooms.

Select the statement that best expresses the main idea of the paragraph.

_____ a. People in beautiful rooms tend to give higher ratings to photographs of faces than people in ugly rooms.

_____ b. The color and general appearance of a room influence the behavior and attitudes of the people in it.

_____ c. The University of Kansas has studied the effects of the color of a room on people's behavior.

_____ d. Beautifully decorated, light-colored rooms make people more comfortable than ugly, dark rooms.

From Jeffrey Schrank, *Deception Detection* (Boston: Beacon Press).

Paragraph 3

Teaching is supposed to be a professional activity requiring long and complicated training as well as official certification. The act of teaching is looked upon as a flow of knowledge from a higher source to an empty container. The student's role is one of receiving information; the teacher's role is one of sending it. There is a clear distinction assumed between one who is supposed to know (and therefore not capable of being wrong) and another, usually younger person who is supposed not to know. However, teaching need not be the province of a special group of people nor need it be looked upon as a technical skill. Teaching can be more like guiding and assisting than forcing information into a supposedly empty head. If you have a certain skill you should be able to share it with someone. You do not have to get certified to convey what you know to someone else or to help them in their attempt to teach themselves. All of us, from the very youngest children to the oldest members of our cultures should come to realize our own potential as teachers. We can share what we know, however little it might be, with someone who has need of that knowledge or skill.

Select the statement that best expresses the main idea of the paragraph.

_____ a. The author believes that it is not difficult to be a good teacher.

_____ b. The author believes that every person has the potential to be a teacher.

_____ c. The author believes that teaching is a professional activity requiring special training.

_____ d. The author believes that teaching is the flow of knowledge from a higher source to an empty container.

From Herbert Kohl, *Reading: How To* (New York: Bantam Books).

Paragraph 4   Albert Einstein once attributed the creativity of a famous scientist to the fact that he "never went to school, and therefore preserved the rare gift of thinking freely." There is undoubtedly truth in Einstein's observation; many artists and geniuses seem to view their schooling as a disadvantage. But such a truth is not a criticism of schools. It is the function of schools to civilize, not to train explorers. The explorer is always a lonely individual whether his or her pioneering be in art, music, science, or technology. The creative explorer of unmapped lands shares with the genius what William James described as the "faculty of perceiving in an unhabitual way." Insofar as schools teach perceptual patterns they tend to destroy creativity and genius. But if schools could somehow exist solely to cultivate genius, then society would break down. For the social order demands unity and widespread agreement, both traits that are destructive to creativity. There will always be conflict between the demands of society and the impulses of creativity and genius.

Select the statement that best expresses the main idea of the paragraph.

_____ a. Albert Einstein and other geniuses and artists have said that schools limit creativity and genius.

_____ b. Schools should be designed to encourage creativity.

_____ c. Explorers can be compared to geniuses because both groups look at the world differently from the way most people do.

_____ d. Schools can never satisfy the needs of both geniuses and society as a whole.

From Jeffrey Schrank, *Deception Detection* (Boston: Beacon Press).

Paragraph 5

Perhaps the most startling theory to come out of kinesics, the study of body movement, was suggested by Professor Ray Birdwhistell. He believes that physical appearance is often culturally programmed. In other words, we learn our looks—we are not born with them. A baby has generally unformed facial features. A baby, according to Birdwhistell, learns where to set the eyebrows by looking at those around—family and friends. This helps explain why the people of some regions of the United States look so much alike. New Englanders or Southerners have certain common facial characteristics that cannot be explained by genetics. The exact shape of the mouth is not set at birth, it is learned after. In fact, the final mouth shape is not formed until well after permanent teeth are set. For many, this can be well into adolescence. A husband and wife together for a long time often come to look somewhat alike. We learn our looks from those around us. This is perhaps why in a single country there are areas where people smile more than those in other areas. In the United States, for example, the South is the part of the country where the people smile most frequently. In New England they smile less, and in the western part of New York state still less. Many Southerners find cities such as New York cold and unfriendly, partly because people on Madison Avenue smile less than people on Peachtree Street in Atlanta, Georgia. People in densely populated urban areas also tend to smile and greet each other in public less than do people in rural areas and small towns.

Select the statement that best expresses the main idea of the paragraph.

_____ a. Ray Birdwhistell can tell what region of the United States a person is from by how much he or she smiles.

_____ b. Ray Birdwhistell is a leader in the field of kinesics.

_____ c. Ray Birdwhistell says that our physical appearance is influenced by the appearance of people around us.

_____ d. People who live in the country are more friendly than people who live in densely populated areas.

From Jeffrey Schrank, *Deception Detection* (Boston: Beacon Press).

Paragraph 6   There is widespread fear among policymakers and the public today that the family is disintegrating. Much of that anxiety stems from a basic misunderstanding of the nature of the family in the past and a lack of appreciation for its resiliency in response to broad social and economic changes. The general view of the family is that is has been a stable and relatively unchanging institution through history and is only now undergoing changes; in fact, change has always been characteristic of it.

Write a sentence that expresses the main idea of the paragraph. _____

_____

Paragraph 7   Enough is now known about the ancient Maya, those sophisticated artists and architects, astronomers and calendar keepers of South America, to realize that much remains to be learned before all the mysteries can be unraveled. Once considered peaceful stargazers, they are now suspected of being bloodthirsty and warlike. Dogged and brilliant scholars have wrestled with the problems for a century and a half. There has been a steady revision of ideas, regular expansion of the boundaries of knowledge, and there is certain to be more.

Write a sentence that expresses the main idea of the paragraph. _____

_____

Paragraph 6 adapted from Maris Vinovskis, "Historical Perspectives on the Development of the Family and Parent-Child Interactions," in _Parenting Across the Life Span,_ ed. Jane B. Lancaster, Jeanne Altman, Alice S. Rossi, and Lonni R. Sherrod (Aldine de Gruyter).
Paragraph 7 adapted from William Weber Johnson, "Two New Exhibitions Explore the Dark Mysteries of the Maya," _Smithsonian._

Poem

Fueled

Fueled
by a million
man-made
wings of fire—
the rocket tore a tunnel
through the sky—
and everybody cheered.
Fueled
only by a thought from God—
the seedling
urged its way
through the thicknesses of black—
and as it pierced
the heavy ceiling of the soil—
and launched itself
up into outer space—
no
one
even
clapped.

Marcie Hans

Write a sentence that expresses the main idea of the poem. _____

_____

Marcie Hans, "Fueled," from *Serve Me a Slice of Moon,* by Marcie Hans (Harcourt Brace Jovanovich).

Discourse Focus

Scanning

We read differently depending on our goal for reading. Sometimes we only need to locate a particular piece of information. For example, we might read the newspaper to discover the final score of a sports event, or to find out when and where a lecture will be held. To scan is to read quickly in order to locate specific information. The steps involved in scanning are the following:

1. Decide exactly what information you are looking for, and think about the form it may take. For example, if you want to know when something happened, you would look for a date. If you want to find out who did something, you would look for a name.
2. Next, decide where you need to look to find the information you want. You probably would not look for sports scores on the front page of the newspaper, nor look under the letter *S* for the telephone number of Sam Potter.
3. Move your eyes as quickly as possible down the page until you find the information you need. Read it carefully.
4. When you find what you need, do not read further.

The four exercises in this section are designed to give you practice in the various skills necessary for scanning.

Exercise 1

The index on page 23 is from the World Almanac, *a general reference text that provides a variety of information on a large number of topics.*

Scan to find the answers to the following questions.

1. If you wanted to learn about world religions, where might you begin your search?

2. Where could you find information on the current population of your country?

3. Where would you look to find information on the Chinese Lunar Calendar?

4. Where would you look to find a map of Africa?

QUICK REFERENCE INDEX

From *The World Almanac and Book of Facts.*

Exercise 2

The chart on page 25 was also taken from the World Almanac.

Scan to find the answers to the following questions.

1. What is the name of the highest waterfall listed here?

2. What is the name of the highest single-leap waterfall listed here?

3. What is the height of the shortest waterfall listed here?

4. What is the height of Catarata de Candelas in Columbia? What is the name of the river that feeds it?

5. How many waterfalls are listed for Japan?

6. How many of California's waterfalls run full force throughout the year?

7. How many waterfalls are listed for Colorado?

Famous Waterfalls

Source: National Geographic Society, Washington, D.C.

The earth has thousands of waterfalls, some of considerable magnitude. Their importance is determined not only by height but volume of flow, steadiness of flow, crest width, whether the water drops sheerly or over a sloping surface, and in one leap or a succession of leaps. A series of low falls flowing over a considerable distance is known as a cascade.

Sete Quedas or Guaira is the world's greatest waterfall when its mean annual flow (estimated at 470,000 cusecs, cubic feet per second) is combined with height. A greater volume of water passes over Boyoma Falls (Stanley Falls), though not one of its seven cataracts, spread over nearly 60 miles of the Congo River, exceeds 10 feet.

Estimated mean annual flow, in cusecs, of other major waterfalls are: Niagara, 212,200; Paulo Afonso, 100,000; Urubupunga, 97,000; Iguazu, 61,000; Patos-Maribondo, 53,000; Victoria, 35,400; and Kaieteur, 23,400.

Height = total drop in feet in one or more leaps. † = falls of more than one leap; * = falls that diminish greatly seasonally; ** = falls that reduce to a trickle or are dry for part of each year. If river names not shown, they are same as the falls. R. = river; L. = lake; (C) = cascade type.

Africa

Name and location	Ht.
Angola	
Duque de Braganca, Lucala R.	344
Ruacana, Cuene R.	406
Ethiopia	
Dal Verme, Dorya R.	98
Fincha	508
Tesissat, Blue Nile R.	140
Lesotho	
*Maletsunyane	630
Zimbabwe-Zambia	
*Victoria, Zambezi R.	343
South Africa	
*Augrabies, Orange R.	480
Howick, Umgeni R.	364
† Tugela	2,014
Highest fall	597
Tanzania-Zambia	
*Kalambo	726
Uganda	
Kabalega (Murchison) Victoria Nile R.	130

Asia

Name and location	Ht.
India—*Cauvery	330
*Gokak, Ghataprabha R.	170
*Jog (Gersoppa), Sharavathi R.	830
Japan	
*Kegon, Daiya R.	330
Laos	
Khon Cataracts, Mekong R. (C)	70

Australasia

Name and location	Ht.
Australia	
New South Wales	
Wentworth	614
Highest fall	360
Wollomombi	1,100
Queensland	
Coomera	210
Tully	885
† Wallaman, Stony Cr.	1,137
Highest fall	937
New Zealand	
Bowen	540
Helena	890
Stirling	505
† Sutherland, Arthur R.	1,904
Highest fall	815

Europe

Name and location	Ht.
Austria—† Gastein	492
Highest fall	280
† *Golling, Schwarzbach R.	250
† Krimml	1,312
France—*Gavarnie	1,385

Name and location	Ht.
Great Britain—Scotland	
Glomach	370
Wales	
Cain	150
Rhaiadr	240
Iceland—Detti	144
† Gull, Hvita R.	105
Italy—Frua, Toce R. (C)	470
Norway	
Mardalsfossen (Northern)	1,535
† Mardalsfossen (Southern)	2,149
† **Skjeggedal, Nybuai R.	1,378
**Skykje	984
Vetti, Morka-Koldedola R.	900
Voring, Bjoreio R.	597
Sweden	
† Handol	427
† Tannforsen, Are R.	120
Switzerland	
† Diesbach	394
Giessbach (C)	984
Handegg, Aare R.	150
Iffigen	120
Pissevache, Salanfe R.	213
† Reichenbach	656
Rhine	79
† Simmen	459
Staubbach	984
† Trummelbach	1,312

North America

Name and location	Ht.
Canada	
Alberta	
Panther, Nigel Cr.	600
British Columbia	
† Delia	1,443
† Takakkaw, Daly Glacier	1,200
Northwest Territories	
Virginia, S. Nahanni R.	294
Quebec	
Montmorency	274
Canada—United States	
Niagara: American	182
Horseshoe	173
United States	
California	
*Feather, Fall R.	640
Yosemite National Park	
*Bridalveil	620
*Illilouette	370
*Nevada, Merced R.	594
**Ribbon	1,612
**Silver Strand, Meadow Br.	1,170
*Vernal, Merced R.	317
† **Yosemite	2,425
Yosemite (upper)	1,430
Yosemite (lower)	320
Yosemite (middle) (C)	675
Colorado	
† Seven, South Cheyenne Cr.	300
Hawaii	
Akaka, Kolekole Str.	442

Name and location	Ht.
Idaho	
**Shoshone, Snake R.	212
Twin, Snake R.	120
Kentucky	
Cumberland	68
Maryland	
*Great, Potomac R. (C)	71
Minnesota	
**Minnehaha	53
New Jersey	
Passaic	70
New York	
*Taughannock	215
Oregon	
† Multnomah	620
Highest fall	542
Tennessee	
Fall Creek	256
Washington	
Mt. Rainier Natl. Park	
Narada, Paradise R.	168
Sluiskin, Paradise R.	300
Palouse	197
**Snoqualmie	268
Wisconsin	
*Big Manitou, Black R. (C)	165
Wyoming	
Yellowstone Natl. Pk. Tower	132
*Yellowstone (upper)	109
*Yellowstone (lower)	308
Mexico	
El Salto	218
**Juanacatlan, Santiago R.	72

South America

Name and location	Ht.
Argentina-Brazil	
Iguazu	230
Brazil	
Glass	1,325
Patos-Maribondo, Grande R.	115
Paulo Afonso, Sao Francisco R.	275
Urubupunga, Parana R.	40
Brazil-Paraguay	
Sete Quedas	
Parana R.	130
Colombia	
Catarata de Candelas, Cusiana R.	984
*Tequendama, Bogota R.	427
Ecuador	
*Agoyan, Pastaza R.	200
Guyana	
Kaieteur, Potaro R.	741
Great, Kamarang R.	1,600
† Marina, Ipobe R.	500
Highest fall	300
Venezuela—	
† *Angel	3,212
Highest fall	2,648
Cuquenan	2,000

From *The World Almanac and Book of Facts*.

Exercise 3

The calendar on page 27 is typical of the list of social events provided by many newspapers in the United States and Canada.

Scan to find the answers to the following questions.

1. Under which section(s) would you look if you wanted to go to a play?

2. Under which section(s) would you look if you wanted to spend an evening eating, drinking, and dancing?

3. When do the Detroit Pistons play basketball this week?

4. Is Lou Rawls singing at a Detroit area night club this week?

5. Is there a pop concert Thursday night?

6. Could you attend a classical music concert Saturday night?

7. What is the topic of Seymour Hersh's lecture Wednesday morning?

Detroit Free Press

The Calendar

James Tatum and his trio play reverent jazz Thursday night in the Hamtramck Public Library.

Journalist Seymour Hersh speaks at Detroit Town Hall Wednesday at the Fisher.

Lou Rawls sings at db's Club in the Hyatt Regency, Dearborn's newest hotel.

Theater

SAME TIME, NEXT YEAR—Comedy-romance. 7 tonight; 8:30 p.m. Mon.-Sat.; matinee at 2 p.m. Wed. and Sat. Fisher Theatre, Second at Grand Blvd.

GODSPELL—The story of Jesus in rock at 2 and 7:30 p.m. today; 8:30 p.m. Tues.-Fri.; 2 and 8:30 p.m. Sat. Music Hall, 350 Madison, downtown.

HILBERRY THEATRE, Cass at Hancock:
● **"As You Like It,"** delightful Shakespeare at 2:30 p.m. Wed. and 8:30 p.m. Thur.
● **"The Miser,"** Moliere folderol at 2:30 p.m. Thur. and 8:30 p.m. Fri.-Sat.

THE ME NOBODY KNOWS—U-D-Marygrove production once only, 8:30 p.m. Tues. at Northwest Activities Center, Meyers at Curtis.

OAKLAND UNIVERSITY, University Drive east of I-75, Rochester:
● **"An Italian Straw Hat"**—Lots of people run through flapping doors and joyous misunderstandings. 8:15 p.m. Thur.-Sat. and 2 and 6:30 p.m. Sun. Studio Theatre.
● **"An Italian Straw Hat"**—Lots of people run through flapping doors and joyous misunderstandings. 8:15 p.m. Thur.-Sat. and 2 and 8:30 p.m. Sun. Studio Theatre.

Children's Theater

THE MIDNIGHT RIDE OF PAUL REVERE follows the famed horseman through every Middlesex village and town, 10 a.m. and 1 p.m. Mon.-Fri.; 11 a.m. and 2 p.m. Sat. Detroit Institute of Arts, 5200 Woodward.

THE SIGNIFYING MONKEY is fun in the jungle. 10 a.m. and 1:30 p.m. Mon.-Fri. Langston Hughes Theatre, Livernois at Davison.

Community Theater

GEORGE WASHINGTON SLEPT HERE is not Bicentennial, despite the title. By the Ibex Club at 8:30 p.m. Fri.-Sat. Grosse Pointe War Memorial, 32 Lake Shore, Grosse Pointe Farms.

ONCE UPON A MATTRESS, a grown-up fairy tale by the Southfield Civic Theatre at 2 p.m. today. Civic Center, 26000 Evergreen, Southfield.

THE TIME OF YOUR LIFE—Saroyan by Red Door Players, 2 p.m. today. Unitarian Church, Forest at Cass.

Nightlife

HYATT REGENCY HOTEL—**Lou Rawls** changes the singing mood at the new db's Club. Strutters Ball plays for dancing. Tues.-Sat., Michigan at Southfield, Dearborn.

TOP HAT—**Bob Taylor** sings show, classic and pop songs Mon.-Sat. 73 E. University, Windsor.

BLOOMFIELD CANOPY—**Elaine Philpot** with music from '20s-'70s Tues.-Sat. 6560 Orchard Lake Rd., West Bloomfield.

ROOSTERTAIL turns comic **Marv Welch** loose with the American Scene in the Palm River Club Tues.-Sun. 100 Marquette at the river.

HOTEL PONTCHARTRAIN introduces **Laurie Seaman** and Celebration Roadshow to downtown at the Top. Two Washington Blvd.

GINO'S SURF—Chicago singer **Deanna Guest** sings and **Lyla** and **Bahia** dance Tues.-Sun. 37400 E. Jefferson, Mt. Clemens.

GOLDEN COACH—**Terry Moretti** and the Las Vegas '76 revue Tues.-Sun. Him and I play bluegrass Mon. 30450 Van Dyke, Warren.

PALOMBO'S has **Donna Marie** and Motion Mon.-Sat. 20401 W. Eight Mile.

MONEY TREE—Guitarist **Mickey Stein** 7-10 p.m. Mon.-Tues.; **Pat Tollas, Monica Stoval** and **Kathy Caesar** Thur.-Fri. when the French restaurant stays open late for the theater crowd. 33 W. Fort, downtown.

WARREN HOLIDAY INN—**Michael Strika** and guitar entertain Tues.-Sat. 32035 Van Dyke.

ROMAN TERRACE—**Gary Primo** Duo, he's the piano, Mon.-Sat. Orchard Lake at Twelve Mile, Farmington Hills.

DEARBORN INN—**Dennis Day** plays piano Tues.-Thur. and Sun. **Mack Ferguson** provides dance music Sat. Oakwood Blvd. south of Michigan Ave.

THE OLD PLACE—Dancing and entertainment Wed.-Sat. **Sherry Johnson,** piano, **Mark Van Haaken,** guitar. 15301 E. Jefferson.

DETROIT TONIGHT TOURS—Visit night places in a British double-decker bus. 961-5180.

Classical Music & Dance

DETROIT SYMPHONY—**Aldo Ceccato** and the Trio di Trieste, 8:30 p.m. Thur. and Sat. and in an NBD Coffee Concert at 9:30 a.m. Fri. Ford Aud., Jefferson at Woodward, downtown.

MISCHA LEFKOWITZ, violin, as part of the Kolego Concert Series at 3 p.m. today at Detroit Institute of Arts, 5200 Woodward.

BRUNCH WITH BACH and harpsichordist **Evelyne Scheyer** at 10 and 11:15 a.m. today. Detroit Institute of Arts, 5200 Woodward.

OAKWAY SYMPHONY, Francesco Di Blasi, conducting, and Dance Detroit in a Gershwin spectacular at 8 p.m. Sat. Redford Theatre, Lahser at Grand River.

THE ELIJAH, Mendelssohn's dramatic oratorio by WSU Symphonic Choir and Temple Beth El Choir. Free at 8 p.m. Fri. Temple Beth El, Fourteen Mile at Telegraph, Bloomfield Township.

WARREN COMMUNITY BAND CONCERT at 3:30 p.m. today. Van Dyke Lincoln High, Nine Mile at Federal, Warren.

Discotheque

SUBWAY sometimes has live music but usually doesn't. Shelby Hotel, 525 W. Lafayette, downtown.

SINDROME—Disco all week, instructions Mon. Telegraph at Ford Road, Dearborn Heights.

PERFECT BLEND—Nightly after 9 p.m. South side of Northwestern at Ten Mile, Southfield.

CLAM SHOP UPSTAIRS Thur.-Fri. Grand Blvd. west of Woodward.

THE LANDING nightly from 6 p.m. to 2 a.m. Southfield at Ten Mile, Southfield.

Pop Concerts

GEORGE CARLIN discusses the world's funnies at 8 and 11 p.m. Fri. Royal Oak Theatre, Fourth at Washington.

AIRTIGHT rocks for Jazz Development Workshop at 8:15 and 10:15 p.m. Mon.-Wed. Langston Hughes Theatre, Livernois at Davison.

JAMES TATUM TRIO returns jazz to Hamtramck Public Library at 7 p.m. Thur. Albert J. Zak Memorial Bldg., 2360 Caniff.

FOLK MUSIC by Patricia Hadecki, Monty Parks and Joe DiPasquale at 7:30 p.m. Tues. Unitarian Church, Cass at Forest.

BLUEGRASS GOES TO COLLEGE in a benefit concert at 7:30 tonight at Marygrove, Outer Drive at Southfield.

Jazz, Folk & Rock

GABOR SZABO, jazz guitarist, Tues.-next Sun. **Sonny Fortune,** sax, **closes tonight.** Baker's Keyboard Lounge, Livernois at Eight Mile.

LITTLE SONNY blows authentic harmonica blues out of the Depression in Greensboro, Ala. Tues.-Sun. at the Raven Gallery, Greenfield at Twelve Mile, Southfield.

JUDY ROBERTS, electronic jazz piano, Wed.-Sat. at Inn Between, Huron at Elizabeth Lake Road, Pontiac.

BOBBY LAUREL'S smooth Suburban Renewal plays Thur.-Sat. in the Gazebo, Mound at Thirteen Mile, Warren.

SHADES OF GREY rocks Tues.-Sun. at Belanger House, Main at Twelve Mile, Royal Oak.

COPELAND BLUES BAND Thur.-Sat. at That Gnu Joint, Cass at Palmer.

EDDY KAY, folk, rock and comedy, Fri.-Sat. Colonial Lounge, Farmington Road at Seven Mile, Livonia.

CONNIE GRAHAM and band sing pops Wed.-Sat. at Bobbies, Telegraph between Twelve and Thirteen Mile roads, Bingham Farms.

JIM FREEMAN joshes the girls and sings Wed.-Sat. Dirty Helen's, Cass at Bagley, downtown.

GREG HOWARD leads Fourth Edition and **Karen Johnson** in Top 40 stuff Mon.-Sat. **AMIRA AMIR** lectures on the mystic art of the belly dance. Fri.-Sat. Playboy Club, James Couzens at Eight Mile.

MIDTOWN FOLK—**Bruce Hambright** Mon.-Wed. and **Fresh Air** Thur.-Sat. Midtown Cafe, 139 S. Woodward, Birmingham.

PHIL ESSER sings solo folk Mon.-Tues. **Ron Coden** does the rest of the week at his club, the Railroad Crossing, 6640 E. Eight Mile.

FEATHER CANYON rolls along Mon.-Tues., followed by Travis Wed.-next Sun. Wagon Wheel, Rochester at Big Beaver, Troy.

RIOT rocks Wed.-Sat. at the Library, 37235 Groesbeck, Mt. Clemens.

JOHN AMORE puts his high-energy songs to work Tues.-Sat. Old-time rocker **Del Shannon** closes tonight. Golden Spur, 14315 Northline, Southgate.

TIM HAZEL in a western mood, Mon.-Sat. Dearborn Towne House, Telegraph south of Michigan Ave.

GEORGE YOUNG heads the instrumental, vocal and comedy show Wed.-Sun. at Bimbo's beer emporium, 22041 Michigan Ave., Dearborn.

Fun Stuff

ICE SHOW—200 skaters in a flag-waving mood. 2 and 7 p.m. Sat.-next Sun. Oak Park Ice Arena, 13950 Oak Park Blvd.

BICENTENNIAL AUCTION for mentally handicapped. 7-11 p.m. Fri. Wing Lake Development Center, 6490 Wing Lake Rd., Bloomfield Hills.

BLUE ENGELS, Humperdinck fans, throw a diabetes research benefit fashion show-dinner at 7:30 p.m. Tues. Salvatore's Italian Villa, Middlebelt between Warren and Ford Roads, Garden City.

Films/Lectures

FAMILY FILM FESTIVAL, comedy, classics and selected short subjects, 9 a.m.-3 p.m. today. Howard Johnson's, West Grand Blvd. at Third, downtown.

DETROIT INSTITUTE OF ARTS, 5200 Woodward:
● **George Pierrot**—Stan Midgley takes a Bicentennial tour of the U.S. at 3 p.m. today.
● **"Basic Training,"** a documentary about Ft. Knox. 7 tonight.
● **"Blonde Venus"**—Josef von Sternberg made Marlene Dietrich wear an ape suit and sing "Hot Voodoo" in 1932. 2 p.m. Wed.-Fri.
● **"Distant Thunder,"** a Bengal doctor and wife are caught up in a corrupt system. 7 and 9:30 p.m. Fri.
● **"My Night at Maud's"** is French and why not? 7 and 9:30 p.m. Sat.

THE EVIL WEED, a slapstick movie by the man who brought you Sha Na Na. 8 and 10 p.m. Fri.-Sat. Cass City Cinema, Unitarian Church, Cass at Forest.

SITDOWN AT DODGE and **"I Am Somebody,"** films about union ordeals at 7:30 p.m. Sun. Trinity Church, 13100 Woodward, Highland Park.

VEGETABLE GARDENING, a free lecture to help you raise a bumper crop by **Gerald Drahelm** of MSU. 5 p.m. today. Detroit Science Center, 52 E. Forest.

SIX WIVES OF HENRY VIII is running at 10 a.m. and 7 p.m. Fri. in Macomb County Service Center, Groesbeck at Elizabeth, Mt. Clemens.

SEYMOUR HERSH, Pulitzer Prize-winning journalist, speaks at Detroit Town Hall at 11 a.m. Wed. Fisher Theatre, Second at Grand Blvd.

Sports

RED WINGS meet Pittsburgh in the Wings' last hockey game of their season tonight at 7 on Olympia ice, 5920 Grand River.

PISTONS play three home basketball games—Philadelphia at 7 tonight; Milwaukee at 7:35 p.m. Wed. and Atlanta, to finish the season, at 8:05 p.m. Fri. Cobo Arena, downtown.

THOROUGHBREDS race at 3:20 p.m. Mon.-Fri. and 2:20 p.m. Sat. Hazel Park, Dequindre at Ten Mile.

NORTH AMERICAN SPEED SKATING qualifying tryouts after 1:30 p.m. today. Further information at 284-1124. Yack Recreation Center, 3131 Third, Wyandotte.

HARNESS RACES:
● **Northville Downs,** Mon.-Sat. Post time, 8:15 p.m. W. Seven Mile at Sheldon, Northville.
● **Windsor Raceway,** 8 p.m. Tues.-Sat. and 1:30 p.m. Sun. Windsor, Ont.

Exhibits

OUTDOOR LIVING SHOW noon-6 p.m. today, 9:30 a.m.-9 p.m. the rest of the week. Pontiac Mall, Telegraph north of Elizabeth Lake Road.

BOAT SHOW, campers and equipment 5-10 p.m. Thur.-Fri. and noon-10 p.m. next Sat.-Sun. Yack Arena, 3131 Third St., Wyandotte.

BEHOLD YOUR BODY, an exhibit to acquaint you with yourself. 9 a.m.-5 p.m. Mon.-Fri. and noon-5 p.m. Sun. Detroit Science Center, 52 E. Forest.

SPRING ARTS AND CRAFTS show and sale from 11 a.m.-9 p.m. Fri.-Sat. Plymouth Cultural Center, 525 Farmer St.

compiled by
CHUCK THURSTON

Adapted from "The Calendar," *Detroit Free Press*.

Exercise 4

A variety of publications provide information for students considering attending colleges and universities. The guide on page 29 contains information for international students.

You are interested in attending a school in Oregon, and a friend has sent you a photocopy of Admission Requirements for International Students *so that you can learn something about colleges and universities in that state. Scan to answer the following questions. Your teacher may want you to write out the answers in the space provided or merely underline the appropriate portions of text.*

1. What level of English proficiency is required at most of the schools?

2. Which school has the largest number of international students? Which school has the largest percentage of international students?

3. What schools have intensive English programs?

4. What is the cost of attending school at Concordia? Who would you call to get more information?

5. Which school(s) offer graduate work?

6. If you do not want to take the TOEFL, which schools might you apply to?

7. Which school(s) do you think you might apply to? Why?

Director of Admissions
Central Oregon Community College
College Way
Bend, Oregon 97701
(503) 382-6112

Undergraduate TOEFL: 500
GPA: 2.5

Type of institution: Two-year undergraduate.
Number of international students: 20 (1% of total students enrolled).
Intensive English language program: No.
Deadlines for admission: One month prior to the beginning of the term.

Undergraduate: ELS Level 108 or 109 will substitute for TOEFL requirement. No other tests are required. GPA for transfer students is 2.5. Admission requirements are higher for nursing.

Admissions Office
Chemeketa Community College
P.O. Box 14007
Salem, Oregon 97309
(503) 399-5006

Undergraduate TOEFL: 450
GPA:

Type of institution: Two-year undergraduate.
Number of international students: 35 (1% of total students enrolled).
Intensive English language program: Yes, must meet college admission requirements.
Deadlines for admission: None.

Undergraduate: There are no substitutes for the TOEFL requirement. No other tests are required. College's placement test is recommended.

Director of Admissions
Clackamas Community College
19600 South Molalla Avenue
Oregon City, Oregon 97045
(503) 657-8400

Undergraduate TOEFL: 500
GPA: 3.0

Type of institution: Two-year undergraduate.
Number of international students: 40 (2% of total students enrolled).
Intensive English language program: No.
Deadlines for admission: Fall-July 31; Winter-October 31; Spring-January 31; Summer-March 31.

Undergraduate: The MTELP, CELT, or ESL will substitute for the TOEFL requirement. No other tests are required. GPA for transfer students is 2.5.

Admissions Office
Clatsop Community College
Sixteenth and Jerome
Astoria, Oregon 97103
(503) 325-0910

Undergraduate TOEFL: 520
GPA:

Type of institution: Two-year undergraduate.
Number of international students: 4 (<1% of total students enrolled).
Intensive English language program: No.
Deadlines for admission:

Undergraduate: The MTELP or previous college-level classes will substitute for the TOEFL requirement. No other tests are required. GPA for transfer students is 2.0.

Director of Admissions
Columbia Christian College
200 Northeast 91st Avenue
Portland, Oregon 97220
(503) 255-7060

Undergraduate TOEFL: 500
GPA: 2.5

Type of institution: Four-year undergraduate.
Number of international students: 7 (2% of total students enrolled).
Intensive English language program: No.

Deadlines for admission: Fall-September 15; Winter-December 15; Spring-March 15.

Undergraduate: There are no substitutes for the TOEFL requirement. The SAT or ACT is required. GPA for transfer students is 2.0.

Admissions Office
Concordia College
2811 Northeast Holman
Portland, Oregon 97211
(503) 288-9371

Undergraduate TOEFL: 500
GPA: 2.5

Type of institution: Four-year undergraduate.
Number of international students: 100 (20% of total students enrolled).
Intensive English language program: Yes, separate admission.
Deadlines for admission: Fall-August 31; Winter-December 15; Spring-February 15; Summer-June 15.

Undergraduate: A score of 5 on the MTELP will substitute for the TOEFL requirement. A score of 400 on the SAT or the ACT is required. GPA for transfer students is 2.0. Students who do not meet the TOEFL requirement are admitted for part- or full-time, non-credit English study.

International Student Admissions
Eastern Oregon State College
Eighth and K Streets
La Grande, Oregon 97850
(503) 963-2171

Undergraduate TOEFL: 500
GPA: 2.75
Graduate TOEFL: 550
GPA: 2.5

Type of institution: Four-year undergraduate; graduate.
Number of international students: 70 (10% of total students enrolled).
Intensive English language program: No.
Deadlines for admission: Fall-September 1; Winter-December 1; Spring-March 1; Summer-May 15.

Undergraduate: Verification of sufficient proficiency or a recommendation will substitute for the TOEFL requirement. No other tests are required. GPA for transfer students is 2.0.

Graduate: Verification of sufficient proficiency or a recommendation will substitute for the TOEFL requirement. No other tests are required.

Director of Admissions
George Fox College
Newberg, Oregon 97132
(503) 538-8383

Undergraduate TOEFL: 500
GPA: 2.5

Type of institution: Four-year undergraduate.
Number of international students: 7 (1.13% of total students enrolled).
Intensive English language program: No.
Deadlines for admission: Fall-September 1.

Undergraduate: There are no substitutes for the TOEFL requirement. No other tests are required.

Director of Admissions
Lane Community College
4000 East 30th Avenue
Eugene, Oregon, 97405
(503) 747-4501

Undergraduate TOEFL: 475
GPA: 3.0

Type of institution: Two-year undergraduate.
Number of international students: 105 (1.4% of total students enrolled).

Intensive English language program: No.
Deadlines for admission: Fall-September; Winter-December; Spring-March. Deadline dates vary each year.

Undergraduate: There are no substitutes for the TOEFL requirement. No other tests are required. GPA for transfer students is 2.5.

2

Essays

The articles that follow address issues that arise when one lives in or visits a foreign culture.

Selection 1A   Essay

The article that follows is one of the classic articles on a "disease" known as culture shock. This is a condition often experienced by visitors to foreign cultures.

Before You Begin   Consider: when you have lived in foreign cultures, did you:

—wash your hands a lot?
—worry about the food?
—find the native people unfriendly and unsympathetic?
—prefer the company of people from your home culture?
—feel homesick?
—make jokes about the host culture?

If you answered yes to some or all of these, you may be familiar with the condition called culture shock. Read the article below to discover the symptoms and stages of this condition; can it be cured? Then complete the exercises that follow.

Your teacher may want you to do Vocabulary from Context exercise 1 on page 34 before you begin.

Culture Shock and the Problem of Adjustment in New Cultural Environments

Kalvero Oberg

1   Culture shock might be called an occupational disease of people who have been suddenly transplanted abroad. Like most ailments, it has its own symptoms and cure.

2   Culture shock is precipitated by the anxiety that results from losing all our familiar signs and symbols of social intercourse. Those signs or cues include the thousand and one ways in which we orient ourselves to the situation of daily life: when to shake hands and what to say when we meet people, when and how to give tips, how to make purchases, when to accept and when to refuse invitations, when to take statements seriously and when not. These cues, which may be words, gestures, facial expressions, customs, or norms, are acquired by all of us in the course of growing up and are as much a part of our culture as the language we speak or the beliefs we accept. All of us depend for our peace of mind and our efficiency on hundreds of these cues, most of which we do not carry on the level of conscious awareness.

3   Now when an individual enters a strange culture, all or most of these familiar cues are removed. He or she is like a fish out of water. No matter how broad-minded or full of goodwill you may be, a series of props have been knocked from under you, followed by a feeling of frustration and anxiety. People react to the frustration in much the same way. First they reject the environment which causes the discomfort. "The ways of the host country are bad because they make us feel bad." When foreigners in a strange land get together to grouse about the host country and its people, you can be sure they are suffering from culture shock. Another phase of culture shock is regression. The home environment suddenly assumes a tremendous importance. To the foreigner everything becomes irrationally glorified. All the difficulties and problems are forgotten and only the good things back home are remembered. It usually takes a trip home to bring one back to reality.

4   Some of the symptoms of culture shock are excessive washing of the hands, excessive concern over drinking water, food dishes, and bedding; fear of physical contact with attendants, the absent-minded stare; a feeling of helplessness and a desire for dependence on long-term residents of one's own nationality; fits of anger over minor frustrations; great concern over minor pains and eruptions of the skin; and finally, that terrible longing to be back home.

5   Individuals differ greatly in the degree in which culture shock affects them. Although not common, there are individuals who cannot live in foreign countries. However, those who have seen people go

Adapted from *Readings in Intercultural Communication,* ed. David S. Hoopes (Washington, D.C.: Society for Intercultural Education, Training and Research), vol. 2.

through culture shock and on to a satisfactory adjustment can discern steps in the process. During the first few weeks most individuals are fascinated by the new. They stay in hotels and associate with nationals who speak their language and are polite and gracious to foreigners. This honeymoon stage may last from a few days or weeks to six months, depending on circumstances. If one is very important, he or she will be shown the show places, will be pampered and petted, and in a press interview will speak glowingly about goodwill and international friendship.

6   But this mentality does not normally last if the foreign visitor remains abroad and has seriously to cope with real conditions of life. It is then that the second stage begins, characterized by a hostile and aggressive attitude toward the host country. This hostility evidently grows out of the genuine difficulty which the visitor experiences in the process of adjustment. There are house troubles, transportation troubles, shopping troubles, and the fact that people in the host country are largely indifferent to all these troubles. They help, but they don't understand your great concern over these difficulties. Therefore, they must be insensitive and unsympathetic to you and your worries. The result, "I just don't like them." You become aggressive, you band together with others from your country and criticize the host country, its ways, and its people. But this criticism is not an objective appraisal. Instead of trying to account for the conditions and the historical circumstances which have created them, you talk as if the difficulties you experience are more or less created by the people of the host country for your special discomfort.

7   You take refuge in the colony of others from your country which often becomes the fountainhead of emotionally charged labels known as stereotypes. This is a peculiar kind of offensive shorthand which caricatures the host country and its people in a negative manner. The "dollar grasping American" and the "indolent Latin Americans" are samples of mild forms of stereotypes. The second stage of culture shock is in a sense a crisis in the disease. If you come out of it, you stay; if not, you leave before you reach the stage of a nervous breakdown.

8   If visitors succeed in getting some knowledge of the language and begin to get around by themselves, they are beginning to open the way into the new cultural environment. Visitors still have difficulties but they take a "this is my problem and I have to bear it" attitude. Usually in this stage visitors take a superior attitude to people of the host country. Their sense of humor begins to exert itself. Instead of criticizing, they joke about the people and even crack jokes about their own difficulties. They are now on the way to recovery.

9   In the fourth stage, your adjustment is about as complete as it can be. The visitor now accepts the customs of the country as just another way of living. You operate within the new surroundings without a feeling of anxiety, although there are moments of social strain. Only with a complete grasp of all the cues of social intercourse will this strain disappear. For a long time the individual will understand what the national is saying but is not always sure what the national means.

With a complete adjustment you not only accept the food, drinks, habits, and customs, but actually begin to enjoy them. When you go home on leave, you may even take things back with you; and if you leave for good, you generally miss the country and the people to whom you became accustomed.

Comprehension

Answer the following questions according to your understanding of the article. Your teacher may want you to answer these questions orally, in writing, or by underlining appropriate parts of the text. True/false items are indicated by a T / F preceding a statement.

1. What precipitates culture shock?

   _____

2. Oberg outlines four steps in adjusting to a new culture. Describe each stage and its characteristics.

   _____

   _____

   _____

   _____

3. T / F   Culture shock can never be cured.

4. T / F   We should try to avoid culture shock.

Discussion/Composition

1. Have you ever experienced culture shock? Describe your symptoms. What advice do you have for people who suffer from culture shock?

2. Using examples, describe the behavior of visitors to your home culture who suffer from culture shock.

3. This article deals with the anxiety of visiting another culture. Once one has adjusted to a foreign culture, however, one may experience "reverse culture shock" upon returning home. What do you think are the symptoms of this related "disease"?

Vocabulary from Context

Both the ideas and the vocabulary in the exercise below are taken from "Culture Shock and the Problem of Adjustment in New Cultural Environments." Use the context provided to determine the meanings of the italicized words. Write a definition, synonym, or description of each of the italicized vocabulary items in the space provided.

1. _____

2. _____

   Illnesses specific to workers in a particular occupation are known as *occupational diseases*. Culture shock is an occupational disease for people who travel. It is *precipitated* by the anxiety of living in a strange culture.

3. _____

4. _____
5. _____
6. _____

7. _____

8. _____

   Suddenly finding yourself in a strange country can be rather frightening. You lose all of the *props* that generally support you, all of the familiar *cues* that provide information about what to do. Without familiar props and cues to *orient* you in unfamiliar situations, it becomes difficult *to cope with* life in a new setting. Everything can seem different. You don't even know how much to *tip* a cab driver or a waiter in a restaurant. In this situation, you can lose a sense of logic, developing *irrational* fear of the local people.

9. _____

   People react differently to visiting different cultures. People who are very important, like the leaders of a country, will be treated very carefully. Because they are *pampered* and *petted*, they may not become uncomfortable. Others may feel very uncomfortable and spend their time *grousing* to whomever will listen about how unfriendly the natives are.

10. _____
11. _____

12. _____

13. _____

14. _____

15. _____

   One symptom of culture shock is the inability to see the host *nationals* as real people. Instead one tends to create *caricatures*, exaggerating the characteristics of the culture. Perhaps you will decide that your hosts are lazy, and grouse about the *indolence* of the local people. In any event, you may decide to spend a good deal of time with people from your country, and their conversation will become the *fountainhead* of your stereotyping.

Exercise 2

This exercise should be completed after you have finished reading "Culture Shock and the Problem of Adjustment in New Cultural Environments." The exercise is designed to see how well you have been able to use your knowledge of stems and affixes, and context, to guess the meaning of unfamiliar vocabulary items. Give a definition, synonym, or description of each of the words below. The number in parentheses indicates the paragraph in which the word can be found. Your teacher may want you to do these orally or in writing.

1. (1) transplanted _____

2. (2) intercourse _____

3. (6) mentality_____

Figurative Language and Idioms

In the paragraph indicated by the number in parentheses, find the phrase that best fits the meaning given. Your teacher may want to read these aloud as you quickly scan the paragraph to find the answer.

1. (3) Which phrase means *out of place, not at home*?

2. (6) Which phrase means to *remain together as a group*?

Selection 1B   Essay

Before You Begin   There is a saying in the United States: "Your actions speak louder than
words."

1. What do you think this saying means? Can you give examples where
   actions speak louder than words?

2. When traveling or living in a foreign culture, have you ever been
   misunderstood because of your actions?

This article originally appeared in a Peace Corps publication. It was written to familiarize people
who would live abroad with elements of nonverbal communication. Read the article in order to get
a general idea of the categories of nonverbal communication. Then do the exercises that follow.

Your Actions Speak Louder . . .

Melvin Schnapper

1   A Peace Corps staff member is hurriedly called to a town in
Ethiopia to deal with reports that one of the volunteers is treating
Ethiopians like dogs. What could the volunteer be doing to
communicate that?

2   A volunteer in Nigeria has great trouble getting any discipline in
his class, and it is known that the students have no respect for him
because he has shown no self-respect. How has he shown that?

3   Neither volunteer offended his hosts with words. But both of them
were unaware of what they had communicated through their nonverbal
behavior.

4   In the first case, the volunteer working at a health center would go
into the waiting room and call for the next patient. She did this as she
would in America—by pointing with her finger to the next patient and
beckoning him to come. Acceptable in the States, but in Ethiopia her
pointing gesture is for children and her beckoning signal is for dogs. In
Ethiopia one points to a person by extending the arm and hand and
beckons by holding the hand out, palm down, and closing it repeatedly.

5   In the second case, the volunteer insisted that students look him
in the eye to show attentiveness, in a country where prolonged eye
contact is considered disrespectful.

6   While the most innocent American-English gesture may have
insulting, embarrassing, or at least confusing connotations in another
culture, the converse is also true. If foreign visitors were to bang on

---

Adapted from *Peace Corps: The Volunteer.*

the table and hiss at the waiter for service in a New York restaurant, they would be fortunate if they were only thrown out. Americans might find foreign students overly polite if they bow.

7   It seems easier to accept the arbitrariness of language—that dog is *chien* in French or *aja* in Yoruba—than the differences in the emotionally laden behavior of nonverbal communication, which in many ways is just as arbitrary as language.

8   We assume that our way of talking and gesturing is "natural" and that those who do things differently are somehow playing with nature. This assumption leads to a blindness about intercultural behavior. And individuals are likely to remain blind and unaware of what they are communicating nonverbally, because the hosts will seldom tell them that they have committed a social blunder. It is rude to tell people they are rude; thus the hosts grant visitors a "foreigner's license," allowing them to make mistakes of social etiquette, and they never know until too late which ones prove disastrous.

9   An additional handicap is that the visitors have not entered the new setting as free agents, able to detect and adopt new ways of communicating without words. They are prisoners of their own culture and interact within their own framework. Yet the fact remains that for maximum understanding the visitor using the words of another language also must learn to use the tools of nonverbal communication of that culture.

10   Nonverbal communication—teaching it and measuring effect—is more difficult than formal language instruction. But now that language has achieved its proper recognition as being essential for success, the area of nonverbal behavior should be taught to people who will live in another country in a systematic way, giving them actual experiences, awareness, sensitivity. Indeed, it is the rise in linguistic fluency which now makes nonverbal fluency even more critical. A linguistically fluent visitor may tend to offend even more than those who don't speak as well if that visitor shows ignorance about interface etiquette; the national may perceive this disparity between linguistic and nonlinguistic performance as a disregard for the more subtle aspects of intercultural communication. Because nonverbal cues reflect emotional states, both visitor and host national might not be able to articulate what's going on.

11   While it would be difficult to map out all the nonverbal details for every language that Peace Corps teaches, one can hope to make visitors aware of the existence and emotional importance of nonverbal channels. I have identified five such channels: kinesic, proxemic, chronemic, oculesic, and haptic.

12   *Kinesics*—movement of the body (head, arms, legs, etc.). The initial example from the health center in Ethiopia was a problem caused by a kinesic sign being used which had different meaning cross-culturally. Another example, the American gesture of slitting one's throat implying "I've had it" or "I'm in trouble," conveys quite a different message in Swaziland. It means "I love you."

13   Americans make no distinction between gesturing for silence to an adult or to a child. An American will put one finger to the lips for both,

while an Ethiopian will use only one finger to a child and four fingers for an adult. To use only one finger for an adult is disrespectful. On the other hand, Ethiopians make no distinction in gesturing to indicate emphatic negation. They shake their index finger from side to side to an adult as well as to a child, whereas this gesture is used only for children by Americans. Thus, if visitors are not conscious of the meaning of such behavior, they not only will offend their hosts but they will be offended by them.

14   Drawing in the cheeks and holding the arms rigidly by the side of the body means "thin" in Amharic. Diet-conscious Americans feel complimented if they are told that they are slim and so may naturally assume that to tell an Ethiopian friend this is also complimentary. Yet in Ethiopia and a number of other countries, this is taken pejoratively, as it is thought better to be heavy-set, indicating health and status and enough wealth to ensure the two.

15   *Proxemics*—the use of interpersonal space. South Americans, Greeks, and others find comfort in standing, sitting, or talking to people at a distance which Americans find intolerably close. We give their unusual closeness the social interpretation of aggressiveness and intimacy, causing us to have feelings of hostility, discomfort, or intimidation. If we back away to our greater distance of comfort, we are perceived as being cold, unfriendly, and distrustful. Somalis would see us as we see South Americans, since their interface distance is greater still than ours.

16   *Chronemics*—the timing of verbal exchanges during conversation. As Americans, we expect our partner to respond to our statement immediately. In some other cultures, people time their exchanges to leave silence between each statement. For Americans this silence is unsettling. To us it may mean that the person is shy, inattentive, bored, or nervous. It causes us to repeat, paraphrase, talk louder, and "correct" our speech to accommodate our partner. In the intercultural situation, it might be best for the visitor to tolerate the silence and wait for a response.

17   *Oculesics*—eye-to-eye contact or avoidance. Americans are dependent upon eye contact as a sign of listening behavior. We do not feel that there is human contact without eye contact. In many countries there are elaborate patterns of eye avoidance which we regard as inappropriate.

18   *Haptics*—the tactile form of communication. Where, how, and how often people can touch each other while conversing are culturally defined patterns. We need not go beyond the borders of our own country to see groups (Italians and black Americans, for example) which touch each other more often than Anglo-Americans do. Overseas, Americans often feel crowded and pushed around by people who have much higher toleration for public physical contact and even need it as part of their communication process. A visitor may feel embarrassed when a host national friend continues to hold his or her hand long after the formal greetings are over.

19   These five channels of nonverbal communication exist in every culture. The patterns and forms are completely arbitrary, and it is arguable as to what is universal and what is culturally defined.

20   Of course, there is no guarantee that heightened awareness will change behavior. Indeed, there may be situations where visitors should not alter their behavior, depending on the status, personalities, and values in the social context. But the approach seeks to make people aware of an area of interpersonal activity which for too long has been left to chance or to the assumption that visitors to other countries will be sensitive to it because they are surrounded by it.

Comprehension

Answer the following questions according to your understanding of the article. You may need to scan* the article for the answers to specific questions. Your teacher may want you to work on these individually, in small groups, or in pairs. True/false items are indicated by a T / F preceding a statement.

1. T / F   In Ethiopia you should not beckon an adult.

2. T / F   As people become more proficient in a language, their nonverbal errors are not considered serious.

3. T / F   Americans make no distinction between nonverbal communication with a child and an adult.

4. T / F   Eye-to-eye contact can be an important form of communication.

5. T / F   There are important differences in the proxemics of North and South Americans.

6. Match the following channels of nonverbal communication with their definition.

   _____ chronemics   a. eye-to-eye contact or avoidance

   _____ haptics   b. the timing of verbal exchanges during conversation

   _____ kinesics   c. the use of interpersonal space

   _____ oculesics   d. movement of the body

   _____ proxemics   e. communication by touching

7. Demonstrate the gesture the American doctor used to beckon patients in Ethiopia described in paragraph 4. What should she have done? How does one gesture for silence to adults in Ethiopia?

8. Demonstrate the gesture "to slit one's throat" described in paragraph 12. What does this mean to you?

---

*For an introduction to scanning, see Unit 1.

Discussion/Composition

1. From your experience, give examples from each of the five channels of nonverbal communication. Which of the five do you think is the most important? Why?

2. Demonstrate for the class gestures you find strange in other cultures or gestures of your own that have caused misunderstanding. What nonverbal behaviors tell you that someone is a stranger to your culture? Demonstrate nonverbal behavior that you think characterizes people from the United States.

3. Can nonverbal communication be taught? Cite examples to support your point of view.

Vocabulary from Context

This exercise is designed to give you additional clues to determine the meanings of unfamiliar vocabulary items in context. In the paragraph indicated by the number in parentheses, find the word or phrase that best fits the meaning given. Your teacher may want to read these aloud as you quickly scan the paragraph to find the answer.

1. (5)   Which word means *lengthy, extended*?

2. (7)   Which word means *without logic or reason*?

3. (10)   Which word means *face to face*?

4. (11)   Which phrase means *to outline, to describe in detail*?

5. (19)   Which word means *methods of communication*?

Reading Selection 2

Mystery

Mystery stories are written to involve readers in solving a problem. The problem is presented early in the passage and the tension grows gradually until it is solved.

In this story, a man named Ausable will certainly die unless he can outsmart his enemy. Read the story carefully. You should be able to solve the problem before the end of the story.

The Midnight Visitor

Robert Arthur

1   Ausable did not fit the description of any secret agent Fowler had ever read about. Following him down the musty corridor of the gloomy French hotel where Ausable had a room, Fowler felt disappointed. It was a small room, on the sixth and top floor, and scarcely a setting for a romantic figure.

2   Ausable was, for one thing, fat. Very fat. And then there was his accent. Though he spoke French and German passably, he had never altogether lost the New England accent he had brought to Paris from Boston twenty years ago.

3   "You are disappointed," Ausable said wheezily over his shoulder. "You were told that I was a secret agent, a spy, dealing in espionage and danger. You wished to meet me because you are a writer, young and romantic. You envisioned mysterious figures in the night, the crack of pistols, drugs in the wine."

4   "Instead, you have spent a dull evening in a French music hall with a sloppy fat man who, instead of having messages slipped into his hand by dark-eyed beauties, gets only an ordinary telephone call making an appointment in his room. You have been bored!" The fat man chuckled to himself as he unlocked the door of his room and stood aside to let his frustrated guest enter.

5   "You are disillusioned," Ausable told him. "But take cheer, my young friend. Presently you will see a paper, a quite important paper for which several men and women have risked their lives, come to me in the next-to-last step of its journey into official hands. Some day soon that paper may well affect the course of history. In that thought is drama, is there not?" As he spoke, Ausable closed the door behind him. Then he switched on the light.

6   And as the light came on, Fowler had his first authentic thrill of the day. For halfway across the room, a small automatic pistol in his hand, stood a man.
     Ausable blinked a few times.
     "Max," he wheezed, "you gave me quite a start. I thought you were in Berlin. What are you doing in my room?"

7   Max was slender, not tall, and with a face that suggested the look

Adapted from "The Midnight Visitor" from *Mystery and More Mystery,* by Robert Arthur (New York: Random House).

of a fox. Except for the gun, he did not look very dangerous.

"The report," he murmured. "The report that is being brought to you tonight concerning some new missiles. I thought I would take it from you. It will be safer in my hands than in yours."

8   Ausable moved to an armchair and sat down heavily. "I'm going to raise the devil with the management this time; I am angry," he said grimly. "This is the second time in a month that somebody has gotten into my room off that confounded balcony!" Fowler's eyes went to the single window of the room. It was an ordinary window, against which now the night was pressing blackly.

9   "Balcony?" Max asked curiously. "No, I had a passkey. I did not know about the balcony. It might have saved me some trouble had I known about it."

10   "It's not my balcony," explained Ausable angrily. "It belongs to the next apartment." He glanced explanatorily at Fowler. "You see," he said, "this room used to be part of a large unit, and the next room—through that door there—used to be the living room. *It* had the balcony, which extends under *my* window now. You can get onto it from the empty room next door, and somebody did, last month. The management promised to block it off. But they haven't."

11   Max glanced at Fowler, who was standing stiffly a few feet from Ausable, and waved the gun with a commanding gesture. "Please sit down," he said. "We have a wait of a half an hour, I think."

"Thirty-one minutes," Ausable said moodily. "The appointment was for twelve-thirty. I wish I knew how you learned about the report, Max."

12   The little spy smiled evilly. "And we wish we knew how your people got the report. But, no harm has been done. I will get it back tonight. What is that? Who is at the door?"

13   Fowler jumped at the sudden knocking at the door. Ausable just smiled, "That will be the police," he said. "I thought that such an important paper as the one we are waiting for should have a little extra protection. I told them to check on me to make sure everything was all right."

14   Max bit his lip nervously. The knocking was repeated.

"What will you do now, Max?" Ausable asked. "If I do not answer the door, they will enter anyway. The door is unlocked. And they will not hesitate to shoot."

15   Max's face was black with anger as he backed swiftly toward the window; with his hand behind him, he opened the window and put his leg out into the night. "Send them away!" he warned. "I will wait on the balcony. Send them away or I'll shoot and take my chances!"

What will happen now? How will Ausable escape? Do you think he has a plan? In a few words, tell how you think the story will end.

_____

_____

Now continue reading.

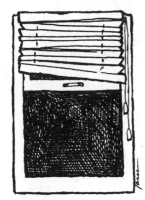

16   The knocking at the door became louder and a voice was raised. "Mr. Ausable! Mr. Ausable!"

Keeping his body twisted so that his gun still covered the fat man and his guest, the man at the window grasped the frame with his free hand to support himself as he rested his weight on one thigh. Then he swung his other leg up and over the window sill.

17   The doorknob turned. Swiftly Max pushed with his left hand to free himself and drop to the balcony. And then as he dropped, he screamed once, shrilly.

18   The door opened and a waiter stood there with a tray, a bottle and two glasses. "Here is the drink you ordered, sir." He set the tray on the table, deftly uncorked the bottle, and left the room.

19   White faced and shaking, Fowler stared after him. "But . . . but . . . what about . . . the police?" he stammered.

"There never were any police." Ausable sighed. "Only Henry, whom I was expecting."

"But what about the man on the balcony . . . ?" Fowler began.

"No," said Ausable, "he won't return."

Why won't Max return? _____

Comprehension Clues

If you were not able to write an ending to the story, perhaps answering the following questions will help you. Mark each of the following statements true (T) or false (F).

1. _____ Max had never been to Ausable's room before.

2. _____ Max knew about the balcony because he had used it to enter the apartment.

3. _____ Ausable knew that someone would knock on the door.

4. _____ The apartment was on the sixth floor of the building.

5. _____ Max knew about the balcony because Ausable told him about it.

Now: Why won't Max return? _____

Discussion/Composition

Prepare alternative ending(s) to this story. Your endings might require that you add or change elements of the story.

Reading Selection 3

Conversation

This passage is taken from the book *Iberia* by James Michener. The author describes the book as a "nineteenth-century English-style travel book with much personal observation, much reflection, and much affection."

Before You Begin

1. How do you feel when you encounter unusual food when you travel? Do you enjoy trying new foods or do you try to avoid them?

2. How do you feel when you are disappointed by one of your "experiments"?

3. Have you ever felt that you were being cheated in a foreign restaurant?

The author of this passage, James Michener, expresses his philosophy of travel in the following quotation: "If you reject the food, ignore the customs, fear the religion and avoid the people, you might better stay home: you are like a pebble thrown into water; you become wet on the surface, but you are never part of the water."

"Toledo: A Problem of Menus" provides a humorous account of Michener's attempt to put his philosophy to work in Spain.

Read the passage and do the exercises that follow. You may want to do the Vocabulary from Context exercise on page 49 before you begin.

Toledo: A Problem of Menus

James Michener

1   The Spanish government, aware that the golden rewards of tourism could evaporate as quickly as they appeared, has taken sensible steps to protect the tourist. . . . Restaurants are required to offer, in addition to their à la carte menus, a special tourist menu from which one can get a good <u>meal</u> and a bottle of wine at a fixed price. By ordering from this menu one can eat really well in Spain and at about half the price one would <u>expect</u> to pay in either France or Italy.

2   But. I sat down, in a restaurant in Toledo, looked at the menu and said, "I'll take fish soup, Spanish omelette and flan."

"And what wine?"

"Whatever comes with the meal."

"Nothing comes with the meal."

"But it says right here . . ."

The first quotation is from the jacket flap of Michener's book *Iberia*. The second is from *Reader's Digest*. The story is adapted from *Iberia: Spanish Travels and Reflections* by James Michener (New York: Random House).

"You have to order that. Then it's extra."

"But the menu says . . ."

"You're pointing at the tourist menu."

"That's what I ordered."

"Oh, no! You didn't mention the tourist menu."

"I'm mentioning it now."

"You can't mention it now. You've got to mention it when you sit down."

3 "But you haven't even given the order to the kitchen."

"True. But I've written it in my book. And it's the writing that counts."

"You mean that if I'd said 'tourist menu' at the start, my meal would have cost me a dollar and sixty cents?"

"Clearly."

"But since I delayed three minutes the same meal is going to cost me two-sixty?"

"Plus sixty cents for the wine."

4 I tried to point out how ridiculous such a situation was, but the waiter was adamant, and soon the manager came up, looked at his waiter's book and shrugged his shoulders. "If you wanted the tourist menu you should have said so," he grumbled.

"I'm saying so now."

"Too late."

I rose and left the restaurant, with the waiter abusing me and the manager claiming loudly that I owed him for having soiled a napkin, which I admit I had unfolded.

5 I escaped but projected myself into an even worse mess, for I chose what seemed to be the best restaurant in Toledo, where I announced quickly and in a clear voice that I wanted the tourist menu.

"What a pity! With the tourist menu you can't have partridge."

"I don't believe I'd care for partridge." I had had it on a previous visit and was not too taken with it. "Just the tourist menu."

"But on the tourist menu you get only three dishes."

"That's exactly what I want."

"But on that menu you don't get special wine, and I know you Americans prefer a special wine."

"I'll drink whatever you Spaniards drink."

"We drink the special wine."

6 I insisted that I be served from the tourist menu, and grudgingly the waiter handed me a menu which offered an enticing choice of five soups, eleven egg or fish dishes, seven meat courses and six promising desserts, but of the twenty-nine dishes thus available, twenty-six carried a surcharge if ordered on the tourist menu. Technically, tourists could order a dinner that would cost the price advertised by the government, but if they did so they would have two soups, one cheap fish and no dessert. Madrid had laid down the law, but Toledo was interpreting it.

7 As a traveler I work on the principle which I commend to others: No one should ever protest two abuses in a row. Few people can be right twice running, and never three times straight, so I ordered three dishes, each of which carried a surcharge: soup, roasted chicken, flan.

The soup was delicious and the ordinary wine was palatable and I sat back to enjoy the meal which had started off so badly.

8   Unfortunately, I had chosen a table that put me next to a good-looking, ruddy-faced Englishman whose tweed suit gave the impression that he must at home have been a hunting man. As he finished his soup he said to his wife, "First class, absolutely first class." He had, as I suspected he might, ordered the partridge, but when the waiter deposited the steaming casserole before him, the Englishman looked at it suspiciously, waited till the waiter had gone, then asked his wife quietly, "Do you smell something?"

"I think I do," she replied.

"And do you know what it is?"

9   Without speaking she pointed her fork at the partridge, whereupon her husband nodded silently and brought his nose closer to the casserole. "My goodness," he said in a whisper, "this is fairly raunchy." In gingerly manner he tasted the bird, folded his hands in his lap and said, "My goodness."

10   His wife got a piece of the bird onto her fork and tasted it, looked gravely at her husband and nodded.

"What to do?" he asked.

"You obviously can't eat it."

"I wonder should I call the waiter."

"I think you'd better."

11   I was now in a relaxed mood and had no desire to see the Englishman make a fool of himself, because obviously he wanted to avoid a scene. "With your permission, sir," I said, waiting for him to acknowledge me.

"Of course."

"I'm afraid there's nothing wrong with your partridge, sir. It's how they serve it in Spain. A delicacy. Well hung."

12   With admirable restraint the Englishman looked at me, then at the offending bird and said, "My good man, I've been accustomed to well-hung fowl all my life. Gamy. But this bird is rotten."

13   "May I, sir?" I tasted the partridge and it was exactly the way it should have been by Toledo standards. Gamy. Tasty. A little like a very strong cheese. Special taste produced by hanging the bird without refrigeration and much admired by Spanish hunters and countrymen. "It's as it should be," I concluded.

14   The Englishman, not one to make a scene, tasted the bird again but found it more objectionable than before. "I've shot a good many birds in my lifetime," he said, "but if I ever got one that smelled like this I'd shoot it again." He picked at the casserole for a moment and added, "This poor bird was hung so long it required no cooking. It had begun to fall apart of its own weight."

15   Once more I tried to console him: "I've had Toledo partridge twice before, and I promise you, it tasted just like yours."

"And you lived?" He pushed his plate away but refrained from complaining to the waiter. He did, however, look rather unpleasantly at me, as if to reprimand me for trying to convince him that he should eat such a bird.

16   At this point the waiter brought my chicken, and I am embarrassed to report that it smelled just like the partridge. It was one of the worst-cooked, poorly presented and evilest-smelling chickens I had ever been served and was obviously inedible. I tried cutting off a small piece, but blood ran out the end and the smell increased. I followed through and tasted it, but it was truly awful and I must have made a face, for the Englishman reached over, cut himself a helping, cut it into pieces and tried one while giving the other to his wife. Neither could eat the sample, whereupon the Englishman smiled indulgently and said very softly, "See what I mean?"

Comprehension

Answer the following questions. Your teacher may want you to answer the questions orally, in writing, or by underlining appropriate parts of the text. True/False items are indicated by a T / F preceding a statement.

1. T / F   The Spanish government does not want Spanish merchants to take unfair advantage of tourists.

2. How does the tourist menu protect tourists? _____

_____

3. T / F   In the first restaurant Michener wanted to order from the tourist menu.

4. T / F   Wine is included in the price of a tourist menu.

5. Why did the waiter refuse to give Michener the tourist menu in the first restaurant? _____

_____

6. T / F   Michener left the first restaurant without paying anything.

7. T / F   Michener hoped to have better luck in the second restaurant because it looked better than the first.

8. T / F   Michener changed his manner of ordering in the second restaurant.

9. In the second restaurant, what were the objections the waiter offered concerning the tourist menu?

   a. _____

   b. _____

   c. _____

10. T / F   For the price of the tourist menu in the second restaurant, one could choose from twenty-nine dishes.

11. Write a definition, synonym, or description of *in a row* (paragraph 7). _____

    What two words in the same paragraph are synonyms of *in a row*? _____

12. T / F   Michener's meal cost more than the government's fixed price for the tourist menu.

13. What made Michener think that the Englishman was a hunter?

    _____

14. The Englishman describes his partridge casserole as "raunchy." What synonyms of *raunchy*

    appear in paragraph 12? _____

15. What was wrong with the Englishman's partridge? _____

    _____

16. What is "well-hung" partridge? _____

17. T / F   The Englishman ate his casserole in spite of its foul odor.

18. Why did Michener speak up when the Englishman was thinking of returning his dinner?

    _____

19. Write a definition, synonym, or description of *inedible* (paragraph 16). _____

    _____

20. Do you think Michener returned his chicken? Why or why not? _____

    _____

Discussion/Composition

1. "When in Rome, do as the Romans do." Do you agree with this saying? Does Michener agree with it?

   a. Write a brief composition that explains why this is a wise philosophy. Give examples of activities and opportunities that might develop from such an approach to travel. Be specific. Use your own experiences or the experiences of others as examples.

   or

   b. Write a brief composition that explains the dangers and drawbacks of this philosophy.

2. We can learn a great deal about a writer from a story such as "Toledo." What is your opinion of Michener as a person? as a traveler? Write a brief composition that explains why you would like to travel through Europe with him. Or explain why you would not like to travel with him. Be specific. Use information from the story to support your position.

Vocabulary from Context

Use the context provided to determine the meanings of the italicized words. Write a definition, synonym, or description of each of the italicized vocabulary items in the space provided.

1. _____ At the Regal Restaurant, there are two menus. On one menu, an entire meal is listed for a single price. On the other, an *à la carte* menu, each dish is priced individually and may be ordered separately. In many cases, ordering from the first kind of menu is the cheapest way to get a complete meal. On such

2. _____ menus, however, if you order something that is not included in the meal, there is a *surcharge,* which makes the meal more expensive.

3. _____ I could not convince my friend to go on a picnic instead of to a restaurant. He was *adamant* in his desire to eat a formal meal.

4. _____ At a famous restaurant, I was once served food so old that it had gone bad. I could smell the *rotten* meat before the waiter put it on my table. Foolishly, I screamed insults at him. I should have realized that it wasn't the waiter's fault. I should

5. _____ have screamed those *abuses* at the cook.

6. _____ Usually if restaurant food is poorly prepared, I don't criticize the waiter. Instead, I *reprimand* the manager.

7. _____ When I am served bad food, I assume a very serious manner and say to the manager *gravely* that I will not pay for the

8. _____ *objectionable* meal.

9. _____ After eating at bad restaurants, the meals at the Elite Café look wonderfully *enticing,* as appealing as water to a person in a desert.

10. _____ Restaurants sometimes keep food unrefrigerated until it is
11. _____ almost bad, until it smells *gamy* and looks *raunchy.*

12. _____ Although I enjoy a pleasant atmosphere when I dine at restaurants, what is most important to me is the quality of the food. Nothing can *console* me after the disappointment of a poor meal.

13. _____ Knowing that the slightest mistake meant losing his job, the waiter carried the expensive wine glasses *gingerly* from the kitchen.

3

Nonprose Reading

Newspaper Advertisements

Classified advertisements, or "want ads," like the ones on page 51 appear in most newspapers.

Before You Begin   1. Have you ever tried to use this kind of advertisement? For what purpose(s)?

2. In what ways does the writing differ from normal prose writing?

The ads on page 51 come from a university newspaper. If you were living in this university community, you might use the ads in this newspaper to find a job, to rent an apartment, or to advertise something you wanted to sell. Reread each question. Then scan the ads to find the answer.*

1. If you had lost your watch, under which section might you look? _____

2. If you wanted to earn money, under which section would you place an ad? _____

3. If you were looking for an apartment, under which section would you place an ad? _____

4. If you needed somebody to share your apartment, under which section would you place an

   ad? _____

5. If you were looking for a house to rent, which telephone number(s) would you call? _____

6. What is the earliest date on which you could sublet an apartment? _____

7. If you wanted to live in an apartment by yourself without spending more than $500, which ads would you be sure to answer? Circle them.

8. If you had trouble getting to work on time every morning, which business service could you

   call? _____

(Continued on page 52)

---

*For an explanation of nonprose reading and an introduction to scanning, see Unit 1.

classified ads

FOR DIRECT CLASSIFIED SERVICE CALL 800-0557—10 A.M.-4 P.M. Monday-Friday

FOR RENT

BEST ON CAMPUS

Excellent room for women begins Jan., 2, 4 or 8 month lease. Singles, $335-$375. Double, $450. Call for appointment. 800-1932.

LUXURY A/C STUDIO, modern kitchen, wall to wall carpet. Available immediately. On-campus location. $495/mo. 800-5808 persistently.

AVAILABLE IMMEDIATELY: MODERN, FURNISHED EFFICIENCY & 1-BEDRM. APTS.
DAHLMANN APARTMENTS
800-7600

ONE BDRM. modern furn. apt., $550 mo., air cond., balcony, avail. Jan. 1 or immediate occupancy. Close to campus. Call Rick. 800-0119 after 10 p.m.

FAMILY HOME, 3 bdrm., full partition basement, 2 car garage, large yard, children and well trained pets welcome. $1175. See 11-21-94. Call Renter's Aid. 800-4300.

APT. 2-bedroom, air conditioned, furnished, convenient to Med. Center, for Jan. 1. 800-9846.

EFFICIENCY $490. Nice kitchen, basement storage space. Renter's Aid, 800-4300. Fee.

2 BEDROOM furnished apartment. Parking, laundry facilities. Dec.-Aug., $800 /month. 800-9715.

APT. 2-bedroom, air conditioned, furnished, convenient to Med. Center, for Jan. 1. 800-9846.

SUBLET

SUBLETS: as of Jan. 1. 2-bedroom furnished apartments. $750; also, roommates wanted. Call Modern Apartments, 418 East Washington, 800-6906.

ASSUME LEASE 3-bdrm. 1½ bath apt. Hospital-campus area, carpeted, stove and refrig.$1200/month plus elec. Avail. 1 Dec. Free bus to downtown and campus 10 times daily weekdays. Coin Laundry and free storage in basement. Underground parking avail. 800-7487.

TO SUBLET: Apt., 2½ rooms and bath, near campus, completely furnished, $450/mo. All utilities included. Available after Xmas. Call Larry persistently, 800-7213.

3-BEDROOM
apartment available for sublet in January. Furnished. 2 blocks from campus. Price negotiable. Call 800-2134.

SUBLET

DOUBLE ROOM in furnished house near campus. Parking. 800-5854.

WANTED TO RENT

2-BDRM. PLACE wanted. Hopefully under $750/mon. Thanks. 800-6839.

GARAGE OR PARKING SPACE wanted near campus. Call Rob, 800-4992 before 10:00 a.m. or after 6:00 p.m.

WANTED: ONE-BEDROOM APARTMENT for Jan. 1 through August. Preferably near campus, but not necessary. Call 800-7129.

ROOMMATES

FEMALE Grad Student wanted: to share a 2-bdrm., furnished apt., own rm. ½ block from Frieze Bldg. $425/mo. Starting Jan. 800-1090 after 5:30. Call persistently.

NEED PERSON to assume lease for own bedroom in apt. near campus, $350/mo. starting Jan. 1. Call 800-6157 after 5:00.

FEMALE ROOMMATE WANTED Own room near campus. Available December 1. Rent $325 per month until March 1st. $375 thereafter. Call Jill for details, 800-7839.

FOURTH WOMAN NEEDED: bi-level, modern apartment, near campus. $300/mo. Beginning January. 800-7866.

BUSINESS SERVICES

TUTORING, EE, Statistics, Math, Computers. Call Walt, 800-3594.

EARLY HOUR WAKE-UP SERVICE For prompt, courteous wake-up service. 800-0760.

WEDDING INVITATIONS—Mod. or traditional. Call 800-0942 anytime.

PASSPORT and Application Photos. Call 800-0552 or 800-9668, ask for Steve.

MATURE STUDENT would take care of children during Christmas vacation. 800-0441 eves.

TYPING AND EDITING. Call Jean. 800-3594. 10 a.m.-10 p.m.

EXPERIENCED GUITAR TEACHER wants students. Folk/jazz. Bob. 800-7535.

LOST AND FOUND

FOUND: Cat, 6 months old, black and white markings Found near Linden and South U. Steve. 800-4661.

LOST: Gold wire rim glasses in brown case. Campus area. Reward. Call Gregg 800-2896.

FOUND: Set of keys on Tappan near Hill intersection. Identify key chain. Call 800-9662 around 6.

FEMALE CAT: Black, white, and brown. Found two weeks ago at E. Ann and Glenn. 800-9286.

FOUND Nov. 8—A black and white puppy in Packard-Jewett area. 800-5770.

FOR SALE

COME to our moving sale—Plants, pottery, books, clothes, etc. Sat., Dec. 14—9:00-5:00. 1612 Ferndale, Apt. 1, 800-4696.

SHEEPSKIN COAT, man's size 42, 1 year old. $160. After 6 p.m., 800-5224.

MOVING: Must sell. TV b/w 12", $50; AM/FM transistor radio A/C or battery, $15; cassette tape recorder, $10; misc. records. Call Jon or Pat, 800-0739 after 5 or weekends.

USED FUR COATS and JACKETS. Good condition. $100-$300. Call 800-0436 after 12 noon.

SNOW TIRES: 12", used one winter. 800-7473.

PERSONAL

OVERSEAS JOBS — Australia, Europe, S. America, Africa. Students all professions and occupations $1000 to $5000 monthly. Expenses paid, overtime, sight-seeing. Free information.

UNSURE WHAT TO DO? Life-Planning Workshop, Dec. 13-15. Bob and Margaret Blood, 800-0046.

THE INTERNATIONAL CENTER plans to publish a booklet of student travel adventures. If you'd like to write about your foreign experience, unusual or just plain interesting, call us (800-9310) and ask for Mike or Janet.

WITCHCRAFT ANYONE? Wish to join or organize people into witchcraft or the occult. Call Don, 800-6762.

HELP WANTED

BABYSITTER—MY HOME

If you are available a few hours during the day, some evenings and occasional weekends to care for 2 school-age children, please call Gayle Moore days 800-1111, evenings and weekends 800-4964.

HELP WANTED for housework ½ day per week. When—to be discussed for mutual convenience. Good wages. Sylvan Street. Call 800-2817.

PERSONS WANTED for delivery work. Own transportation. Good pay. Apply 2311 E. Stadium. Office 101, after 9 a.m.

TELEPHONE RECEPTIONIST wanted. No experience necessary. Good pay. Apply 2311 E. Stadium. Office 101. After 9 a.m.

WAITPERSON WANTED: 10 a.m.-2 p.m. or 10:30 a.m.-5 p.m. Apply in person, 207 S. Main. Curtis Restaurant.

PLANT LOVERS interested in working part-time at The Greenhouse apply in person. Liberty at Division.

9. Whom would you call if you wanted to buy a radio? _____

10. If you were a man and wanted to share an apartment, which telephone number(s) would

   you be sure to call? _____

11. Whom would you call if you wanted to learn to play the guitar? _____

12. If you wanted a job taking care of children, which ad would you answer? _____

13. Which number(s) would you be sure to call if you were interested in apartments near the

   Medical Center? _____

14. If you wanted to place an ad, what number would you call? _____

   If you placed an ad at 4:00 P.M. on Wednesday, when would it appear? _____

15. Would you answer the ad offering a job as a delivery person if you didn't have a car? ____

16. Rewrite the following ad using complete grammatical sentences: For Rent: 1-bdrm. mod.

   furn. apt. $600/mo. A/C avail. after Xmas. _____

   _____

   _____

   _____

17. Write an ad from the following statement using abbreviations and eliminating unnecessary
   words.

   I am leaving the country before January 31, and I must sell everything. I have a television,
   an air conditioner, miscellaneous clothing and a used refrigerator. I also want to sell an
   artificial Christmas tree and my electric typewriter. The typewriter will be available after
   January 20. Please call 800-7351 before 9:00 in the evening. Ask for Bob.

   _____

   _____

   _____

   _____

Word Study

Stems and Affixes

Below is a list of some commonly occurring stems and affixes.* Study their meanings, then do the exercises that follow. Your teacher may ask you to give examples of other words you know that are derived from these stems and affixes.

Prefixes

ante-	before	anterior, ante meridiem (A.M.)
circum-	around	circumference
contra-, anti-	against	anti-war, contrast
inter-	between	international, intervene
intro-, intra-	within	introduce, intravenous
post-	after	post-game, post-graduate
sub-, suc-, suf-, sug-, sup-, sus-	under	subway, support
super-	above, greater, better	superior, supermarket
trans-	across	trans-Atlantic, transportation

Stems

-ced-	go, move, yield	precede
-duc-	lead	introduce
-flect-	bend	reflect, flexible
-mit-, -miss-	send	remit, missionary
-pon-, -pos-	put, place	postpone, position
-port-	carry	portable
-sequ-, -secut-	follow	consequence, consecutive
-spir-	breathe	inspiration, conspiracy
-tele-	far	telegraph, telephone
-ven-, -vene-	come	convene, convention
-voc-, -vok-	call	vocal, revoke

Suffixes

-able-, -ible-, -ble	capable of, fit for	trainable, defensible
-ous, -ious, -ose	full of, having the qualities of	poisonous, anxious, verbose

Exercise 1

In each item, select the best definition of the italicized word or phrase or answer the question.

1. The first thing Jim did when he got off the train was look for a *porter*.

____ a. person who sells tickets   ____ c. person who carries luggage
____ b. taxi cab   ____ d. door to the luggage room

*For a list of all stems and affixes taught in *Reader's Choice,* see the Appendix.

2. No matter what Fred said, Noam *contradicted him*.

    ____ a. said the opposite   ____ c. laughed at him
    ____ b. yelled at him   ____ d. didn't listen to him

3. The doctor is a specialist in the human *respiratory* system. She is an expert on _____

    ____ a. bones.   ____ c. nerves.
    ____ b. lungs.   ____ d. the stomach.

4. He *circumvented* the problem.

    ____ a. described   ____ c. went around, avoided
    ____ b. solved   ____ d. wrote down, copied

5. Which is a postscript?

    ____ a.
    ____ b.
    ____ c.
    ____ d.

6. Use what you know about stems and affixes to explain how the following words were derived:

    a. telephone _____

    b. telegram _____

    c. television _____

7. When would a photographer use a telephoto lens for his camera? _____

_____

8. Use word analysis to explain what *support* means _____

_____

9. What is the difference between interstate commerce and intrastate commerce? _____

_____

10. At one time, many European towns depended on the system of aqueducts built by the

    Romans for their water supply. What is an aqueduct? _____

_____

11. If a person has a *receding* hairline, what does he look like? _____

_____

12. The abbreviation A.M. (as in 10:30 A.M.) stands for *ante meridiem*. What do you think P.M.

(as in 10:30 P.M.) stands for? _____

_____

13. Consider these sentences:

   a. He *subscribes* to *Time* magazine.
   b. He *subscribes* to the theory that the moon is made of green cheese.

   Explain how these meanings of *subscribe* developed from the meanings of *sub* and *scribe*.

_____

_____

_____

Exercise 2

Word analysis can help you to guess the meaning of unfamiliar words. Using context clues and what you know about word parts, write a synonym, description, or definition of the italicized words.

1. _____   Despite evidence *to the contrary,* Mark really believes that he can pass an exam without studying.

2. _____   I haven't finished the report you asked for yet; let's *postpone* our meeting until next Tuesday.

3. _____   Ask your *supervisor* if you can take your vacation next month.

4. _____   Please *remit* your payment in the enclosed envelope.

5. _____   Something must be wrong with this machine. It won't type *superscripts* correctly: $\frac{2}{x}$ x2 x_2 x^2

6. _____   *Antibiotics,* such as penicillin, help the body fight bacterial but not viral infections.

7. _____   Nowadays, very little mail is *transported* by train.

8. _____   Don't invite Frank again; his behavior tonight was *inexcusable*.

9. _____   Scientists study the *interaction* between parents and their babies to better understand how infants learn.

10. _____ After the plane crash, the pilot had to fix his radio before he could *transmit* his location.

11. _____ The committee decided to stop working at noon and to *reconvene* at 1:30.

12. _____ The State of Texas *revoked* his driver's license because he had had too many accidents.

13. _____ This material is very useful because it is strong yet *flexible*.

14. _____ Barbara wanted to buy a *portable* typewriter.

15. _____ The Portugese sailor Magellan was the first person to *circumnavigate* the world.

16. _____ The King *imposed* a heavy tax on his people to pay for his foreign wars.

Exercise 3

Following is a list of words containing some of the stems and affixes introduced in this unit and the previous one. Definitions of these words appear on the right. Put the letter of the appropriate definition next to each word.

1. ____ anteroom

2. ____ antecedent

3. ____ vociferous

4. ____ vocation

5. ____ subsequent

a. characterized by a noisy outcry or shouting

b. a room forming an entrance to another one

c. the career one believes oneself called to; one's occupation or profession

d. something that happened or existed before another thing

e. following in time, order, or place

---

6. ____ subscript

7. ____ superscript

8. ____ intervene

9. ____ introspection

10. ____ convene

11. ____ consequence

a. the observation or examination of one's own thought processes

b. a letter or symbol written immediately below and to the right of another symbol

c. a logical result or conclusion; the relation of effect to cause

d. a letter or symbol written immediately above and to the right of another symbol

e. to come between people or points in time

f. to come together as a group

Word Study

Dictionary Use

In Unit 1, you were introduced to the types of information that a dictionary can provide. In this exercise, you will again scan* for information from a dictionary page, but here you will concentrate only on the definition of words. Read the questions, then scan the dictionary page (page 59) to find the answers.

1. In the following sentences, first determine the part of speech of the italicized word, then use the dictionary page to find a synonym for the word.

   a. Because of her all-night study sessions, Sandy is *run-down*.

      1. noun, verb, adjective, adverb

      2. synonym: _____

   b. John's telephone call to Peter caused a *rupture* in their four-year friendship.

      1. noun, verb, adjective, adverb

      2. synonym: _____

2. Find a synonym for *running* as it is used in the following sentence.

   We have won the contest four years *running*. _____

3. Check all the following words that are synonyms of *rural*.

   _____ a. rustic   _____ b. rubric   _____ c. pastoral

4. Under which word would you find synonyms of *run-of-the-mill*?

   _____ a. mill   _____ b. average   _____ c. run

5. Which word must you look up to find a description of a running knot?

   _____ a. slipknot   _____ b. running   _____ c. knot

6. According to this dictionary, a running mate can be either _____

      _____ a. a horse or a person.
      _____ b. a horse or a machine.
      _____ c. a person or a machine.

Dictionary page from *The American Heritage Dictionary of the English Language* (Boston: Houghton Mifflin).
*For an introduction to scanning, see Unit 1.

7. Which word must you look up to find the definition of *rung* as used in the following sentence:

   I would have rung you earlier but I didn't have time.

   _____ a. ring
   _____ b. rang
   _____ c. rung

8. From the dictionary definitions give the number of the appropriate definition for each of the italicized words in the following sentences.

   a. We put a *runner* in the hall from the front door to the kitchen. _____

   b. The singer walked onto the *runway* in order to get closer to the audience. _____

   c. There were 24 *runes* in the Germanic alphabet. _____

9. Which of the following runes is a modern *m*?

   _____ a. ᛉ
   _____ b. ᛗ
   _____ c. ᛖ

10. What is the meaning of the italicized word in the following sentence?

    John complained that *Ruse* was dangerous.

    _____ a. a misleading action
    _____ b. a city
    _____ c. an artifice

11. Complete the following sentence with the appropriate form of the word *rural*.

    Because of his anti-urban feelings Kenworthy Piker is known as the leading

    _____ of his time.

12. Choose the word that correctly completes the following sentences.

    a. Let me give you a brief _____ of what we talked about before you arrived.

       1. run-off
       2. run-down

    b. We must have a _____ in order to decide which person will be the new president.

       1. run-off
       2. run off

runcinate
Runcinate leaf of dandelion

rune

f u th a r k
g w h n i j e
p z s t b e
m l ng o d

basic Germanic runic alphabet

edh yogh

two later runes used in English

run·a·gate (rŭn′ə-gāt′) *n. Archaic.* **1.** A renegade or deserter. **2.** A vagabond. [Variant of RENEGADE (influenced by RUN).]

run-a·round (rŭn′ə-round′) *n.* Also **run·round** (rŭn′round′). **1.** Deception, usually in the form of evasive excuses. **2.** *Printing.* Type set in a column narrower than the body of the text, as on either side of a picture.

run·a·way (rŭn′ə-wā′) *n.* **1.** One that runs away. **2.** An act of running away. **3.** *Informal.* An easy victory. *—adj.* **1.** Escaping or having escaped from captivity or control. **2.** Of or done by running away. **3.** Easily won, as a race. **4.** Of or pertaining to a rapid price rise.

run·back (rŭn′băk′) *n.* **1.** The act of returning a kickoff, punt, or intercepted forward pass. **2.** The distance so covered.

run·ci·ble spoon (rŭn′sə-bəl). A three-pronged fork, as a pickle fork, curved like a spoon and having a cutting edge. [*Runcible,* a nonsense word coined by Edward Lear.]

run·ci·nate (rŭn′sə-nāt′, -nĭt) *adj. Botany.* Having saw-toothed divisions directed backward: *runcinate leaves.* [Latin *runcinātus,* past participle of *runcināre,* to plane, from *runcina,* carpenter's plane (formerly taken also to mean a saw), from Greek *rhukanē*†.]

run down. **1. a.** To slow down and stop, as a machine. **b.** To exhaust or wear out. **c.** To lessen in value. **2.** To pursue and capture. **3.** To hit with a moving vehicle. **4.** To disparage; decry. **5.** To give a brief or summary account of. **6.** *Baseball.* To put out a runner after trapping him between two bases.

run-down (rŭn′doun′) *n.* **1.** A summary or résumé. **2.** *Baseball.* A play in which a runner is put out when he is trapped between bases. *—adj.* **1.** In poor physical condition; weak or exhausted. **2.** Unwound and not running.

rune (ro͞on) *n.* **1.** One of the letters of an alphabet used by ancient Germanic peoples, especially by the Scandinavians and Anglo-Saxons. **2.** Any poem, riddle, or the like written in runic characters. **3.** Any occult characters. **4.** A Finnish poem or canto. [In sense 4, from Finnish *runo.* In other senses, Middle English *roun, rune,* secret writing, rune, from Old Norse *rūn* (unattested). See **rūno-** in Appendix.*] *—run′ic adj.*

rung¹ (rŭng) *n.* **1.** A rod or bar forming a step of a ladder. **2.** A crosspiece supporting the legs or back of a chair. **3.** The spoke in a wheel. **4.** *Nautical.* One of the spokes or handles on a ship's steering wheel. [Middle English *rung, rong,* Old English *hrung,* akin to Old High German *runga,* Gothic *hrugga*†.]

rung². Past tense and past participle of **ring.** See Usage note at **ring.**

run in. **1.** To insert or include as something extra. **2.** *Printing.* To make a solid body of text without a paragraph or other break. **3.** *Slang.* To take into legal custody.

run-in (rŭn′ĭn′) *n.* **1.** A quarrel; an argument; a fight. **2.** *Printing.* Matter added to a text. *—adj.* Added or inserted in text.

run·let (rŭn′lĭt) *n.* A rivulet. [Diminutive of RUN (stream).]

run·nel (rŭn′əl) *n.* **1.** A rivulet; a brook. **2.** A narrow channel or course, as for water. [Middle English *rynel,* Old English *rynel,* from *rinnan,* to run, flow. See **er-¹** in Appendix.*]

run·ner (rŭn′ər) *n.* **1.** One who or that which runs, as: **a.** One that competes in a race. **b.** A fugitive. **c.** A messenger or errand boy. **2.** An agent or collector, as for a bank or brokerage house. **3.** One who solicits business, as for a hotel or store. **4.** A smuggler. **5.** A vessel engaged in smuggling. **6.** One who operates or manages something. **7.** A device in or on which a mechanism slides or moves, as: **a.** The blade of a skate. **b.** The supports on which a drawer slides. **8.** A long narrow carpet. **9.** A long narrow tablecloth. **10.** A roller towel. **11.** *Metallurgy.* A channel along which molten metal is poured into a mold; gate. **12.** *Botany.* **a.** A slender, creeping stem that puts forth roots from nodes spaced at intervals along its length. **b.** A plant, such as the strawberry, having such a stem. **c.** A twining vine, such as the **scarlet runner** *(see).* **13.** Any of several marine fishes of the family Carangidae, such as the blue runner, *Caranx crysos,* of temperate waters of the American Atlantic coast.

run·ner-up (rŭn′ər-ŭp′) *n.* One that takes second place.

run·ning (rŭn′ĭng) *n.* **1.** The act of one that runs. **2.** The power or ability to run. **3.** Competition: *in the running.* **4.** An operating: *the running of a machine.* **5. a.** That which runs or flows. **b.** The amount that runs. *—adj.* Continuous: *a running commentary.* *—adv.* Consecutively: *four years running.*

running board. A narrow footboard extending under and beside the doors of some automobiles and other conveyances.

running gear. **1.** The working parts of an automobile, locomotive, or other vehicle. **2. Running rigging** *(see).*

running hand. Writing done rapidly without lifting the pen from the paper.

running head. *Printing.* A title printed at the top of every page or every other page. Also called "running title."

running knot. A **slipknot** *(see).*

running light. **1.** One of several lights on a boat or ship kept lighted between dusk and dawn. **2.** One of several similar lights on an aircraft; a navigation light.

running mate. **1.** A horse used to set the pace in a race for another horse. **2.** The candidate or nominee for the lesser of two closely associated political offices.

running rigging. The part of a ship's rigging that comprises the ropes with which sails are raised, lowered, or trimmed, booms and gaffs are operated, etc. Also called "running gear."

running stitch. One of a series of small, even stitches.

run·ny (rŭn′ē) *adj.* **-nier, -niest.** Inclined to run or flow.

Run·ny·mede (rŭn′ĭ-mēd). A meadow on the Thames, 19 miles west of London, where King John is thought to have signed the Magna Carta in 1215. [Middle English *Runimede,* "meadow on the council island" : Old English *Rūnieg,* council island : *rūn,* secret, secret council (see **rūno-** in Appendix*) + *ieg, ig,* island (see **akwā-** in Appendix*) + *mede,* MEAD (meadow).]

run off. **1.** To print, duplicate, or copy. **2.** To run away; elope. **3.** To spill over; to overflow. **4.** To decide a contest or competition by a run-off.

run-off (rŭn′ôf′, -ŏf′) *n.* **1. a.** The overflow of a fluid from a container. **b.** Rainfall that is not absorbed by the soil. **2.** Eliminated waste products from manufacturing processes. **3.** An extra competition held to break a tie.

run-of-the-mill (rŭn′əv-*thə*-mĭl′) *adj.* Ordinary; not special; average. See Synonyms at **average.** [From *run of (the) mill,* products of a mill that are not graded for quality.]

run on. **1.** To continue on and on. **2.** *Printing.* To continue a text without a formal break.

run-on (rŭn′ŏn′, -ôn′) *n. Printing.* Matter that is appended or added without a formal break. *—adj.* Being run on.

run·round. Variant of **run-around.**

runt (rŭnt) *n.* **1.** An undersized animal; especially, the smallest animal of a litter. **2.** A person of small stature. Often used disparagingly. [Possibly from Dutch *rund,* small ox. See **ker-¹** in Appendix.*] *—runt′i·ness n.* *—runt·y adj.*

run through. **1.** To pierce. **2.** To use up (money, for example) quickly. **3.** To examine or rehearse quickly.

run-through (rŭn′thro͞o′) *n.* A complete but rapid review or rehearsal of something, such as a theatrical work.

run·way (rŭn′wā′) *n.* **1.** A path, channel, or track over which something runs. **2.** The bed of a water course. **3.** A chute down which logs are skidded. **4.** *Bowling.* A narrow track on which balls are returned after they are bowled. **5.** A smooth ramp for wheeled vehicles. **6.** A narrow walkway extending from a stage into an auditorium. **7.** A strip of level ground, usually paved, on which aircraft take off and land.

Run·yon (rŭn′yən), **(Alfred) Damon.** 1884–1946. American journalist and author of short stories.

ru·pee (ro͞o-pē′, ro͞o′pē) *n. Abbr.* **Re., r., R.** **1. a.** The basic monetary unit of Ceylon and Mauritius, equal to 100 cents. **b.** The basic monetary unit of India, equal to 100 paise. **c.** The basic monetary unit of Nepal, equal to 100 pice. **d.** The basic monetary unit of Pakistan, equal to 100 paisas. See table of exchange rates at **currency.** **2.** A coin worth one rupee. [Hindi *rupaiyā,* from Sanskrit *rūpya,* wrought silver, from *rūpa*†, shape, image.]

Ru·pert (ro͞o′pərt). A river of Quebec, Canada, flowing 380 miles westward from Mistassini Lake to James Bay.

Ru·pert (ro͞o′pərt), **Prince.** 1619–1682. German-born English military, naval, and political leader; supporter of Charles I; inventor.

Ru·pert's Land (ro͞o′pərts). The Canadian territory granted the Hudson's Bay Company in 1670, most of which was incorporated in The Northwest Territories after its purchase by Canada in 1870.

ru·pi·ah (ro͞o-pē′ä) *n., pl.* **rupiah** or **-ahs.** **1.** The basic monetary unit of Indonesia, equal to 100 sen. See table of exchange rates at **currency.** **2.** A note worth one rupiah. [Hindi *rupaiyā,* RUPEE.]

rup·ture (rŭp′chər) *n.* **1. a.** The act of breaking open or bursting. **b.** The state of being broken open or burst. **2.** A break in friendly relations between individuals or nations. **3.** *Pathology.* **a.** A **hernia** *(see),* especially of the groin or intestines. **b.** A tear in bodily tissue. *—v.* **ruptured, -turing, -tures.** *—tr.* To break open; burst. *—intr.* To undergo or suffer a rupture. —See Synonyms at **break.** [Middle English *ruptur,* from Old French *rupture,* from Latin *ruptūra,* from *rumpere* (past participle *ruptus*), to break. See **reup-** in Appendix.*] *—rup′tur·a·ble adj.*

ru·ral (ro͝or′əl) *adj.* **1.** Of or pertaining to the country as opposed to the city; rustic. **2.** Of or pertaining to people who live in the country. **3.** Of or relating to farming; agricultural. Compare **urban.** [Middle English, from Old French, from Latin *rūrālis,* from *rūs* (stem *rūr-*), country. See **rewe-** in Appendix.*] *—ru′ral·ism′ n.* *—ru′ral·ist n.* *—ru′ral·ly adv.*

Synonyms: *rural, arcadian, bucolic, rustic, pastoral, sylvan.* These adjectives are all descriptive of existence or environment which is close to nature; those with a literary flavor are often used facetiously. *Rural* applies to sparsely settled or agricultural country, as distinct from settled communities. *Arcadian* implies ideal or simple country living. *Bucolic* is often used derisively of country people or manners. *Rustic,* sometimes uncomplimentary, applies to country people who seem unsophisticated, but may also apply favorably to living conditions or to natural environments which are pleasingly primitive. *Pastoral* implies the supposed peace of rural living and the shepherd's life, with a suggestion of artificiality. *Sylvan* refers to wooded as opposed to cultivated country, and carries the sense of unspoiled beauty.

rural free delivery. *Abbr.* **R.F.D., RFD** Free government delivery of mail in rural areas.

ru·ral·i·ty (ro͞o-răl′ə-tē) *n., pl.* **-ties.** **1.** The state or quality of being rural. **2.** A rural trait or characteristic.

ru·ral·ize (ro͝or′əl-īz′) *v.* **-ized, -izing, -izes.** *—tr.* To make rural. *—intr.* To live or visit in the country. *—ru′ral·i·za′tion n.*

rural route. *Abbr.* **R.R.** A rural mail route.

Ru·rik (ro͞o′rĭk). Died A.D. 879. Scandinavian warrior; founder of the dynasty that ruled Russia until 1598.

Rus. Russia; Russian.

Ru·se (ro͞o′sā). *Turkish* **Rus·chuk** (ro͞os′cho͝ok). A Danubian port in northeastern Bulgaria. Population, 118,000.

ruse (ro͞oz) *n.* An action or device meant to confuse or mislead. See Synonyms at **artifice.** [Middle English, detour of a hunted animal, from Old French, from *ruser,* to repulse, detour. See **rush** (to dash off).]

ă pat/ā pay/âr care/ä father/b bib/ch church/d deed/ĕ pet/ē be/f fife/g gag/h hat/hw which/ĭ pit/ī pie/îr pier/j judge/k kick/l lid, needle/m mum/n no, sudden/ng thing/ŏ pot/ō toe/ô paw, for/oi noise/ou out/o͝o took/o͞o boot/p pop/r roar/s sauce/sh ship, dish/

Sentence Study

Introduction

The exercises in this book provide you with practice in using a number of reading skills and strategies to understand a reading passage. Context Clues, Stems and Affixes, and Dictionary Use exercises provide you with practice in quickly finding specific pieces of information in a passage. Skimming, introduced later in this unit, focuses on reading a passage quickly for a general idea of its meaning.

When you have difficulty understanding a passage, just reading further will often make the passage clearer. Sometimes, however, comprehension of an entire passage depends on your being able to understand a single sentence. Sentences that are very long and sentences that contain difficult vocabulary or difficult grammatical patterns often cause comprehension problems for readers. The sentence study exercise that follows as well as similar ones in later units gives you the opportunity to develop strategies for understanding complicated sentences.

Although there is no easy formula that will help you to arrive at an understanding of a difficult sentence, you should keep the following points in mind.

1. Try to determine what makes the sentence difficult:

   a. If the sentence contains a lot of difficult vocabulary, it may be that the sentence can be understood without knowing the meaning of every word. Try crossing out unfamiliar items:

      The West had sent armies to ~~capture and~~ hold Jerusalem; instead they themselves fell ~~victim~~ to ~~a host of~~ new ideas and ~~subtle~~ influences which left their mark on the development of European literature, ~~chivalry,~~ warfare, ~~sanitation,~~ commerce, political institutions, medicine, ~~and the papacy itself.~~

   b. If the sentence is very long, try to break it up into smaller parts:

      The West had sent armies to capture and hold Jerusalem. The West fell victim to a host of new ideas and subtle influences. These ideas and influences left their mark on the development of European literature, chivalry, warfare, sanitation, commerce, political institutions, medicine, and the papacy.

   c. Also, if the sentence is very long, try to determine which parts of the sentence express specific details supporting the main idea. Often clauses which are set off by commas, or introduced by words such as *which, who,* and *that,* are used to introduce extra information or to provide supporting details. Try crossing out the supporting details in order to determine the main idea:

      These ideas, ~~which left their mark on the development of European literature, chivalry, warfare, sanitation, commerce, political institutions, medicine, and the papacy,~~ greatly changed Western culture.

Be careful! A good reader reads quickly but accurately.

2. Learn to recognize the important grammatical and punctuation clues that can change the meaning of a sentence.

   a. Look for single words and affixes that can change the entire meaning of a sentence:

      Summery weather is *not un*common.
      The *average* daytime *high* temperature is *approximately* 56°.

   b. Look for punctuation clues:

      Wally ☺sings☺ at all of his friends' parties.
      Barry said, "George has been elected president?"

   Note that all of the italicized words or affixes and the circled punctuation above are essential to the meaning of the sentences; if any of these are omitted, the meaning of the sentences change significantly.

   c. Look for key words that tell you of relationships within a sentence:

      The school has grown *from* a small building holding 200 students *to* a large institute that educates 4,000 students a year.

      From . . . to indicates the beginning and end points of a period of change.

      Many critics have proclaimed Doris Lessing as *not only* the best writer of the postwar generation, *but also* a penetrating analyst of human affairs.

      Not only . . . but also indicates that both parts of the sentence are of equal importance.

      In order to graduate on time, you will need to take five courses each semester.

      In order to is like *if*; it indicates that some event must occur before another event can take place.

      The West had sent armies to capture and hold Jerusalem; *instead* they themselves fell victim to new ideas and subtle influences.

      Instead indicates that something happened contrary to expectations.

      As a result of three books, a television documentary, and a special exposition at the Library of Congress, the mystery has aroused considerable public interest.

      As a result of indicates a cause and effect relationship. The clause that follows *as a result of* is the cause of some event. The three books, television program, and exposition are the *cause*; the arousal of public interest is the *effect*.

      Because of the impact of these ideas, *which* had been introduced originally to Europe by soldiers returning from the East, the West was greatly changed.

      Because of indicates a cause and effect relationship. The West was changed as a result of these ideas. The information between the word *which* and the final comma (,) refers to *these ideas*.

Sentence Study

Comprehension

Read the following sentences carefully. The questions that follow are designed to test your comprehension of complex grammatical structures. Select the *best* answer.

Example

The student revolt is not only a thorn in the side of the president's newly established government, but it has international implications as well.

Whom or what does this revolt affect?
_____ a. the students
_____ b. the side of the president's body
_____ c. only the national government
_____ d. national and international affairs

Explanation

_____ a. According to the sentence, the students are the cause of certain events, not among those affected.
_____ b. Although you may not have been familiar with the idiom *a thorn in someone's side,* context clues should have told you that this phrase means *a problem* and does not actually refer to the side of the president's body.
_____ c. National government is an incomplete answer. The construction *not only . . . but . . . as well* should tell you that more than one element is involved. The president's newly established government (the national government) is not the only area affected by the revolt.
__✓__ d. The revolt affects both national and international affairs.

1. I disagreed then as now with many of John Smith's judgments, but always respected him, and this book is a welcome reminder of his big, honest, friendly, stubborn personality.
    How does the author of this sentence feel about John Smith?
    _____ a. He dislikes him but agrees with his ideas.
    _____ b. He considers him to be a disagreeable person.
    _____ c. He disagrees with his ideas but respects him.
    _____ d. He disagreed with him then but agrees with him now.

2. Concepts like *passivity, dependence,* and *aggression* may need further research if they are to continue to be useful ways of thinking about human personalities.
    What might require more research?
    _____ a. human thought processes
    _____ b. certain concepts
    _____ c. human personalities
    _____ d. useful ways of thinking

3. In order for you to follow the schedule set by the publisher, your paper must be looked over over the weekend, revised, and handed in in its final form on Monday.

What must you do on Saturday and Sunday?

_____ a. meet the publisher _____ c. hand in a paper

_____ b. examine your paper _____ d. look over the weekend

4. The real reason why prices were, and still are, too high is complicated, and no short discussion can satisfactorily explain this problem.

What word or phrase best describes prices?

_____ a. complicated _____ c. too high in the past, but low now

_____ b. adequately explained _____ d. too high in the past and in the present

5. This is not just a sad-but-true story; the boy's experience is horrible and damaging, yet a sense of love shines through every word.

How does the author of this sentence feel about the story?

_____ a. It transmits a sense of love. _____ c. It is not true.

_____ b. It is just sad. _____ d. It is horrible and damaging.

6. In the past five years the movement has grown from unorganized groups of poorly armed individuals to a comparatively well-armed, well-trained army of anywhere from 10,000 to 16,000 members.

What is the present condition of this movement?

_____ a. The members are poorly armed.

_____ b. There are only a few poor individuals.

_____ c. There are over 16,000 members.

_____ d. The members are organized and well armed.

7. The financial situation isn't bad yet, but we believe that we have some vital information and, if it is correct, unemployment will soon become a serious problem.

What do we know about the financial situation?

_____ a. It won't change. _____ c. It is not bad now.

_____ b. It will become a serious problem. _____ d. It will improve.

8. The general then added, "The only reasonable solution to the sort of problems caused by the current unstable political situation is one of diplomacy and economic measures and not the use of military force."

What type of solution does the general support?

_____ a. economic and diplomatic action

_____ b. diplomatic and economic action if military force fails

_____ c. only diplomatic action

_____ d. military actions in response to political problems

9. Because the supply of natural gas was plentiful in comparison to other choices like coal and fuel oil, and because it burns cleaner, many people changed their heating systems to natural gas, thereby creating shortages.

Why did people prefer gas?

_____ a. It was natural.

_____ b. There were no other choices.

_____ c. The other fuels were dirtier and less plentiful.

_____ d. There is, even today, a plentiful supply of it.

Paragraph Reading

Main Idea

This exercise is similar to the one you did in Unit 1. Read the following paragraphs and poem quickly. Concentrate on discovering the author's main idea. Remember, don't worry about details in the selections. You only want to determine the author's general message.

    After each of the first five paragraphs, select the statement that best expresses the writer's main idea. After paragraphs 6 and 7 and the poem, write a sentence that expresses the main idea in your own words. When you have finished, your teacher may want to divide the class into small groups for discussion.

Paragraph 1

        John Cabot was the first Englishman to land in North America. However, this man who legitimized England's claim to everything from Labrador to Florida, left no sea journal, no diary or log, not even a portrait or a signature. Until 1956 most learned encyclopedias and histories indicated that Cabot's first landfall in America was Cape Breton, Nova Scotia. Then a letter was discovered in the Spanish archives, making it almost certain that he had touched first at the northernmost tip of Newfoundland, within five miles of the site of Leif Ericson's ill-fated settlement at L'Anse aux Meadows. Researchers studying the voyages of Columbus, Cartier, Frobisher, and other early explorers had a wealth of firsthand material with which to work. Those who seek to recreate the life and routes used by Cabot must make do with thirdhand accounts, the disloyal and untruthful boasts of his son, Sebastian, and a few hard dates in the maritime records of Bristol, England.

Select the statement that best expresses the main idea of the paragraph.

_____ a. John Cabot claimed all the land from Labrador to Florida for England.

_____ b. Much of what is known about Cabot is based on the words of his son, Sebastian, and on records in Bristol, England.

_____ c. The lack of firsthand accounts of Cabot's voyage has left historians confused about his voyages to North America.

_____ d. Historians interested in the life and routes used by Cabot recently discovered an error they made in describing his discovery of North America.

From Allan Keller, "The Silent Explorer: John Cabot in North America," *American History Illustrated.*

Paragraph 2   The Bible, while mainly a theological document written with the purpose of explaining the nature and moral imperatives of the Christian and Jewish God, is secondarily a book of history and geography. Selected historical materials were included in the text for the purpose of illustrating and underlining the religious teaching of the Bible. Historians and archaeologists have learned to rely upon the amazing accuracy of historical memory in the Bible. The smallest references to persons and places and events contained in the accounts of the Exodus, for instance, or the biographies of such Biblical heroes as Abraham and Moses and David, can lead, if properly considered and pursued, to extremely important historical discoveries. The archaeologists' efforts are not directed at "proving" the correctness of the Bible, which is neither necessary nor possible, any more than belief in God can be scientifically demonstrated. It is quite the opposite, in fact. The historical clues in the Bible can lead the archaeologist to a knowledge of the civilizations of the ancient world in which the Bible developed and with whose religious concepts and practices the Bible so radically differed. It can be considered as an almost unfailing indicator, revealing to the experts the locations and characteristics of lost cities and civilizations.

Select the statement that best expresses the main idea of the paragraph.

_____ a. The holy writings of the world's religions can provide valuable geographical information.

_____ b. The Bible is primarily a religious document.

_____ c. The Bible was intended by its authors to be a record of the history of the ancient world.

_____ d. The Bible, though primarily a religious text, is a valuable tool for people interested in history.

Paragraph 3   At one time it was the most important city in the region—a bustling commercial center known for its massive monuments, its crowded streets and commercial districts, and its cultural and religious institutions. Then, suddenly, it was abandoned. Within a generation most of its population departed and the once magnificent city became all but a ghost town. This is the history of a pre-Columbian city called Teotihuacán (the Aztec Indians' word for "the place the gods call home"), once a metropolis of as many as 200,000 inhabitants 33 miles northeast of present-day Mexico City and the focus of a far-flung empire that stretched from the arid plains of central Mexico to the mountains of Guatemala. Why did this city die? Researchers have

Paragraph 2 from Nelson Glueck, "The Bible as Divining Rod," *Horizon.*
Paragraph 3 from "Twilight of the Gods," *Time.*

found no signs of epidemic disease or destructive invasions. But they have found signs that suggest the Teotihuacanos themselves burned their temples and some of their other buildings. Excavations revealed that piles of wood had been placed around these structures and set afire. Some speculate that Teotihuacán's inhabitants may have abandoned the city because it had become "a clumsy giant . . . too unwieldy to change with the times." But other archaeologists think that the ancient urbanites may have destroyed their temples and abandoned their city in rage against their gods for permitting a long famine.

Select the statement that best expresses the main idea of the paragraph.

_____ a. Teotihuacán, once the home of 200,000 people, was the center of a large empire.

_____ b. Many archaeologists are fascinated by the ruins of a pre-Columbian city called Teotihuacán.

_____ c. Teotihuacán, once a major metropolitan area, was destroyed by an invasion.

_____ d. A still unsolved mystery is why the people of Teotihuacán suddenly abandoned their city.

Paragraph 4

In any archaeological study that includes a dig, the procedures are basically the same: 1) selecting a site 2) hiring local workers 3) surveying the site and dividing it into sections 4) digging trenches to locate levels and places to excavate 5) mapping architectural features 6) developing a coding system that shows the exact spot where an object is found 7) and recording, tagging, cleaning and storing excavated materials. Neilson C. Debevoise, writing on an expedition to Iraq in the early 1930's, described the typical "route" of excavated pottery. Workers reported an object to staff members before removing it from the ground. The date, level, location and other important information were written on a piece of paper and placed with the object. At noon the objects were brought in from the field to the registry room where they were given a preliminary cleaning. Registry numbers were written with waterproof India ink on a portion of the object previously painted with shellac. The shellac prevented the ink from soaking into the object, furnished a good writing surface, and made it possible to remove the number in a moment. From the registry room objects were sent to the drafting department. If a clay pot, for example, was of a new type, a scale drawing was made on graph paper. Measurements of the top, greatest diameter, base, height, color of the glaze, if any, the quality and texture of the body and the quality of the workmanship were recorded on paper with the drawing. When the drafting department had completed its work the materials were placed on the storage shelves, grouped according to type for division with the

Paragraph 4 from "Unearthing the Past," *Research News.*

Iraq government and eventually shipped to museums. Today, the steps of a dig remain basically the same, although specific techniques vary.

Select the statement that best expresses the main idea of the paragraph.

_____ a. For a number of years, archaeologists have used basically the same procedure when conducting a dig.

_____ b. Neilson C. Debevoise developed the commonly accepted procedure for organizing a dig.

_____ c. Archaeologists take great care to assure that all excavated objects are properly identified.

_____ d. A great deal of important historical and archaeological information can be provided by a dig.

Paragraph 5

The unprecedented expansion of Modern architecture throughout the world must be considered one of the great events in the history of art. Within the space of the last generation, the contemporary movement has become the dominant style of serious building not only in the United States and Europe, where pioneers had been at work since the late nineteenth century, but also in nations such as Brazil and India, where almost no Modern architecture existed until much later. Only the Gothic perhaps, among all the styles of the past, gained popular acceptance with anything like the speed of the Modern. And like the Gothic—which required a full seventy-five years of experimentation before it produced the cathedral of Chartres—the Modern has continually improved its structural techniques, gained in scale, and revised its aesthetics as it has attempted to meet the full range of people's civilized needs.

Select the statement that best expresses the main idea of the paragraph.

_____ a. Gothic architecture gained popular acceptance faster than Modern architecture did.

_____ b. Modern architecture has not changed fast enough to meet the needs of civilization.

_____ c. The rapid growth and development of Modern architecture (as an art form) is nearly unequaled in the history of art.

_____ d. If architectural styles are to endure, they must develop and improve in an attempt to meet society's needs.

Paragraph 5 adapted from Allan Temko, "The Dawn of the 'High Modern'," *Horizon.*

Paragraph 6

A summit is not any old meeting between two heads of state. Potentates have been visiting each other since the beginning of time. The Queen of Sheba came to visit King Solomon and exchanged riddles with him. Mark Antony came to visit Cleopatra and stayed on. Royalty, presidents and prime ministers of allied nations have sometimes got together after a victorious war to divide the spoils, as they did at the Congress of Vienna in 1814 and then at Paris after World War I. But a summit, in the sense in which Winston Churchill introduced the word into the language when he called for one in 1950, is something quite different and quite specific: it is a meeting between the leaders of two or more rival or enemy Great Powers trying to satisfy their mutual demands and head off future conflict.

Write a sentence that expresses the main idea of the paragraph. _____

_____

Paragraph 7

The ideals that children hold have important implications for their school experiences. Children who believe in the value of hard work and responsibility and who attach importance to education are likely to have higher academic achievement and fewer disciplinary problems than those who do not have these ideals. They are also less likely to drop out of school. Such children are more likely to use their out-of-school time in ways that reinforce learning. For example, high school students who believe in hard work, responsibility, and the value of education spend about 3 more hours a week on homework than do other students. This is a significant difference since the average student spends only about 5 hours a week doing homework.

Write a sentence that expresses the main idea of the paragraph. _____

_____

Paragraph 6 from Robert Wernick, "Summits of Yore: Promises, Promises and a Deal or Two," *Smithsonian.*
Paragraph 7 from "Ideals," in *What Works: Research about Teaching and Learning* (U.S. Department of Education).

Poem

Looking in the Album

Here the formal times are surrendered
to the camera's indifferent gaze: weddings,
graduations, births and official portraits taken
every ten years to falsify appearances.
Even snapshots meant to gather afternoons
with casual ease are rigid. Smiles
are too buoyant. Tinny laughter echoes
from the staged scene on an artificial
beach. And yet we want to believe
this is how it was: That children's hair
always bore the recent marks of combs;
that trousers, even at picnics, were always
creased and we traveled years with the light
but earnest intimacy of linked hands or arms
arranged over shoulders. This is the record
of our desired life: Pleasant, leisurely on vacations,
wryly comic before local landmarks, competent
auditors of commencement speakers, showing
in our poses that we believed what we were told.
But this history contains no evidence
of aimless nights when the wilderness of ourselves
sprang up to swallow the outposts of what
we thought we were. Nowhere can we see
tears provoked by anything but joy. There
are no pictures of our brittle, lost intentions.
We burned the negatives that we felt did not give a true
account and with others made this abridgement of our lives.

Vern Rutsala

Write a sentence that expresses the main idea of the poem. _____

_____

Vern Rutsala, "Looking in the Album," in *The Window* by Vern Rutsala (Middletown: Wesleyan University Press).

Discourse Focus

Skimming

It is sometimes useful to obtain a general impression of a book, article, or story before deciding whether or not to read more carefully. *To skim* is to read quickly in order to get a general idea of a passage. Unlike scanning,* which involves searching for details or isolated facts, skimming requires you to note only information and clues that provide an idea of the central theme or topic of a piece of prose.

When you skim, it is necessary to read only selected sentences in order to get the main idea. You should also use textual clues such as italicized or underlined words, headlines or subtitles, spacing, paragraphing, etc. Do not read every word or sentence.

Once you have a general idea about an article, you may decide to read the entire selection carefully, or only to scan for specific pieces of information in order to answer questions that have occurred to you.

This exercise is designed to give you practice in skimming. The following partial entries from an encyclopedia are from biographies of famous people. Preceding each selection is a question concerning a research topic. You must skim each passage to decide if a careful reading would provide information on the topic given. Indicate your answer by checking *Yes* or *No*.

Example

In one minute, skim this passage and indicate if the selection should be read carefully.

Would you do more research on Jane Addams if you were interested in women's contribution to modern elementary education?

_____ Yes
_____ No

ADDAMS, JANE (1860–1935), American social worker who founded the Chicago social welfare center known as Hull House. She was born in Cedarville, Ill., on Sept. 6, 1860, the daughter of a prosperous merchant. She graduated from Rockford College (then Rockford Seminary) in 1881. Traveling in Europe, she was stirred by the social reform movement in England and especially by a visit to Toynbee Hall, the first university settlement. In 1889, with her college classmate Ellen Gates Starr, she founded Hull House in the slums of Chicago.

Hull House grew rapidly and soon became the most famous settlement house in America. Many reformers came there, not so much to serve as to learn. Jane Addams was the leader and dominant personality. Hull House pioneered in child labor reform and in the fight for better housing, parks, and playgrounds. It initiated steps toward progressive education and attempts to acclimatize immigrants to America.

Jane Addams was a practical idealist and an activist. She favored

prohibition and woman suffrage, and she campaigned for the Progressive party in 1912. She went beyond politics, however, for politics to her was part of a larger movement to humanize the industrial city.

She had always been a pacifist, and when World War I broke out in 1914, she became chairman of the Woman's Peace party and president of the International Congress of Women. In 1915 she visited many countries in Europe, urging the end of the war through mediation. She remained a pacifist when the United States entered the war in 1917, and as a result she was denounced by many Americans. In 1931 she was awarded the Nobel Peace Prize (sharing the award with Nicholas Murray Butler).

Jane Addams continued to be in the vanguard of social reform movements until her death in Chicago on May 21, 1935. She wrote ten books (including her famous *Twenty Years at Hull House*) and more than 400 articles. The influence that had begun at Hull House continued to spread around the world.

Explanation

You should have checked *No*. The first sentence identifies Jane Addams as an ". . . American social worker who founded the Chicago social welfare center known as Hull House." A brief glance at the second and fourth paragraphs indicates that she worked for child labor reform,

---

Example from *The Encyclopedia Americana* (Danbury, Conn.: Grolier).
*For an introduction to scanning, see Unit 1.

that she was a pacifist, and that she was chair of the Women's Peace party. Her publications, mentioned at the end of the article, do not deal with elementary education. Note that it is necessary to read only selected parts of each paragraph in order to obtain the main idea.

The selections that follow are similar to the example. You should skim each selection in one minute, then indicate if careful reading would be valuable.

Selection 1

Would you want to read more about Jane Austen if you were interested in British authors active in politics?

_____ Yes
_____ No

AUSTEN, JANE (1775-1817), English novelist, whose narrative world — "the little bit (two Inches wide) of Ivory on which I work with so fine a Brush" — has gained in literary reputation with the passage of the years.

Life. Jane Austen was born in Steventon, near Basingstoke, on Dec. 16, 1775. She was one of many children of a clergyman whose income was sufficient to support his family's gentility and whose literate tastes created an urbane atmosphere in the Austen home. She enjoyed an affectionate intimacy with her brothers and her sister, Cassandra. Jane never married but resided and worked in her family's home. The Austens lived largely in the English countryside, and Jane came to know all of county society, from the village apothecary to the landed aristocracy. She died in Winchester on July 18, 1817, and was buried in the cathedral.

Writings. The principles of English neoclassicism as expressed in the critical essays of Joseph Addison, the ethics of Samuel Johnson, and the fiction of Henry Fielding provided Jane Austen with a literary heritage.

In _Sense and Sensibility_ (1811) sentimentality is seriously attacked as a source of emotional insufficiency; here the values are more complex — reason and imagination are no longer set in opposition but are ironically interrelated. _Pride and Prejudice_ (1813), the most popular and wittiest of her novels, resembles the 18th-century comedy of manners with which her work has been too generally associated, and she herself was later dissatisfied with the sustained "playfulness and epigrammatism of the general style." _Mansfield Park_ (1814), though it includes sequences of brilliant comedy and bitter verisimilitude, has seemed too serious for some generations of readers; but a growing awareness of the figurative and ironic elements in her novels may alter this response. It is clear that irony is a pervasive and significant element in her fiction, and in _Emma_ (1816), perhaps the most perfectly patterned of her narratives, she employs her ironic vision to explore the heroine's delusions. By contrast, _Persuasion_ (published posthumously in 1818) reveals a delicately lyric insight characterized by an especially poetic use of natural imagery. _Persuasion_ was her last completed novel; during the final months of her life she began to write _Sanditon_, a fragment reverting partly to the manner of her earlier parody.

Selection 2

Would you want more information about the Dionne Quintuplets if you were interested in social and governmental reaction to multiple births?

_____ Yes
_____ No

DIONNE QUINTUPLETS, the five daughters born in Callander, Ontario, on May 28, 1934, to Oliva and Elzire Dionne, who already had six children. The quintuplets, Annette, Émilie, Yvonne, Marie, and Cécile, were delivered at the Dionne farmhouse (now preserved and restored). They were cared for by Dr. Allan Roy Dafoe, a local general medical practitioner. The Canadian Red Cross provided them with incubators and nursing care, and the Dafoe Memorial Hospital was built nearby by public subscription as a nursery. In 1935 the Ontario legislature made them wards of the province to avoid exploitation by theatrical managers and show producers; their father regained custody in 1941.

In 1943 a new family home was built, and the quintuplets were educated there until they entered Nicolet College in 1952. Marie (Mrs. Florian Houle) died in Montreal on Feb. 27, 1970. Émilie died of an epileptic seizure on Aug. 6, 1954, in Ste.-Agathe-des-Monts, Quebec. Yvonne trained as a nurse and spent several years in convents. Annette married Germain Allard of Montreal, and Cécile married Philippe Langlois of Quebec.

"Austen, Jane," "Dionne Quintuplets," "Curie, Pierre and Marie," and "Eddy, Mary Baker" from _The Encyclopedia Americana_ (Danbury, Conn.: Grolier). "Jenner, Edward" from _Encyclopedia Britannica_.

Selection 3

Would you read more about the Curies if you were interested in scientific contributions to modern transportation?

_____ Yes
_____ No

CURIE, PIERRE (1859–1908), and MARIE (1867–1934), French scientists, whose isolation of polonium and radium marked the beginning of a new era in the study of atomic structure.

Pierre Curie was born in Paris on May 15, 1859, the son of a physician. Until the age of 14 he was trained in science by his father, receiving only a minimum of the classical education that was standard in his time. He went to the Sorbonne at 16 and majored in physics. When he was only 19, he was appointed a teaching assistant and director of laboratory instruction at the Paris Faculty of Sciences.

Early Careers. In 1880, Pierre Curie and his brother Jacques discovered piezo-electricity, the appearance of electrical charges on the surface of certain insulating crystals when subjected to mechanical stresses. About 1891, Pierre began an intense investigation of magnetism at elevated temperatures. This led to the discovery of the _Curie point_ — the temperature at which ferromagnetic substances lose their magnetism. Further research

led to the formulation of _Curie's law_, which states that the magnetic susceptibility of ferromagnetic substances above the Curie point is inversely proportional to the absolute temperature. This law is not strictly true and was modified by Pierre Weiss in 1907.

In 1895, Pierre married Marie Sklowdoska, a young student from Poland, who had begun her scientific career with an investigation of the magnetic properties of different kinds of steel. In fact, it was their mutual interest in magnetism that drew them together. Marie Sklowdoska was born in Warsaw on Nov. 7, 1867. She made a brilliant record as a student but found no outlet for her talents in her native country. She became a private tutor and might have remained in that position had it not been for her sister Bronislawa, who lived in Paris. Marie joined her sister in 1891 and studied mathematics, physics, and chemistry at the Sorbonne. Her marriage to Pierre Curie thrust her into the mainstream of French science. Their scientific careers were to remain intertwined until Pierre's tragic death.

Selection 4

Would you want to read more about Mary Baker Eddy if you were interested in religious leaders and writers?

_____ Yes
_____ No

EDDY, MARY BAKER (1821–1910). The subject of sharp controversy in her own day, she is now recognized as a pioneer of modern spiritual healing, but her position as a Christian thinker is still variously estimated. Mrs. Eddy herself urged that her life and her works be submitted to the New Testament test "By their fruits ye shall know them" (Matthew 7:20), and any responsible estimate of her must be determined by one's understanding of Christian Science.

Life. Mary Morse Baker, the daughter of a farmer, was born at Bow, near Concord, N.H., on July 16, 1821. Because of her poor health her education was sporadic, but she received valuable mental stimulus and guidance from her elder brother Albert, a brilliant student at Dartmouth. Although deeply religious, she was also independent and early took issue with her father's strict Calvinism. Largely because of the sense of New Testament Christianity she imbibed from her mother, she found it impossible to accept the doctrine that most of the human race had been born to inevitable damnation. A sharp confrontation on this issue with the minister of the Congregational Church at Sanbornton Bridge (now Tilton),

N.H., when she was 17, resulted surprisingly in her being accepted into membership despite her doctrinal protest.

In 1866 her years of illness came to an abrupt climax when she was critically injured by a fall and restored suddenly to health while reading in the Bible of one of Jesus' healings (Matthew 9:1–8). This was the genesis of Christian Science. The remainder of her long life was given to study, writing, healing, teaching, and finally to organizing and guiding the Church of Christ Scientist. In 1877 she married Asa Gilbert Eddy, a practitioner of Christian Science healing. One of her last acts, when she was 87, was the founding of the international daily newspaper the _Christian Science Monitor_ in 1908. She died in Chestnut Hill, Mass., on Dec. 3, 1910, leaving behind her a church with nearly 100,000 members.

Thought. During her years of invalidism Mrs. Eddy's faith in orthodox medicine had waned and she had sought relief through homeopathy, hydropathy, and other systems then popular. Gradually she came to the conclusion that all disease was mental rather than physical. This was confirmed by her experience in the early 1860's with a healer named Phineas P. Quimby, in Portland, Me.

Selection 5

Would you read more about Edward Jenner if you were interested in the lives of physicians who made important medical discoveries?

_____ Yes
_____ No

JENNER, EDWARD. Jenner was born May 17, 1749, in Berkeley, Gloucestershire, at a time when the patterns of British medical practice and education were undergoing gradual change. Slowly the division between the Oxford- or Cambridge-trained physicians and the apothecaries or surgeons — who were much less educated and who acquired their medical knowledge through apprenticeship rather than through academic work — was becoming less sharp and hospital work was becoming much more important.

Jenner was a country youth, the son of a clergyman who died when the boy was only five. Brought up largely by an older brother who was also a clergyman, Edward acquired a love of nature that remained with him all his life. He attended grammar school and at the age of 13 was apprenticed to a nearby surgeon. In the following eight years Jenner acquired a sound knowledge of medical and surgical practice. On completing his apprenticeship at the age of 21, he went to London and became the house pupil of John Hunter, who was on the staff of St. George's Hospital and was soon to become one of the most prominent surgeons in London. Even more important, however, he was an anatomist, biologist, and ex-

perimentalist of the first rank; not only did he collect biological specimens but he also concerned himself with problems of physiology and function.

The firm friendship that grew between the two men lasted until the death of Hunter in 1793. From no one else could Jenner have received the stimuli that so confirmed his natural bent — a catholic interest in biological phenomena, disciplined powers of observation, sharpening of critical faculties, and a reliance on experimental investigation. From Hunter, Jenner received the characteristic advice: "Why think [i.e., speculate] — why not try the experiment?"

In addition to his training and experience in biology, Jenner made progress in clinical surgery. At the end of two years in London, he returned, in 1773, to country practice in Berkeley and enjoyed substantial success. He was capable, skillful, and popular. In addition to practicing medicine, he joined two medical groups for the promotion of medical knowledge and wrote occasional medical papers. He played the violin in a musical club, wrote light verse, and, as a naturalist, made many observations, particularly on the nesting habits of the cuckoo and on bird migration. He also

4

Reading Selections 1A–1B

News and Information

In our modern world an education is rapidly becoming a necessity if one hopes to earn a good living. The readings that appear below provide you with the opportunity to examine your ideas about education. Your teacher may want you to talk over some of the issues in small groups before discussing answers with the class as a whole.

The following questions are intended to focus your thoughts on education. The questions have no absolute right or wrong answer; each society has different opinions on the importance and structure of education. Indicate if you believe each statement is true (T) or false (F). Be prepared to give reasons and examples to support your answers.

1. _____ An education is a basic human right—every child is entitled to an education.

2. _____ Society must take responsibility for the education of all individuals.

3. _____ It is the responsibility of the family to provide an education for children.

4. _____ All children must attend school.

5. _____ School is not necessary for all children.

6. _____ A good education includes music, art, sports, social activities, etc.

7. _____ Schools should focus only on the "basics": reading, writing, and arithmetic.

8. _____ Education policy should be made at the national level, and all schools should follow a uniform plan.

9. _____ Schools should be controlled by the community in which they are located.

Selection 1A   **Textbook**

Below is an excerpt from an American textbook for school children. Read the selection and answer the questions that follow.

American Values in Education

Our school system has developed as it has because the American people value education highly. Some of the traditional values which have developed over the years are:

1. Public education should be *free*. There should be no hidden charges to prevent any citizen from receiving a good education at public expense.

2. Schooling should be *equal* and open to all. No one should be discriminated against because of race, religion, or financial status.

3. The public schools should be *free of any creed or religion*. The schools of the United States are open to all Americans regardless of their religious beliefs. The Supreme Court has held that no special prayer or Bible reading shall be required. However, religious schools (sometimes called parochial schools) are permitted outside of the public school system.

4. Public schools are *controlled by the state and local governments* within which they are located. Local school boards run the public schools under laws passed by the state legislature. The State Board of Education assists the local schools, but does not give orders to the district board. The United States Office of Education also assists with advice and information, but the actual control is located in the local school district, where the people know the local situation.

5. Attendance at school is *compulsory*. Parents cannot decide to keep their children out of school. Each state compels the attendance of young people, usually between the ages of 7 and 16.

6. Schooling should be *enriched* and not just confined to the fundamentals. Most Americans believe that schools should be places where young people can grow in body, mind, and spirit. Athletics, clubs, social events, and creative arts are a part of each person's education. Schools should be lively places where individuals are encouraged to develop to their greatest potential.

Discussion

1. Using the six "traditional values" of American education described above, summarize the educational philosophy of your country. Where do you find similarities? What are the differences?

2. Who should make decisions about the schools—parents? professional educators? elected officials? religious leaders? specially appointed experts? the children themselves? Read the statements below and discuss the pros and cons of each. With whom do you agree?

   a. Parents: "They are our kids. We know what is best for them. We should decide what they learn and how they are taught."

   b. Teachers: "What do parents know? We have been to college. We are the ones with the special training. We should make the decisions."

   c. Government officials: "We have the best view of the issues. We know the budget and we understand the laws and how they apply. Only we can make the best decisions."

   d. Religious authorities: "Schools that teach facts but no values weaken the moral strength of the country. We can provide the wisdom and insight on which all teaching should be based."

From *American Civics,* 2d ed. (New York: Harcourt Brace Jovanovich).

e. University experts: "We have studied the problems and done the research. We should be consulted before any decisions are made."

f. Children: "It is our lives and education that are at stake. No decisions should be made without our advice and agreement."

3. Do you think your country fulfills its educational goals? Does the United States live up to the philosophical ideals listed above? To what extent can a country live up to its educational ideals? Give examples to support your opinions.

Selection 1B   **Newspaper Article**

An automobile accident has caused heartache and trouble for the Espino family of Brownsville, Texas. It has also caused difficulties for the Brownsville school system. In many ways, the following article challenges the ideas discussed in the previous article. Read the article, imagining that you know the little boy, Raul. Decide what you would do to solve his problems. Answer the comprehension and discussion questions that follow. You may want to do the Vocabulary from Context exercise 1 on pages 79–80 before reading.

Parents Seeking Cool Classroom for Son

1 BROWNSVILLE, Texas (AP) — School bells and the swelter of a waning Texas summer will greet children in Brownsville when they resume classes in a few weeks, but Raul Espino Jr. hopes that will not mean another semester of peering at his classmates from inside a plexiglass box that protects him from the heat.

2 The 7-year-old's parents asked a federal judge this week to order their son's entire classroom air-conditioned to free him from the transparent cubicle. An auto accident when he was an infant left the boy a paraplegic and his body unable to control its temperature.

3 NONE OF THE Brownsville Intermediate District's 28 primary or junior high schools, which open Aug. 25, have air conditioning. The district's solution to Raul's problem was to put him in the box.

4 U.S. District Judge Filemon Vela said he would decide by Aug. 15 whether to grant the request from Ana and Raul Espino.

5 "Other alternatives have not been considered," Vela said. "We may be able to find a solution with the present setting."

6 The accident damaged the hypothalamus gland in Raul's brain that controls the body's temperature and some movement. He is confined to a wheelchair and must stay in an environment between 72 and 78 degrees.

7 Doctors say the injury did not affect his intelligence, and teachers call him an above-average student.

8 WHEN HE transferred last year from a school for the handicapped to Egly Elementary School, the box with a portable air conditioning unit was built for him to use when temperatures climbed above 78 degrees. A two-way sound system was installed so he could converse with his teacher and classmates.

9 Mrs. Espino testified Monday that she was overjoyed to hear her son would be with normal children last school year, but then she became dismayed to learn that he would be confined to the cubicle.

10 After failing to persuade the Texas Education Agency and the state Board of Education to order classroom air conditioning, the Espinos took their case to federal court, arguing that the district is violating a law that requires handicapped children be educated in the "least restrictive environment."

11 Local Superintendent Raul Besteio testified that he decided to build the box instead of air conditioning the room for fear of jealousy among other parents and teachers. Besteio said he turned down a woman from Pennsylvania who offered to pay for air conditioning because that would have been "discrimination."

12 THE DISTRICT, with a relatively low tax base in the Rio Grande Valley, cannot afford to air condition the classroom, he said.

13 No estimates of the cost of air conditioning were available, but based on costs at the three high schools in the 28,000-student district, it could come to $5,700 a room.

Comprehension

Answer the following questions. Your teacher may want you to answer orally, in writing, or by underlining appropriate portions of the text. True/False items are indicated by a T / F preceding the statement. Some items may have more than one right answer.

1. Why is Raul in a wheelchair? _____

_____

---

2. Why does Raul need an air-conditioned environment? _____

_____

3. Brownsville, Texas, must be a warm place. From reading the article, what do you think are

typical temperatures during the school year? _____

4. How did the Brownsville school district solve Raul's need for an air-conditioned

environment? _____

5. T / F   Raul must stay in the plexiglass box all of the time.

6. T / F   Raul cannot see or hear his classmates from inside the plexiglass box.

7. Why do Raul's parents object to the box? _____

_____

8. T / F   The school district has worked cooperatively with the parents to solve Raul's
problems.

9. T / F   The Brownsville school system cannot afford to air-condition any of its classrooms.

10. T / F   The Brownsville school district cannot afford to air-condition Raul's classroom.

11. How much would it cost to air-condition Raul's rooom? _____

_____

12. T / F   Apparently the Brownsville school district believes that primary and junior high
school students can endure the heat better than high school students.

13. Judge Vela reports that he is exploring other options. What might they be? What
alternatives can you think of that have not been mentioned? How would the problem be
solved in your country?

_____

_____

_____

_____

14. The superintendent of schools cited considerations of discrimination as one of the reasons
that the situation had not been resolved (paragraph 11). In your opinion, which of the
following situations constitute discrimination?

a. A classroom whose environment makes it impossible for a handicapped student to work

    b. Providing air-conditioning for handicapped students but not for nonhandicapped students

    c. Providing air-conditioning for high school students but not for primary or junior high students

    d. Air-conditioning paid for by private sources rather than by public funds

    e. Air-conditioning only one classroom in a school

15. Do you think the superintendent's office is air-conditioned? _____

16. Do you think the writer of the newspaper article agrees with the Espinos or with the

    superintendent? _____

17. Use the six points from the textbook article to evaluate the Brownsville school district.

    What grade would you give it? _____

Discussion/Composition

1. Pretend you are one of the following people involved in the legal battle you have been reading about:

    a. the attorney representing the Espinos
    b. the attorney representing the Brownsville Intermediate District

    State your position on the issue of how Raul's special needs should be met, and explain the reasoning behind your position.

2. Pretend you are the federal court judge responsible for deciding how to resolve the dispute between the Espinos and the Brownsville Intermediate District. What would your decision be? Explain your reasoning.

Vocabulary from Context

Exercise 1

Use the context provided to determine the meanings of the italicized words. Write a definition, synonym, or description of each italicized vocabulary item in the space provided.

1. _____   For most children in North America, school vacation begins in June. Classes *resume* in late August or early September.

2. _____ Because the walls of the room were *transparent* we could see everything that was going on in the next room.

3. _____ The problem was complex and several different solutions were offered by teachers, parents, and administrators. It was the director's job to choose the best solution from among these *alternatives*.

4. _____ We did not like the solution that was proposed, and we argued for several days with the director, but we could not *persuade* her to change her mind.

5. _____ The boy was in a box where he could not move around or participate in all of the class activities. His parents felt that the box was far too *restrictive* and demanded a change.

Exercise 2

This exercise is designed to give you additional clues to determine the meanings of unfamiliar words in context. In the paragraph indicated by the number in parentheses, find the word that best fits the meaning given. Your teacher may want to read these aloud as you quickly scan the paragraph to find the answer.

1. (1)   Which word means *extreme heat*?

2. (1)   Which word means *looking at*?

3. (2)   Which word means *a small enclosed space, box*?

4. (2)   Which word means *a person who cannot move his or her legs due to disease or injury*?

5. (6, 10)   Which word means *all that surrounds a person, including air, objects, etc.*?

6. (9)   Which word means *surprised, alarmed, discouraged*?

7. (11)   Which word means *envy, unhappiness caused by wanting what someone else has*?

8. (11)   Which word means *unfair or unequal treatment*?

Reading Selection 2
Newspaper Questionnaire

Before You Begin   1. If you have a problem, what do you do? Do you try to avoid the problem? Do you simply worry about it? Or do you do something about it?

2. Do you think all people handle problems in the same way? Do you think people from different backgrounds and cultures respond differently to crises?

Efficient reading requires an understanding of the attitudes and experiences of the writer. Unless one has knowledge about or is able to infer an author's beliefs, it is possible to understand all of the sentences in a passage and yet not comprehend a writer's ideas.

Reading a newspaper in another language is an excellent way of drawing inferences about another culture. The following selection is a quiz which appeared in a newspaper in the United States. It was designed to provide people with the opportunity to measure their ability to handle problems. By taking the quiz, you should be able to gain an understanding of the kinds of problems experienced in the United States and the ways in which people attempt to deal with them.

Answer each of the questions. If you have trouble deciding what you would do in a given situation, choose the response that is closest to what you would do.

How Do You Handle Everyday Stress?

Psychologists are now convinced that day-to-day problems, which frequently seem unimportant, are what "take a lot out of you." Moreover, they can even affect the length of your life. Everybody faces day-to-day problems, but some can handle them better than others.

Would you like to know how well you can cope? In this quiz, circle the answer closest to the way you actually react in the situation described. If the situation is unfamiliar, circle the answer closest to the way you think you would handle it.

Answers at the end will tell you how well you are coping with everyday stress and may help you to improve your methods of dealing with problems.

1. Birthdays, weddings, anniversaries . . . it seems impossible to avoid spending money.
   a. You tell everyone to take you off their gift list so that you don't have to buy a gift.
   b. In spite of the expense you continue to enjoy selecting small, special gifts for any occasion.
   c. You give only to those who are most important to you.
2. You had an automobile accident with another car and you have to appear in court.
   a. The anxiety and inconvenience of appearing in court causes you to lose sleep.
   b. It's an unimportant event, one of those things that happen in life. You will reward yourself with a little gift after court.
   c. You forget about it. You will cope with it when the day comes.

3. Some furniture and carpeting in your house was damaged by a leak in the water pipes and you discover that your insurance doesn't cover the loss.
   a. You become depressed and complain bitterly about the insurance company.
   b. You recover the furniture yourself.
   c. You think about canceling your insurance and writing a letter of complaint to the Better Business Bureau.
4. You've had a fight with your neighbor and nothing was resolved.
   a. You go home, fix a strong drink, try to relax and forget about it.
   b. You call your lawyer to discuss a possible lawsuit.
   c. You work off your anger by taking a walk.
5. The pressures of modern day living have made you and your spouse irritable.

Adapted from "How Do You Handle Everyday Stress?" by Dr. Syvil Marquit and Marilyn Lane. Features and News Service.

a. You decide to take it easy and not be forced into any arguments.

b. You try to discuss irritating matters with a third person so that you can make your feelings known without an argument.

c. You insist on discussing the problems with your spouse to see how you can take off some of the pressure.

6. A close friend is about to get married. In your opinion, it will be a disaster.

a. You convince yourself that your early fears are incorrect, and hope for the best.

b. You decide not to worry because there's still time for a change of plans.

c. You decide to present your point of view; you explain your reasoning seriously to your friend.

7. You are worried about rising food prices.

a. Despite rising prices, you refuse to change your eating habits.

b. Your anger level rises every time you see an increase in price from the week before, but you buy anyway.

c. You try to spend less and plan good menus anyway.

8. Finally your abilities have been recognized; you've been offered an important job.

a. You think of turning down the chance because the job is too demanding.

b. You begin to doubt if you can handle the added responsibility successfully.

c. You analyze what the job requires and prepare yourself to do the job.

9. You suspect that your rent or some other monthly expense will increase.

a. You pick up the mail anxiously each day and give a sigh of relief when the letter isn't there.

b. You decide not to be caught by surprise and you plan how to handle the situation.

c. You feel everyone is in the same situation and that somehow you'll cope with the increase.

10. Someone close to you has been seriously injured in an accident, and you hear the news by phone.

a. You hold back your feelings for the moment because other friends and relatives have to be told the news.

b. You hang up and burst into tears.

c. You call your doctor and ask for tranquilizers to help you through the next few hours.

11. You've won a big luxury car in a competition. You could use a car but it seems this is going to change your life considerably.

a. You worry about the added problems your good luck will bring.

b. You sell it and buy a smaller car, banking the money left over.

c. You decide to enjoy the car and to worry about the added expense later.

12. Every holiday there is a serious argument in the family about whether to visit your parents or those of your spouse.

a. You make a rigid 5-year plan, which will require you to spend each holiday with different members of the family.

b. You decide that you'll spend important holidays with the members of the family you like best, and ask others to join you for the lesser holidays.

c. You decide the fairest thing is not to celebrate with the family at all — and it's less trouble.

13. You're not feeling well.

a. You diagnose your own illness, then read about it.

b. You gather up your courage, talk about it at home and go to see your doctor.

c. You delay going to the doctor thinking that you will eventually feel better.

14. Your youngest child is leaving home and going into the world.

a. You discuss the development with friends to see how they're handling it.

b. You give all the help you can and plan new interests for yourself.

c. You try to talk the young person into staying home a bit longer.

Now that you have indicated how you would react to these situations, return to the questions to predict the behaviors of others:

1. For each item, place a *C* (for native culture) next to the response you believe would describe the behavior of people from your culture.

2. Place a *U* (for U.S. natives) next to the response that you believe best describes the behavior of most people in the United States.

When you have finished, continue reading the article. You will learn how to score your responses and discover what the authors of this questionnaire consider appropriate behavior. Be sure to score responses for yourself, others from your culture, and natives of the United States.

To find out how you cope with stress, score your answers according to the following chart:

Questions 1–3:   A = 3, B = 1, C = 2
Questions 4–8:   A = 3, B = 2, C = 1
Questions 9–14: A = 2, B = 1, C = 3

The lower your total score, the better able you are to cope with your problems. If you scored 23 or less, the advice that follows may be normal behavior for you. (Perhaps you can teach others how to be calm.)

If you scored over 23, here are some ways to handle stress conditions effectively. Don't put difficult situations to one side thinking they will go away. Eventually you will have to deal with them anyway.

Don't make decisions that will cause you stress later. It's better to face reality at the beginning. For example, don't accept an invitation if you know you won't be able to attend when the time comes.

In order to avoid problems later, think things through in advance. In facing a problem, don't guess about the future or let your imagination run away with you; find out what the true situation is, then handle it.

Most of the time what you may be fearing will never happen. When you get upset about an unavoidable stress-filled event, do something physical to work it off. When tragedy strikes, as it does to all of us, don't be afraid to show your emotions.

Discussion/Composition

1. What can you infer from this quiz about the kinds of problems faced by people in the United States? How are these similar to and different from problems faced by people everywhere?

2. The choices below each question in the quiz describe some of the ways people in the United States cope with problems. Compare and contrast the ways in which you, people from your culture, and a "typical American" might respond to these situations. Which responses are similar? Which do you find strange? Be sure to give examples.

Vocabulary

Circle the word or phrase that is not similar in meaning.

deal with   attempt   handle   cope with

Reading Selection 3

Magazine Article

Read the following article quickly to determine the author's main ideas. You may want to do the Vocabulary from Context exercise on pages 88–89 before you begin reading.

Before You Begin   Have you ever heard of the Bermuda Triangle, an area of the Caribbean where ships disappear? What have you heard about it?

Before Christopher Columbus discovered the New World, Europeans commonly believed that the world was flat. They believed that if you sailed too far from land you would fall off the edge of the earth to be eaten by fire-breathing monsters. Ridiculous, you say? Don't be too sure. Before making a final judgment, read about the:

Graveyard of the Atlantic

1   At 2 P.M. on Dec. 5, 1945, five Navy bombers took off in perfect flying weather from the Naval Air Station at Fort Lauderdale, Fla., on a routine training mission over the Atlantic Ocean. Less than two hours later, the flight commander radioed that he was "completely lost." Then there was silence. A rescue plane was sent to search for the missing aircraft and it, too, disappeared. In all, six planes and 27 men vanished that day without a trace. Despite one of history's most extensive search efforts, involving more than 300 planes and dozens of ships, the Navy was unable to discover even floating wreckage or a telltale oil slick.

2   This is just one of the many chilling stories told of "The Bermuda Triangle," a mysterious area of the Atlantic Ocean roughly stretching south from Bermuda to the Florida coast and Puerto Rico. During the past 30 years, the triangle has claimed the lives of some 1,000 seamen and pilots. Among sailors, it is known variously as "The Triangle of Death," "The Hoodoo Sea" and "The Graveyard of the Atlantic" because of the mysterious calms, waterspouts, and sudden storms that have bothered seafarers in its water. When he entered this stretch of the Atlantic, Christopher Columbus noted curious glowing streaks of "white water." The mysterious patches of light and foam are still visible today and so bright that they have been seen by U.S. astronauts from outer space.

3   The triangle has aroused considerable public interest through three hot-selling books, a television documentary (narrated by horror master Vincent Price) and a special exposition at the Library of Congress. None of these investigations has produced convincing answers to the mystery of the triangle, but there is no shortage of interesting theories. Some scientists and popular authors go

Adapted from "Graveyard of the Atlantic," *Newsweek*.

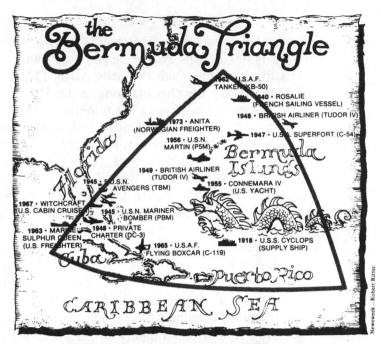

Limbo of the lost: Some of the triangle's victims and where they vanished

so far as to suggest that the triangle is a hunting ground of extraterrestrial beings in search of human specimens for their "cosmic zoos."

4   Whatever the truth may be, planes and ships disappear in the triangle with eerie regularity. On July 3, 1947, a U.S. Army C-54 Superfort disappeared 100 miles off Bermuda without broadcasting any word of difficulty. An immediate search over 100,000 square miles of sea failed to turn up a single piece of wreckage. On Jan. 30, 1948, a Tudor IV British airliner, the Star Tiger, vanished over the triangle with 31 passengers and crew aboard. A year later, the Star Tiger's sister plane, the Star Ariel, disappeared en route to Jamaica. Seventy-two search planes, plus dozens of ships, failed to turn up any sign of the missing aircraft.

5   One of the largest ships claimed by the mysterious triangle was the U.S.S. Cyclops, a 500-foot coaling ship that disappeared on March 4, 1918. Investigations revealed no evidence of foul weather, no messages for help, no wreckage and no sign of the 309 men aboard. Stranger yet are the numerous "ghost" ships that have been found floating crewless within the triangle. On one weird occasion in 1881, the cargo ship Ellen Austin discovered a schooner, sails flapping in the wind, a full cargo of mahogany intact, but no sign of human life. The captain of the Ellen Austin installed a new crew to sail it, but two days later, during a rough storm, the two ships temporarily lost sight of each other. When the captain again boarded the schooner, he found his crew had disappeared. After a second crew was assigned, the ship was again lost in a fog bank. This time, no trace of the schooner—or the crew—was ever found.

6   Officially, the U.S. Navy does not recognize the triangle as a danger zone and the U.S. Coast Guard is convinced that "the majority of disappearances [in the triangle] can be attributed to the area's unique environmental features." These include the swift Gulf Stream current, the unexplored underwater canyons of the Atlantic and the

often violent weather patterns within the mystery zone. Then too, the triangle is one of only two places on earth where a compass needle points to true rather than magnetic north. (The other is "The Devil's Sea," an equally treacherous zone in the Pacific, southeast of Japan.) Thus, a navigator who does not remember this may find himself well off course. "There are mysterious and strange things going on out there," admits Richard Winer, author of *The Devil's Triangle* . . . a paperback that has sold 500,000 copies since its publication three months ago. "But I believe that all the answers lie in human error, mechanical malfunctions, freak weather or magnetic abnormalities."

7   Officials of the National Oceanic and Atmospheric Administration are not so certain. "Despite efforts by the U.S. Air Force, Navy and Coast Guard," NOAA reports, "no reasonable explanation to date has been made for the vanishings." Because of these uncertainties, private investigators have sought more fanciful explanations. John Wallace Spencer, author of *Limbo of the Lost,* a paperback that has sold 1.5 million copies in the past fifteen months, argues that beings from outer space have established a highly advanced civilization in the unexplored depths of the Atlantic inside the triangle. There, he believes, most of the missing vessels—and their crews—may still be on display for study by these higher intelligences. "It sounds weird," Spencer admits, "until you realize that it's the only explanation that covers all the facts."

8   These and other theories are all examined in Charles Berlitz's current volume, *The Bermuda Triangle* . . . which has climbed onto the best-seller list less than three months after publication. A Yale graduate with a fascination for Atlantis, the legendary lost continent, Berlitz expands upon the theory that a giant solar crystal, which once supplied power for Atlantis, lies on the ocean floor. Periodically, he theorizes, passing ships and planes trigger the crystal, which confuses their instruments and sucks them into the impassable deep.

9   To test such theories, a parapsychological institute called the Isis Center for Research and Study of the Esoteric Arts, based in Silver Springs, Md., is planning to take 300 psychics and scientists on a cruise into the triangle. The researchers hope to make contact with whatever "higher intelligence" may lie under the sea. A similar expedition into the Devil's Sea was made by a group of Japanese scientists in 1955. Nothing has been heard of them since.

Comprehension

Exercise 1

Indicate if each statement is true (T) or false (F) according to your understanding of the passage. Do not refer to the passage as you mark your answers.

1. _____ The Bermuda Triangle is an area of the Atlantic Ocean where a number of ships and planes have disappeared.

2. _____ The triangle has been a source of mystery for only thirty years.

3. ____ In spite of great public interest in the triangle, no theory has yet been suggested to explain the disappearances.

4. ____ According to the article, important information regarding the disappearances has come from people who lived through the experiences themselves.

5. ____ The U.S. Navy does not recognize the triangle as a danger zone.

6. ____ Although a great deal of publicity has been given to the mystery of the triangle, officials of the U.S. government all agree that natural causes account for the disappearances.

7. ____ If the team from the Isis Center for Research and Study of the Esoteric Arts is as successful as the team of Japanese scientists was in 1955, the mystery will soon be solved.

Exercise 2

This section tests your comprehension of details. You may refer to the passage to answer the following questions.

1. How many people have disappeared in the triangle in the last thirty years?

2. What curiosity of the triangle was reported by both Columbus and U.S. astronauts?

3. From the information you have here, what is the date of the most recent disappearance in the triangle?

4. What is meant by the term *ghost ship*?

5. What environmental features of the triangle make it unique?

6. In the triangle, a compass needle points to true north rather than to magnetic north. How might this fact help explain the disappearances?

7. Richard Winer, John Wallace Spencer, and Charles Berlitz all offer theories concerning the triangle. What is your opinion of each of these theories?

8. Has the group from the Isis Center completed its voyage? How would you find this information?

Discussion/Composition

Do you believe that the Bermuda Triangle is a truly mysterious place, or do you believe that the events described can be explained by science?

Write an essay supporting your point of view. Use evidence from the article and/or other evidence with which you are familiar.

Vocabulary from Context

Use the context provided and your knowledge of stems and affixes to determine the meanings of the italicized words. Write a definition, synonym, or description of each of the italicized vocabulary items in the space provided.

The Bermuda Triangle is an area of the Atlantic Ocean that has puzzled people for several centuries.

1. _____   There are a number of environmental features that can be found only in the Bermuda Triangle. Because of these *unique* characteristics, the triangle is one of the most dangerous areas in the Atlantic Ocean.

2. _____   The weather in the triangle is *treacherous;* its sudden changes often endanger the lives of sailors.

3. _____   The triangle is well known for unexpected storms, hurricanes that are out of season, and other unnatural events. Many people feel that this *freak* weather can explain most of the strange events that have occurred there.

4. _____   Because of the many violent storms, the triangle is often *impassable*.

5. _____   Many ships leave land and disappear completely; the U.S.S. Cyclops, for example, *vanished* in 1918.

6. _____   Some missing ships carried *cargo* such as coal, oil, mahogany, and military supplies, while other ships carried only passengers.

7. _____   Engine *malfunction* might explain the disappearance of old ships, but investigators must look for other explanations when a new ship disappears.

8. _____   When a ship is reported missing, searchers rush to the area to look for *evidence* that might explain the disappearance.

9. _____   One author tries to explain the disappearances of the ships by *attributing* them to natural events or human error.

10. _____   Another author believes that intelligences from another world are responsible for the disappearances. He says that these *extraterrestrial* beings have a zoo where they keep all the missing sailors.

11. _____   Many people agree that natural causes cannot explain the strange events in the triangle. "It just isn't natural for a ship to completely disappear like this. It's *weird*, no matter how you try to explain it," declared the sailor.

12. _____   "These *eerie* events make me afraid to sail out of sight of land."

5

Nonprose Reading

Questionnaire

This questionnaire requires following the same kind of directions you will encounter when applying for insurance or a visa, or in dealing with some government agencies. The directions on such forms are often complicated and difficult to understand. This exercise is designed to give you practice in following directions and providing information required by a questionnaire.*

Before You Begin Is it possible to use science and statistics to predict the future? Is it possible to predict, for example, how long you will live?

The questionnaire beginning on this page is designed to make just such a prediction. It appeared in a magazine in the United States. Fill it out carefully, then decide how you feel about this use of statistics.

THE ODDS FOR LONG LIFE

This questionnaire came from Robert Collins, coordinator for health education in the Bellevue, Washington, Public Schools, who has used it to encourage class discussion of life expectancy. We thought we'd use it to stimulate personal thinking on that subject among our readers. We hope you'll get a pencil and fill in the blanks.

But beware. The figures are unscientific and extremely imprecise — merely indicators of *some* characteristics and practices that may contribute to long life. Furthermore, the predictions here are based on the "average" person. They will predict for any one of us only in terms of very rough odds. As a result, if you are past middle age you may find that the "prediction" for you is death several years ago.

1) Year of Birth
Find the year of your birth (or the closest year shown), and then write your basic life expectancy in the space provided.

Write down your basic life expectancy._____ years

YEARS OF LIFE EXPECTED AT BIRTH

Year	Total	Male	Female
1920[a]	54.1	53.6	54.6
1930	59.7	58.1	61.6
1940	62.9	60.8	65.2
1950	68.2	65.6	71.1
1955	69.6	66.7	72.8
1960	69.7	66.6	73.1
1965	70.2	66.8	73.7
1970	70.8	67.1	74.7
1971	71.1	67.4	75.0
1972	71.2	67.4	75.1
1973	71.4	67.6	75.3
1974	72.0	68.2	75.9
1975	72.6	68.8	76.6
1976	72.9	69.1	76.8
1977	73.3	69.5	77.2
1978	73.5	69.6	77.3
1979	73.9	70.0	77.8
1980	73.7	70.0	77.5
1981	74.2	70.4	77.9
1982	74.6	70.9	78.2
1983p	74.7	71.0	78.3
1984p	74.7	71.1	78.3

Source: National Center for Health Statistics.
p = preliminary

[a]Data prior to 1940 for death-registration states only

Adapted from "The Odds for Long Life" by Robert Collins, *Harper's*. Life expectancy data from *The World Almanac and Book of Facts.*
*For an explanation of nonprose reading, see Unit 1.

2) Present Age

Age	Add	Age	Add
1–4 yrs.	1 yr.	46–50 yrs.	4.5 yrs.
5–10	2 yrs.	51–55	5.5
11–15	2	56–60	6.5
16–20	2	61–65	8
21–25	2.5	66–70	9.5
26–30	3	71–75	11.5
31–35	3	76–80	12
36–40	3.5	81–85	6.5
41–45	4	85 plus	4.5

New total _____ years

3) Family History
Add 1 year for each 5-year period your father has lived past 70. Do the same for your mother.

New total _____ years

4) Marital Status
If you are married, add 5 years.
If you are over 25 and not married, deduct 1 year for every unwedded decade.

New total _____ years

5) Where You Live
Small town — add 3–5 years.
City — subtract 2 years.

New total _____ years

6) Economic Status
If wealthy or poor for greater part of life, deduct 3 years.

New total _____ years

7) Your Shape
If you are over 40, deduct 1 year for every 5 lbs. you are overweight. For each inch your stomach measurement exceeds your chest measurement, deduct 2 years.

New total _____ years

8) Exercise
Regular and moderate add 3 years; regular and vigorous, add 5 years.

New total _____ years

9) Disposition
Good-natured and placid add 1–5 years. Tense and nervous subtract 1–5 years.

New total _____ years

10) Alcohol
Heavy drinker — subtract 5 years. Very heavy drinker — subtract 10 years.

New total _____ years

11) Smoking

½ to 1 pack per day	subtract 3 years
1 to 1½ packs per day	subtract 5 years
1½ to 2 packs per day	subtract 10 years
Pipe or cigar	subtract 2 years

New total _____ years

12) Family Environment
Regular medical checkups and regular dental care add 3 years. Frequently ill subtract 2 years.

Final total _____ years

Discussion

1. Why would marital status be a factor in life expectancy?

2. The questionnaire implies that living in a small town is healthier than living in a city. Do you agree? Why or why not?

3. Three years must be deducted from your life expectancy if you have been either wealthy or poor for a long period of time. How do you explain this?

4. The questionnaire implies that your personality affects your life expectancy. How do you explain this?

5. The basic life expectancy chart gives different life expectancies for men and women. Why is this? In your society is there a difference in life expectancy for the two sexes?

6. What are the credentials and qualifications of Mr. Collins, the author of the questionnaire? On what does he base his facts and figures?

Word Study

Context Clues

Exercise 1

In the following exercise, do NOT try to learn the italicized words. Concentrate on developing your ability to guess the meaning of unfamiliar words using context clues. Read each sentence carefully, and write a definition, synonym, or description of the italicized word on the line provided.

1. _____   The major points of your plan are clear to me, but the details are still *hazy.*

2. _____   By *anticipating* the thief's next move, the police were able to arrive at the bank before the robbery occurred.

3. _____   All of the palace's laundry, when gathered for washing, formed a *massive* bundle that required the combined efforts of all the servants to carry.

4. _____   "Give me specific suggestions when you criticize my work," said the employee. "*Vague* comments do not help me improve."

5. _____   The apple *appeased* my hunger temporarily, but I could still eat a big dinner.

6. _____   After the attacks on civilians by army troops, a committee met to try to discover what could have *provoked* such action.

7. _____   The king *manifested* his pleasure with a hearty laugh.

8. _____   The nation's highway death *toll* has increased every year since the invention of the automobile.

9. _____   The workers' lives were *wretched;* they worked from morning to night in all kinds of weather, earning only enough money to buy their simple food and cheap clothes.

10. _____   In a series of bold moves, government attorneys attacked the *mammoth* auto industry, saying that the size of the business endangered the financial freedom of the individual buyer.

Exercise 2

This exercise is designed to give you practice using context clues from a passage. Use your general knowledge along with information from the entire text below to write a definition, synonym, or description of the italicized word on the line provided. Read through the entire passage before making a decision. Note that some of the words appear more than once; by the end of the passage you should have a good idea of their meaning. Do not worry if your definition is not exact; a general idea of the meaning will often allow you to understand the meaning of a written text.

People in Americas before Last Ice Age?

A *site* in northeastern Brazil has yielded evidence of the earliest known human *occupation* in the Americas, approximately 32,000 years ago, according to a report by two French scientists.

Although the discovery, reported in June 19 *NATURE,* does not *resolve* long-standing archaeological *disputes* over when and how people first arrived in the New World, the *site* is much older than others where human *occupation* has been *firmly* established. Several such finds in the southwestern United States date to 11,500 years ago, and a rock shelter near Pittsburgh is thought to contain evidence of use by humans 19,000 years ago; previously, the earliest known *site* occupied by humans in South America was 14,200 years old.

site: _____

occupation: _____

NATURE: _____

resolve: _____

disputes: _____

firmly: _____

From *Science News.*

Word Study

Stems and Affixes

Below is a list of some commonly occurring stems and affixes.* Study their meanings; then do the exercises that follow. Your teacher may ask you to give examples of other words you know that are derived from these stems and affixes.

Prefixes

a-, an-	without, lacking, not	atypical, apolitical
bene-	good	benefit, benefactor
bi-	two	bicycle, binary
mis-	wrong	misspell, mistake
mono-	one, alone	monarch, monopoly
poly-	many	polynomial, polytechnic
syn-, sym-, syl-	with, together	symphony, sympathy

Stems

-anthro-, -anthropo-	human	anthropology
-arch-	first, chief, leader	patriarch, monarch, archbishop
-fact-, -fect-	make, do	affect, benefactor, factory
-gam-	marriage	monogamy, polygamous
-hetero-	different, other	heterosexual, heterogeneous
-homo-	same	homogenized milk
-man-, -manu-	hand	manually, manage
-morph-	form, structure	polymorphous
-onym-, -nomen-	name	synonym, nomenclature
-pathy-	feeling, disease	sympathy, telepathy, pathological
-theo-, -the-	god	theology, polytheism

Suffixes

-ic, -al	relating to, having the nature of	comic, musical
-ism	action or practice, theory or doctrine	Buddhism, communism
-oid	like, resembling	humanoid

Exercise 1

In each item, select the best definition of the italicized word or phrase, or answer the question.

1. The small country was ruled by a *monarch* for 500 years.

    ____ a. king or queen   ____ c. group of the oldest citizens
    ____ b. single family   ____ d. group of the richest citizens

---

*For a list of all stems and affixes taught in *Reader's Choice,* see the Appendix.

2. He was interested in *anthropology*.

    _____ a. the study of apes
    _____ b. the study of insects
    _____ c. the study of royalty
    _____ d. the study of humans

3. Some citizens say the election of William Blazer will lead to *anarchy*.

    _____ a. a strong central government
    _____ b. a government controlled by one person
    _____ c. the absence of a controlling government
    _____ d. an old-fashioned, out-dated government

4. If a man is a *bigamist*, he

    _____ a. is married to two women.
    _____ b. is divorced.
    _____ c. has two children.
    _____ d. will never marry.

5. Which of the following pairs of words are *homonyms*?

    _____ a. good   bad
    _____ b. Paul   Peter
    _____ c. lie   die
    _____ d. two   too

6. Which of the following pairs of words are *antonyms*?

    _____ a. sea   see
    _____ b. wet   dry
    _____ c. read   read
    _____ d. Jim   Susan

7. The reviewer criticized the poet's *amorphous* style.

    _____ a. unimaginative
    _____ b. unusual
    _____ c. stiff, too ordered
    _____ d. lacking in organization and form

8. Dan says he is an *atheist*.

    _____ a. one who believes in one god
    _____ b. one who believes there is no god
    _____ c. one who believes in many gods
    _____ d. one who is not sure if there is a god

9. There was a great *antipathy* between the brothers.

    _____ a. love
    _____ b. difference
    _____ c. dislike
    _____ d. resemblance

10. Which circle is *bisected*?

    a.   b.   c.   d.

11. This design is symmetric:

Which one of the following designs is *asymmetric*?

    a.   b.   c.   d.

12. Consider the following sentences:

Many automobiles are *manufactured* in Detroit.
The authors must give the publisher a *manuscript* of their new book.

How are the meanings of *manufacture* and *manuscript* different from the meanings of

the stems from which they are derived? _____

_____

Exercise 2

Word analysis can help you to guess the meaning of unfamiliar words. Using context clues and what you know about word parts, write a synonym, description, or definition of the italicized words.

1. _____   Doctors say that getting regular exercise is *beneficial to* your health.

2. _____   He's always *mislaying* his car keys, so he keeps an extra set in the garage.

3. _____   Because some of our patients speak Spanish and some speak English, we need a nurse who is *bilingual*.

4. _____   My parents always told me not to *misbehave* at my grandparents' house.

5. _____   Some people prefer to remain *anonymous* when they call the police to report a crime.

Exercise 3

Following is a list of words containing some of the stems and affixes introduced in this unit and the previous one. Definitions of these words appear on the right. Put the letter of the appropriate definition next to each word.

1. ____ archenemy   a. care of the hands and fingernails

2. ____ archetype   b. the saying of a blessing

3. ____ anthropoid   c. resembling humans

4. ____ benediction   d. one who performs good deeds

5. ____ benefactor   e. a chief opponent

6. ____ manicure   f. the original model or form after which a thing is made

7. _____ monotheism

8. _____ polytheism

9. _____ polygamy

10. _____ monogamy

11. _____ heterogeneous

12. _____ homogeneous

a. made up of similar parts

b. belief in one god

c. the practice of having one marriage partner

d. the practice of having several marriage partners

e. consisting of different types; made up of different types

f. belief in more than one god

Sentence Study

Comprehension

Read the following sentences carefully.* The questions that follow are designed to test your comprehension of complex grammatical structures. Select the *best* answer.

1. My discovery of Tillie Olsen was a gift from a friend; years ago she gave me her copy of *Tell Me a Riddle* because she liked the stories and wanted to share the experience.
   What do we know about Tillie Olsen?
   _____ a. She is a friend.
   _____ b. She likes stories.
   _____ c. She gives gifts.
   _____ d. She is an author.

2. A few government officials even estimate that the war has created more than half a million refugees who need immediate food, clothing, and shelter.
   Exactly how many refugees are there?
   _____ a. half a million
   _____ b. over half a million
   _____ c. We don't know exactly.
   _____ d. Only a few government officials know the exact figure.

3. The Green Tiger Press believes that the relatively unknown works of great children's illustrators are sources of vast beauty and power, and is attempting to make these treasures more easily available.
   What is the goal of this printing company?
   _____ a. to publish more children's books
   _____ b. to develop powerful stories
   _____ c. to make children's illustrations more easily available
   _____ d. to encourage artists to become children's illustrators

4. Although he calls the $1,000 donation "a very generous amount, especially in these times," the president expresses hope that the project will attract additional funds from companies and other sources so that it can continue beyond this first year.
   What does the president know about the project?
   _____ a. It will cost only $1,000.
   _____ b. It is very special.
   _____ c. Special sources will support it.
   _____ d. It cannot continue without additional funding.

5. Any thought that this new custom will remain unchanged—or in Europe will remain uniquely English—is ridiculous.
   What does the author believe about the new custom?
   _____ a. It will remain limited.
   _____ b. The custom will change.
   _____ c. Acceptance of the custom is ridiculous.
   _____ d. The custom will remain in Europe.

*For an introduction to sentence study, see Unit 3.

6. These robust and persistent sailors gathered from all the nations of western Europe, and set out on the voyages that laid foundations for four great empires with no other power than sail and oar.

    Why were these voyages important?

    _____ a. Sailors came from many countries in Europe.

    _____ b. The voyages laid the foundations for western Europe.

    _____ c. The foundations for empires were established.

    _____ d. Western Europe lost its power.

7. Young people need to develop the values, attitudes, and problem-solving skills essential to their participation in a political system that was designed, and is still based, on the assumption that all citizens would be so prepared.

    What is a basic assumption of this political system?

    _____ a. All people will be capable of participation.

    _____ b. All people participate in the system.

    _____ c. All people should have the same values and attitudes.

    _____ d. Most people cannot develop the skills to participate in the system.

8. While we may be interested in the possibilities of social harmony and individual fulfillment to be achieved through nontraditional education, one cannot help being cautious about accepting any sort of one-sided educational program as a cure for the world's ills.

    How does the author feel about nontraditional education?

    _____ a. He believes that it has no possibility of success.

    _____ b. He doubts that it can cure the world's ills.

    _____ c. He feels that it is a cure for the world's ills.

    _____ d. He believes it will bring social harmony.

9. The complexity of the human situation and the injustice of the social order demand far more fundamental changes in the basic structure of society itself than some politicians are willing to admit in their speeches.

    What is necessary to correct the problems of society?

    _____ a. basic changes in its structure

    _____ b. fewer political speeches

    _____ c. honest politicians

    _____ d. basic changes in political methods

Paragraph Reading

Restatement and Inference

Each paragraph below is followed by five statements. The statements are of four types:
1. Some of the statements are *restatements* of ideas in the original paragraph. They give the same information in a different way.
2. Some of the statements are *inferences* (conclusions) that can be drawn from the information given in the paragraph.
3. Some of the statements are not true based on the information given.
4. Some of the statements cannot be judged true or false based on the information given in the original paragraph.

Put a check (✓) next to all restatements and inferences (types 1 and 2). Note: do not check a statement that is true of itself but cannot be inferred from the paragraph.

Example

Often people who hold higher positions in a given group overestimate their performance, while people in the lowest levels of the group underestimate theirs. While this may not always be true, it does indicate that often the actual position in the group has much to do with the feeling of personal confidence a person may have. Thus, members who hold higher positions in a group or feel that they have an important part to play in the group will probably have more confidence in their own performance.

_____ a. If people have confidence in their own performance, they will achieve high positions in a group.

_____ b. If we let people know they are an important part of a group, they will probably become more self-confident.

_____ c. People who hold low positions in a group often overestimate their performance.

_____ d. People in positions of power in a group may feel they do better work than they really do.

_____ e. People with higher positions in a group do better work than other group members.

Explanation

_____ a. This cannot be inferred from the paragraph. We know that people who hold high positions have more self-confidence than those who don't. However, we don't know that people with more confidence will achieve higher status. Confidence may come only *after* one achieves a higher position.

✓ b. This is an inference that can be drawn from the last sentence in the paragraph. We know that if people feel they have an important part to play in a group, they will probably have more self-confidence. We can infer that if we let people know (and therefore make them feel) that they have an important part to play, they will probably become more self-confident.

_____ c. This is false. The first sentence states that the people in the lowest levels of a group underestimate, not overestimate, their performance.

__✓__ d. This is a restatement of the first sentence. People who hold higher positions tend to overestimate their performance: they may feel they do better work than they really do.

_____ e. We do not know this from the paragraph. We know that people who hold higher positions often *think* they do better work than others in a group. (They "overestimate their performance.") We do not know that they actually do better work.

Paragraph 1   Like any theory of importance, that of social or cultural anthropology was the work of many minds and took on many forms. Some, the best known of its proponents, worked on broad areas and attempted to describe and account for the development of human civilization in its totality. Others restricted their efforts to specific aspects of the culture, taking up the evolution of art, or the state, or religion.

_____ a. Social anthropology concerns itself with broad areas while cultural anthropology concerns itself with specific aspects of culture.

_____ b. Cultural anthropologists, also known as social anthropologists, may work in either broad or restricted areas.

_____ c. Cultural anthropology is a new field of study.

_____ d. Any important area of study requires the work of many minds and is therefore likely to have different approaches.

_____ e. The best-known people in cultural anthropology attempted to describe the development of human civilization.

Paragraph 2   I saw by the clock of the city jail that it was past eleven, so I decided to go to the newspaper immediately. Outside the editor's door I stopped to make sure my pages were in the right order; I smoothed them out carefully, stuck them back in my pocket, and knocked. I could hear my heart thumping as I walked in.

_____ a. The teller of this story has just left the city jail.

_____ b. He has been carrying his papers in his pocket.

_____ c. We know that the storyteller is a newspaper writer by profession.

_____ d. We might infer that the storyteller is going to show his papers to the editor.

_____ e. The meeting is important for the storyteller.

Paragraph 3   In recent years there have been many reports of a growing impatience with psychiatry, with its seeming foreverness, its high cost, its debatable results, and its vague, esoteric terms. To many people it is like a blind man in a dark room looking for a black cat that isn't there. The magazines and mental health associations say psychiatric treatment is a good thing, but what it is or what it accomplishes has not been made clear.

_____ a. Even mental health associations haven't been able to demonstrate the value of psychiatry.

_____ b. The author believes that psychiatry is of no value.

_____ c. People are beginning to doubt the value of psychiatry.

_____ d. In recent years psychiatry has begun to serve the needs of blind people.

_____ e. Only magazines and mental health associations believe that psychiatry is a good thing.

Paragraph 4   The Incas had never acquired the art of writing, but they had developed a complicated system of knotted cords called *quipus*. These were made of the wool of the alpaca or llama, dyed in various colors, the significance of which was known to the officials. The cords were knotted in such a way as to represent the decimal system. Thus an important message relating to the progress of crops, the amount of taxes collected, or the advance of an enemy could be speedily sent by trained runners along the post roads.

_____ a. Because they could not write, the Incas are considered a simplistic, poorly developed society.

_____ b. Through a system of knotted cords, the Incas sent important messages from one community to another.

_____ c. Because runners were sent with the cords, we can safely assume that the Incas did not have domesticated animals.

_____ d. Both the color of the cords and the way they were knotted formed part of the message of the *quipus*.

_____ e. The *quipus* were used for important messages.

Paragraph 5

There was a time when scholars held that early humans lived in a kind of beneficent anarchy, in which people were granted their rights by their fellows and there was no governing or being governed. Various early writers looked back to this Golden Age but the point of view that humans were originally *children of nature* is best known to us in the writings of Rousseau, Locke, and Hobbes. These men described the concept of *social contract,* which they said had put an end to the *state of nature* in which the earliest humans were supposed to have lived.

_____ a. For Rousseau, Locke, and Hobbes, the concept of *social contract* put an end to the time of beneficent anarchy in which early humans lived.

_____ b. According to the author, scholars today do not hold that early humans lived in a state of anarchy.

_____ c. Only Rousseau, Locke, and Hobbes wrote about early humans as *children of nature.*

_____ d. The early writers referred to in this passage lived through the Golden Age of early humans.

_____ e. We can infer that the author of this passage feels that concepts of government have always been present in human history.

Discourse Focus

Careful Reading / Drawing Inferences

Mystery stories, like most other texts, require readers to note important facts and draw inferences based on these. To solve the following mysteries, you must become a detective, drawing inferences from the clues provided. Each mystery below has been solved by the fictional Professor Fordney, a master detective—the expert the police call for their most puzzling cases. Your job is to match wits with the great professor. Your teacher may want you to work with your classmates to answer the question following each mystery. Be prepared to defend your solution with details from the passage.

Mystery 1: Class Day

"I shall tell you," Fordney said to his class some years ago, of an exploit of the famed scientist, Sir Joshua Beckwith, Professor of Egyptology in London.

"He had uncovered an ancient tomb in Egypt and, through his undisputed knowledge and ability to read hieroglyphics, had definitely established the date of the birth and the reign of a great Pharaoh whose mummy he had discovered. A man of volatile temper, and emphatic scientific views which he did not hesitate to express in exposing charlatanism, he had many enemies.

"The British Museum soon received a message, signed by Sir Joshua, which in part read as follows: 'Have discovered the tomb of an important Pharaoh who reigned from 1410 to 1428 B.C. and who died at the age of 42 years, leaving two sons and two daughters. Great wealth found in sarcophagus. One of his sons died shortly after his reign began, etc. . . .'

"The Museum officials at first were astonished," continued Fordney, "but examination of the communication quickly told them it was either a very stupid fake or an attempt at a 'practical joke'!

"They were right in their belief that the message did not come from Sir Joshua Beckwith. He did make a most important discovery— but how did the Museum authorities know the communication was not authentic?"

How did they know? _____

_____

Mystery 2: Ruth's Birthday

A multitude of small accidents had delayed Ruth Mundy. The battery in her car had gone dead and she had to call a cab; she had mislaid the key to the strong box! Just as the taxi pulled up she located it. Hastily snatching from the dresser drawer two twenty-dollar bills, one old and crumpled, one crisp and new, she thrust them loosely into her bag. In her hurry, the perfume bottle on the dresser upset, spilling

From *Minute Mysteries* by Austin Ripley (New York: Pocket Books).

perfume on her lovely moire purse! If this kept up she'd be late for her birthday party! Now, where was that book she was to return? She was sure she had just put it on the dresser! Finally locating it under her coat on the bed, she grabbed it and ran.

Once in the taxi she opened her bag and fumbled for her vanity case. Its clasp opened and she stuck her finger in the paste rouge. Another casualty! Well, it didn't get on anything else, that was one break. Removing all traces of the rouge with her handkerchief, she threw it away.

Arriving at the Mayflower Hotel she handed the driver a bill. While she waited for her change Professor Fordney alighted from his car and greeted her with a "Hello, Ruth."

Acknowledging the greeting she turned to the driver. "You've made a mistake. This is change for five. I gave you a twenty."

"Oh no, lady! You gave me five dollars!"

Fordney listened amused while Ruth excitedly proved she'd given the driver a twenty-dollar bill.

"How's that, Professor?" she laughed.

How did Ruth prove her story? _____

_____

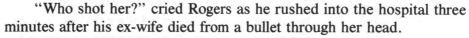

Mystery 3:

The Ex-Wife Murder

"Who shot her?" cried Rogers as he rushed into the hospital three minutes after his ex-wife died from a bullet through her head.

"Just a minute," Professor Fordney said. "I'd like to ask you a few questions . . . routine, you know. Although divorced for the past six months, you have been living in the same house with your ex-wife, have you not?"

"That's right."

"Had any trouble recently?"

"Well . . . yesterday when I told her I was going on a business trip, she threatened suicide. In fact, I grabbed a bottle of iodine from her as she was about to drink it. When I left last evening at seven, however, telling her I was spending the night with friends in Sewickley, she made no objections. Returning to town this afternoon," he continued, "I called my home and the maid answered."

"Just what did she say?"

" 'Oh, Mr. Rogers, they took poor mistress to St. Anne's hospital 'bout half an hour ago. Please hurry to her!' She was crying so I couldn't get anything else out of her; then I hurried here. Where is she?"

"The nurse here will direct you," responded the Professor.

"A queer case this, Joe," said Inspector Kelley who had been listening to the conversation. "These moderns are a little too much for me! A man and woman living together after being divorced six months!"

"A queer case, indeed, Jim," sighed Fordney. "You'd better detain Rogers. If he didn't shoot her himself, I'm confident he knows who did."

Why did the Professor advise the Inspector to detain Rogers? _____

_____

Mystery 4: Case #463

At 8:10 P.M., July 4, 1945, Miss Ruby Marshall left her apartment on the fifth floor of the Hotel Oakwood. As she walked toward the elevator she passed Jane McGuire. The fourteen-year-old child had her Scottish terrier on a long leash and as they came opposite each other the dog growled and leaped at Miss Marshall. The woman screamed and ran back to her apartment.

Thirty minutes later Mrs. McGuire had a call from police headquarters informing her that Miss Marshall had received first aid at Mercy Hospital for a wound on the knee where the McGuire dog had bitten her. Invalided for the past two years, Mrs. McGuire was unable to look into the situation herself. She immediately called her friend, Professor Fordney, informing him of the above and asking him to look into the matter.

He found Miss Marshall sitting on a chair in the emergency ward, about to leave the hospital. Receiving permission to examine the wound from the doctor who had just taken care of her, Fordney raised Miss Marshall's immaculate evening dress, noticed her hose were rolled below her knees, removed the bandage and found cauterized marks on the right knee cap. Turning to the physician he inquired, "Are you sure those are teeth marks?"

"Why . . . they look like it to me!"

Lowering the woman's dress, the Professor told her, "You certainly didn't show much intelligence in trying to frame this charge against Mrs. McGuire, toward whom you hold a personal grudge. Her dog did not bite you!"

How did he know? _____

_____

6

Reading Selections 1A–1D

News and Editorials

Before You Begin   1. Do you smoke?

2. Do you believe that people should be allowed to smoke whenever and wherever they wish?

3. Are there actions that governments and individuals should take to control smoking?

The following reading selections document the continuing controversy over smoking.

Selection 1A   **Magazine Editorial**

The issue of smokers' and nonsmokers' rights can be a very emotional one. The editorial on page 109 is a debate about controlling smoking in the workplace. The writer on the left (Ian M. Rolland) believes it makes good business sense to create a smoke-free working environment. The writer on the right (Bernard J. Dushman) worries that controlling smoking on and off the job discriminates against employees who smoke.

Debate

Choose one side of the debate (it may be more fun to choose the side with which you do NOT agree). Carefully read this side only. Paraphrase *the author's* argument in a debate with your classmates. If you and your classmates accurately paraphrase both sides of the argument, you should be able to complete the Comprehension exercise below *after* your debate.

    Your teacher may want you to do Vocabulary from Context exercise 1 on page 110 before you begin reading.

Comprehension

Indicate if each statement below is true (T) or false (F) according to your understanding of the debate.

1. ＿＿ Rolland believes that employees should not be hired if they smoke at home.

2. ＿＿ Dushman does not believe that smoking is a health hazard.

3. ＿＿ Dushman believes that discrimination against smokers is becoming at least as serious as that against women and minorities.

4. ＿＿ Rolland believes that smoking is a victimless crime.

5. ＿＿ Rolland claims his decision to control smoking is a business decision.

A Burning Issue on the Job and Off

BY IAN M. ROLLAND

1 The corporation I head took a deep breath of clean air last week and went cold turkey. Smoking on the job in the home office was absolutely forbidden. Since 1982 it had been restricted to work areas and cafeterias; the hard line stiffened last February when employees were permitted to smoke only at their desks.

2 Now we provide a smoke-free working environment. Why? To paraphrase the slogan on President Harry Truman's desk, "The butt stops here."

3 Anything that kills 350,000 Americans each year deserves decisive action, and all the brawny cowpokes and tawny-haired sirens cannot blow enough advertising smoke to obscure the fact that one out of every seven deaths in this country is linked to smoking. The costs related to it are also sapping our economy. One recent report estimates that smokers utilize the health-care system at least 50 percent more than nonsmokers; they waste 30 minutes each workday fumbling with matches and lighters, sucking seductive poisons. If time is going to be wasted, I'd rather it be frittered away on daydreams and chatter than flicked into a valley of ashes. Furthermore, smoking may not be a victimless vice.

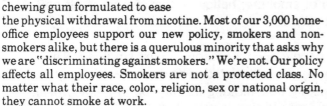

The butt stops here; you can't smoke at work

4 Still, a ban can create serious personnel problems. Since 25 percent of our employees smoke, we are offering them on-the-job smoking-cessation classes and counseling. Our medical office provides Nicorettes, a sugarless chewing gum formulated to ease the physical withdrawal from nicotine. Most of our 3,000 home-office employees support our new policy, smokers and nonsmokers alike, but there is a querulous minority that asks why we are "discriminating against smokers." We're not. Our policy affects all employees. Smokers are not a protected class. No matter what their race, color, religion, sex or national origin, they cannot smoke at work.

5 We are not trying to dictate personal lifestyles. We encourage our employees to stop smoking altogether, but they cannot smoke on the job. We simply can't afford their habit. According to a congressional study, the cost to the economy averages $65 billion annually in increased medical bills, premature death and time lost from work. And as a major participant in the field of health-care financing, we have an obligation to prove that, if properly conceived, a smoke-free working environment is attainable. This isn't a crusade. This is a business decision.

Rolland is president of Lincoln National Corp., an insurance holding company based in Ft. Wayne, Ind.

BY BERNARD J. DUSHMAN

6 Less than two decades after Congress outlawed job discrimination on the basis of race, sex, national origin, religion and age, discrimination in hiring is raising its ugly head again. Today's new targets are smokers. Scores of employers, including a police department in Holden, Mass., and a fire department in Janesville, Wis., won't hire them. It doesn't matter if the employees do not smoke during working hours or if they limit their smoking to the privacy of their homes. If they smoke at all, they won't be hired.

7 Robert E. Mercer, the chairman of Goodyear Tire and Rubber Co., has predicted that "we'll get to the point where nonsmoking is a condition of employment." Radar Electric in Seattle is one such firm. At others, nonsmokers are given preference in hiring and promotion. You can track this new wave of discrimination by reading the classified pages of major newspapers across the country. "Nonsmoker" ads appear regularly.

8 While no sane person would suggest that discrimination against smokers rises to the moral obscenity of discrimination based on race, sex or religion, the trend is still pernicious. One might have hoped that one of the lessons we learned in the struggle to outlaw job discrimination is that the use of non-job-related criteria to control the distribution of jobs is perverse, counterproductive and dumb.

No boss has the right to control your private life

9 Well, here we go again!

10 Don't ask whether an applicant is bright, creative, conscientious or dependable. If the applicant smokes, he or she can't be hired. What makes this new kind of discrimination particularly dangerous is that we are not talking about smoking on the job. Whatever justification there might be for regulating smoking in the workplace, some companies are going a giant step beyond. They are denying people jobs because of what they do on their own time; they are using the powerful incentive of a job to control how people act in their homes.

11 Sure, smokers as a class have not been subjected to the systemic maltreatment suffered by blacks and women. But employers ought not to be able to impose their concepts of morality, or health, on employees on pain of loss of a job or on denial of the opportunity to compete. No employer ought to have the power to decide what we do in private. Isn't an honest day's work all an employer has a right to demand?

A nonsmoker, Dushman is assistant dean at Yale Law School and president of the Ohio Civil Liberties Union.

Vocabulary from Context

Exercise 1

Both the ideas and the vocabulary in the exercise below are taken from "A Burning Issue On and Off the Job." Use the context provided to determine the meanings of the italicized words. Write a definition, synonym, or description of each of the italicized vocabulary items in the space provided.

1. _____

2. _____

3. _____

4. _____

Cigarette advertising can be very effective. The people we see advertising cigarettes sell attractive images. For example, we might be shown very attractive women and strong cowboys. These *sirens* and *brawny cowpokes* are *seductive* images, designed to make us desire cigarettes.

5. _____

6. _____

7. _____

Some people believe that cigarette smoking is a moral weakness that affects individuals and society. They argue that this *vice* is *linked to* a good deal of illness every year. Cigarette smoking, they argue, can *sap* the strength of individuals and of the national economy.

8. _____

9. _____

Other people think discussions of the dangers of cigarette smoking *obscure* the real issue, hiding the fact that curbing smokers' rights makes them the *target* of discrimination.

10. _____

11. _____

12. _____

Both sides in this debate can become very emotional, using very strong language. Some people believe that smoking in public is immoral. Others believe that curbing smokers' rights is equally *obscene* and *perverse*. Still others focus on the evil of smoking, believing that the act itself and its effects are *pernicious*.

13. _____

14. _____

15. _____

In the end, people need a reason to stop smoking. This *incentive* to stop can be job-related. For example, we may be on the way to making nonsmoking a *condition of employment*: smokers may have a hard time getting hired, and *personnel* who smoke may be fired.

16. _____

17. _____

18. _____

19. _____

It can be argued that making smoking a job-related issue is not fair. Whether or not you smoke does not make you a good employee. Some people will always waste time either smoking or talking. Does it matter if you *fritter away* your time *chattering* or smoking? Similarly, smokers do not necessarily create more dirt in the workplace. Not all smokers *flick* ashes on the floor while they talk, or press cigarette *butts* into the floor. People are individuals.

Exercise 2

This exercise should be completed after you have finished reading the debate. The exercise is designed to see how well you have been able to use your knowledge of stems and affixes and context to guess the meaning of unfamiliar vocabulary items. Give a definition, synonym, or description of each of the words below. The number in parentheses indicates the paragraph in which the word can be found. Your teacher may want you to do these orally or in writing.

1. (4)   formulated _____

2. (4)   withdrawal _____

3. (5)   dictate _____

4. (5)   premature _____

5. (8)   counterproductive _____

6. (11) maltreatment _____

7. (11) impose _____

Figurative Language and Idioms

In the paragraph indicated by the number in parentheses, find the phrase that best fits the definition given. Your teacher may want to read these aloud as you quickly scan the paragraph to find the answer.

1. (1)   What phrase means *firm or strict policy*?

2. (1)   What phrase means *stopped a habit suddenly and absolutely*?

3. (2)   What phrase is a pun on a saying meaning *to take responsibility*?

4. (6)   What phrase means that *something unpleasant is returning*?

5. (10) What phrase means *moving a great distance quickly*?

Selection 1B   **Newspaper Advertisement**

Before You Begin   If you were trying to develop a prosmoking advertisement at a time when cigarette smoking is under attack, what kind of advertisement would you create?

Below is an advertisement in favor of smokers' rights. Read it through once, then complete the exercises that follow. Your teacher may want you to work in groups or pairs.

Smoking in Public:
Live and Let Live

Ours is a big world, complex and full of many diverse people. People with many varying points of view are constantly running up against others who have differing opinions. Those of us who smoke are just one group of many. Recently, the activism of non-smokers has reminded us of the need to be considerate of others when we smoke in public.

But, please! Enough is enough! We would like to remind non-smokers that courtesy is a two-way street. If you politely request that someone not smoke you are more likely to receive a cooperative response than if you scowl fiercely and hurl insults. If you speak directly to someone, you are more likely to get what you want than if you complain to the management.

Many of us have been smoking for so long that we sometimes forget that others are not used to the aroma of burning tobacco. We're human, and like everyone else we occasionally offend unknowingly. But most of us are open to friendly suggestions and comments, and quite willing to modify our behavior to accommodate others.

Smokers are people, too. We laugh and cry. We have hopes, dreams, aspirations. We have children, and mothers, and pets. We eat our hamburgers with everything on them and salute the flag at Fourth of July picnics. We hope you'll remember that the next time a smoker lights up in public.

Just a friendly reminder from your local Smokers Rights Association.

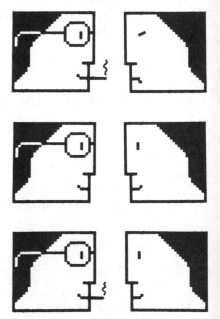

Recognizing a Point of View

This exercise should be completed after you have finished reading "Smoking in Public: Live and Let Live." Below you will find portions of the advertisement followed by four statements. Put a check (3) next to those statements that reflect the underlying beliefs or point of view of the original text.

1. Ours is a big world, complex and full of many diverse people. People with many varying points of view are constantly running up against others who have differing opinions. Those of us who smoke are just one group of many.

   _____ a. Smokers are simply another group in the U.S., such as Greek Americans.
   _____ b. Smokers can be thought of as people with a different point of view rather than as a group who engage in a particular behavior.
   _____ c. People should like smokers.
   _____ d. Smokers are people too.

2. We would like to remind nonsmokers that courtesy is a two-way street. If you politely request that someone not smoke, you are more likely to receive a cooperative response than if you scowl fiercely and hurl insults. If you speak directly to someone, you are more likely to get what you want than if you complain to the management.

   _____ a. Nonsmokers have not been polite to smokers.
   _____ b. Nonsmokers should never complain to the management.
   _____ c. Smokers have always been cooperative.
   _____ d. If nonsmokers were more polite, smokers would be more cooperative.

3. Smokers are people, too. We laugh and cry. We have hopes, dreams, aspirations. We have children and mothers and pets. . . . We hope you'll remember that the next time a smoker lights up in public.

   _____ a. Smokers are not always treated like people.
   _____ b. Nonsmokers should be nicer to smokers because they have mothers.
   _____ c. When smokers light up in public, we should remember that we all have many things in common.
   _____ d. Having a pet makes you a nice person.

Evaluating a Point of View

1. Check (✓) all of the following that are assumptions of this passage.

_____ a. Secondary smoking (being near people who smoke) can kill you.
_____ b. Smokers might be uncooperative if nonsmokers are not polite.
_____ c. Smokers are people too.

2. Now look at the statements listed under 1 above. Check (3) all those with which you agree.

Discussion

1. Who do you think wrote this advertisement? What purpose does it serve?

2. What is your reaction to this advertisement? Is your opinion of smokers different now than before you read it?

3. What do you think made the ad persuasive? Unpersuasive?

Composition

Develop an anti- or prosmoking advertisement.

Selection 1C   **Magazine Graphic**

The map and the accompanying paragraph on page 117 are taken from a magazine that reports on international issues. They give information about smoking patterns in various countries around the world. When reading magazines, one often skims and scans* articles and illustrations before deciding whether or not to read more carefully. At this point, do NOT read the map and paragraph carefully. Skim and scan to answer the Overview questions. Then do the Comprehension exercise on this page.

Overview

Skim the map and paragraph for the answers to the following questions.

1. What kinds of information do the map and paragraph provide?

2. What does each cigarette on the map mean?

3. Why are some countries on the map shaded gray?

4. Is total world consumption of cigarettes increasing or decreasing?

Comprehension

1. In 1990, what was the total world consumption of cigarettes?

2. Did world consumption increase or decrease between 1989 and 1990?

3. Is world consumption expected to increase or decrease in the future? Why?

4. What country is the world's leading exporter of tobacco?

5. What country has the greatest adult cigarette consumption per capita?

6. In what country has adult cigarette consumption per capita increased the most?

7. In what country has adult cigarette consumption per capita decreased the most?

8. What is the adult cigarette consumption per capita in Costa Rica? In your country? Why are the figures for some countries not shown?

---

*For an introduction to skimming, see Unit 3; for an introduction to scanning, see Unit 1.

Critical Reading

1. What does "adult cigarette consumption per capita" mean? How would you calculate "adult cigarette consumption per capita" for a country?

2. Compare the figures on the map for several countries you are somewhat familiar with. Do the comparisons agree with your impressions of how much people in these countries smoke? If not, can you think of possible reasons for the disagreement?

3. How reliable do you find this graphic?

Smoke Alert

Who's puffing 5 trillion cigarettes

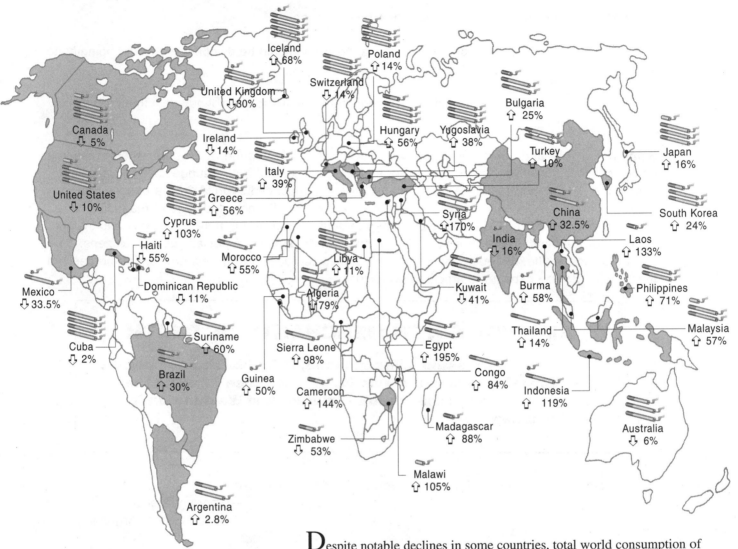

Iceland ⬆ 68%

Poland ⬆ 14%

Switzerland ⬇ 14%

United Kingdom ⬇ 30%

Bulgaria ⬆ 25%

Canada ⬇ 5%

Ireland ⬇ 14%

Hungary ⬆ 56%

Yugoslavia ⬆ 38%

Turkey ⬆ 10%

Japan ⬆ 16%

Italy ⬆ 39%

United States ⬇ 10%

Greece ⬆ 56%

Syria ⬆ 170%

China ⬆ 32.5%

South Korea ⬆ 24%

Cyprus ⬆ 103%

India ⬇ 16%

Laos ⬆ 133%

Haiti ⬇ 55%

Morocco ⬆ 55%

Libya ⬆ 11%

Mexico ⬇ 33.5%

Dominican Republic ⬇ 11%

Algeria ⬆ 79%

Kuwait ⬇ 41%

Burma ⬆ 58%

Philippines ⬆ 71%

Suriname ⬆ 60%

Thailand ⬆ 14%

Malaysia ⬆ 57%

Cuba ⬇ 2%

Sierra Leone ⬆ 98%

Egypt ⬆ 195%

Brazil ⬆ 30%

Guinea ⬆ 50%

Congo ⬆ 84%

Cameroon ⬆ 144%

Indonesia ⬆ 119%

Australia ⬇ 6%

Zimbabwe ⬇ 53%

Madagascar ⬆ 88%

Malawi ⬆ 105%

Argentina ⬆ 2.8%

Represents 1,000 cigarettes per capita
(Adults only)

Leading tobacco exporters

Source: World Health Organization

Despite notable declines in some countries, total world consumption of cigarettes continues to rise—from an estimated 5.2 trillion in 1989 to 5.37 trillion in 1990. Overall tobacco use, according to UN's Food and Agriculture Organization, is likely to go up close to 2% a year in coming years, most likely because of population growth in developing countries—target for tobacco exporters from some countries whose own people are smoking less. The map shows adult cigarette consumption per capita for 1985 in major tobacco exporting and/or consuming nations as well as those with a rise or fall of more than 50% between 1970 and 1985. There was a decline of 10% in the United States, the world's No. 1 tobacco producer and exporter, and declines from 2% to 53% in six other major exporting nations. The figures suggest some effect from various national and international antismoking efforts dramatized by the annual Great American Smokeout next month and the global No-Tobacco Day sponsored by the United Nations in May. But smoking has skyrocketed in many places, including Indonesia (up 119%), Syria (170%), and Egypt (195%).

Selection 1D   **Magazine Exposé**

Before You Begin 1. Why do children begin to smoke?

2. Do you believe that children should be discouraged from beginning to smoke?

3. Should governments take actions to control advertising aimed at children?

Some magazines and newspapers present "special reports," often the result of long-term research, on topics of particular interest to their readers. When this kind of report suggests that it has uncovered hidden information, it is called an exposé (pronounced *expozAY*). The exposé that follows is from *Reader's Digest,* which claims to be the "world's most widely read magazine." Originating in the United States, it is published throughout the world, in 14 languages and in editions for the blind. The article that follows, however, is directed especially at U.S. citizens.

Below is the title, the epigram, and some emphasized quotes from this article. On the basis of these, what do you expect the article to be about?

AMERICA'S NEW MERCHANTS OF DEATH

Pushed by decreasing sales at home, U.S. tobacco companies are marketing cigarettes abroad. Among those lured by their clever advertising: the world's children. And Washington is lending a hand.

"From television ads we know that everyone in America smokes."

—Georgina Becci, age 13,
Buenos Aires, Argentina

"I feel a lot more important smoking Lucky Strike—it costs more and has a lot of class. It's an American original!"

—Francisco Queman, 16,
Santiago, Chile

"I like Parliaments the best, but if I were a boy I'd probably be smoking Marlboros. They make the boys feel like men."

—Huang Mei-Chun, 13,
Taipei, Taiwan

Skimming

The theme or main idea of this article is found in paragraphs 5 and 6. Read these first, then skim the article to discover how children worldwide are made smokers. Your teacher may want you to do Vocabulary from Context exercise 1 on pages 122–23 before you begin reading.

AMERICA'S NEW MERCHANTS OF DEATH

1 IN GERMANY, three women in black miniskirts set up a table beside a Cadillac in the center of Dresden. In exchange for an empty pack of local cigarettes, they offer passersby a pack of Lucky Strikes and a leaflet that reads: "You just got hold of a nice piece of America. Lucky Strike is the original . . . a real classic." Says German physician Bernhard Humburger, who studies youth smoking, "Adolescents time and again receive cigarettes at such promotions."

2 • A Jeep decorated with the yellow Camel logo pulls up in front of a high school in Buenos Aires. The driver, a blond woman, begins handing out free cigarettes to 15- and 16-year-olds during their lunch break.

3 • In Malaysia, a man responds to a television commercial for "Salem High Country Holidays." When he tries to book a trip, he is refused; the $2.5-million-a-year operation exists only to advertise Salem on TV. This promotes Salem cigarettes without breaking the law.

4 • At a video arcade in Taipei, free U.S. cigarettes lie atop each game. "As long as they're here, I may as well try one," says a high-school girl in a Chicago Bears T-shirt. Before the United States entered the Taiwanese cigarette market, such giveaways were uncommon at places frequented by adolescents.

5 A *Reader's Digest* investigation covering 20 countries on five continents has revealed that millions of children are being lured into nicotine addiction by U.S. cigarette makers. In several nations, U.S. tobacco companies have been fighting laws that curtail cigarette use by young people and are cleverly violating the spirit of curbs on advertising. Their activities clearly show a disregard for public health.

6 But the most shocking finding is that children are being lured into smoking in the name of the United States itself. In some countries, tobacco companies never would have gotten a start without the help of a powerful ally: the U.S. government.

7 Although domestic sales have dropped for eight straight years, and by the year 2000 only one in seven people in the U.S. will likely smoke, sales outside the U.S. have more than tripled since 1985. Smoking rates in developing countries are climbing more than two percent a year. Most troubling is the rise in youth smoking. In the Philippines, 22.7 percent of people under 18 now smoke. In some Latin American cities, the teenage rate is a shocking 50 percent. In Hong Kong, children as young as seven are smoking.

8 Why are the young so important? Because millions of adult smokers either kick their habit or die each year, the cigarette industry depends on attracting new customers. Most smokers begin between ages 12 and 16; if a young person hasn't begun by 18, he or she is unlikely ever to smoke.

9 "Tobacco is a growth industry, and we are gaining in volume and share in markets around the world," Philip Morris assured stockholders in its 1991 annual report.

10 "Growth prospects internationally have never been better," reported Dale Sisel, chief executive officer of R. J. Reynolds (RJR) Tobacco International at last summer's international tobacco conference in Raleigh, N.C. "We all produce and sell a legal product that more than one billion consumers around the world use every single day."

11 Unmentioned at the conference was the fact that smoking is one of the leading causes of premature death, linked to cancers of the mouth, lung, esophagus, kidney, pancreas, bladder and cervix, as well as to heart disease. Or that, according to the World Health Organization, tobacco will prematurely kill 200 million who are now children and eventually wipe out ten percent of the world's population. This grim prospect is due in no small part to the spectacular U.S. invasion of international markets.

12 "The American people need to know precisely how their companies and government are promoting smoking among the world's children," says Dr. Carlos Ferreyra Nunez, president of the Argentine Association of Public Health. "If they knew the full story, I believe they would stop this outrage."

13 Here is that story.

Pervasive Influence

14 TOBACCO ADVERTISING is more pervasive in other parts of the world than in the U.S. African merchants can get their shops painted to look like a pack of Marlboros. The Camel logo appears on store awnings and taxis in Warsaw. Christmas trees in Malaysian discos are decorated free by Kent—with balls and stars bearing the Kent logo. In Mexico, one in five TV commercials is for cigarettes. On an average day, 60 spots for U.S. brands appear on Japanese TV, many of them during programs watched by teens.

15 Although their marketing budgets are secret, tobacco companies have increased their spending for international advertising, adding substantially to the $4 billion spent yearly in the United States. "It's crucial for them," says Richard Pollay, professor of marketing at the University of British Columbia. "Familiarity in advertising leads to trust."

16 Tobacco spokespeople insist that cigarette advertising draws only people who already smoke. But an ad executive who worked until recently on the Philip Morris account disagrees. "You don't have to be a genius to figure out what's going on. Just look at the ads. It's ridiculous for them to deny that a cartoon character like Joe Camel isn't attractive to kids."

17 Dr. John L. Clowe, president of the American Medical Association, says, "It is clear that advertising encourages tobacco use among children. And, despite tobacco-industry denials, ads like Joe Camel are especially appealing to adolescents, equating smoking with sex, athleticism, even success."

18 Numerous independent studies support this view. Time and again they have shown that cigarette advertising creates an environment in which young people are more likely to smoke. That may explain why the U.S. Centers for Disease Control found that smokers between ages 12 and 18 prefer Marlboro, Newport and Camel—three of the most advertised brands.

Brand-Stretching

19 LIKE THE UNITED STATES, some developing countries have banned cigarette commercials on TV and radio. This doesn't stop the tobacco companies, however. To keep their logos before the public, they use "brand-stretching"— advertising nontobacco products and services named after their brands. Most of these items have special appeal to young people: Marlboro jeans and jackets, for example.

20 In Malaysia, a music store called Salem Power Station wraps customers' tapes and CDs in plastic bags bearing the Salem logo, and television carries an MTV-like show called "Salem Powerhits." A Budapest radio station broadcasts a rock program called the Marlboro Hit Parade, and in China, Philip Morris sponsors the Marlboro American Music Hour. Rock concerts are especially effective.

21 Sports sponsorship is even more insidious, for it implies that smoking and fitness mix. Tobacco logos appear at events of every description, from cycling in Morocco to badminton in Indonesia. There's the Salem Open Tennis Tournament in Hong Kong and the Kent International Sailing Regatta, to name just two. U.S. tobacco companies spent $100 million sponsoring sports last year.

22 Tobacco companies regularly skirt laws against TV commercials. In Shanghai, Philip Morris sponsors spots for "The World of Marlboro." Except that cigarettes aren't mentioned, they are identical to a Marlboro commercial: the Marlboro man and his horse splash across a stream, the man dismounts and gazes toward mountains that look like the Rockies.

23 Unfortunately, many of the children who succumb to brand-stretching find habits that begin as cobwebs end up as steel cables. At a McDonald's in Malaysia, Sunil Ramanathan, 16, finishes off a Big Mac, lights a Marlboro and inhales deeply. He says he's smoked since he was ten. "I know smoking is bad for me, but I can't stop. I try to quit, but after one day I start again."

Easy Access

24 JUST OFF Taipei's busy Keelung Road, high-school students begin arriving at the Whisky A Go-Go disco about 9 P.M., and soon the room is a sea of denim. On each table are free packs of Salems. Before long, the place is full of smoke.

25 "American tobacco companies spend more than a quarter of a billion dollars every year giving away cigarettes, many of which are smoked by children and teenagers," says Joe Tye, editor of the newsletter *Tobacco Free Youth Reporter*, "If they can get a youngster to smoke a few packs, chances are he'll be a customer for life."

26 Of seven under-18 students assembled at the Beltram High School in Buenos Aires, five say they have been offered free Camels. None was asked his age. One, Ruben Paz, 16, said he got his from a "blond, American-looking girl" handing out cigarettes from "the Camel Jeep" at the school door.

Sell America

27 "MANY AFRICAN children have two hopes," says Paul Wangai, a physician in Nairobi, Kenya. "One is to go to heaven, the other to America. U.S. tobacco companies profit from this by associating smoking with wealth. It's not uncommon to hear children say they start because of the glamorous lifestyle associated with smoking."

28 Cigarette advertising outside the United States focuses heavily on U.S. lifestyles; indeed, the ads are seen as a way of learning about the United States itself. A letter from secretarial students in China appeared in the Petaluma, California, *Argus-Courier*: "Every day we listen to the Marlboro American Music Hour. We enjoy Elvis Presley and Michael Jackson. We smoke American cigarettes and wear American clothes. We are eager to gain more information about American life."

29 To hear the children of the rest of the world tell it, everyone in the U.S. smokes. The truth is, the United States has one of the *lowest* smoking rates—25.5 percent of the population.

30 Yet because of advertising, U.S. cigarettes are considered a sign of style and sophistication. In Bangkok, young Thais sew Marlboro logos on their jackets and jeans. At the city's Wat Nai Rong High School, 17-year-old Wasana Warathongchai says smoking makes her feel "sophisticated and cosmopolitan, like America." She associates Marlboros with "jeans and denim jackets, Pizza Hut, everything we like about America."

Friends in High Places

31 THE THEME of last summer's Raleigh conference was "The Tobacco Industry to the Year 2000," and on hand were two experts from the U.S. Department of Agriculture to help the industry sell tobacco overseas.

32 . . . Wait a minute. Didn't the U.S. government decide in 1964 that cigarettes are a major cause of death and disease, and doesn't the U.S. government discourage its own citizens from smoking? Then how can we encourage people of other nations to smoke?

33 For many years, Japan, Korea, Taiwan and Thailand imposed strong trade restrictions on imported cigarettes. But U.S. tobacco companies joined forces with the Office of the U.S. Trade Representative (USTR) to enter these Asian markets.

34 The weapon Washington has used was Section 301 of the old Trade Act of 1974. It empowers the USTR to retaliate—with punitive tariffs—against any nation thought to have imposed unfair barriers on U.S. products.

35 Here is a recent example. When the USTR began an investigation of Japanese trading practices, a U.S. senator stepped in on behalf of the tobacco industry. He sent a letter to the Japanese prime minister suggesting he could not support a substantial U.S. military presence in the Pacific or help change anti-Japanese trade attitudes in Congress unless Japan opened its cigarette market.

36 "I urge that you establish a timetable for allowing U.S. cigarettes a specific share of your market," the senator wrote. "I suggest a total of 20 percent within 18 months." Three months later, the Japanese government agreed to open its markets more.

37 The results have been devastating. Before the U.S. tobacco companies arrived, smoking rates were declining slightly in Japan, but in the past 5 years, cigarette consumption by minors has increased 16 percent. Among Taiwanese high-school students, the smoking rate climbed 14 percent. The number of Thai smokers ages 15 to 19 increased 24 percent, with similar increases for Korean high-school boys.

38 "We were making progress in discouraging smoking, but all has been washed away by the flood of American advertising," says David D. Yen, chair of an antismoking group in Taiwan. "We want your friendship, but not your tobacco."

39 The U.S. cigarette business is booming. Exports are soaring, factories being built. And at the end of the rainbow lies China, with 300 million smokers—30 percent of the world market.

40 "This vastly larger marketplace means a whole new world of opportunities," RJR's Dale Sisel told the Raleigh conference. Expansion abroad, he continued, would "pave the way for a bigger and brighter future."

41 That kind of talk makes Argentina's Dr. Ferreyra Nunez shake with anger. "U.S. tobacco companies know their product causes death. Yet they promote smoking among children. What must these people think? Don't they have children of their own?"

You Can Stop This Outrage

42 PUBLIC OPINION is more powerful than the tobacco lobby. If you agree that it's wrong for the United States to promote the sale abroad of a health hazard that we discourage at home, write a letter to the President. Ask him to order the United States Trade Representative to stop helping the tobacco companies open cigarette markets overseas. Urge him to support curbs on tobacco advertising in other countries like those already in place here. And send copies of your letter to your Representatives in Congress.

43 The President's address is The White House, Washington, D.C. 20500. (Fax number: 202-456-2461)

AUTHOR'S NOTE: William Ecenbarger is a *Reader's Digest* staff writer. He is a previous winner of the George Polk Award for Investigative Journalism.

Comprehension

1. T / F U.S. tobacco companies encourage young people to smoke.

2. T / F The tobacco companies deny that their advertising causes people to begin to smoke.

3. Why are young people an important market for cigarette makers?

   _____

4. T / F Tobacco advertising is more pervasive in other parts of the world than in the U.S.

5. The article states that the investigation has covered five continents. What are the five continents from which examples are given in this article?

   _____

6. T / F U.S. tobacco companies often break the law in other countries by their advertising.

7. What is "brand-stretching"?

8. T / F Research shows that cigarette advertising creates an environment in which young people are more likely to smoke.

9. According to the article, why is sports sponsorship "insidious"?

10. T / F The younger you are when you begin to smoke, the easier it is to quit.

11. Why does cigarette smoking outside the U.S. focus heavily on U.S. lifestyles?

    _____

12. T / F In Asia, unlike other parts of the world, cigarette advertising has had little effect on smoking rates among minors.

13. The article states (paragraph 39) "at the end of the rainbow lies China." What does this mean?

    _____

14. T / F Doctors and public health officials in developing countries are not aware of the health risks of smoking.

15. The article refers to the U.S. government as a "powerful ally" of the tobacco industry. What has been the role of the U.S. government in helping sell cigarettes?

    _____

16. What does the author of this article want readers in the U.S. to do?

    _____

Critical Reading

1. Why do you think the advertising practices described in this article continue? Who benefits from them in the U.S.? Who might benefit from them in your country/community? Are there ways that you benefit from them?

2. Did this article affect your attitudes toward
   —cigarette companies?
   —government officials?
   In your opinion, what made the article effective? Not effective?

Discussion/Composition

1. The following is from a report prepared for a tobacco company by a company specializing in marketing and research. The report recommends that the following types of advertising should be targeted at young people:

   —Present the cigarette as one of a few initiations into the adult world.
   —Present the cigarette as part of the illicit pleasure category of products and activities.
   —To the best of your ability (considering some legal constraints), relate the cigarette to "pot [marijuana]," wine, beer, sex, etc.
   —Don't communicate health or health-related points.

   Do you believe that there should be any control on the advertising of cigarettes targeted at young people? Support your position.

2. Write a letter to the President of the United States giving your opinion about the practices of U.S. cigarette companies internationally.

Vocabulary from Context

Exercise 1

Both the ideas and the vocabulary in the exercise below are taken from "America's New Merchants of Death." Use the context provided to determine the meanings of the italicized words. Write a definition, synonym, or description of each of the italicized vocabulary items in the space provided.

1. _____   Usually *merchants* sell objects that people need, that make their lives better. However, the salespeople who
2. _____   *promote* cigarette smoking among young people may be making America a "merchant of death." Increasingly, American cigarette companies advertise, not in the U.S.,
3. _____   but *overseas*. Outside the U.S., advertising shows cigarettes as part of the American lifestyle. In these ads, cigarettes ARE America, and smokers are presented as rich, attractive,

4. _____

5. _____

6. _____

7. _____

8. _____

9. _____

10. _____

11. _____

12. _____

13. _____

14. _____

15. _____

16. _____

17. _____

18. _____

19. _____

20. _____

21. _____

22. _____

and romantic. These ads are meant to *appeal to* young people, and as a result of these romantic pictures, children around the world are being *lured* into cigarette smoking at a very young age. Once they begin to smoke, they are unlikely to be able to stop; cigarette smoking becomes a *habit.* This nicotine *addiction* is very hard to break. If children *succumb to* this advertising and begin to smoke before they are 18 years old, they may become smokers for life.

Tobacco companies *deny* that they create new smokers; instead, they say that they only appeal to those who already smoke. However, experts say that it is clear that advertising encourages children to smoke.

The health effects on nations can be *devastating:* every year, millions of people die from the effects of smoking, and nations spend millions of dollars on related health costs.

The problem for U.S. cigarette companies is that smoking in the United States is decreasing. *Stockholders* want to see the companies they own make money. Because their sales in the U.S. have decreased, they are expanding their markets *abroad.* If companies can create more smokers internationally, particularly young smokers, they will be rich.

Many nations realize the dangers of smoking and have tried to *ban* ads completely so that children never see them, or at least *curtail* smoking advertisements so that they are not widespread. But these controls are often not successful; by and large, they have not *curbed* cigarette advertising. Through their activities, U.S. companies *violate* the meaning of these laws even if they obey the wording of the laws. There are a number of ways in which these companies violate the *spirit* of laws intended to protect young people from cigarettes.

As one example, some companies don't advertise their cigarettes, but they give them away free. Even more *insidious* is the involvement of cigarette companies in sports events. They appear to be promoting a sports event when, in fact, they are selling cigarettes. It is harmful in the long run when cigarette companies *sponsor* sports events and music concerts which otherwise might not be performed for lack of money. At these events, young people see the names and familiar pictures of cigarette *brands* such as Camels all around them. If they see the familiar camel *logo,* for example, even if cigarettes are not mentioned, the young people will be more likely to choose that brand when they begin to smoke. As a result of advertising at sponsored events, youth live in an environment in which cigarette smoking is all around them and, when these ads are *pervasive,* smoking seems normal.

23. _____

24. _____

25. _____

26. _____

27. _____

28. _____

29. _____

For those who worry about youth smoking, these actions are an *outrage,* but there is little they can do about their anger. Some governments have tried to pass laws to keep U.S. cigarettes out of their countries; however, these *barriers* have been met with counteractions on the part of the U.S. It has *retaliated* by making it more difficult for these governments to sell their products in the U.S. The U.S. government creates trade *tariffs* that add costs to any products bought from these countries. These *punitive* actions punish nations for trying to protect their youth.

The result has been an increase in young smokers worldwide. Cigarette sales are *soaring,* with great increases around the world. For U.S. companies in particular, the sale of cigarettes internationally is *booming*—new factories are being built and they have an increasing share of the world market.

Exercise 2

This exercise is designed to give you additional clues to determine the meaning of unfamiliar vocabulary items in context. In the paragraph of "America's Merchants of Death" indicated by the number in parentheses, find the word that best fits the meaning given. Your teacher may want to read these aloud as you quickly scan the paragraph to find the answer.

1. (1)   Which word means *a printed sheet of paper?*

2. (1)   Which word means *not a copy; the first?*

3. (1)   Which word means *a perfect example; first class?*

4. (5)   Which word means *lack of concern?*

5. (6)   Which word means *friend; helper?*

6. (10)   Which word means *expectations; chances?*

7. (21)   Which word means *health?*

8. (31)   Which word means *topic; subject; focus?*

Exercise 3

This exercise should be done after you have finished reading "America's New Merchants of Death." The exercise is designed to determine how well you have been able to use context clues to guess the meaning of unfamiliar vocabulary in the article. Give a definition, synonym, or description of each of the words below. The number in parentheses indicates the paragraph in which the word can be found. Your teacher may want you to do these orally or in writing.

1. (1)   passersby _____

2. (4)   giveaways _____

3. (4)   frequented _____

4. (7)   domestic _____

5. (9)   growth industry _____

6. (36) timetable _____

Figurative Language and Idioms

In the paragraph indicated by the number in parentheses, find the phrase that best fits the definition given. Your teacher may want to read these aloud as you quickly scan the paragraph to find the answer.*

1. (8)   What phrase means *quit; become free of their addiction?*

2. (23) What phrase means are *harmless and easy to free oneself from in the beginning but become traps and are impossible to give up?*

3. (24) What phrase means *full of young people in blue jeans?*

4. (33) What phrase means *worked together?*

5. (39) What phrase means *the biggest prize; the greatest dream?*

6. (40) What phrase means *make possible; prepare the way?*

_____

*For an introduction to scanning, see Unit 1.

Stems and Affixes

The words in the left column are taken from "America's New Merchants of Death." Using your knowledge of stems and affixes and their context, match each word on the left with its synonym or definition on the right. The number in parentheses indicates the paragraph in which the word can be found.

1. _____ miniskirt (1)   a. put in place; established; brought about

2. _____ invasion (11)   b. items sent or carried out of one country to another

3. _____ sophistication (30)   c. a short skirt worn several inches above the knee

4. _____ imposed (33)   d. arrival or incoming of something harmful

5. _____ imported (33)   e. knowing in the ways of the world

6. _____ exports (39)   f. brought in from another country

Dictionary Study

Many words have more than one meaning. When you use the dictionary to discover the meaning of an unfamiliar word or phrase, you need to use the context to determine which definition is appropriate. Use the portions of the dictionary provided to select the best definition for each of the italicized words below.

1. In Malaysia, a man responds to a television commercial for "Salem High Country Holidays"; when he tries to *book* a trip, he is refused by the office manager.

2. Tobacco spokespeople insist that cigarette advertising *draws* only people who already smoke.

3. Tobacco companies regularly *skirt* laws against TV commercials.

4. On TV in Shanghai, Philip Morris sponsors *spots* for "The World of Marlboro."

book \'bùk\ *n* [ME, fr. OE *bōc;* akin to OHG *buoh* book, Goth *boka* letter] (bef. 12c) **1 a :** a set of written sheets of skin or paper or tablets of wood or ivory **b :** a set of written, printed, or blank sheets bound together into a volume **c :** a long written or printed literary composition **d :** a major division of a treatise or literary work **e :** a record of a business's financial transactions or financial condition — often used in pl. 〈the ∼*s* show a profit〉 **2** *cap* : BIBLE **1 3 :** something that yields knowledge or understanding 〈the great ∼ of nature〉 〈her face was an open ∼〉 **4 a :** the total available knowledge and experience that can be brought to bear on a task or problem 〈tried every trick in the ∼〉 〈the ∼ on him is that he can't hit a curveball〉 **b :** the standards or authority relevant in a situation 〈run by the ∼〉 **5 a :** all the charges that can be made against an accused person 〈threw the ∼ at him〉 **b :** a position from which one must answer for certain acts : ACCOUNT 〈bring criminals to ∼〉 **6 a :** LIBRETTO **b :** the script of a play **c :** a book of arrangements for a musician or dance orchestra : musical repertory **7 :** a packet of items bound together like a book 〈a ∼ of stamps〉 〈a ∼ of matches〉 **8 a :** BOOKMAKER **b :** the bets registered by a bookmaker; *also* : the business or activity of giving odds and taking bets **9 :** the number of tricks a cardplayer or side must win before any trick can have scoring value — **book·able** \'bù-kə-bəl\ *adj* — **book·ful** \'bùk-,fùl\ *n* — **in one's book** : in one's own opinion — **in one's good books** : in favor with one — **one for the book** : an act or occurrence worth noting — **on the books** : on the records

²**book** *adj* (13c) **1 :** derived from books and not from practical experience 〈∼ learning〉 **2 :** shown by books of account 〈∼ assets〉

³**book** *vt* (1807) **1 a :** to register (as a name) for some future activity or condition (as to engage transportation or reserve lodgings) 〈∼ed to sail on Monday〉 **b :** to schedule engagements for 〈∼ the band for a week〉 **c :** to set aside time for **d :** to reserve in advance 〈∼ two seats at the theater〉 〈were all ∼ed up〉 **2 a :** to enter charges against in a police register **b** *chiefly Brit* : to charge (as a soccer player) with an infraction of the rules ∼ *vi* **1 :** to make a reservation 〈∼ through your travel agent〉 **2** *chiefly Brit* : to register in a hotel — usu. used with *in* — **book·er** *n*

draw \'dró\ *vb* **drew** \'drü\; **drawn** \'drón, 'drän\; **draw·ing** [ME *drawen, dragen,* fr. OE *dragan;* akin to ON *draga* to draw, drag] *vt* (bef. 12c) **1 :** to cause to move continuously toward or after a force applied in advance : PULL 〈∼ your chair up by the fire〉: as **a :** to move (as a covering) over or to one side 〈∼ the drapes〉 **b :** to pull up or out of a receptacle or place where seated or carried 〈∼ water from the well〉 〈*drew* a gun〉; *also* : to cause to come out of a container 〈∼ water for a bath〉 **2 :** to cause to go in a certain direction (as by leading) 〈*drew* him aside〉 **3 a :** to bring by inducement or allure : ATTRACT 〈honey ∼*s* flies〉 **b :** to bring in or gather from a specified group or area 〈a college that ∼*s* its students from many states〉 **c :** BRING ON, PROVOKE 〈*drew* enemy fire〉 **d :** to bring out by way of response : ELICIT 〈*drew* cheers from the audience〉 **e :** to receive in the course of play 〈the batter *drew* a walk〉 〈∼ a foul〉 **4 :** INHALE 〈*drew* a deep breath〉 **5 a :** to extract the essence from 〈∼ tea〉 **b :** EVISCERATE 〈plucking and ∼*ing* a goose before cooking〉 **c :** to derive to one's benefit 〈*drew* inspiration from the old masters〉 **6 :** to require (a specified depth) to float in 〈a ship that ∼*s* 12 feet of water〉 **7 a :** ACCUMULATE, GAIN 〈∼*ing* interest〉 **b :** to take (money) from a place of deposit **c :** to use in making a cash demand 〈∼*ing* a check against his account〉 **d :** to receive regularly or in due course 〈∼ a salary〉 **8 a :** to take (cards) from a stack or from the dealer **b :** to receive or take at random

skirt \'skərt\ *n* [ME, fr. ON *skyrta* shirt, kirtle — more at SHIRT] (14c) **1 a** (1) : a free-hanging part of an outer garment or undergarment extending from the waist down (2) : a separate free-hanging outer garment or undergarment usu. worn by women and girls covering some or all of the body from the waist down **b :** either of two usu. leather flaps on a saddle covering the bars on which the stirrups are hung **c :** a cloth facing that hangs loosely and usu. in folds or pleats from the bottom edge or across the front of a piece of furniture **d :** the lower branches of a tree when near the ground **2 a :** the rim, periphery, or environs of an area **b** *pl* : outlying parts (as of a town or city) **3 :** a part or attachment serving as a rim, border, or edging **4 :** a girl or woman — **skirt·ed** *adj*

²**skirt** *vt* (1602) **1 :** to form or run along the border or edge of : BORDER **2 a :** to provide a skirt for **b :** to furnish a border or shield for **3 a :** to go or pass around or about; *specif* : to go around or keep away from in order to avoid danger or discovery **b :** to avoid esp. because of difficulty or fear of controversy 〈∼ed the issue〉 **c :** to evade or miss by a narrow margin 〈having ∼ed disaster —Edith Wharton〉 ∼ *vi* : to be, lie, or move along an edge or border — **skirt·er** *n*

spot \'spät\ *n* [ME; akin to MD *spotte* stain, speck, ON *spotti* small piece] (13c) **1 :** a taint on character or reputation : FAULT 〈the only ∼ on the family name〉 **2 a :** a small area visibly different (as in color, finish, or material) from the surrounding area **b** (1) : an area marred or marked (as by dirt) (2) : a circumscribed surface lesion of disease (as measles) or decay 〈∼*s* of rot〉 〈rust ∼*s* on a leaf〉 **c :** a conventionalized design used on playing cards to distinguish the suits and indicate values **3 :** an object having a specified number of spots or a specified numeral on its surface **4 :** a small quantity or amount : BIT **5 a :** a particular place, area, or part **b :** a small extent of space **6** *pl usu* **spot :** a small croaker (*Leiostomus xanthurus*) of the Atlantic coast with a black spot behind the opercula **7 a :** a particular position (as in an organization or a hierarchy) **b :** a place or appearance on an entertainment program **8 :** SPOTLIGHT **9 :** a position usu. of difficulty or embarrassment **10 :** a brief announcement or advertisement broadcast between scheduled radio or television programs **11 :** a brief segment or report on a broadcast esp. of news — **on the spot 1 :** at once : IMMEDIATELY **2 :** at the place of action **3 a :** in a responsible or accountable position **b :** in a difficult or trying situation

²**spot** *vb* **spot·ted; spot·ting** *vt* (14c) **1 :** to stain the character or reputation of : DISGRACE **2 :** to mark in or with a spot **3 :** to locate or identify by a spot **4 a :** to single out : IDENTIFY; *esp* : to note as a known criminal or a suspicious person **b :** DETECT, NOTICE 〈∼ a mistake〉 **c** (1) : to locate accurately 〈∼ an enemy position〉 (2) : to cause to strike accurately 〈∼ the battery's fire〉 **5 a :** to lie at intervals in or over : STUD **b :** to place at intervals or in a desired spot 〈∼ field telephones〉 **c :** to fix in or as if in the beam of a spotlight **d :** to schedule in a particular spot or at a particular time **6 :** to remove a spot from **7 :** to allow as a handicap ∼ *vi* **1 :** to become stained or discolored in spots **2 :** to cause a spot **3 :** to act as a spotter; *esp* : to locate targets **4 :** to experience abnormal and sporadic bleeding in small amounts from the uterus — **spot·ta·ble** \'spä-tə-bəl\ *adj*

Vocabulary Review

Two of the words on each line in the following exercise are similar in meaning. Circle the word that does not belong.

1. exported	curbed	curtailed
2. overseas	abroad	sophisticated
3. addiction	invasion	habit
4. tariff	barrier	addiction
5. devastating	booming	soaring
6. spots	machines	ads
7. glamorous	sophisticated	insidious

Reading Selection 2

Magazine Article

Before You Begin   1. Why do people get married? Why do some people choose never to marry?

2. How do you think young people who are considering marriage should be prepared? Is it the responsibility of the family, the school, or religious institutions?

3. If you were to design a high school course to prepare young people for married life, what topics would you include?

A high school teacher in Oregon has developed an unusual course for helping young people make intelligent decisions about marriage. Read the following article to see how you feel about Mr. Allen's "Conjugal Prep." Then answer the Comprehension questions. You may want to do the Vocabulary from Context exercise on page 131 before you begin reading.

Conjugal Prep

1   The bridegroom, dressed in a blue blazer and brown suede Adidas sneakers, nervously cleared his throat when his bride, in traditional white, walked down the classroom aisle. As the mock minister led the students—and ten other couples in the room—through the familiar marriage ceremony, the giggles almost drowned him out. But it was no laughing matter. In the next semester, each "couple" would buy a house, have a baby—and get a divorce.

2   In a most unusual course at Parkrose (Ore.) Senior High School, social-science teacher Cliff Allen leads his students through the trials and tribulations of married life. Instead of the traditional course, which dwells on the psychological and sexual adjustments young marrieds must face, Allen exposes his students to the nitty-gritty problems of housing, insurance and child care. "No one tells kids about financial problems," says Allen, 36. "It's like sex—you don't talk about it in front of them."

3   Students act out in nine weeks what normally takes couples ten years to accomplish. In the first week, one member of each couple is required to get an after-school job—a real one. During the semester, the salary, computed on a full-time basis with yearly increases factored in, serves as the guideline for their lifestyle. The third week, the couples must locate an apartment they can afford and study the terms of the lease.

4   **Disaster:** In the fifth week, the couples "have a baby" and then compute the cost by totaling hospital and doctor bills, prenatal and postnatal care, baby clothes and furniture. In week eight, disaster strikes: the marriages are strained to the breaking point by such calamities as a mother-in-law's moving in, death, or imprisonment. It's all over by week nine (the tenth year of marriage). After lectures by marriage counselors and divorce lawyers and computations of alimony and child support, the students get divorced.

5   Allen's course, which has "married" 1,200 students since its inception five years ago, is widely endorsed by parents and students. Some of the participants have found the experience chastening to their real-life marital plans. "Bride" Valerie Payne, 16, and her "groom," David Cooper, 19, still plan to marry in July, but, said Cooper, the course pointed out "the troubles you can have." The course was more unsettling to Marianne Baldrica, 17, who tried "marriage" last term with her boyfriend Eric Zook, 18. "Eric and I used to get along pretty well before we took the course together," Marianne said. "But I wanted to live in the city, he wanted the country. He wanted lots of kids, I wanted no kids. It's been four weeks since the course ended and Eric and I are just starting to talk to each other again."

—LINDA BIRD FRANCKE with MARY ALICE KELLOGG
in Parkrose, Ore.

"Conjugal Prep," *Newsweek.*

Comprehension

Answer the following questions. Your teacher may want you to answer the questions orally, in writing, or by underlining appropriate parts of the text. True/False items are indicated by a T / F preceding the statement.

1. T / F   The course taught by Cliff Allen requires students to marry, buy a house, and get a divorce.

2. T / F   Allen believes that traditional courses do not adequately prepare young people for married life.

3. What are the nitty-gritty problems that Allen's students must face during the course?

_____

_____

4. T / F   One member of a "newlywed couple" must get a job.

5. How long does the course last? _____ How long are the couples "married"?

_____

6. What are some of the events of married life that the students "experience"? _____

_____

7. What are examples of the disasters that strike couples in the 8th week of the course? _____

_____

_____

8. How has the course affected the marriage plans of some of the students? _____

_____

9. Do you think young people in your country should be required to take such a course? _____

10. Would this course be of interest to gay and lesbian students? _____

Discussion/Composition

1. Compare and contrast the customs and values of the United States (as revealed in this article) with those of your country or community with respect to the following areas:

   a. age at which people marry
   b. role of the school in preparing young people for marriage
   c. amount of individual freedom in choosing marriage partners
   d. "crises" likely to be faced by married couples

2. Marriage rates in the United States are dropping. Here are some facts about marriage from the 1990 Census:

   —The proportion of men and women in their twenties and thirties who have never married grew substantially during the past two decades.
   —Men and women are waiting longer to marry, and the number of unmarried couples living together has more than quadrupled in the past 20 years.

   a. Are the facts cited above true also of your country/community? Why do you think this is or isn't the case?
   b. What do you think are reasons why people in general in the U.S. are marrying later? Why do you think more people never marry?
   c. Why do you think courses such as the one described in "Conjugal Prep" are being developed?

Vocabulary from Context

Both the ideas and the vocabulary from the passage below are taken from "Conjugal Prep."
Use the context provided to determine the meanings of the italicized words. Write a definition,
synonym, or description of each of the italicized vocabulary items in the space provided.

1. _____

2. _____

3. _____

4. _____

5. _____

6. _____

7. _____
8. _____

9. _____

10. _____

11. _____

In Mr. Allen's high school class, all the students have to
"get married." However, the wedding ceremonies are not real
ones but imitations. These *mock* ceremonies sometimes
become so noisy that the loud laughter *drowns out* the voice
of the "minister." Even the two students getting married often
begin to *giggle*.

The teacher, Mr. Allen, believes that marriage is a difficult
and serious business. He wants young people to understand
that there are many changes that must take place after marriage. He believes that the need for these psychological and
financial *adjustments* should be understood before people marry.

Mr. Allen doesn't only introduce his students to major
problems faced in marriage such as illness or unemployment.
He also *exposes* them to the *nitty-gritty* problems they will
face every day. He wants to introduce young people to all the
trials and tribulations that can *strain* a marriage to the
breaking point. He even familiarizes his students with the
problems of divorce and the fact that divorced men must pay
child support money for their children and sometimes pay
monthly *alimony* to their wives.

It has been *unsettling* for some of the students to see the
problems that a married couple often faces. Until they took
the course, they had not worried much about the problems of
marriage. However, both students and parents feel that
Mr. Allen's course is valuable and have *endorsed* the course
publicly. Their statements and letters supporting the class have
convinced the school to offer the course again.

Cartoonists Look at Marriage

On page 133 are some cartoonists' views of marriage that have appeared in newspapers in the United States.

1. Which cartoons do you find amusing? Which ones would not be found amusing in your country/community?

2. Do any of these cartoons illustrate problems for which Allen's course attempts to prepare young people?

3. Are there situations presented here that reveal universal problems presented by marriage?

LOVE HANDLES By H. Brown

Doonesbury   By Garry Trudeau

Reading Selection 3

Magazine Article

Popular magazines sometimes contain articles on technical topics. This is particularly true when technology can be used to help people.

"Sonar for the Blind" is a magazine article that describes a new type of equipment designed to help blind people. Read the passage quickly to determine the author's main ideas. Then use the questions that follow to guide you in a careful reading of the article. You will need to do the Vocabulary from Context exercise on page 137 before you begin reading.

Sonar for the Blind

1   A blind baby is doubly handicapped. Not only is it unable to see, but because it cannot receive the visual stimulus from its environment that a sighted child does, it is likely to be slow in intellectual development. Now the ten-month-old son of Dr. and Mrs. Dennis Daughters of San Ramon, Calif., is the subject of an unusual psychological experiment designed to prevent a lag in the learning process. With the aid of a sonar-type electronic device that he wears on his head, infant Dennis is learning to identify the people and objects in the world around him by means of echoes.

2   Dennis and a twin brother, Daniel, were born last September almost three months too early. Daniel died after five days, and Dennis developed retrolental fibroplasia, an eye disorder usually caused by overexposure to oxygen in an incubator.* He went blind, but through a pediatrician at the premature unit where he was treated, the Daughterses were contacted by Dr. Tom Bower, a psychologist from the University of Edinburgh then serving a fellowship at the Stanford University Center for Advanced Study in the Behavioral Sciences. Bower wanted to see how a blind infant might respond if given an echo-sounding device to help him cope with his surroundings—and the Daughterses agreed to help.

3   By the time the child was six weeks old, his parents noticed that he continuously uttered sharp clicking sounds with his tongue. Bower explained that blind people often use echoes to orient themselves, and that the clicking sounds were the boy's way of creating echoes. This, Bower believed, made the child an ideal subject for testing with an electronic echo-sounding device.

4   Signals: The device used in the study is a refinement of the "Sonicguide," an instrument produced by Telesensory Systems, Inc., of Palo Alto, Calif., and used by blind adults in addition to a cane or guide dog. As adapted for Dennis, it consists of a battery-powered system about the size of a half dollar that is worn on a headgear. A transmitter emits an ultrasonic pulse that creates an 80-degree cone of sound at 6 feet. Echoes from objects within the cone are changed by

---

Adapted from "Sonar for the Blind," *Newsweek.*
*incubator: a machine for the protection of small weak babies in which temperature and oxygen are controlled

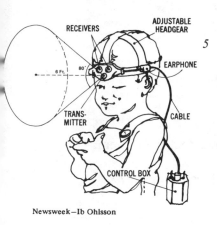

RECEIVERS · ADJUSTABLE HEADGEAR · EARPHONE · TRANS-MITTER · CABLE · CONTROL BOX · 6 Ft. · 80°

Newsweek—Ib Ohlsson

two receivers into audible signals fed into each ear. The signals are perceived as sounds that vary in pitch and volume with the size and distance of the object.

5   The closer an object is, the lower the pitch, and the larger the object, the louder the signal. Hard surfaces produce a sharp ping, while soft ones send back signals with a slightly fuzzy quality. An object slightly to the right of Denny's head sends back a louder sound to his right ear than to the left. Thus, by simply moving his head right and left and up and down, he can not only locate an object but also get some notion of its shape and size, thanks to the varying qualities of sounds reaching his ears as the cone of ultrasound passes its edges. Dennis likes to use the device to play a kind of peek-a-boo with his mother. Standing on her knee and facing her directly, he receives a strong signal in both ears. By turning his head away, he makes her seem to disappear. "From the first time he wore it," says Mrs. Daughters, "it was like a light going on in his head."

6   The boy also learned to identify many objects, including his favorite toy, a rubber caterpillar with six antenna-like projections coming out of its body. And at six-and-a-half months, when a teething biscuit was held in front of Dennis, the child immediately grabbed it with both hands and put it into his mouth.

7   So far, the study has shown that a normal blind baby can employ echoes as well as, or even better than, an unsighted adult can. What remains to be determined is how well the device will help Dennis cope with his surroundings as he begins to walk and venture further into his environment. Meanwhile, Telesensory, Inc., is working on the development of a sonar device with somewhat the same sensitivity as Dennis's for use by school-age children.

Comprehension

Exercise 1

Answer the following questions. Your teacher may want you to answer the questions orally, in writing, or by underlining appropriate parts of the text. True/False items are indicated by a T / F preceding a statement.

1. Why does the writer say that a blind baby is doubly handicapped in comparison to a sighted

   child? _____

   _____

2. T / F   Dennis was blind at birth.

3. Why did Bower believe Dennis would be an ideal subject for this experiment? _____

   _____

4. T / F   Dennis is the first blind person to use a sonar-type electronic device to help in identifying objects.

5. T / F   Dennis doesn't hear the sounds made by the transmitter.

6. T / F   With the headgear on, Dennis can identify objects behind him.

7. T / F   Dennis cannot identify anything closer than six feet from him.

8. T / F   Dennis has a wider range of "vision" 6 feet from his eyes than 2 feet from them.

9. There are two receivers on the headgear. How does this help Dennis locate objects?

_____

10. If someone holds a book 6 feet directly in front of Dennis and then moves it to only 1 foot directly in front of him, what change in sound does Dennis hear?

____ a. a lower-pitched sound   ____ c. a sharper sound
____ b. a higher-pitched sound   ____ d. a softer sound

11. How could Dennis distinguish between a small ball and a large ball from a distance of 3 feet? The small ball would produce _____

____ a. a sharper sound.   ____ c. a softer sound.
____ b. a higher-pitched sound.   ____ d. a louder sound.

12. How could Dennis distinguish between a book and a pillow of the same size and at an equal distance in front of him? A book would produce _____

____ a. a higher-pitched sound.   ____ c. a sharper sound.
____ b. a louder sound.   ____ d. a fuzzier sound.

13. How do you think the child's game of peek-a-boo is usually played? _____

_____

14. T / F   It seems that blind babies are at least as good as blind adults at using echoes to "see."

Exercise 2

Indicate which of the following statements are inferences or conclusions that can be drawn from this article. Check (✓) all the correct inferences. Be prepared to defend your answers with portions of the text.

1. ____ Visual stimuli are helpful to intellectual development.

2. ____ When Dennis grows up he will not need to use a guide dog or a cane like other blind people.

3. ____ Dennis has learned the relationship between the echoes he hears and the shape and distance of an object in front of him.

4. ____ It is hoped that school-aged children will be able to use a device similar to Dennis's.

Discussion/Composition

1. The article you just read describes how an electronic echo-sounding machine works. Describe, in detail, how another machine operates. For example: How does a camera take a picture? How does an airplane fly? How does a telephone work?

2. Imagine you want to teach your friends how to do something they've never done before. Give them step-by-step instructions explaining how to perform a certain task. Consider tasks such as how to make an overseas telephone call, catch a fish, change a car tire, make your favorite meal, buy a used car.

Vocabulary from Context

Use the context provided to determine the meanings of the italicized words. Write a definition, synonym, or description of each italicized vocabulary item in the space provided.

1. _____   Sue has been blind from birth, but she did not let her *handicap* stop her from going to college.

2. _____   Rick spent all of his time playing sports instead of studying; as a result his reading ability has been handicapped. His mental development *lags* behind his physical development.

3. _____   Alice shouted into the cave calling for her brother, but the only sound she heard was the *echo* of her own voice bouncing off the stone walls.

4. _____   When the child moved to the city she frequently got lost if she went out alone. She could never remember which direction she had come from; she was unable to *orient* herself in her new surroundings.

5. _____   The singer's performance was not very good; the notes he sang were often the wrong *pitch*—sometimes they were too low and sometimes too high.

6. _____   Blind people face countless difficulties in their lives but, happily, they succeed in *coping* with many of them so they can live near-normal lives.

7

Nonprose Reading

Poetry

Because the goal of reading is to (re)create meaning, we can say that reading involves solving a puzzle for which the clues are the words we read.* Reading poetry can be the most exciting kind of reading because more of the meaning seems hidden. The author provides the fewest but the richest clues. All of your reading skills will be needed if you are to "solve" the poems in this section.

    Each of the following poems describes something. Read each poem carefully to discover what is being described; do not be concerned if you do not know the meaning of some vocabulary items. If you are having trouble arriving at an answer, read the poem again. If the poem is still not clear, answering the questions on page 141 will give you more clues.

Living Tenderly

My body a rounded stone
with a pattern of smooth seams.
My head a short snake,
retractive, projective,
My legs come out of their sleeves
or shrink within,
and so does my chin.
My eyelids are quick clamps.
My back is my roof.
I am always at home.
I travel where my house walks.
It is a smooth stone.
It floats within the lake,
or rests in the dust.
My flesh lives tenderly
inside its bone.

May Swenson

What is it? _____

Poems from *Poems to Solve,* by May Swenson (New York: Charles Scribner's Sons).
*For an explanation of nonprose reading, see Unit 1.

Southbound on the Freeway

A tourist came in from Orbitville,
parked in the air, and said:

The creatures of this star
are made of metal and glass.

Through the transparent parts
you can see their guts.

Their feet are round and roll
on diagrams—or long

measuring tapes—dark
with white lines.

They have four eyes.
The two in the back are red.

Sometimes you can see a 5-eyed
one, with a red eye turning

on the top of his head.
He must be special—

The others respect him,
and go slow,

when he passes, winding
among them from behind.

They all hiss as they glide,
like inches, down the marked

tapes. Those soft shapes,
shadowy inside

the hard bodies—are they
their guts or their brains?

May Swenson

What is it? _____

By Morning

Some for everyone
    plenty

    and more coming

Fresh dainty airily arriving
    everywhere at once

Transparent at first
    each faint slice
    slow soundlessly tumbling
    then quickly thickly a gracious fleece
    will spread like youth like wheat
    over the city

Each building will be a hill
    all sharps made round

        dark worn noisy arrows made still
        wide flat clean spaces

Streets will be fields
    cars be fumbling sheep

A deep bright harvest will be seeded
    in a night

By morning we'll be children
    feeding on manna

    a new loaf on every doorsill

May Swenson

What is it? _____

Comprehension Clues

"Living Tenderly": What is it?

1. What is the shape of its body?

2. What does its head look like?

3. T / F   Its legs don't move.

4. T / F   It carries its home wherever it goes.

5. T / F   It lives only in dry places.

"Southbound on the Freeway": What does the tourist see?

1. From where is the tourist observing the creatures?

2. What are the creatures made of?
   a. Describe their feet.
   b. Describe their eyes.

3. What is it that is described as "dark with white lines"?

4. What is different about the special ones:
   a. in appearance?
   b. in the way they affect the behavior of the other creatures?

5. What is a freeway?

"By Morning": What is it?

1. Which adjectives describe how it arrives?

2. How does it look at first?

3. What could make buildings suddenly look like hills?

4. What happens to the cars?

5. What could happen in the night to change a city like this?

Word Study

Context Clues

Exercise 1

In the following exercise do NOT try to learn the italicized words. Concentrate on developing your ability to guess the meaning of unfamiliar words using context clues. Read each sentence carefully, and write a definition, synonym, or description of the italicized word on the line provided.

1. _____   It is difficult to list all of my father's *attributes* because he has so many different talents and abilities.

2. _____   Mary, the president of the family council, *conferred* upon Robert the title of vice-president, because she thought he would do a good job.

3. _____   Mother was tall, fat, and middle-aged. The principal of the school was an older woman, almost as *plump* as Mother, and much shorter.

4. _____   When Mark was in one of his *pedantic* moods, he assumed the manner of a distinguished professor and lectured for hours, on minute, boring topics.

5. _____   Many members of the old wealthy families in society held themselves *aloof* from Gatsby, refusing even to acknowledge his existence.

6. _____   I became angrier and angrier as Don talked, but I *refrained* from saying anything.

7. _____   Mr. Doodle is always busy in an *ineffectual* way; he spends hours running around accomplishing nothing.

8. _____   Ian was proud of the neat rows of *marigolds* in his flower beds, which he tended with great care.

9. _____   Most dentists' offices are *drab* places, but Emilio's new office is a bright, cheerful place.

10. _____   The inner and outer events of a plant are interdependent; but this isn't saying that the *skin, cortex, membrane,* or whatever you want to call the boundary of the individual, is meaningless.

Exercise 2

This exercise is designed to give you practice using context clues from a passage. Use your general knowledge along with information from the entire text below to write a definition, synonym, or description of the italicized word on the line provided. Read through the entire passage before making a decision. Note that some of the words appear more than once; by the end of the passage you should have a good idea of their meaning. Do not worry if your definition is not exact; a general idea of the meaning will often allow you to understand the meaning of a written text.

Babies Sound Off: The Power of Babble

There is more to the *babbling* of a baby than meets the ear. A handful of scientists are picking apart infants' utterances and finding that not only is there an ordered *sequence* of vocal stages between birth and the first words, but in *hearing-impaired* babies a type of *babbling* thought to signal an emerging capacity for speech is delayed and distorted.

"The traditional wisdom [among developmental researchers] is that deaf babies *babble* like hearing babies," says linguist D. Kimbrough Oller of the University of Miami (Fla.). "This idea is a *myth.*" Oller reported his latest findings on hearing and deaf infants last week at a National Institutes of Health seminar in Bethesda, Md. He and his colleagues demonstrated 8 years ago that hearing babies from a variety of language communities start out by cooing and gurgling; at about 7 months of age, they start to produce *sequences* of the same syllables (for instance, "da-da-da" or "dut-dut-dut") that are classified as *babbling* and can be recorded and acoustically measured in the laboratory, with words or wordlike sounds appearing soon after 1 year of age. *Babbling*—the emitting of identifiable consonant and vowel sounds—usually disappears by around 18 to 20 months of age.

In a just-completed study, Oller and his co-workers found that repeated *sequences* of syllables first appeared among 21 hearing infants between the ages of 6 and 10 months; in contrast, these vocalizations emerged among 9 severely to profoundly deaf babies between the ages of 11 and 25 months. In addition, deaf babies *babbled* less frequently than hearing babies, produced fewer syllables and were more likely to use single syllables than repeated *sequences*.

babbling: _____

sequence: _____

hearing-impaired: _____

myth: _____

From *Science News.*

Word Study

Stems and Affixes

Below is a list of some commonly occurring stems and affixes.* Study their meanings; then do the exercises that follow. Your teacher may ask you to give examples of other words you know that are derived from these stems and affixes.

Prefixes

multi-	many	multiply, multiple
peri-	around	periscope, perimeter
semi-	half, partly	semisweet, semicircle
tri-	three	triangle
ultra-	beyond, excessive, extreme	ultramodern
uni-	one	unicycle, unify, universe

Stems

-aster-, -astro-, -stellar-	star	astronomy, stellar
-auto-	self	automobile, automatic
-bio-	life	biology
-cycle-	circle	bicycle, cycle
-mega-	great, large	megaton, megalopolis
-mort-	death	mortal, immortality
-phil-	love	philosophy
-polis-	city	metropolis
-psych-	mind	psychology
-soph-	wise	philosophy, sophomore

Suffixes

-ity	condition, quality, state of being	unity, ability
-ness	condition, quality, state of being	sadness, happiness

Exercise 1

In each item, select the best definition of the italicized word or phrase or answer the question.

1. To apply to some universities, you must fill out the application form and include a short *autobiography*.

 _____ a. sample of your writing   _____ c. list of courses you have taken
 _____ b. account of your life written by you   _____ d. list of schools you have attended

---

*For a list of all stems and affixes taught in *Reader's Choice,* see the Appendix.

2. The police officer used a *megaphone*.

_____ a. a portable radio   _____ c. an instrument to make one's
_____ b. a long stick   voice louder
                                _____ d. a telephone in the car

3. Dr. Swanson has written articles about *interstellar* travel.

_____ a. underwater   _____ c. high-speed
_____ b. long-distance   _____ d. outer space

4. Janet is interested in *autographs* of famous people.

_____ a. pictures   _____ c. families
_____ b. personalities   _____ d. signatures

5. An *asterisk* is a written symbol that looks like _____

_____ a. /.   _____ c. %.
_____ b. *.   _____ d. @.

6. The government is financing a study of the effects on humans of living in a *megalopolis*.

_____ a. an apartment in a large building   _____ c. a dangerous part of a city
_____ b. an extremely large city   _____ d. a city with a large police force

7. Children learning to ride bicycles probably already know how to ride a _____

_____ a. unicycle.   _____ c. tricycle.
_____ b. megacycle.   _____ d. motorcycle.

8. What is the *perimeter* of this rectangle?

_____ a. 14   _____ c. 2
_____ b. 4   _____ d. 5

9. *Nautical* means *pertaining to sailors, ships, or navigation*. Explain how the word *astronaut* is formed.

_____

_____

10. Why are the clothes that nurses, police officers, and soldiers wear called *uniforms*?

_____

_____

11. People who study population often speak of the world mortality rate. What is the opposite of *mortality rate*?

_____

Exercise 2

Word analysis can help you to guess the meaning of unfamiliar words. Using context clues and what you know about word parts, write a synonym, description, or definition of the italicized words.

1. _____ I enjoy reading *biographies* of kings and queens.

2. _____ The Morrises hired a full-time nurse to help them care for their newborn *triplets*.

3. _____ The new art museum will be named for the *multimillionaire* who donated the money to build it.

4. _____ About 4 million people live in the Detroit *metropolitan* area.

5. _____ All the hospital's private rooms were occupied, so Michelle had to stay in a *semiprivate* one.

6. _____ Winston Churchill wrote a *multivolume* history of World War II.

7. _____ Race car drivers need to have good *peripheral* vision so they can see another car driving alongside them without turning their heads.

8. _____ That jeweler doesn't cut diamonds; he works mainly with *semiprecious* stones such as opals.

9. _____ He was shot during the robbery, but it is not a *mortal wound*.

10. _____ My teeth are falling out; my dentist wants me to make an appointment with a *periodontist*.

11. _____ The president's *popularity* with the voters has never been greater than it is today.

Exercise 3

Following is a list of words containing some of the stems and affixes introduced in this unit and the previous ones. Definitions of these words appear on the right. Put the letter of the appropriate definition next to each word.

1. _____ psychologist

2. _____ philanthropist

3. _____ sophisticated

4. _____ biochemist

5. _____ biology

6. _____ antibiotic

a. worldly-wise; knowing; finely experienced

b. a substance capable of killing microorganisms

c. the science of life or living matter

d. one who studies the chemistry of living things

e. one who shows love for humanity by doing good works for society

f. one who studies mental processes and behavior

---

7. _____ multicolored

8. _____ asteroid

9. _____ periscope

10. _____ astronomer

11. _____ unilateral

12. _____ bilateral

a. starlike; shaped like a star

b. affecting two sides or parties

c. having many colors

d. pertaining to, involving, or affecting only one side

e. a scientific observer of the planets, stars, and outer space

f. an optical instrument that allows a submarine to observe the surface from below the water

---

13. _____ cycle

14. _____ semicircle

15. _____ trilogy

16. _____ astrology

17. _____ ultraviolet

18. _____ ultranationalism

a. a recurring period of time in which certain events repeat themselves in the same order and at the same intervals

b. the study of the influence of the stars on human affairs

c. excessive devotion to national interests as opposed to international considerations

d. a series or group of three related dramas, operas, novels, etc.

e. invisible rays of the spectrum lying beyond the violet end of the visible spectrum

f. a half circle

Sentence Study

Restatement and Inference

Each sentence below is followed by five statements.* The statements are of four types:
1. Some of the statements are restatements of the original sentence. They give the same information in a different way.
2. Some of the statements are inferences (conclusions) that can be drawn from the information given in the original sentence.
3. Some of the statements are false based on the information given.
4. Some of the statements cannot be judged true or false based on the information given in the original sentence.

Put a check (✓) next to all restatements and inferences (types 1 and 2). Note: do not check a statement that is true of itself but cannot be inferred from the sentence given.

Example   Heavy smokers and drinkers run a fifteen-times greater risk of developing cancer of the mouth and throat than nonsmokers and nondrinkers.

_____ a. Cancer of the mouth and throat is more likely to occur in heavy smokers and drinkers than in nonsmokers and nondrinkers.

_____ b. People who never drink and smoke will not get mouth or throat cancer.

_____ c. Heavy drinkers who run have a greater risk of developing cancer than nondrinkers.

_____ d. People who don't smoke and drink have less chance of getting cancer of the mouth and throat than those who smoke and drink heavily.

_____ e. People would probably be healthier if they did not drink and smoke too much.

Explanation

✓ a. This is a restatement of the original sentence. If heavy smokers and drinkers run a greater risk of developing cancer than those who do not drink or smoke, then cancer is more likely to occur in heavy smokers and drinkers.

_____ b. It is not true that people who never smoke and drink will never get mouth or throat cancer. We only know that they are *less likely* to get this kind of cancer.

_____ c. The word *run* in the original sentence is part of the phrase *to run a risk* which means *to be in danger*. The sentence does not tell us anything about heavy drinkers who enjoy the sport of running.

---

*For an introduction to sentence study, see Unit 3.

✓ d. This is a restatement of the original sentence. If people who drink and smoke heavily have a greater chance of getting mouth and throat cancer than those who don't, then it must be true that those who don't smoke and drink heavily have less chance of developing this kind of cancer.

✓ e. This is an inference that can be drawn from the information given. If people who smoke and drink heavily run a high risk of developing cancer, then we can infer that people probably would be healthier if they didn't smoke and drink too much (heavily).

1. Nine out of ten doctors responding to a survey said they recommend our product to their patients if they recommend anything.

    _____ a. Nine out of ten doctors recommend the product.

    _____ b. Of the doctors who responded to a survey, nine out of ten doctors recommend the product.

    _____ c. If they recommend anything, nine out of ten doctors responding to a survey recommend the product.

    _____ d. Most doctors recommend the product.

    _____ e. We don't know how many doctors recommend the product.

2. This organization may succeed marvelously at what it wants to do, but what it wants to do may not be all that important.

    _____ a. The organization is marvelous.

    _____ b. The organization may succeed.

    _____ c. Although the organization may reach its goals, the goals might not be important.

    _____ d. What the organization wants is marvelous.

    _____ e. The author questions the goals of the organization.

3. This book contains a totally new outlook that combines the wisdom of the past with scientific knowledge to solve the problems of the present.

    _____ a. Problems of the past and present are solved in this book.

    _____ b. In this book, current knowledge and past wisdom are combined to solve current problems.

    _____ c. Only by using knowledge of the past and present can we solve problems.

    _____ d. None of today's problems can be solved without scientific knowledge.

    _____ e. This book is different because it combines the wisdom of the past with scientific knowledge.

4. Like other timeless symbols, flags have accompanied mankind for thousands of years, gaining ever wider meaning, yet losing none of their inherent and original force.

        a. In spite of losing some of their original force, flags are a timeless symbol that has accompanied mankind for thousands of years.

        b. Flags have existed for thousands of years.

        c. Timeless symbols typically gain wider meaning while not losing their inherent force.

        d. Thousands of years ago flags accompanied mankind but through time they have lost their force.

        e. Because flags are considered a timeless symbol, they have gained continually wider meaning without losing their inherent original force.

5. When there is an absence of reliable information about drugs, the risks involved in using them are greatly increased.

        a. There is no reliable information about drugs.

        b. Using drugs is more dangerous when we don't know what effects and dangers are involved.

        c. The risks involved in using drugs have increased.

        d. People should try to find out about drugs before using them.

        e. There are no risks involved in using drugs if we have reliable information about them.

6. The project of which this book is the result was first suggested in the summer of 1992, in the course of some leisurely conversations at the foot of and (occasionally) on top of the Alps of western Austria.

        a. This book was written in 1992.

        b. This book was written in Austria.

        c. This book is a collection of conversations held in 1992.

        d. This book is the end result of a project.

        e. This book is about western Austria.

7. Los Angeles' safety record with school buses is generally a good one, but of course this record is only as good as the school bus drivers themselves.

        a. In spite of a generally good safety record for their school buses, Los Angeles school bus drivers are not very good.

_____ b. If school bus drivers are not very good, the town's school bus safety record will not be very good either.

_____ c. If cities wish to maintain good safety records with school buses, they should hire good school bus drivers.

_____ d. With better school buses, drivers will be able to maintain better safety records.

_____ e. Los Angeles' safety record with school buses has improved because better bus drivers have been hired.

8. Taxes being so high, the descendents of the wealthy class of the nineteenth century are being forced to rent out their estates to paying guests.

_____ a. In the nineteenth century, the wealthy class rented out its estates.

_____ b. Because of high taxes, families that were rich one hundred years ago now rent out their estates.

_____ c. Guests pay high taxes when they rent old estates.

_____ d. Some families that were once wealthy are having trouble paying their taxes.

_____ e. High taxes have changed the lives of some of the old wealthy families.

9. According to the definition of Chinese traditional medicine, acupuncture is the treatment of disease—not just the alleviation of pain—by inserting very fine needles into the body at specific points called loci.

_____ a. The author believes some people do not know that acupuncture can be used to treat illness.

_____ b. Finely pointed needles called loci are used in acupuncture.

_____ c. In Chinese traditional medicine, acupuncture is known to treat disease and alleviate pain.

_____ d. Those using acupuncture treat disease by placing needles into the body at specific points.

_____ e. Only those who practice traditional Chinese medicine use acupuncture.

10. It would be difficult to overpraise this book.

_____ a. This is a difficult book.

_____ b. This book deserves much praise.

_____ c. It is difficult not to overpraise this book.

_____ d. It is difficult to praise this book.

_____ e. The author of this sentence thinks this is an excellent book.

Paragraph Analysis

Reading for Full Understanding

The paragraph exercises in Units 1 and 3 require you to determine the main idea of a passage. This exercise and the one in Unit 11 require much more careful reading. Each selection is followed by a number of questions. The questions are designed to give you practice in:

1. determining the main idea
2. understanding supporting details
3. drawing inferences
4. guessing vocabulary items from context
5. using syntactic and stylistic clues to understand selected portions of the paragraphs

Read each paragraph carefully. Try to determine the author's main idea while attempting to remember important details. For each of the questions below, select the *best* answer. You may refer to the passage to answer the questions.

Example

1　　It is not often realized that women held a high place in southern
2　European societies in the 10th and 11th centuries. As a wife, the
3　woman was protected by the setting up of a dowry or *decimum*.
4　Admittedly, the purpose of this was to protect her against the risk of
5　desertion, but in reality its function in the social and family life of the
6　time was much more important. The *decimum* was the wife's right to
7　receive a tenth of all her husband's property. The wife had the right to
8　withhold consent, in *all* transactions the husband would make. And
9　more than just a right: the documents show that she enjoyed a real
10　power of decision, equal to that of her husband. In no case do the
11　documents indicate any degree of difference in the legal status of
12　husband and wife.
13　　The wife shared in the management of her husband's personal
14　property, but the opposite was not always true. Women seemed
15　perfectly prepared to defend their own inheritance against husbands
16　who tried to exceed their rights, and on occasion they showed a fine
17　fighting spirit. A case in point is that of María Vivas, a Catalan woman
18　of Barcelona. Having agreed with her husband Miró to sell a field she
19　had inherited, for the needs of the household, she insisted on
20　compensation. None being offered, she succeeded in dragging her
21　husband to the scribe to have a contract duly drawn up assigning her a
22　piece of land from Miró's personal inheritance. The unfortunate
23　husband was obliged to agree, as the contract says, "for the sake of
24　peace." Either through the dowry or through being hot-tempered, the
25　Catalan wife knew how to win herself, within the context of the family,
26　a powerful economic position.

From Sylvia L. Thrupp, ed., *Early Medieval Society* (New York: Appleton-Century Crofts).

1. A *decimum* was _____

    _____ a. the wife's inheritance from her father.
    _____ b. a gift of money to the new husband.
    _____ c. a written contract.
    _____ d. the wife's right to receive one-tenth of her husband's property.

2. In the society described in the passage, the legal standing of the wife in marriage was _____

    _____ a. higher than that of her husband.
    _____ b. lower than that of her husband.
    _____ c. the same as that of her husband.
    _____ d. higher than that of a single woman.

3. What compensation did María Vivas get for the field?

    _____ a. some of the land Miró had inherited
    _____ b. a tenth of Miró's land
    _____ c. money for household expenses
    _____ d. money from Miró's inheritance

4. Could a husband sell his wife's inheritance?

    _____ a. no, under no circumstances
    _____ b. yes, whenever he wished to
    _____ c. yes, if she agreed
    _____ d. yes, if his father-in-law agreed

5. Which of the following is NOT mentioned as an effect of the dowry system?

    _____ a. The husband had to share the power of decision in marriage.
    _____ b. The wife was protected from desertion.
    _____ c. The wife gained a powerful economic position.
    _____ d. The husband was given control over his wife's property.

Explanation

1. (d) This is a restatement of a part of the passage. If you did not remember the definition of the word *decimum,* you could have scanned for it quickly and found the answer in lines 6 and 7.

2. (c) This is the main idea of the paragraph. The high place of women in the society is introduced in the first sentence. In lines 9 and 10 the author states that a woman enjoyed a legal power of decision equal to that of her husband. The last sentence tells us that, within the context of the home, women held a powerful economic position.

3. (a) This tests your understanding of details. In lines 20, 21, and 22 the author states that María Vivas forced her husband to agree to a contract giving her a piece of land from his inheritance.

4. (c) This is an inference. In lines 7 and 8 the author states that the wife could refuse to agree to any business agreements the husband might want to make. Thus, we can infer that a husband could only sell his wife's inheritance if she agreed. Furthermore, in lines 18 and 19, the fact that María Vivas allowed her husband to sell a field she had inherited indicates that her agreement was necessary.

5. (d) Items a, b, and c serve as a summary of the ideas of the passage.

   (a) Lines 9 and 10 tell us that wives enjoyed a real power of decision; lines 13 and 14 state that a wife shared in the management of her husband's estate.

   (b) Lines 4 and 5 state that the purpose of the dowry was to protect wives from desertion.

   (c) The final sentence states that, within the context of the family, the wife was able to win a powerful economic position.

   (d) Nowhere does it state that a husband was given control over a wife's property, and in several instances the opposite is stated (see questions 3 and 4).

Paragraph 1

1   Today is the anniversary of that afternoon in April a year ago that
2 I first saw the strange and appealing doll in the window of Abe
3 Sheftel's stationery and toy shop on Third Avenue near Fifteenth
4 Street, just around the corner from my office, where the plate on the
5 door reads: Dr. Samuel Amory. I remember just how it was that day:
6 the first hint of spring floated across the East River, mixing with the
7 soft-coal smoke from the factories and the street smells of the poor
8 neighborhood. As I turned the corner on my way to work and came to
9 Sheftel's, I was made once more aware of the poor collection of toys in
10 the dusty window, and I remembered the approaching birthday of a
11 small niece of mine in Cleveland, to whom I was in the habit of
12 sending modest gifts. Therefore, I stopped and examined the window
13 to see if there might be anything appropriate, and looked at the
14 confusing collection of unappealing objects—a red toy fire engine,
15 some lead soldiers, cheap baseballs, bottles of ink, pens, yellowed
16 stationery, and garish cardboard advertisements for soft-drinks. And
17 thus it was that my eyes eventually came to rest upon the doll tucked
18 away in one corner, a doll with the strangest, most charming expression
19 on her face. I could not wholly make her out, due to the shadows and
20 the film through which I was looking, but I was aware that a
21 tremendous impression had been made upon me as though I had run
22 into a person, as one does sometimes with a stranger, with whose
23 personality one is deeply impressed.

From Paul Gallico, "The Enchanted Doll," in *Story and Structure,* ed. Laurence Perrine (New York: Harcourt, Brace and World, Inc.).

1. What made an impression on the narrator?

   _____ a. the doll's unusual face
   _____ b. the collection of toys
   _____ c. a stranger he met at the store
   _____ d. the resemblance of the doll to his niece

2. Why does the narrator mention his niece?

   _____ a. She likes dolls.
   _____ b. The doll looks like her.
   _____ c. She lives near Sheftel's.
   _____ d. He was looking for a gift for her.

3. Why did the narrator go past Sheftel's?

   _____ a. He was on his way to work.
   _____ b. He was looking for a present for his niece.
   _____ c. He wanted to buy some stationery.
   _____ d. He liked to look in the window.

4. The story takes place in the _____

   _____ a. early summer.
   _____ b. midsummer.
   _____ c. early spring.
   _____ d. late spring.

5. When was the story written?

   _____ a. one year after the incident
   _____ b. right after the incident
   _____ c. in the narrator's old age
   _____ d. on the narrator's birthday

6. Most of the things in the store window were _____

   _____ a. expensive.
   _____ b. appealing.
   _____ c. neatly arranged.
   _____ d. unattractive.

Paragraph 2

1   The great advance in rocket theory 60 years ago showed that
2 liquid-fuel rockets were far superior in every respect to the skyrocket
3 with its weak solid fuel, the only kind of rocket then known. However,
4 in the 1960s, large solid-fuel rockets with solid fuels about as
5 powerful as liquid fuels have made their appearance, and it is a favorite
6 layperson's question to inquire which one is "better." The question is
7 meaningless; one might as well ask whether a gasoline or a diesel
8 engine is "better." It all depends on the purpose. A liquid-fuel rocket is
9 complicated, but has the advantage that it can be controlled beautifully.
10 The burning of the rocket engine can be stopped completely; it can be
11 reignited when desired. In addition, the thrust can be made to vary by
12 adjusting the speed of the fuel pumps. A solid-fuel rocket, on the other
13 hand, is rather simple in construction, though hard to build when a
14 really large size is desired. But once you have a solid-fuel rocket, it is
15 ready for action at very short notice. A liquid-fuel rocket has to be
16 fueled first and cannot be held in readiness for very long after it has
17 been fueled. However, once a solid-fuel rocket has been ignited, it will
18 keep burning. It cannot be stopped and reignited whenever desired (it
19 could conceivably be stopped and reignited after a precalculated time
20 of burning has elapsed) and its thrust cannot be varied. Because a
21 solid-fuel rocket can be kept ready for a long time, most military
22 missiles employ solid fuels, but human-piloted spaceflight needs the
23 fine adjustments that can only be provided by liquid fuels. It may be
24 added that a liquid-fuel rocket is an expensive device; a large solid-fuel
25 rocket is, by comparison, cheap. But the solid fuel, pound per pound,
26 costs about 10 times as much as the liquid fuel. So you have, on the
27 one hand, an expensive rocket with a cheap fuel and on the other hand
28 a comparatively cheap rocket with an expensive fuel.

1. The author feels that a comparison of liquid- and solid-fuel rockets shows that ____

   ____ a. neither type is very economical.   ____ c. each type has certain advantages.
   ____ b. the liquid-fuel rocket is best.   ____ d. the solid-fuel rocket is best.

2. The most important consideration for human-piloted space flight is that the rocket be ____

   ____ a. inexpensive to construct.   ____ c. easily controlled.
   ____ b. capable of lifting heavy spacecraft into orbit.   ____ d. inexpensive to operate.

3. Solid-fuel rockets are expensive to operate because of their ____

   ____ a. size.   ____ c. burning time.
   ____ b. fuel.   ____ d. complicated engines.

4. Which of the following statements is *not* characteristic of liquid-fuel rockets?

   ____ a. The fuel is cheap.   ____ c. They are cheap to build.
   ____ b. They can be stopped and reignited.   ____ d. They must be used soon after fueling.

Adapted from Willy Ley, "Space Race," in *Information Please Almanac*, ed. D. Golenpaul (New York: Simon and Schuster).

Paragraph 3

1   It was not yet eleven o'clock when a boat crossed the river with a
2   single passenger who had obtained his transportation at that unusual
3   hour by promising an extra fare. While the youth stood on the landing-
4   place searching in his pockets for money, the ferryman lifted a lantern,
5   by the aid of which, together with the newly risen moon, he took a
6   very accurate survey of the stranger's figure. He was a young man of
7   barely eighteen years, evidently country bred, and now, as it seemed,
8   on his first visit to town. He was wearing a rough gray coat, which was
9   in good shape, but which had seen many winters before this one. The
10   garments under his coat were well constructed of leather, and fitted
11   tightly to a pair of muscular legs; his stockings of blue yarn must have
12   been the work of a mother or sister, and on his head was a three-
13   cornered hat, which in its better days had perhaps sheltered the grayer
14   head of the lad's father. In his left hand was a walking stick, and his
15   equipment was completed by a leather bag not so abundantly stocked
16   as to inconvenience the strong shoulders on which it hung. Brown,
17   curly hair, well-shaped features, bright, cheerful eyes were nature's
18   gifts, and worth all that art could have done for his adornment. The
19   youth, whose name was Robin, paid the boatman, and then walked
20   forward into the town with a light step, as if he had not already
21   traveled more than thirty miles that day. As he walked, he surveyed his
22   surroundings as eagerly as if he were entering London or Madrid,
23   instead of the little metropolis of a New England colony.

1. What time of year was it in this story?

_____ a. spring   _____ c. fall
_____ b. summer   _____ d. winter

2. At what time of day did Robin cross the river?

_____ a. morning   _____ c. late afternoon
_____ b. midday   _____ d. night

3. The boatman was willing to take Robin across the river because _____

_____ a. he wanted to make extra money.
_____ b. he saw that Robin was young and rich.
_____ c. he was going to row across the river anyway.
_____ d. he felt sorry for him because Robin looked poor.

4. The stockings that Robin wore were obviously _____

_____ a. well worn.   _____ c. handmade.
_____ b. very expensive.   _____ d. much too big.

From Nathaniel Hawthorne, *Selected Tales and Sketches,* ed. H. Waggooner Hyatt (Chicago: Holt, Rinehart and Winston).

5. From the way he looked, it was evident that Robin was ____

____ a. a wealthy merchant's son.   ____ c. a soldier.
____ b. a country boy.   ____ d. a foreigner.

6. Robin was apparently going to the town ____

____ a. to buy new clothes.   ____ c. for the first time in several years.
____ b. for the first time.   ____ d. on one of his regular trips there.

7. How did Robin appear as he walked into town?

____ a. He was cheerful and excited.
____ b. He was tired.
____ c. He seemed very sad.
____ d. He seemed frightened by his strange surroundings.

8. How far had Robin traveled?

____ a. over thirty miles   ____ c. from a nearby town
____ b. from Madrid   ____ d. from London

Paragraph 4

1   Fifty volunteers were alphabetically divided into two equal groups,
2 Group A to participate in a 7 week exercise program, and Group B to
3 avoid deliberate exercise of any sort during those 7 weeks. On the day
4 before the exercise program began, all 50 men participated in a step-
5 test. This consisted of stepping up and down on a 16-inch bench at 30
6 steps a minute for 5 minutes. One minute after completion of the step-
7 test, the pulse rate of each subject was taken and recorded. This
8 served as the pretest for the experiment. For the next 7 weeks,
9 subjects in the experimental group (Group A) rode an Exercycle (a
10 motor-driven bicycle-type exercise machine) for 15 minutes each day.
11 The exercise schedule called for riders to ride relaxed during the first
12 day's ride, merely holding on to the handle bars and foot pedals as the
13 machine moved. Then, for the next 3 days, they rode relaxed for 50
14 seconds of each minute, and pushed, pulled, and pedaled actively for
15 10 seconds of each minute. The ratio of active riding was increased
16 every few days, so that by the third week it was half of each minute,
17 and by the seventh week the riders were performing 15 solid minutes of
18 active riding.
19   At the end of the 7 weeks, the step-test was again given to both
20 groups of subjects, and their pulses taken. The post-exercise pulse
21 rates of subjects in the experimental group were found to have
22 decreased an average of 30 heart beats per minute, with the lowest
23 decrease 28 and the highest decrease 46. The pulse rates of subjects in
24 the control group remained the same or changed no more than 4 beats,
25 with an average difference between the initial and final tests of zero.

From James E. Haney, "Health and Motor Behavior: Measuring Energy Expenditures," *Research News*.

1. How many people were in each group?

   ____ a. 100   ____ c. 25
   ____ b. 50   ____ d. 15

2. The step-test was given ____

   ____ a. after each exercise period.
   ____ b. at the beginning and at the end of the seven week period.
   ____ c. only once, at the beginning of the seven week period.
   ____ d. twice to the men in Group A and once to the men in Group B.

3. When were pulse rates taken?

   ____ a. after every exercise period
   ____ b. every day
   ____ c. after the step-tests
   ____ d. every time the ratio of active riding was increased

4. The exercise schedule was planned so that the amount of active riding ____

   ____ a. increased every few days.
   ____ b. varied from day to day.
   ____ c. increased until the third week and then was kept constant.
   ____ d. increased every exercise period.

5. What did Group A do in their program?

   ____ a. They stepped up and down on a bench each day.
   ____ b. They pushed and pulled on exercise handles every day.
   ____ c. They rode on an Exercycle every day.
   ____ d. They refrained from any exercise.

6. The post-exercise pulse rates of Group B were found on the average to have ____

   ____ a. not changed.   ____ c. gone down 30 beats per minute.
   ____ b. gone down 28 beats per minute.   ____ d. gone down 4 beats per minute.

7. This paragraph implies that ____

   ____ a. most people do not get enough exercise.
   ____ b. a high pulse rate is desirable.
   ____ c. regular exercise can strengthen your heart.
   ____ d. everyone should exercise 15 minutes a day.

Paragraph 5

1 In the second half of each year, many powerful storms are born in
2 the tropical Atlantic and Caribbean seas. Of these, only about a half a
3 dozen generate the strong, circling winds of 75 miles per hour or more
4 that give them hurricane status, and several usually make their way to
5 the coast. There they cause millions of dollars of damage, and bring
6 death to large numbers of people.
7   The great storms that hit the coast start as innocent circling
8 disturbances hundreds—even thousands—of miles out to sea. As they
9 travel aimlessly over water warmed by the summer sun, they are
10 carried westward by the trade winds. When conditions are just right,
11 warm, moist air flows in at the bottom of such a disturbance, moves
12 upward through it and comes out at the top. In the process, the
13 moisture in this warm air produces rain, and with it the heat that is
14 converted to energy in the form of strong winds. As the heat increases,
15 the young hurricane begins to swirl in a counter-clockwise motion.
16   The average life of a hurricane is only about nine days, but it
17 contains almost more power than we can imagine. The energy in the
18 heat released by a hurricane's rainfall in a single day would satisfy the
19 entire electrical needs of the United States for more than six months.
20 Water, not wind, is the main source of death and destruction in a
21 hurricane. A typical hurricane brings 6- to 12-inch downpours resulting
22 in sudden floods. Worst of all is the powerful movement of the sea—
23 the mountains of water moving toward the low-pressure hurricane
24 center. The water level rises as much as 15 feet above normal as it
25 moves toward shore.

1. When is an ordinary tropical storm called a hurricane?

       ____ a. when it begins in the Atlantic and Caribbean seas
       ____ b. when it hits the coastline
       ____ c. when it is more than 75 miles wide
       ____ d. when its winds reach 75 miles per hour

2. What is the worst thing about hurricanes?

       ____ a. the destructive effects of water
       ____ b. the heat they release
       ____ c. that they last about nine days on the average
       ____ d. their strong winds

3. The counter-clockwise swirling of the hurricane is brought about by ____

       ____ a. the low-pressure area in the center of the storm.   ____ c. the trade winds.
       ____ b. the force of waves of water.   ____ d. the increasing heat.

4. Apparently the word *downpour* means ____

       ____ a. heavy rainfall.   ____ c. the progress of water to the hurricane center.
       ____ b. dangerous waves.   ____ d. the energy produced by the hurricane.

From E. Hughes, "Hurricane Warning," *Reader's Digest.*

Discourse Focus

Prediction

Reading is an active process. Meaning does not exist only on the page or in the mind of the reader. It is created by an active *interaction* between reader and text. Based on their general knowledge and the information in a text, good readers develop predictions about what they will read next; then they read to see if their expectations will be confirmed. If they are not confirmed, readers reread, creating new predictions. Most often, however, readers are not greatly surprised; readers continue reading. This exercise is designed to give you practice in the process of consciously developing and confirming expectations. You will read an article, stopping at several points to consider what you expect to read about next. Readers cannot always predict precisely what an author will talk about next, but you can practice using clues from the text and your general knowledge to more efficiently predict content.

The Troubled State of Calculus
A Push to Revitalize College Calculus Teaching Has Begun

Calculus: a large lecture hall, 200 or so bored students, a lecturer talking to a blackboard filled with Greek symbols, a thick, heavy textbook with answers to even-numbered problems, a seemingly endless chain of formulas, theorems and proofs.

Example

1. Above are the title, subtitle, and an inset from an article on calculus. On the basis of these, what aspect of calculus do you think the article might be about? List two possibilities:

   _____

   _____

2. Does the author seem to think that calculus instruction is successful

   or unsuccessful at the present time? _____ What words give

   you this impression? _____

   _____

Adapted from *Science News*.

Explanation

1. The main title indicates that calculus instruction is *troubled*. The subtitle tells us that there is a movement to improve calculus teaching. The inset describes a "typical," boring calculus class, suggesting what is troubled, and what needs to be improved. Based on this information in the text you might have decided that the article would be about such things as current problems with calculus instruction, and proposals for improving instruction. If you have personal knowledge of calculus instruction, you may have some more specific ideas about the kinds of problems and solutions that might be mentioned.

2. Obviously the author has a negative opinion of calculus instruction. He refers to it as *troubled* in the main title, and indicates a need to *revitalize* (to give new life to) it in the subtitle. The inset describes a *large* lecture hall, with *bored* students and *heavy* books: the opposite of a lively situation.

---

3. Before you continue reading the article, decide how you expect it to begin. Remember, you cannot always predict precisely what an author will do, but you can use knowledge of the text and your general knowledge to make good guesses. Which of the following seems the most likely beginning?

   a. The author will describe traditional ways of teaching calculus.
   b. The author will describe math instruction in general.
   c. The author will describe new ways to teach calculus.
   d. The author will describe the general state of calculus instruction.

Now read to see if your expectations are confirmed.

by Ivar Peterson

More than half a million students take an introductory calculus course in any given year, and the number is growing. A large proportion have no choice. Calculus is a barrier that must be overcome on the way to a professional career in medicine or engineering. Even disciplines like history now sometimes require some college mathematics. But for many people who in the last few years have passed through such a course, the word "calculus" brings back painful memories.

4. The article appears to be critical of current teaching practices. Is this what you expected?

5. Did you expect the article to begin with a general description of calculus instruction?

6. What do you expect to read about next? What words or phrases point in this direction? What do you know about calculus and schools in general that would lead you to predict this?

_____

_____

_____

Now read to see if your expectations are confirmed.

In many universities about half of the students who take introductory calculus fail the course. A surprisingly large number must take the course several times to get through. At the same time, engineering and physical sciences professors complain that even the students who pass don't know very much about calculus and don't know how to use it.

"The teaching of calculus is a national disgrace," says Lynn A. Steen, president of the Mathematical Association of America, based in Washington, D.C., and a professor at St. Olaf College in Northfield, Minn. "Too often calculus is taught by inexperienced instructors to ill-prepared students in an environment with insufficient feedback," he says. "The result is a serious decline in the number of students pursuing advanced mathematics, and a majority of college graduates who have learned to hate mathematics."

7. Were your expectations confirmed? If not, why not? Did you misunderstand something in the previous section? Do you think your expectations were valid? Would they provide a better outline for the author than the one he used?

8. At this point, the author has summarized his criticisms of the teaching of calculus. What do you think he will say next?

_____

_____

Discuss your choices with your classmates. Then read to see if your expectations are confirmed.

Now a small group of educators has started a movement to change what is taught in an introductory calculus course, to improve the way it is taught and to bring the teaching of calculus into the computer age. Earlier this year, 25 faculty members, administrators, scientists and others representing diverse interests met at Tulane University in New Orleans to see what could be done.

One big surprise was a general agreement that there is room for change. When participants came to the meeting, says mathematician Peter L. Renz of Bard College in Annandale-on-Hudson, N.Y., although they recognized the problem, "we all believe that there was nothing we could do about calculus." Yet despite this pessimism, many of the participants brought worthwhile suggestions.

9. Were your expectations confirmed in these two paragraphs?

10. What do you think the author will do next? What aspects of the text and your general knowledge help you to create this prediction?

_____

_____

_____

Read to see if your expectations are confirmed.

A key question is the role of hand-held calculators and computers. For the price of a calculus textbook, students can buy a scientific calculator. "The first thing that one can do on that basis is to eliminate an awful lot of the routine problems," says mathematician Ronald G. Douglas, dean of the physical sciences school at the State University of New York at Stony Brook. The ideas are still important, and instructors may need some of these techniques to illustrate what is going on, he says, but drilling students in something that any calculator or computer can now do becomes much less important.

The conference participants agreed that the routine use of calculators would help shift the focus of calculus back to its fundamental ideas and away from students mechanically plugging numbers into formulas to get "nice" answers. Until now, says Douglas, "all we've been teaching people in some sense has been a kind of pattern recognition."

11. Were your predictions confirmed?

12. What other kinds of problems and solutions do you predict are discussed in the final sections of this article? Be prepared to defend your predictions.*

_____

_____

_____

---

*The rest of this article is not reprinted here; however, a summary of the ideas can be found in the Answer Key.

Reading Selections 1A–1B

Technical Prose

Following are two magazine articles that discuss issues and patterns of population growth. When writing about technical subjects, authors sometimes include graphs and tables because such visual aids present information clearly and concisely. You will need to use information from the graphs and chart as well as the prose sections of the following articles in order to complete the comprehension exercises.

Before You Begin   1. How many people live in your community?

2. Now imagine that twice as many people lived there. What effects would the increased population have on the way you live, travel, eat, work?

Selection 1A   **Magazine Article**

Read "Crowded Earth—Billions More Coming" quickly to get a general understanding of the article; do not be concerned if you do not know the meanings of some vocabulary items. Then scan* to answer the comprehension questions.

Comprehension

Answer the following questions according to information given in the article and accompanying chart and graphs. Indicate if statements 1 through 18 are true (T) or false (F).

1. _____ In the year 2000, the world population may be 12 billion people.

2. _____ The population estimate of 6.4 billion for the year 2000 is based on the present growth rate of 2 percent per year.

3. _____ The population is increasing fastest in the more highly industrialized countries.

4. _____ Generally speaking, the nations with the highest rates of population increase are the same countries that even today find it difficult to feed all their people.

---

*For an introduction to scanning, see Unit 1.

5. _____ By the year 2000, approximately four-fifths of the world's population will live in the "poorer" nations.

6. _____ By the year 2000, 37 percent of the world population will be living in urban areas.

7. _____ It took millions of years for the world population to reach 1 billion.

8. _____ The world population doubled between 1830 and 1930.

9. _____ The world population doubled between 1930 and 1960.

10. _____ The world's birth rate is increasing while the death rate is decreasing.

11. _____ Graph I shows that the world population is increasing faster now than it ever has before.

12. _____ The percentage figures in Graph II indicate the expected percentage increase in population between 1972 and 2000.

13. _____ The population of Russia is increasing about twice as fast as the population of Europe.

14. _____ By the year 2000, it is estimated that Asia alone will have more people than are alive in the whole world today.

15. _____ Chart III lists the 25 countries with the highest rate of population increase.

16. _____ No figures are available on the rate of population increase in West Germany.

17. _____ The population of Poland is increasing faster than the population of Italy.

18. _____ According to Chart III, the United Kingdom has the lowest rate of population increase of any country in the world.

19. What two results of medical advances does the author say have caused the change in the world death rate? _____

_____

_____

20. The author mentions that it will be difficult to feed 6 billion people. What other danger of an overcrowded world is mentioned? _____

_____

21. In Chart III, the column titled "Years Until Population Will Double" is an estimation. What is it based on? What factors affect population growth? _____

_____

_____

CROWDED EARTH—BILLIONS MORE COMING

MORE THAN 6 BILLION people in a world that already is having trouble supporting about 4 billion—

That is the prospect now being held out by population experts, and it frightens them.

A new projection by the United Nations shows that, if the present growth rate of 2 per cent per year continues, today's world population of 3.9 billion will hit 6.4 billion by the year 2000.

What's more, the great bulk of the growth—9 of every 10 people added to the earth's population—will be in the poorer, undeveloped countries. These are the nations where feeding billions of people already is proving a near-insurmountable challenge.

By the year 2000, today's "have not" nations will have a combined population of 5 billion people, comprising nearly four fifths of the world's population.

Food isn't the only problem that such a population explosion presents. The more people there are and the more crowded their living conditions, authorities warn, the greater grows the likelihood of violence and upheaval.

According to U. N. projections, half of all the earth's people will be living in urban areas by the year 2000, up from 37 per cent today.

From time of Christ—. To put this growth in perspective—

At the time of Christ, millions of years after man first appeared on the earth, demographers estimate there were 250 million people.

In 1830, world population reached 1 billion. It took only 100 more years to add another billion to world population; just 30 more to add a third billion. And it will have taken just 15 more years to reach the 4-billion mark in 1975.

Actually, the world's birth rate is on a decline. But so are death rates, as medical advances have increased life spans and reduced infant mortality.

Average world life expectancy, the U. N. says, has increased by 20 years over the past three decades.

It's mainly in advanced nations that population growth is being curbed.

The outlook beyond 2000 is even more threatening. Unless population growth is curtailed, a world population of 12 billion is foreseen in a century. One question raised by demographers:

Is the earth capable of providing a decent life for 12 billion people?

I.

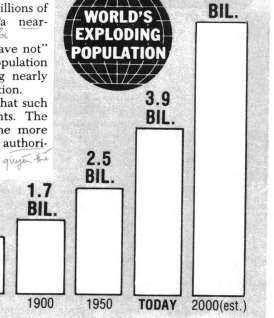

791 MIL.	978 MIL.	1.3 BIL.	1.7 BIL.	2.5 BIL.	3.9 BIL.	6.4 BIL.
1750	1800	1850	1900	1950	TODAY	2000(est.)

WORLD'S EXPLODING POPULATION

II.

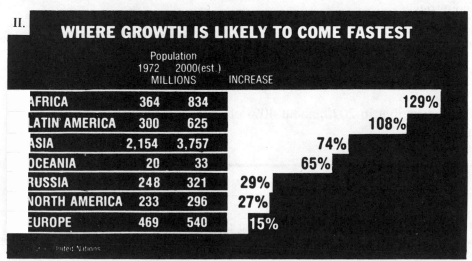

WHERE GROWTH IS LIKELY TO COME FASTEST

	Population 1972 MILLIONS	2000(est.)	INCREASE
AFRICA	364	834	129%
LATIN AMERICA	300	625	108%
ASIA	2,154	3,757	74%
OCEANIA	20	33	65%
RUSSIA	248	321	29%
NORTH AMERICA	233	296	27%
EUROPE	469	540	15%

United Nations

III.

THE 25 MOST POPULATED COUNTRIES

		Population 1973	Years Until Population Will Double*
1.	China	792,677,000	41
2.	India	596,000,000	32
3.	U.S.S.R.	248,626,000	77
4.	United States	209,123,000	116
5.	Indonesia	128,121,000	26
6.	Japan	106,663,000	53
7.	Brazil	101,582,000	25
8.	Bangladesh	75,382,000	26
9.	Pakistan	64,461,000	24
10.	West Germany	61,806,000	†
11.	Nigeria	58,148,000	29
12.	United Kingdom	55,956,000	231
13.	Mexico	54,963,000	20
14.	Italy	54,642,000	116
15.	France	51,921,000	116
16.	Philippines	41,288,000	22
17.	Thailand	39,075,000	25
18.	Turkey	37,737,000	27
19.	Egypt	34,705,000	32
20.	Spain	34,675,000	63
21.	Korea	33,435,000	35
22.	Poland	33,202,000	77
23.	Iran	32,778,000	22
24.	Burma	29,213,000	30
25.	Ethiopia	26,947,000	27

*Years to double assumes continuation of 1972 rate of increase.

†No increase in 1972

Source: U.S. Census Bureau

Reprinted from *U.S. News and World Report.*

Selection 1B   **Magazine Article**

The article you just read was written in the 1970s. "World Population Growth Rate Slows" (opposite page) appeared in 1990. Read this article. As you read, ask yourself if the two articles make similar or different predictions.

Comprehension

Answer the following questions using information from the article and the accompanying chart.

1. T / F   The U.S. Census Bureau expects world population to decline in the future.

2. T / F   The United Nations' high, medium, and low population predictions mentioned in this article all assume that the world fertility rate will decline in the future.

3. T / F   The world mortality rate has been declining.

4. T / F   According to the Bureau of the Census, world population will probably stop growing in 2020.

5. T / F   The PRB believes that world population will probably not stop growing until 2130.

6. Where is population growing fastest? Put a *1* next to the area with the fastest growth rate, a *2* next to the area with the second highest growth rate, and a *3* next to the area growing at the slowest rate.

   _____ Rural areas in developing countries
   _____ Urban areas in developing countries
   _____ Urban areas in industrialized countries

7. T / F   The Census Bureau predicts that in 2020, less than 20% of the world population will live in developed countries.

8. T / F   Population is no longer increasing in developed countries.

9. T / F   The percentage of world population that lives in developing nations is increasing.

10. T / F   The Census Bureau predicts that in 2020, about 40% of people in the world will live outside urban areas.

Discussion

Do the 1990 predictions about population seem consistent with the predictions made in the 1970s? Cite evidence from the articles to support your answer.

Demographics

World Population Growth Rate Slows

The world population growth rate is expected to decline in the 1990s, falling from 1.8% currently to 1.5% in the year 2000, according to the U.S. Bureau of the Census. However, total population will increase by a billion people during each of the next three decades.

Global population has been estimated at 5.2 billion people for 1989. Seventy-five percent of the earth's inhabitants live in developing nations, and that proportion is projected to reach over 80% by the year 2020, says the Census Bureau.

Even with a reduced growth rate, population increases continue to be large because the population base itself is so large, points out the Population Reference Bureau (PRB). The United Nations' high, medium, and low forecasts for the world's population are based on specific assumptions about fertility and mortality. For instance, if mortality continues to decline and current family-planning programs and other socioeconomic policies continue to lower fertility, the world's population could stop growing after reaching about 10–11 billion people in the latter half of the next century. If fertility declines at a faster pace, world population could stop growing in 2040 at 8 billion. But if fertility declines at a slower pace, the population will not stop growing until 2130 at 14 billion people, according to PRB.

Rural-to-urban migration, combined with natural increase, is leading to a disproportionate growth in urban population, especially in developing nations, says PRB. In 1950, only three cities had populations over 10 million. Now there are 11 such cities, and that number is growing.

Currently, 41% of the world's population live in urban areas. In 2020, this proportion is expected to increase to 60%. Urban populations in developing countries are growing at twice the rural rate, according to the Census Bureau. But rural populations in the Third World are still growing faster than urban populations in industrialized nations.

Sources: *World Population Profile: 1989*, Series WP-89, U.S. Department of Commerce, Bureau of the Census, Washington, D.C. 20230. Copies available from the Superintendent of Documents, U.S. Government Printing Office, Washington, D.C. 20402. *World Population: Toward the Next Century*, Population Reference Bureau, Inc. Copies available from the Circulation Department, Population Reference Bureau, 777 14th Street, N.W., Suite 800, Washington, D.C. 20005. $3.

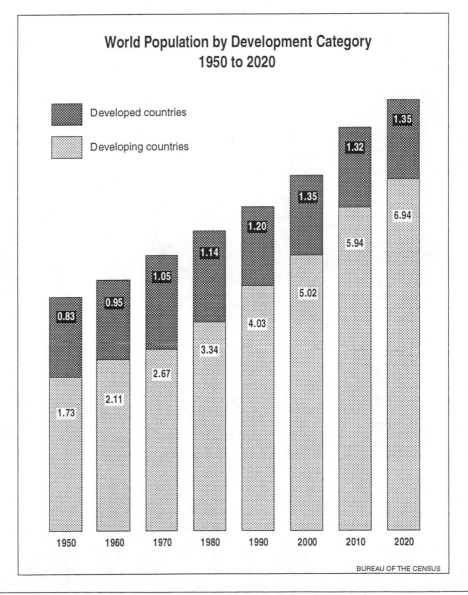

World Population by Development Category 1950 to 2020

Developed countries

Developing countries

Year	Developed	Developing
1950	0.83	1.73
1960	0.95	2.11
1970	1.05	2.67
1980	1.14	3.34
1990	1.20	4.03
2000	1.35	5.02
2010	1.32	5.94
2020	1.35	6.94

BUREAU OF THE CENSUS

World population is expected to increase by a billion people during each of the next three decades.

Discussion/Composition

1. What specific challenges will we face as world population grows? Consider economic, political, environmental, and/or personal challenges. Where possible, support your ideas with information from these two articles.

2. Imagine you are the Minister of Health in your country. What actions, if any, would you take to respond to growing world population? Prepare a speech to present to government leaders supporting your position. You might want to comment on some of the following approaches to the problem.

   a. It is not the role of government to attempt to control population.
   b. The government should plan for population growth through economic development.
   c. The government should take a role in controlling population growth through measures such as educational campaigns or financial incentives for small families.
   d. The government should control population by prohibiting families from having more than one child.

Reading Selection 2

Magazine Article

Before You Begin   1. Why do people laugh? Do people laugh for different reasons?

2. Are there cultural differences that affect when and why people laugh?

3. Do you find jokes in English funny?

The following magazine article attempts to summarize scientific research for the general public. The author of the article on page 172 draws from the work of a number of experts in presenting an explanation for why we laugh.

First skim* the article. In order to facilitate skimming, your teacher may want to read first (and sometimes second or last) lines of each paragraph aloud to you. Then complete Comprehension exercise 1. Read the article a second time, more carefully, before completing the other exercises that follow. You may want to do Vocabulary from Context exercise 1 on pages 175–76 before you begin reading.

Comprehension

Exercise 1

Indicate if each statement is true (T) or false (F) according to your understanding of the article.

1. _____ We laugh as a release for our normally repressed drives.

2. _____ Laughter strengthens social bonds.

3. _____ We laugh to express mastery over anxiety.

4. _____ We laugh to release energy after a crisis.

5. _____ We laugh at jokes of which we are the target.

6. _____ We never laugh when we are alone because we require company to laugh.

7. _____ We laugh immediately at birth.

8. _____ We sometimes laugh in times of sorrow.

9. _____ We sometimes laugh when nothing is funny.

10. _____ The ability to laugh takes a lifetime to perfect.

"Why We Laugh" by Janet Spencer from *Ladies' Home Journal.*
*For an introduction to skimming, see Unit 3.

Are you a quiet giggler? Or can you let loose with hearty laughter? Your ability to laugh may mean more than you think. By Janet Spencer

Picture this cartoon: A man is watering his lawn just as an attractive blonde walks by. As he ogles her, he accidentally turns the hose on his dowdy wife, who is sitting on the porch.

2) Men usually think the cartoon is funny. Women do not. And there's a good reason for the difference in opinion.

3) We start finding things laughable—or not laughable—early in life. An infant first smiles at approximately eight days of age. Many psychologists feel this is an infant's first sign of simple pleasure—food, warmth and comfort. At six months or less, the infant laughs to express complex pleasures—such as the sight of Mother's smiling face.

4) In his book *Beyond Laughter*, psychiatrist Martin Grotjahn says that the earlier infants begin to smile and laugh, the more advanced is their development. Studies revealed that children who did not develop these responses (because they lacked an intimate, loving relationship) "developed a schizophrenic psychosis in later life, or simply gave up and died."

5) Between the ages of six months and one year, babies learn to laugh for essentially the same reasons they will laugh throughout their lives, says Dr. Jacob Levine, associate professor of psychology at Yale University. Dr. Levine says that people laugh to express mastery over an anxiety. Picture what happens when parents toss children into the air. The children will probably laugh—but not the first time. In spite of their enjoyment of "flying," they are too anxious to laugh. How do they know Mommy or Daddy will catch them? Once the children realize they will be caught, they are free to enjoy the game. But more importantly, says Dr. Levine, the children laugh because they have mastered an anxiety.

6) Adult laughter is more subtle, but we also laugh at what we used to fear. The feeling of achievement, or lack of it, remains a crucial factor. Giving a

first dinner party is an anxious event for newlyweds. Will the food be good? Will the guests get along? Will they be good hosts? All goes well; the party is over. Now they laugh freely. Their pleasure from having proved their success is the foundation for their pleasure in recalling the evening's activities. They couldn't enjoy the second pleasure without the first, more important one—their mastery of anxiety.

7) Laughter is a social response triggered by cues. Scientists have not determined a brain center for laughter, and they are perplexed by patients with certain types of brain damage who go into laughing fits for no apparent reason. The rest of us require company, and a reason to laugh.

8) When we find ourselves alone in a humorous situation, our usual response is to smile. Isn't it true that our highest compliment to a humorous book is to say that "it made me laugh out loud"? Of course, we do occasionally laugh alone; but when we do, we are, in a sense, socializing with ourselves. We laugh at a memory, or at a part of ourselves.

9) Practically every philosopher since Plato has written on how humor and laughter are related, but Sigmund Freud was the first to evolve a conclusive theory. Freud recognized that we all repress certain basic but socially "unacceptable" drives, such as sex and aggression. Jokes, not accidentally, are often based on either sex or aggression, or both. We find these jokes funny because they provide a sudden release of our normally suppressed drives. We are free to enjoy the forbidden, and the energy we normally use to inhibit these drives is discharged in laughter.

10) Another reason laughter is pleasurable is because of the physical sensations involved. Laughter is a series of minor facial and respiratory convulsions that stimulates our respiratory and circulatory systems. It activates the secretion of adrenalin and increases the blood flow to the head and brain. The total effect is one of euphoria.

11) Of course, we don't always need a joke to make us laugh. People who survive frightening situations, such as a fire or an emergency plane landing, frequently intersperse their story of the crisis with laughter. Part of the laughter expresses relief that everything is now all right. During a crisis, everyone mobilizes energy to deal with the potential problem. If the danger is averted, we need to release that energy. Some people cry; others laugh.

12) Part of the integral pleasure of a joke *is* getting the point. But if the sexual or aggressive element of the joke is too thinly disguised, as in "sick" humor, the joke will leave us feeling guilty instead of amused. We may laugh—but in em-

barrassment. According to Dr. Grotjahn, "The disguise must go far enough to avoid guilt," but "not so far that the thrill of aggression is lost."

13) Which brings us to why women may not have found the joke about the man watering his wife very funny—because they get the point only too well. Many psychiatrists agree that the reason women aren't amused by this kind of joke is that most sex jokes (a hefty percentage of all jokes) employ women as their target. Women sometimes make poor joke tellers for the same reason; consciously or subconsciously, they express their resentment by "forgetting" the story.

14) When we are made the butt of a joke, either on a personal or impersonal level, we are emotionally involved in it. Consequently, we won't be able to laugh (except as a pretense). While we are feeling, we cannot laugh. The two do not mix. French essayist Henri Bergson called laughter a "momentary anesthesia of the heart." We call it comic relief.

15) Knowing that laughter blunts emotion, we can better understand why we sometimes laugh when nothing is funny. We laugh during moments of anxiety because we feel no mastery over the situation, claims Dr. Levine. He explains, "Very often compulsive laughter is a learned response. If we laugh, it expresses good feelings and the fact that we are able to cope. When we're in a situation in which we *can't* cope, we laugh to reassure ourselves that we *can!*"

16) How often have we laughed at a funeral or upon hearing bad news? We laugh to deny an unendurable reality until we are strong enough to accept it. Laughter also breaks our tension. However, we may also be laughing to express relief that the tragedy didn't happen to us. We laugh before giving a big party, before delivering a speech, or while getting a traffic ticket, to say, "This isn't bothering me. See? I'm laughing."

17) But if we sometimes laugh in sorrow, more often we laugh with joy. Laughter creates and strengthens our social bonds. And the ability to share a laugh has guided many marriages through hard periods of adjustment.

18) According to Dr. Levine, we can measure our adjustment to the world by our capacity to laugh. When we are secure about our abilities, we can poke fun at our foibles. If we can laugh through our anxieties, we will not be overpowered by them.

19) The ability to laugh starts early, but it takes a lifetime to perfect. Says Dr. Grotjahn, "When social relationships are mastered, when individuals have mastered . . . a peaceful relationship with themselves, then they have . . . the sense of humor." And then they can throw back their heads and laugh. **END**

11. _____ We laugh to break tension.

12. _____ Laughter is an unpleasant physical sensation.

13. _____ A sense of humor is a result of the mastery of human relationships.

14. _____ We always laugh when we understand a joke.

Now read the article again and complete the exercises that follow.

___

Exercise 2

The sentences in exercise 1 are general statements about laughter. Often authors will give specific examples to make an argument stronger or clearer. Following is a list of situations that the author of this article uses to illustrate some of the true statements in exercise 1. Match each of the examples below with the number of the appropriate general statement from the previous exercise. Some items have more than one possible answer. Choose what you feel to be the best answer. Be prepared to defend your choice.

___

Example

_3_ Infants laugh when their parent throws them in the air.

1. _____ A newlywed couple laughs after they give their first successful dinner party.

2. _____ People who survive an emergency plane landing intersperse their story with laughter.

3. _____ We laugh before delivering a speech.

4. _____ We sometimes laugh at a funeral or when we hear bad news.

5. _____ We laugh at a sexual joke.

6. _____ Married couples laugh through hard periods of social adjustment.

Critical Reading

___

Exercise 1

In order to evaluate an author's arguments, it is important to notice whom she quotes to support her statements. A number of experts are cited in this article. Next to each name below write the person's profession.

Example

Sigmund Freud _psychiatrist_

1. Henri Bergson _____

2. Martin Grotjahn _____

3. Jacob Levine _____

4. Plato _____

Exercise 2

When an article combines information from many sources, it is sometimes difficult to determine the source of an individual piece of information. In this article it is especially difficult to determine if individual statements are those of the author or are based on the work of the experts cited.

Following is a list of statements made in the article. Indicate if each one has been made by the author or one of her sources.

Example

_____Levine_____ We laugh to express mastery over anxiety.

1. _____ We laugh as a release for our normally repressed drives.

2. _____ Laughter strengthens social bonds.

3. _____ We laugh to release energy after a crisis.

4. _____ A sense of humor is a result of the mastery of human relationships.

5. _____ We sometimes laugh when nothing is funny.

6. _____ Laughter is a pleasurable physical sensation.

Exercise 3

Now that you have examined the experts and information cited by the author, what is your opinion of the article? Why are the experts cited? How could this article be made more persuasive?

Discussion/Composition

1. Tell a joke that you enjoy. How was your joke received? Are there ideas from the article that explain your classmates' reactions?

2. This article discusses situations that bring about laughter in the United States. Which situations given are similar to those in your country? Which are different? Which elements of laughter do you think are the same for all people?

Vocabulary from Context

Exercise 1

Use the context provided to determine the meanings of the italicized words. Write a definition, synonym, or description of each of the italicized vocabulary items in the space provided.

1. _____

2. _____
3. _____
4. _____
5. _____
6. _____
7. _____

Some people feel very nervous when they fly in airplanes. No matter how hard they try, they cannot lower their *anxiety*. Some of them enjoy talking about their fears while others *resent* being asked to discuss their personal feelings. Many are aware that they feel anxious but only a few are *conscious* of the way they express their *tension*. Some people try to hide their nervousness; they try to *disguise* their anxiety by telling jokes. Others become loud and *aggressive*, attacking people by making them the *butt* of cruel jokes.

8. _____
9. _____

Sometimes making someone else the *target* of jokes is an attempt to control one's own fears—to *master* anxiety.

10. _____

A number of *factors* can be mentioned as important in explaining why some people have a fear of flying: early childhood experiences, general sense of security, fear of heights, trust in others, percentage of alcohol in blood, etc.,

11. _____

but the *crucial* factor seems to be a feeling of no control.

12. _____

Usually, we are able to *suppress* our feelings so that they do not affect our behavior.

13. _____

By smiling foolishly and talking loudly, we are able to *repress* the rising feeling of fear so that it does not affect the way we behave.

14. _____

Most of us learn very young in life to control basic *drives* such as sex, hunger, and aggression.

15. _____   Sometimes the tension produced by our fears is so great that we cannot suppress it. At such times we need to *discharge* the tension by laughing or crying.

16. _____   The memory of a bad experience can sometimes *trigger* the same fear caused by that experience. Thus, a child might be frightened by the sight of a dog even though he is safe, merely because he once had a bad experience with a dog. A bad

17. _____   experience can be the *cue* that triggers our fears.

18. _____   Everyone experiences fear during major *crises*—such as fires, automobile accidents, etc.—but some people are even afraid of the dark.

19. _____   At the time of the crime, the man felt no emotion but later he began to feel *guilty,* so he went to the police and told them the whole story.

20. _____   Because it is necessary to recognize a problem before it can be solved, admitting that we are afraid is an *integral* part of the process of mastering our fears.

Exercise 2

The following groups of sentences have been adapted from the article "Why We Laugh." Use context clues to determine the meanings of the italicized words. Write a definition, synonym, or description of each of the italicized vocabulary items in the space provided.

1. People who survive frightening situations frequently *intersperse* their story of the crisis with laughter. Part of the laughter expressed is relief that everything is all right. During a crisis, everyone mobilizes energy to deal with the potential problem. If the danger is avoided we need to release that energy. For example, if a pilot *averts* a plane crash by making a safe emergency landing, he may laugh as he describes his experience.

   intersperse: _____

   averts: _____

2. We find these jokes funny because they provide a sudden release of our normally suppressed drives. We are free to enjoy the forbidden, and the energy we normally use to *inhibit* these drives is discharged as laughter.

   inhibit: _____

3. When we are secure about our abilities, we can joke about our *foibles*. If we can laugh at our small faults, we will not be overpowered by them.

   foibles: _____

4. A man is watering his lawn just as an attractive, well-dressed blond walks by. As he *ogles* her, he accidently turns the hose on his ugly, *dowdy* wife.

ogle: _____

dowdy: _____

Vocabulary Review

Two of the words on each line in the following exercise are similar in meaning. Circle the word that does not belong.

1. cue   butt   target
2. inhibit   suppress   trigger
3. resent   release   discharge
4. crucial   conscious   integral
5. aggression   repression   suppression

Reading Selection 3

Short Story

Before You Begin   1. What is a lottery?

2. Why do you think lotteries have become popular throughout the world?

When "The Lottery" first appeared in the *New Yorker* in 1948, letters flooded the magazine expressing admiration, anger, and confusion at the story. For a long time, Shirley Jackson refused to discuss the story, apparently believing that people had to make their own evaluation of it and come to a personal understanding of its meaning. Whatever people may think of it, they all agree that it is unusual.

Read "The Lottery" carefully and make your own judgment. You may want to do Vocabulary from Context exercise 1 on page 183 before you begin reading.

The Lottery

Shirley Jackson

1 The morning of June 27th was clear and sunny, with the fresh warmth of a full-summer day; the flowers were blossoming profusely, and the grass was richly green. The people of the village began to gather in the square, between the post office and the bank, around ten o'clock; in some towns there were so many people that the lottery took two days and had to be started on June 26th, but in this village, where there were only about three hundred people, the whole lottery took only about two hours, so it could begin at ten o'clock in the morning and still be through in time to allow the villagers to get home for noon dinner.

2 The children assembled first, of course. School was recently over for the summer, and the feeling of liberty sat uneasily on most of them; they tended to gather together quietly for a while before they broke into boisterous play, and their talk was still of the classroom and the teacher, of books and reprimands. Bobby Martin had already stuffed his pockets full of stones, and the other boys soon followed his example, selecting the smoothest and

roundest stones; Bobby and Harry Jones and Dickie Delacroix—the villagers pronounced the name "Dellacroy"—eventually made a great pile of stones in one corner of the square and guarded it against the raids of the other boys. The girls stood aside, talking among themselves, looking over their shoulders at the boys, and the very small children rolled in the dust or clung to the hands of their older brothers or sisters.

3 Soon the men began to gather, surveying their own children, speaking of planting and rain, tractors and taxes. They stood together, away from the pile of stones in the corner, and their jokes were quiet, and they smiled rather than laughed. The women, wearing faded house dresses and sweaters, came shortly after their menfolk. They greeted one another and exchanged bits of gossip as they went to join their husbands. Soon the women, standing by their husbands, began to call to their children, and the children came reluctantly, having to be called four or five times. Bobby Martin ducked under his mother's grasping hand and

ran, laughing, back to the pile of stones. His father spoke up sharply, and Bobby came quickly and took his place between his father and his oldest brother.

4 The lottery was conducted—as were the square dances, the teen-age club, the Halloween program—by Mr. Summers, who had time and energy to devote to civic activities. He was a round-faced, jovial man, and he ran the coal business; and people were sorry for him, because he had no children and his wife was a scold. When he arrived in the square, carrying the black wooden box, there was a murmur of conversation among the villagers, and he waved and called, "Little late today, folks." The postmaster, Mr. Graves, followed him, carrying a three-legged stool; and the stool was put in the center of the square, and Mr. Summers set the black box down on it. The villagers kept their distance, leaving a space between themselves and the stool, and when Mr. Summers said, "Some of you fellows want to give me hand?" there was a hesitation before two men, Mr. Martin and his oldest son, Baxter, came forward to

---

Reprinted from *The Lottery* by Shirley Jackson (New York: Farrar, Straus and Giroux).

hold the box steady on the stool while Mr. Summers stirred up the papers inside it.

5   The original paraphernalia for the lottery had been lost long ago, and the black box now resting on the stool had been put into use even before Old Man Warner, the oldest man in town, was born. Mr. Summers spoke frequently to the villagers about making a new box, but no one liked to upset even as much tradition as was represented by the black box. There was a story that the present box had been made with some pieces of the box that had preceded it, the one that had been constructed when the first people settled down to make a village here. Every year, after the lottery, Mr. Summers began talking again about a new box, but every year the subject was allowed to fade off without anything's being done. The black box grew shabbier each year; by now it was no longer completely black but splintered badly along one side to show the original wood color, and in some places faded or stained.

6   Mr. Martin and his oldest son, Baxter, held the black box securely on the stool until Mr. Summers had stirred the papers thoroughly with his hand. Because so much of the ritual had been forgotten or discarded, Mr. Summers had been successful in having slips of paper substituted for the chips of wood that had been used for generations. Chips of wood, Mr. Summers had argued, had been all very well when the village was tiny, but now that the population was more than three hundred and likely to keep on growing, it was necessary to use something that would fit more easily into the black box. The night before the lottery, Mr. Summers and Mr. Graves made up the slips of paper and put them into the box, and it was then taken to the safe of Mr. Summers' coal company and locked up until Mr. Summers was ready to take it to the square next morning. The rest of the year, the box was put away, sometimes one place, sometimes another; it had spent one year in Mr. Graves's barn and another year underfoot in the post office, and sometimes it was set on a shelf in the Martin grocery and left there.

7   There was a great deal of fussing to be done before Mr. Summers declared the lottery open. There were the lists to make up—of heads of families, heads of households in each

family, members of each household in each family. There was the proper swearing-in of Mr. Summers by the postmaster, as the official of the lottery; at one time, some people remembered, there had been a recital of some sort, performed by the official of the lottery, a perfunctory, tuneless chant that had been rattled off duly each year; some people believed that the official of the lottery used to stand just so when he said or sang it; others believed that he was supposed to walk among the people; but years and years ago this part of the ritual had been allowed to lapse. There had been also a ritual salute, which the official of the lottery had had to use in addressing each person who came up to draw from the box, but this also had changed with time, until now it was felt necessary only for the official to speak to each person approaching. Mr. Summers was very good at all this; in his clean white shirt and blue jeans, with one hand resting carelessly on the black box, he seemed very proper and important as he talked interminably to Mr. Graves and the Martins.

8   Just as Mr. Summers finally left off talking and turned to the assembled villagers, Mrs. Hutchinson came hurriedly along the path to the square, her sweater thrown over her shoulders, and slid into place in the back of the crowd. "Clean forgot what day it was," she said to Mrs. Delacroix, who stood next to her, and they both laughed softly. "Thought my old man was out back stacking wood," Mrs. Hutchinson went on, "and then I looked out the window and the kids was gone, and then I remembered it was the twenty-seventh and came a-running." She dried her hands on her apron, and Mrs. Delacroix said, "You're in time, though. They're still talking away up there."

9   Mrs. Hutchinson craned her neck to see through the crowd and found her husband and children standing near the front. She tapped Mrs. Delacroix on the arm as a farewell and began to make her way through the crowd. The people separated good-humoredly to let her through; two or three people said, in voices just loud enough to be heard across the crowd, "Here comes your Mrs., Hutchinson," and "Bill, she made it after all." Mrs. Hutchinson reached her husband, and Mr. Summers, who had been waiting, said

cheerfully, "Thought we were going to have to get on without you, Tessie." Mrs. Hutchinson said, grinning, "Wouldn't have me leave m'dishes in the sink, now, would you Joe?" and soft laughter ran through the crowd as the people stirred back into position after Mrs. Hutchinson's arrival.

10   "Well, now," Mr. Summers said soberly, "guess we better get started, get this over with, so's we can go back to work. Anybody ain't here?"

"Dunbar," several people said. "Dunbar, Dunbar."

Mr. Summers consulted his list. "Clyde Dunbar," he said. "That's right. He's broke his leg, hasn't he? Who's drawing for him?"

11   "Me, I guess," a woman said, and Mr. Summers turned to look at her. "Wife draws for her husband," Mr. Summers said. "Don't you have a grown boy to do it for you, Janey?" Although Mr. Summers and everyone else in the village knew the answer perfectly well, it was the business of the official of the lottery to ask such questions formally. Mr. Summers waited with an expression of polite interest while Mrs. Dunbar answered.

"Horace's not but sixteen yet," Mrs. Dunbar said regretfully. "Guess I gotta fill in for the old man this year."

"Right," Mr. Summers said. He made a note on the list he was holding. Then he asked, "Watson boy drawing this year?"

12   A tall boy in the crowd raised his hand, "Here," he said. "I'm drawing for m'mother and me." He blinked his eyes nervously and ducked his head as several voices in the crowd said things like "Good fellow, Jack," and "Glad to see your mother's got a man to do it."

"Well," Mr. Summers said, "guess that's everyone. Old Man Warner make it?"

"Here," a voice said, and Mr. Summers nodded.

13   A sudden hush fell on the crowd as Mr. Summers cleared his throat and looked at the list. "All ready?" he called. "Now, I'll read the names—heads of families first—and the men come up and take a paper out of the box. Keep the paper folded in your hand without looking at it until everyone has had a turn. Everything clear?"

14   The people had done it so many times that they only half listened to the directions; most of them were

quiet, wetting their lips, not looking around. Then Mr. Summers raised one hand high and said, "Adams." A man disengaged himself from the crowd and came forward. "Hi, Steve," Mr. Summers said, and Mr. Adams said, "Hi, Joe." They grinned at one another humorlessly and nervously. Then Mr. Adams reached into the black box and took out a folded paper. He held it firmly by one corner as he turned and went hastily back to his place in the crowd, where he stood a little apart from his family, not looking down at his hand.

"Allen," Mr. Summers said. "Anderson . . . Bentham."

15 "Seems like there's no time at all between lotteries any more," Mrs. Delacroix said to Mrs. Graves in the back row. "Seems like we got through with the last one only last week."

"Time sure goes fast," Mrs. Graves said.

"Clark . . . Delacroix."

"There goes my old man," Mrs. Delacroix said. She held her breath while her husband went forward.

"Dunbar," Mr. Summers said, and Mrs. Dunbar went steadily to the box while one of the women said, "Go on, Janey," and another said, "There she goes."

16 "We're next," Mrs. Graves said. She watched while Mr. Graves came around from the side of the box, greeted Mr. Summers gravely, and selected a slip of paper from the box. By now, all through the crowd there were men holding the small folded papers in their large hands, turning them over and over nervously. Mrs. Dunbar and her two sons stood together, Mrs. Dunbar holding the slip of paper.

"Harburt . . . Hutchinson."

"Get up there, Bill," Mrs. Hutchinson said, and the people near her laughed.

"Jones."

17 "They do say," Mr. Adams said to Old Man Warner, who stood next to him, "that over in the north village they're talking of giving up the lottery."

Old Man Warner snorted. "Pack of crazy fools," he said. "Listening to the young folks, nothing's good enough for them. Next thing you know, they'll be wanting to go back to living in caves, nobody work any more, live *that* way for a while. Used to be a saying about 'Lottery in June, **22**

corn be heavy soon.' First thing you know, we'd all be eating stewed chickweed and acorns. There's always been a lottery," he added petulantly. "Bad enough to see young Joe Summers up there joking with everybody."

18 "Some places have already quit lotteries," Mrs. Adams said.

"Nothing but trouble in that," Old Man Warner said stoutly. "Pack of young fools."

"Martin." And Bobby Martin watched his father go forward. "Overdyke . . . Percy."

"I wish they'd hurry," Mrs. Dunbar said to her older son. "I wish they'd hurry."

"They're almost through," her son said.

"You get ready to run tell Dad," Mrs. Dunbar said.

19 Mr. Summers called his own name and then stepped forward precisely and selected a slip from the box. Then he called, "Warner."

"Seventy-seventh year I been in the lottery," Old Man Warner said as he went through the crowd. "Seventy-seventh time."

"Watson." The tall boy came awkwardly through the crowd. Someone said, "Don't be nervous, Jack," and Mr. Summers said, "Take your time, son."

"Zanini."

20 After that, there was a long pause, a breathless pause, until Mr. Summers, holding his slip of paper in the air, said, "All right, fellows." For a minute, no one moved, and then all the slips of paper were opened. Suddenly, all the women began to speak at once, saying, "Who is it?" "Who's got it?" "Is it the Dunbars?" "Is it the Watsons?" Then the voices began to say, "It's Hutchinson. It's Bill." Bill Hutchinson's got it."

"Go tell your father," Mrs. Dunbar said to her older son.

21 People began to look around to see the Hutchinsons. Bill Hutchinson was standing quiet, staring down at the paper in his hand. Suddenly, Tessie Hutchinson shouted to Mr. Summers, "You didn't give him time enough to take any paper he wanted. I saw you. It wasn't fair!"

"Be a good sport, Tessie," Mrs. Delacroix called, and Mrs. Graves said, "All of us took the same chance."

"Shut up, Tessie," Bill Hutchinson said.

22 "Well, everyone," Mr. Summers

said, "that was done pretty fast, and now we've got to be hurrying a little more to get done in time." He consulted his next list. "Bill," he said, "you draw for the Hutchinson family. You got any other households in the Hutchinsons?"

"There's Don and Eva," Mrs. Hutchinson yelled. "Make *them* take their chance!"

"Daughters draw with their husbands' families, Tessie," Mr. Summers said gently. "You know that as well as anyone else."

"It wasn't *fair!*" Tessie said.

23 "I guess not, Joe," Bill Hutchinson said regretfully. "My daughter draws with her husband's family. That's only fair. And I've got no other family except the kids."

"Then, as far as drawing for families is concerned, it's you," Mr. Summers said in explanation, "and as far as drawing for households is concerned, that's you, too. Right?"

"Right," Bill Hutchinson said.

"How many kids, Bill?" Mr. Summers asked formally.

"Three," Bill Hutchinson said. "There's Bill, Jr., and Nancy, and little Dave. And Tessie and me."

"All right, then," Mr. Summers said. "Harry, you got their tickets back?"

24 Mr. Graves nodded and held up the slips of paper. "Put them in the box, then," Mr. Summers directed. "Take Bill's and put it in."

"I think we ought to start over," Mrs. Hutchinson said, as quietly as she could. "I tell you it wasn't *fair.* You didn't give him time enough to choose. *Everybody* saw that."

Mr. Graves had selected the five slips and put them in the box, and he dropped all the papers but those onto the ground, where the breeze caught them and lifted them off.

"Listen, everybody," Mrs. Hutchinson was saying to the people around her.

"Ready, Bill?" Mr. Summers asked, and Bill Hutchinson, with one quick glance around at his wife and children, nodded.

25 "Remember," Mr. Summers said, "take the slips and keep them folded until each person has taken one. Harry, you help little Dave." Mr. Graves took the hand of the little boy, who came willingly with him up to the box. "Take a paper out of the box, Davy," Mr. Summers said. Davy put his hand into the box and laughed. "Take just one paper," Mr.

Summers said. "Harry, you hold it for him." Mr. Graves took the child's hand and removed the folded paper **28** from the right fist and held it while little Dave stood next to him and looked up at him wonderingly.

26   "Nancy next," Mr. Summers said. Nancy was twelve, and her school friends breathed heavily as she went forward, switching her skirt, and took a slip daintily from the box. "Bill, Jr.," Mr. Summers said, and Billy, his face red and his feet overlarge, nearly knocked the box over as he got a paper out. "Tessie," Mr. Summers said. She hesitated for a minute, looking around defiantly, and then set her lips and went up to the box. She snatched a paper out and held it behind her.   **29**

27   "Bill," Mr. Summers said, and Bill Hutchinson reached into the box and felt around, bringing his hand out at last with the slip of paper in it.

The crowd was quiet. A girl whispered, "I hope it's not Nancy," and the sound of the whisper reached the edges of the crowd.

"It's not the way it used to be," Old Man Warner said clearly. "People ain't the way they used to be."

"All right," Mr. Summers said.

"Open the papers. Harry, you open little Dave's."

Mr. Graves opened the slip of paper, and there was a general sigh through the crowd as he held it up and everyone could see that it was blank. Nancy and Bill, Jr., opened theirs at the same time, and both beamed and laughed, turning around to the crowd and holding their slips above their heads.

"Tessie," Mr. Summers said. There was a pause, and then Mr. Summers looked at Bill Hutchinson, and Bill unfolded his paper and showed it. It was blank.

"It's Tessie," Mr. Summers said, and his voice was hushed. "Show us her paper, Bill."

Bill Hutchinson went over to his wife and forced the slip of paper out of her hand. It had a black spot on it, the black spot Mr. Summers had made the night before with the heavy pencil in the coal-company office. Bill Hutchinson held it up, and there was a stir in the crowd.

"All right, folks," Mr. Summers said, "Let's finish quickly."

30   Although the villagers had forgotten the ritual and lost the original black box, they still remembered to

use stones. The pile of stones the boys had made earlier was ready; there were stones on the ground with the blowing scraps of paper that had come out of the box. Mrs. Delacroix selected a stone so large she had to pick it up with both hands and turned to Mrs. Dunbar. "Come on," she said. "Hurry up."

Mrs. Dunbar had small stones in both hands, and she said, gasping for breath, "I can't run at all. You'll have to go ahead and I'll catch up with you."

31   The children had stones already, and someone gave little Davy Hutchinson a few pebbles.

Tessie Hutchinson was in the center of a cleared space by now, and she held her hands out desperately as the villagers moved in on her. "It isn't fair," she said. A stone hit her on the side of the head.

Old Man Warner was saying, "Come on, come on, everyone." Steve Adams was in the front of the crowd of villagers, with Mrs. Graves beside him.

"It isn't fair, it isn't right," Mrs. Hutchinson screamed, and then they were upon her.

Comprehension

Exercise 1

Without referring to the story, indicate if each statement below is true (T) or false (F).

1. _____ The lottery was always held in summer.

2. _____ The lottery had not changed for many generations.

3. _____ The villagers were angry at Mrs. Hutchinson for being late.

4. _____ In the first drawing, only one person from each family drew a paper from the black box.

5. _____ The lottery was a custom only in this small village.

6. _____ Bill Hutchinson thought the first drawing was unfair.

7. _____ Tessie Hutchinson drew the paper with the black dot in the final drawing.

8. ____ The people wanted to finish in a hurry because they didn't like Tessie.

9. ____ The lottery was a form of human sacrifice.

Exercise 2

The following exercise requires a careful reading of "The Lottery." Indicate if each statement below is true (T) or false (F) according to your understanding of the story. Use information in the passage and inferences that can be drawn from the passage to make your decisions. You may refer to the story if necessary.

1. ____ Old Man Warner believed that the lottery assured the prosperity of the village.

2. ____ The date of the lottery was not rigidly fixed but occurred any time in summer when all of the villagers could be present.

3. ____ Mr. Summers never managed to make a new box for the lottery because people were unwilling to change the traditions that remained from the past.

4. ____ A family might contain several households.

5. ____ Mr. Warner felt that stopping the lottery would be equal to returning to prehistoric times.

6. ____ Only Mr. Warner remembered when the lottery was started.

7. ____ The villagers were hesitant to take part in the final step in the lottery.

Drawing Inferences

1. When did you first realize that this was a strange lottery? That winning the lottery was not desirable?

2. What details did the author add to make the lottery seem like a "normal" lottery? What details indicated that the lottery was strange? What details had double meanings?

3. Why do you think everyone had to take part in the final step of the lottery?

4. What was Mr. Warner's attitude toward the lottery? In what way and why did his attitude differ from other members of the community? What group in every society does Mr. Warner represent?

5. Why did Tessie want to include Tom and Eva in the final drawing?

6. Which aspects of the lottery have changed? Which have not changed?

Discussion

1. How do you think the lottery began? Why was it started? Why does it take place at that time of year?

2. Why do you think the community continues the lottery?

3. Would you take part in the lottery if you were a member of the community?

4. This story is about a physical sacrifice in which a person is killed. Sacrifice is characterized by the suffering of one member of a group for the benefit of the group as a whole, and by a sense of relief when one realizes that he or she has not been selected. This relief is so great that it leads to unconcern toward the fate of the person(s) to be sacrificed. Using this definition, can you think of specific institutions in modern societies in which sacrifices take place? Aside from physical sacrifice, what other types of sacrifice are possible?

Discussion/Composition

Was the lottery fair?

Vocabulary from Context

Exercise 1

Use the context provided to determine the meanings of the italicized words. Write a definition, synonym, or description of each of the italicized vocabulary items in the space provided.

1. _____

2. _____

3. _____
4. _____
5. _____
6. _____

7. _____

8. _____

I like any game of chance, but I most enjoy taking part in a lottery. The lottery is like an unchanging religious ceremony, and it is perhaps this *ritual* quality of the lottery that people enjoy. Unlike other games of chance, a lottery does not require a great deal of *paraphernalia*. The only equipment needed is a bowl filled with slips of paper. I enjoy the excitement of watching the official pick the winning number. The moment before the *drawing* is very serious. The judge *gravely* approaches the bowl and looks at the crowd *soberly*. The crowd is quiet except for the low *murmur* of excitement. Suddenly the winner is selected. After the lottery is over, everyone but the winner throws away his or her piece of paper, and the *discarded* slips are soon blown away by the wind. People begin to *disengage* themselves from the crowd and the lottery is over.

Exercise 2

This exercise is designed to give you additional clues to determine the meanings of unfamiliar vocabulary items in context. In the paragraph of "The Lottery" indicated by the number in parentheses, find the word that best fits the meaning given. Your teacher may want to read these aloud as you quickly scan the paragraph to find the answer.

1. (2) Which word means *noisy and excited*?

2. (2) Which word means *criticisms; severe or formal scoldings*?

3. (3) Which word means *information, usually about other people, not always factual*?

4. (7) Which word at the beginning of the paragraph means *taking care of details*?

5. (7) Which word at the bottom of the paragraph means *endlessly*?

Exercise 3

This exercise should be done after you have finished reading "The Lottery." The exercise is designed to determine how well you have been able to use context clues to guess the meaning of unfamiliar vocabulary in "The Lottery." Give a definition, synonym, or description of each of the words and phrases below. The number in parentheses indicates the paragraph in which the word can be found. This exercise can be done orally or in writing.

1. devote (first sentence, paragraph 4) _____

2. stirred up (last sentence, paragraph 4) _____

3. fade off (bottom, paragraph 5) _____

4. shabbier (last sentence, paragraph 5) _____

5. lapse (middle, paragraph 7) _____

6. craned (first sentence, paragraph 9) _____

7. tapped (second sentence, paragraph 9) _____

8. consulted (paragraph 10) _____

Nonprose Reading

Bus Schedule

The United States is a country that has depended heavily on the automobile. In recent years, because of concern about oil resources and the pollution caused by auto emissions, large cities have tried to change commuter habits by encouraging people to ride buses rather than drive their cars. Bus schedules such as the one that follows are a part of this effort.

Before You Begin   Reflect on bus travel in your country:

1. How convenient is the bus service in your country? How often do the buses run? Are there many buses to choose from?

2. Do buses serve small towns as well as cities? Rural areas as well as urban areas? Do many people ride buses?

3. Do drivers adhere to a strict schedule? Do drivers wait for passengers who are running to catch the bus?

4. How do you find out about the buses? Do you use printed schedules to find the appropriate bus routes and times?

Consider bus travel as a visitor to the U.S.:

1. In the U.S., bus travelers rely on printed bus schedules. Why do you think this might be?

2. Imagine you are visiting a large city in the United States for the first time. You plan to take city buses to see some of the city's parks, museums, and important landmarks. What would you need to know about the city's bus system in order to plan your tour?

Bus schedules are often difficult to read.* Following are pages of a Denver, Colorado, bus schedule. The accompanying exercises are designed to help you solve typical problems encountered by bus travelers.

---

*For an explanation of nonprose reading, see Unit 1.

Exercise 1

At the top of page 188 are the cover pages of a Denver bus schedule. Skim them to get a general idea of the kinds of information they provide. Then use questions 1 through 8 to guide you in finding specific information.

1. Within the Denver bus system there are many different bus routes. Each route, or line, has a different name and a separate printed schedule. What bus route is this schedule for?

   _____

2. Do you know if this bus goes to the campus of the University of Colorado at Denver? To the Denver Museum of Natural History?

   _____

3. What are "peak hours"? Why is it important to know if your bus is traveling during peak hours?

   _____

   _____

4. How much would it cost two adults and a 5-year-old child to take a local bus ride on a Saturday?

   _____

5. Suppose that all you have is a five-dollar bill. Will you need to get change before you board the bus?

   _____

6. If you left your umbrella on a Denver bus, what number would you call to see if it had been found?

   _____

7. If you have questions about bus routes, what number should you call? _____

8. How much would it cost a handicapped passenger (with proper RTD identification) to ride a bus at noon on a Monday?

   _____

Exercise 2

The map on the bottom of page 188 shows the routes followed by eastbound and westbound 20th Avenue buses. Use the map to answer the following questions.

1. Can you connect to a route 76 bus from a route 20 bus? _____

2. T / F   The westbound bus passes Mercy Hospital.

3. T / F   The eastbound bus stops in front of Children's Hospital.

4. When do 20th Avenue buses pass the corner of West 26th and Lowell? _____

5. You want to visit a friend at Fitzsimons Hospital. Does the 20th Avenue bus go directly there?

_____

Exercise 3

Within the 20th Avenue bus schedule, there are separate time tables for buses that travel east and buses that travel west. On page 188 are the time tables for the eastbound 20th Avenue buses. Suppose that you are staying near the Denver West Marriott Hotel. Use the time tables to answer the following questions. For some questions you may want to use the map in exercise 2 as well as the time tables.

1. T / F   It costs more to take the 8:55 A.M. weekday bus from the Marriott than to take the 9:57 A.M. bus.

2. If you use a wheelchair, which 20th Avenue bus would you take? _____

3. If you wanted to meet a friend at Mile High Stadium at 10:00 A.M. on a Wednesday, what

   bus would you need to catch from the hotel? _____

4. It's Friday. You want to meet a friend for an 8:00 P.M. dinner at a restaurant on the corner

   of E. 17th and York. What is the latest bus you could catch from your hotel? _____

5. How many buses go from the Marriott Hotel to Union Station? _____

6. T / F   The Marriott is a convenient place to stay if you want to visit downtown Denver on the weekend.

7. T / F   20th Avenue buses do not run on Christmas Day.

8. T / F   The bus schedule is bilingual.

RTD The Ride

20

X Stops

20th Avenue

Service to:
Auraria
Beth Israel Hospital
Children's Hospital
City Park
Colorado Women's College
Denver Museum of
 Natural History
Denver West Marriott
Downtown Denver
Fitzsimons Hospital
Kaiser Permanente
McNichols Arena
Mercy Hospital
Mile High Stadium
Sloans Lake
St. Anthony Hospital Central
St. Joseph's Hospital
St. Luke's Hospital
Union Station

**This route makes "X" stops
on 15th/17th Streets**

For information call: 778-6000

Fares/Tarifas

Type of Service	Peak	Off-Peak	Monthly Passes	
			Regular	Elderly-Handicapped Youth (6–19 yrs.)
Mall Shuttle	free	free	–	–
Circulator	.70	.70	$18.00	$12.00
Boulder City	$1.00	.70	$25.00	$16.00
Local/Ltd	$1.50	.70	$32.00	$24.00
Express	$2.00	$2.00	$54.00	$36.00
Regional long distance	$3.50	$3.50	$90.00	$60.00
Transfers	free	free		

Peak Hours are 6:00-9:00 AM and 4:00-6:00 PM weekdays only.

Off-Peak Hours are all other times including holidays.

Exact Fare, Token or Monthly Pass Only! Drivers carry no change.

Transfers are intended for one continuous trip in the same direction. Request transfers at the time a fare is paid by cash or token.

Passes and Tokens are available at selected RTD offices and all King Soopers and Safeway stores. Tokens are sold at all Albertsons stores. Charge your pass or tokens by the roll to your MasterCard, Visa or Choice Card at selected RTD locations, by mail or by phone. To charge by phone, call 777-8893, seven days a week, 24 hours a day.

Elderly (65+), Handicapped and Youth pass discounts are available at selected RTD locations. Youth show proof of age. Elderly show a Medicare card, driver's license or Colorado ID. Handicapped show an authorized RTD identification card available through RTD, call 777-8600. To receive discounted passes by mail, initial eligibility must be established at an RTD location.

Elderly and Handicapped passengers ride for just 5¢ during off-peak hours by showing identification noted above for pass discounts.

Children 5 and under ride free if accompanied by adult passenger (limit 3).

RTD's Downtown Information Center is located at Civic Center Station, Broadway and Colfax. Passes, tokens and customer schedules are available here. Hours are from 8:00 AM-6:00 PM Monday-Friday.

RTD's Customer Service is located at Civic Center Station, Broadway and Colfax. For compliments or concerns call 573-2343. Hours are from 8:00 AM-5:00 PM Monday-Friday.

Lost and Found articles can be reclaimed at the following locations:

   Denver: Civic Center Station, Broadway and Colfax
   Hours: 8:00 AM-5:00 PM Monday-Friday. Call 573-2288

   Boulder: Boulder Transit Center, 14th and Walnut
   Hours: 7:00 AM-7:00 PM Monday-Friday. Call 442-7332

   Longmont: Longmont Terminal, 815 South Main
   Hours: 8:00 AM-5:00 PM Monday-Friday. Call 776-4141

TTY information service for patrons with hearing and speech impairments ONLY: call 753-9405.

Notice: Although RTD makes every effort to operate its service as scheduled, bus schedules may vary because of road, traffic, equipment, and other conditions. RTD makes no warranty or guarantee, express or implied, that bus service will be provided as scheduled. The RTD's liability is limited to the value of the fare for a one-way ride.

For information call: 778-6000, 5:00 AM to 10:00 PM Mon-Fri and 7:00 AM to 10:00 PM Sat/Sun/Holiday.

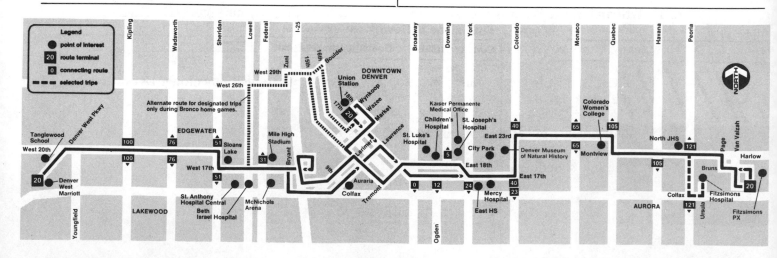

Denver West to Fitzsimons—Eastbound

Monday-Friday   Lunes-Viernes   Times listed are approximate

	Denver West Marriott	West 20th-Youngfield (Lakewood)	West 20th-Wadsworth	West 17th-Sheridan	West 17th-Bryant (Mile High Stadium)	Lawrence-9th (Auraria)	Wynkoop-17th (Union Station)	17th-Champa**	East 17th-York	Colorado-East 17th	East 23rd-Monaco	Montview-Havana	Fitzsimons PX	Fitzsimons Hospital (Aurora)
H	524	528	538	544	549	555	--	601	608	611	618	627	634	--
H	--	--	--	--	--	--	620	623	630	633	640	649	656	--
H	601	605	616	622	627	634	--	641	651	654	701	710	717	--
H	621	625	636	642	647	654	--	701	711	714	721	730	737	--
H	--	--	--	--	--	--	717	721	731	734	741	750	757	--
H	652	656	708	714	719	726	--	735	745	748	755	804	811	--
H	--	--	--	--	--	--	745	750	800	803	810	819	826	--
H	722	726	738	744	749	756	--	805	815	818	825	834	841	--
H	--	--	--	--	--	--	816	820	830	833	840	849	856	--
H	755	759	809	815	820	826	--	835	845	848	855	904	911	--
H	--	--	--	--	--	--	845	850	900	903	910	919	926	--
H	825	829	839	845	850	856	--	905	915	918	925	934	941	--
H	--	--	--	--	--	--	915	920	930	933	940	949	956	--
H	855	859	909	915	920	926	--	935	945	948	955	1004	1011	--
H	--	--	--	--	--	--	945	950	1000	1003	1010	1019	1026	--
H	--	--	--	--	--	--	1000	1005	1015	1018	1025	1034	1041	--
H	--	--	--	--	--	--	1015	1020	1030	1034	1041	1050	1057	--
H	957	1001	1011	1017	1022	1028	--	1035	1045	1049	1056	1105	1112	--
H	--	--	--	--	--	--	1045	1050	1100	1104	1111	1120	1127	--
H	--	--	--	--	--	--	1100	1105	1115	1119	1126	1135	1142	--
H	--	--	--	--	--	--	1115	1120	1130	1134	1141	1150	1157	--
H	1057	1101	1111	1117	1122	1128	--	1135	1145	1149	1156	1205	1212	--
H	--	--	--	--	--	--	1145	1150	1200	1204	1211	1220	1227	--
H	--	--	--	--	--	--	1200	1205	1215	1219	1226	1235	1242	--
H	--	--	--	--	--	--	1215	1220	1230	1234	1241	1250	1257	--
H	1157	1201	1211	1217	1222	1228	--	1235	1245	1249	1256	105	112	--
H	--	--	--	--	--	--	1245	1250	100	104	111	120	127	--
H	--	--	--	--	--	--	100	105	115	119	126	135	142	--
H	--	--	--	--	--	--	115	120	130	134	141	150	157	--
H	1257	101	111	117	122	128	--	135	145	149	156	205	212	--
H	--	--	--	--	--	--	145	150	200	204	211	220	227	--
H	--	--	--	--	--	--	200	205	215	219	226	235	242	--
H	--	--	--	--	--	--	215	220	231	235	243	253	300	--
H	--	--	--	--	--	--	--	--	244	247	255	--	--	--
H	157	201	211	217	222	228	--	235	246	250	258	308	315	--
H	--	--	--	--	--	--	245	250	301	305	313	323	330	--
H	--	--	--	--	--	--	300	305	316	320	328	338	345	--
H	--	--	--	--	--	--	310	315	327	331	339	349	357	--
H	--	--	--	--	--	--	320	325	337	341	349	359	407	--
H	254	258	310	316	321	327	--	335	347	351	359	409	417	--
H	--	--	--	--	--	--	340	345	357	401	409	419	427	--
H	--	--	--	--	--	--	350	355	407	411	419	429	437	--
H	324	328	340	346	351	357	--	405	417	421	429	439	447	--
H	--	--	--	--	--	--	410	415	427	431	439	449	457	--
H	--	--	--	--	--	--	420	425	437	441	449	459	507	--
H	354	358	410	416	421	426	--	435	447	451	459	509	517	--
H	--	--	--	--	--	--	440	445	457	501	509	519	527	--
H	--	--	--	--	--	--	450	455	506	510	518	528	536	--
H	424	428	440	446	451	456	--	505	516	520	528	538	546	--
H	--	--	--	--	--	--	510	515	526	530	538	548	555	--
H	--	--	--	--	--	--	525	530	540	544	552	602	609	--
H	507	511	520	526	531	536	--	545	555	559	607	617	624	--
H	--	--	--	--	--	--	555	600	610	614	622	632	--	639
H	537	541	550	556	601	606	--	615	625	629	637	647	--	654
H	--	--	--	--	--	--	625	630	640	644	652	702	--	709
H	607	611	620	626	631	636	--	645	655	659	707	717	--	724
H	--	--	--	--	--	--	710	715	722	725	731	739	--	748
H	--	--	--	--	--	--	740	745	752	755	801	810	--	817
H	--	--	--	--	--	--	810	815	822	825	831	840	--	847
H	--	--	--	--	--	--	840	845	852	855	901	910	--	917
H	--	--	--	--	--	--	910	915	922	925	931	940	--	947
H	--	--	--	--	--	--	940	945	952	955	1001	1010	--	1017
H	--	--	--	--	--	--	1010	1015	1022	1025	1031	1040	--	1047
H	--	--	--	--	--	--	1040	1045	1052	1055	1101	1110	--	1117
H	--	--	--	--	--	--	1110	1115	1122	1125	1131	1140	--	1147
H	--	--	--	--	--	--	1140	1145	1152	1155	1201	1210	--	1217

**This route makes the following "X" stops on 17th Street
17th - Lawrence
17th - Champa
17th - Welton

H - accessible service - wheelchair lift equipped buses serving local routes

Shaded area indicates peak hours.

El area sombreada indica horas de trafico de gran volumen.

Holidays: New Year's Day, Memorial Day, Independence Day, Labor Day, Thanksgiving Day, and Christmas Day.

Denver West to Fitzsimons—Eastbound

Saturday   Sabado

	Wynkoop-17th (Union Station)	17th-Champa**	East 17th-York	Colorado-East 17th	East 23rd-Monaco	Montview-Havana	Fitzsimons PX	Fitzsimons Hospital (Aurora)
H	508A	511	520	523	530	539	--	546
H	538	541	550	553	600	609	616	--
H	608	611	620	623	630	639	646	--
H	645	648	657	700	707	716	723	--
H	715	718	727	730	737	746	753	--
H	745	748	757	800	807	816	823	--
H	815	818	827	830	837	846	853	--
H	841	846	858	902	909	919	926	--
H	911	916	928	932	939	949	956	--
H	941	946	958	1002	1009	1019	1026	--
H	1011	1016	1028	1032	1039	1049	1056	--
H	1041	1046	1058	1102	1109	1119	1126	--
H	1111	1116	1128	1132	1139	1149	1156	--
H	1141	1146	1158	1202P	1209	1219	1226	--
H	1211P	1216	1228	1232	1239	1249	1256	--
H	1241	1246	1258	102	109	119	126	--
H	111	116	128	132	139	149	156	--
H	141	146	158	202	209	219	226	--
H	211	216	228	232	239	249	256	--
H	241	246	258	302	309	319	326	--
H	311	316	328	332	339	349	356	--
H	341	346	358	402	409	419	426	--
H	411	416	428	432	439	449	456	--
H	441	446	458	502	509	519	526	--
H	511	516	528	532	539	549	556	--
H	541	546	558	602	609	619	626	--
H	605	610	622	626	633	643	--	650
H	635	640	652	656	703	712	--	719
H	715	718	725	728	734	743	--	750
H	745	748	755	758	804	813	--	820
H	815	818	825	828	834	843	--	850
H	845	848	855	858	904	913	--	920
H	915	918	925	928	934	943	--	950
H	945	948	955	958	1004	1013	--	1020
H	1015	1018	1025	1028	1034	1043	--	1050
H	1045	1048	1055	1058	1104	1113	--	1120
H	1115	1118	1125	1128	1134	1143	--	1150

Downtown to Fitzsimons—Eastbound

Sunday/Holiday   Domingo/Dia de Fiesta

	Wynkoop-17th (Union Station)	17th-Champa**	East 17th-York	Colorado-East 17th	East 23rd-Monaco	Montview-Havana	Fitzsimons PX	Fitzsimons Hospital (Aurora)
H	528A	531	539	542	548	557	604	--
H	558	601	609	612	618	627	634	--
H	628	631	639	642	648	657	704	--
H	658	701	709	712	718	727	734	--
H	738	741	749	752	758	807	814	--
H	814	817	825	828	834	843	850	--
H	844	847	855	858	904	913	920	--
H	914	917	925	928	934	943	950	--
H	944	947	955	958	1004	1013	1020	--
H	1014	1017	1025	1028	1034	1043	1050	--
H	1044	1047	1055	1058	1104	1113	1120	--
H	1114	1117	1125	1128	1134	1143	1150	--
H	1144	1147	1155	1158	1204P	1213	1220	--
H	1214P	1217	1225	1228	1234	1243	1250	--
H	1244	1247	1255	1258	104	113	120	--
H	114	117	125	128	134	143	150	--
H	144	147	155	158	204	213	220	--
H	214	217	225	228	234	243	250	--
H	244	247	255	258	304	313	320	--
H	314	317	325	328	334	343	350	--
H	344	347	355	358	404	413	420	--
H	414	417	425	428	434	443	450	--
H	444	447	455	458	504	513	520	--
H	514	517	525	528	534	543	550	--
H	544	547	555	558	604	613	620	--
H	615	618	626	629	635	644	--	651
H	645	648	656	659	705	714	--	721
H	715	718	725	728	734	743	--	750
H	745	748	755	758	804	813	--	820
H	815	818	825	828	834	843	--	850
H	845	848	855	858	904	913	--	920
H	915	918	925	928	934	943	--	950
H	945	948	955	958	1004	1013	--	1020
H	1015	1018	1025	1028	1034	1043	--	1050
H	1045	1048	1055	1058	1104	1113	--	1120
H	1115	1118	1125	1128	1134	1143	--	1150

Word Study

Stems and Affixes

Below is a list of some commonly occurring stems and affixes.* Study their meanings; then do the exercises that follow. Your teacher may ask you to give examples of other words you know that are derived from these stems and affixes.

Prefixes

by-	aside or apart from the common, secondary	bypass, byproduct
de-	down from, away	descend, depart
dia-	through, across	diameter, diagonal
epi-	upon, over, outer	epidermis
hyper-	above, beyond, excessive	hypersensitive
hypo-	under, beneath, down	hypothesis, hypothermia

Stems

-capit-	head, chief	captain, cap, decapitate
-corp-	body	corporation, incorporate
-derm-	skin	epidermis, dermatology
-geo-	earth	geology, geography
-hydr-, -hydro-	water	hydrogen, hydrology
-ortho-	straight, correct	orthodox, orthography
-pod-, -ped-	foot	podiatrist, pedestrian
-son-	sound	sound, sonic
-therm-, -thermo-	heat	thermal, hypothermia
-ver-	true	verity, veritable

Suffixes

-ate	to make	activate
-fy	to make	liquify
-ize	to make	crystallize

Exercise 1

Word analysis can help you to guess the meaning of unfamiliar words. Using context clues and what you know about word parts, write a synonym, description, or definition of the italicized words.

1. _____   Mr. Adams is employed at a *hydroelectric* power plant.

2. _____   Before Cindy gets dressed in the morning, she looks at the *thermometer* hanging outside her kitchen window.

3. _____   Some doctors prescribe medication to slow down *hyperactive* children.

---

*For a list of all stems and affixes taught in *Reader's Choice*, see the Appendix.

4. _____   I'm not sure if that information is correct, but I'll look in our records to *verify* it.

5. _____   Susan wants to replace the *pedals* on her bicycle with a special kind that racers use.

6. _____   After spending so many days lost in the desert, he was suffering from severe *dehydration*.

7. _____   June's father's hobby is photography, so she bought him a top-quality *tripod* for his birthday.

8. _____   He will never learn how to improve his writing unless he stops being so *hypersensitive* to criticism.

9. _____   Dr. Robinson said that just the sight of a *hypodermic* needle is enough to frighten many of his patients.

10. _____   Although she finished her degree in dentistry in 1960, she wants to go back to school next year to specialize in *orthodontics*.

11. _____   The immigration authorities *deported* Mr. Jensen because he did not have a legal passport.

12. _____   The average *per capita* annual income in this country for people between the ages of sixteen and sixty-five has risen dramatically in the last ten years.

13. _____   Mr. Thompson made an appointment with a *dermatologist* because he noticed small red spots on his hands.

14. _____   Scientists have developed a sensitive instrument to measure *geothermal* variation.

15. _____   Anthropologists say that bipedalism played an important role in the cultural evolution of the human species. Because early humans were *bipedal,* their hands were free to make and use tools.

16. _____   They doubted the *veracity* of his story.

17. _____   The Concorde, which flies at *supersonic* speed, can cross the Atlantic in about three hours.

Exercise 2

Following is a list of words containing some of the stems and affixes introduced in this unit and the previous ones. Definitions of these words appear on the right. Put the letter of the appropriate definition next to each word.

1. ____ hyperbole

   a. the tissue immediately beneath the outer layer of the tissue of plants

2. ____ hypodermis

   b. a quotation printed at the beginning of a book or chapter to suggest its theme

3. ____ epicenter

4. ____ epidermis

   c. the outer layer of skin of some animals

5. ____ epigraph

   d. an exaggeration; a description that is far beyond the truth

   e. the part of the earth's surface directly above the place of origin of an earthquake

---

6. ____ orthography

   a. fear of water

7. ____ hydrate

   b. agreeing with established beliefs

8. ____ decapitate

   c. fat; large of body

9. ____ orthodox

   d. to cut off the head of

10. ____ hydrophobia

   e. correct spelling; writing words with the proper, accepted letters

11. ____ corpulent

   f. to cause to combine with water

---

12. ____ bypass

   a. of or related to walking; a person who walks

13. ____ pedestrian

   b. a dead body

14. ____ byproduct

   c. a passage to one side; a route that goes around a town

15. ____ corporeal

   d. a secondary and sometimes unexpected result; something produced (as in manufacturing) in addition to the principal product

16. ____ corpse

17. ____ podiatry

   e. the care and treatment of the human foot in health and disease

   f. bodily; of the nature of the physical body; not spiritual

---

18. ____ deflect

   a. to turn aside from a fixed course

19. ____ decentralize

   b. of or relating to the form of the earth or its surface features

20. ____ diaphanous

   c. to divide and distribute what has been concentrated or united

21. ____ verisimilitude

   d. the quality of appearing to be true

22. ____ geomorphic

   e. characterized by such fineness of texture as to permit seeing through

Sentence Study

Comprehension

Read these sentences carefully.* The questions that follow are designed to test your comprehension of complex grammatical structures. Select the *best* answer.

1. Like physical anthropology, orthodontics (dentistry dealing with the irregularities of teeth) tries to explain how and why men are different; unlike anthropology, it also tries to correct those differences for functional or aesthetic reasons.

    How does orthodontics differ from physical anthropology?

    _____ a. Physical anthropology is concerned with aesthetics; orthodontics is not.

    _____ b. Physical anthropology deals with the irregularities of teeth.

    _____ c. Orthodontics tries to explain why men are different, anthropology does not.

    _____ d. Anthropology does not try to correct differences among men; orthodontics does.

2. What is most obvious in this book are all those details of daily living that make Mrs. Richards anything but common.

    According to this statement, what kind of person is Mrs. Richards?

    _____ a. She is very obvious.

    _____ b. She is an unusual person.

    _____ c. She is anything she wants to be.

    _____ d. She is quite ordinary.

3. A third island appeared gradually during a period of volcanic activity that lasted over four years. Later, the 1866 eruptions, which brought to Santorin those volcanologists who first began archeological work there, enlarged the new island through two new crater vents.

    What enlarged the third island?

    _____ a. the eruptions of 1866

    _____ b. a four-year period of volcanic activity

    _____ c. the activities of the men who came to study volcanoes

    _____ d. archeological work, which created two new crater vents

4. Just before his tenth birthday John received a horse from his father; this was the first of a series of expensive gifts intended to create the impression of a loving parent.

    Why did John receive the horse?

    _____ a. because he was ten

    _____ b. because his father loved him

    _____ c. because his father wanted to seem loving

    _____ d. because his father wouldn't be able to give him expensive gifts in the future

5. Since industry and commerce are the largest users of electrical energy, using less electricity would mean a reduced industrial capacity and fewer jobs in the affected industries and therefore an unfavorable change in our economic structure.

    According to this sentence, decreasing the use of electricity _____

    _____ a. must begin immediately.   _____ c. will cause difficulties.

    _____ b. isn't important.   _____ d. won't affect industry.

---

*For an introduction to sentence study, see Unit 1.

6. The medical journal reported that heart attack victims who recover are approximately five times as likely to die within the next five years as those people without a history of heart disease.

   What did this article say about people who have had a heart attack?
   _____ a. They are more likely to die in the near future than others.
   _____ b. They will die in five years.
   _____ c. They are less likely to die than people without a history of heart disease.
   _____ d. They are likely to recover.

7. Few phenomena in history are more puzzling than this one: that men and women with goals so vague, with knowledge so uncertain, with hopes so foggy, still would have risked dangers so certain and tasks so great.

   What historical fact is puzzling?
   _____ a. that people had such vague goals
   _____ b. that people took such great risks
   _____ c. that people had foggy hopes and uncertain knowledge
   _____ d. that people completed such great tasks

8. Next he had to uncover the ancient secret—so jealously guarded by the ancients that no text of any kind, no descriptive wall painting, and no tomb inscriptions about making papyrus are known to exist.

   What secret did this man want to discover?
   _____ a. how to understand wall paintings
   _____ b. how to read tomb inscriptions
   _____ c. how to read the ancient texts
   _____ d. how to produce papyrus

9. Alexis, ruler of a city where politics was a fine art, concealed his fears, received the noblemen with extravagant ceremonies, impressed them with his riches, praised them, entertained them, bribed them, made promises he had no intention of keeping—and thus succeeded in keeping their troops outside his city walls.

   Why did Alexis give money and attention to the noblemen?
   _____ a. because they praised him
   _____ b. in order to prevent their armies from entering the city
   _____ c. in order to impress them with his riches
   _____ d. because they were his friends

Paragraph Reading

Restatement and Inference

This exercise is similar to the one found in Unit 5. Each paragraph below is followed by five statements. The statements are of four types:

1. Some of the statements are restatements of ideas in the original paragraph. They give the same information in a different way.
2. Some of the statements are inferences (conclusions) that can be drawn from the information given in the paragraph.
3. Some of the statements are false based on the information given.
4. Some of the statements cannot be judged true or false based on information given in the original paragraph.

Put a check (✓) next to all restatements and inferences (types 1 and 2). Note: do not check a statement that is true of itself but cannot be inferred from the paragraph.

Paragraph 1

It was the weekend before the exam. We were at the Walkers' house and it was pouring rain. Jack came in late, drenched to the skin. He explained that a car had broken down on the road and he had stopped to help push it onto the shoulder and out of the traffic. I remember thinking then how typical that was of Jack. So helpful, so accommodating.

_____ a. Jack came in late because it was raining.

_____ b. Jack came in late because his car had broken down.

_____ c. The narrator thinks Jack is typical.

_____ d. The narrator bases his opinion of Jack on this one experience.

_____ e. Jack often helps other people.

Paragraph 2

The illustrations in books make it easier for us to believe in the people and events described. The more senses satisfied, the easier is belief. Visual observation tends to be the most convincing evidence. Children, being less capable of translating abstractions into actualities, need illustration more than adults. Most of us, when we read, tend to create only vague and ghostlike forms in response to the words. The illustrator, when he reads, must see. The great illustrator sees accurately.

_____ a. Illustrations help us to believe events described in words.

_____ b. When most people read, they do not picture events as accurately as can a great illustrator.

_____ c. Children are less able than adults to visualize events described in books.

_____ d. The author believes illustrators are especially able to imagine visual details described with words.

_____ e. The author believes all illustrators see accurately.

Paragraph 3   Surveys reveal that most adults consider themselves "well informed about the affairs of the nation and the world." Yet a regularly taken Roper poll that asks, "From where do you obtain most of your information about the world?" has found the percentage of people who reply, "Television" has been increasing steadily over the past decade. The latest questionnaire found that well over 60 percent of the respondents chose television over other media as their major source of information. These two facts are difficult to reconcile since even a casual study of television news reveals it is only a headline service and not a source of information enabling one to shape a world view.

_____ a. Most adults obtain most of their information about world affairs from the newspaper.

_____ b. The author of this passage does not believe that television provides enough information to make people well informed.

_____ c. The number of people answering the questionnaire has increased.

_____ d. Sixty percent of the people questioned get all their news from television.

_____ e. Most adults are well informed about the affairs of the nation and the world.

Paragraph 4   The dusty book room whose windows never opened, through whose panes the summer sun sent a dim light where gold specks danced and shimmered, opened magic windows for me through which I looked out on other worlds and times than those in which I lived. The narrow shelves rose halfway up the walls, their tops piled with untidy layers that almost touched the ceiling. The piles on the floor had to be climbed over, columns of books flanked the window, falling at a touch.

_____ a. The room is dusty and shadowy, filled with books from floor to ceiling.

_____ b. The sun never enters the room.

_____ c. The author spent time in this room as a child.

_____ d. The author did not like the room.

_____ e. Through the windows in the room, the author saw worlds other than those in which he lived.

Paragraph 5   By voting against mass transportation, voters have chosen to
continue on a road to ruin. Our interstate highways, those much
praised golden avenues built to whisk suburban travelers in and out of
downtown, have turned into the world's most expensive parking lots.
That expense is not only economic—it is social. These highways have
created great walls separating neighborhood from neighborhood,
disrupting the complex social connections that help make a city livable.

_____ a. Interstate highways have created social problems.

_____ b. Highways create complex social connections.

_____ c. By separating neighborhoods, highways have made cities more livable.

_____ d. The author supports the idea of mass transportation.

_____ e. The author agrees with a recent vote by the citizens.

Discourse Focus

Careful Reading/Drawing Inferences

This exercise is similar to the one found in Unit 5. Once again you must match wits with the great Professor Fordney. Solve the following mysteries, drawing inferences from the clues provided. Your teacher may want you to work with your classmates to answer the questions following each mystery. Be prepared to defend your solution with details from the passage.

Mystery 1:
Murder on Board

During a lull in the storm which tossed and rocked the sturdy little steamer *Dauntless,* a shot rang out on A deck.

Professor Fordney threw down the detective story he was somewhat unsuccessfully trying to read and hastened into the companionway. Where it turned at the far corner, he found Steward Mierson bending over the body of a man who had been instantly killed. Just then the heavens opened; lightning flashed and thunder boomed as if in ghoulish mockery.

The dead man's head bore powder burns. Captain Larson and the criminologist started checking the whereabouts of everyone aboard, beginning with those passengers nearest where the body was discovered.

The first questioned was Nathan Cohen, who said he was just completing a letter in his cabin when he heard the shot.

"May I see it?" Larson asked.

Looking over the captain's shoulder, Fordney saw the small, precise handwriting, on the ship's stationery. The letter was apparently written to a woman.

The next cabin was occupied by Miss Margaret Millsworth. On being questioned regarding what she was doing at the time, Miss Millsworth became excited and nervous. She stated that she had become so frightened by the storm, that about fifteen minutes before the shot was fired she had gone to the cabin of her fiancé, James Montgomery, directly opposite. The latter corroborated her statement, saying they hadn't rushed into the passageway because it would have looked compromising were they seen emerging together at that hour. Fordney noticed a dark red stain on Montgomery's dressing gown.

The whereabouts of the rest of the passengers and crew were satisfactorily checked.

Whom did the captain hold on suspicion? Why? _____

_____

From *Minute Mysteries* by Austin Ripley (New York: Pocket Books).

Mystery 2:
Death in the Mountains

While hunting in the Adirondacks, Fordney was informed of a tragedy at one of the camps. Thinking he might be of some help, he went over and introduced himself and was told of the accident by Wylie, the victim's companion.

"When Moore hadn't returned to camp at nine o'clock last night, I was a bit worried, because he didn't know these mountains. There wasn't a star out and it was dark and moonless, so I decided to look around for him. We're five miles from anyone, you know.

"Putting more wood on the fire, I set out. After searching for an hour I was coming up the slope of a ravine when I saw a pair of eyes shining at me.

"Calling twice, and getting no answer, I fired, thinking it was a mountain lion. Imagine my horror when I reached the spot, struck a match, and saw I had nearly blown off Moore's head. A terrible experience!

"I carried him back to camp and then walked to the nearest house to report the accident."

"How far from camp did you find him?"

"About a quarter of a mile."

"How did you manage to shoot with your right hand bandaged?"

"Oh—I use either hand."

"Mind if I look at the gun?"

"Not at all." Wylie handed it over.

"H'mmmm. European make. Had it long?"

"No. It's rather new."

"Why did you deliberately murder Moore?" Fordney abruptly demanded. "For that's what you did!"

How did he know? _____

_____

Mystery 3:
Case #194

Rudolph Mayer stumbled into the police station of the little village of Monroe, shook water from his clothes, and collapsed. A local physician was summoned and brought Mayer around. He told the following story.

"My wife and I, fond of winter sports, registered at the Fox Head Resort this afternoon—I've spent several vacations here. Shortly before dusk we decided to go skating on Lake Howard. We'd been out probably twenty minutes, as nearly as I can figure it, when my wife, who was about ten yards in front of me, suddenly dropped into the water through a large hole. Someone must have been cutting ice. I swerved, took off my skates, and jumped in after her. Despite my efforts, however, I couldn't locate her. I was barely able to pull myself out, and as I called and there was no help at hand, made my way here, somehow. It's about half a mile, I guess, and I didn't think I'd be able to do it. For God's sake send someone out there!"

Again the man fainted but was revived in a few minutes, mumbling incoherently about skates.

Two constables were dispatched through the ten below zero weather to the scene and returned with Mayer's skates found on the edge of a large hole where a local concern had been cutting ice. At the sight of them Mayer again collapsed.

Professor Fordney read no further in the above newspaper account.

"Mayer is certainly lying," he said to himself.

How did he know? _____

_____

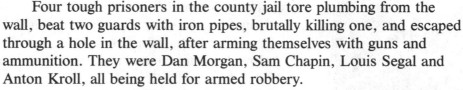

Mystery 4:
The Break

Four tough prisoners in the county jail tore plumbing from the wall, beat two guards with iron pipes, brutally killing one, and escaped through a hole in the wall, after arming themselves with guns and ammunition. They were Dan Morgan, Sam Chapin, Louis Segal and Anton Kroll, all being held for armed robbery.

A posse was quickly organized and the gang surrounded in a small valley fifteen miles from the jail. Two of the mob were wounded and all captured, but not before one of the gang killed State Trooper Don Burton with a bullet through his head.

Professor Fordney interrogated the sullen four separately but each refused any information concerning himself or the others. From outside sources, however, the criminologist learned the following facts.

1. A dancer, one of the four, acted as leader of the gang. He spoke several languages fluently.
2. For some time the ugly Segal and the handsome leader had been suspicious of each other.
3. A week before their arrest, Sam Chapin and the leader won $4,000 each in a crap game at Anton Kroll's lake cabin. Kroll does not gamble.
4. The leader and the prisoner who killed Trooper Don Burton are good friends. They once ran a gambling house in Cuba.
5. Anton Kroll and the killer have been going with twin sisters who knew nothing of their criminal backgrounds.

Fordney sat in his study evaluating the above data. After a few moments he reached for the phone, called the prosecuting attorney and advised him to issue a murder warrant for . . . .

Who killed Trooper Don Burton? _____

_____

Reading Selections 1A–1B

Feature Articles

Before You Begin In his book *With Respect to the Japanese,* John Condon, a specialist in intercultural relations, describes U.S. interest in Japan:

> A New York bookdealer said he had never seen anything like the surge of interest American readers have recently shown for books on Japanese management. . . . Many have argued that Americans have much to learn from the Japanese, while others have raised doubts about transferring methods from one culture to another. In this writer's opinion, the most remarkable fact about the Japan boom in the U.S. is that for the first time Americans have considered the possibility of learning from another culture in areas where Americans had thought they excelled. In that regard Japan deserves special credit, for this might lead to a greater openness and curiosity and learning across other cultural boundaries that rarely occur in the U.S.

1. Why do you think Americans have recently become fascinated by Japan?

2. Why does the author feel that this interest is positive? Do you agree?

Selection 1A **Feature Article**

This first feature article is an example of U.S. interest in Japan. It is reprinted from the *New York Times.* Unlike news articles that seek to inform the public about important events, feature articles are essays that describe persons and topics of general interest. Read this article quickly to discover the major ways in which the author contrasts the Japanese and United States styles of decision-making, and to see whether or not you agree. You will need to do Vocabulary from Context exercise 1 on pages 204–5 before you begin reading.

Quotation from John C. Condon, *With Respect to the Japanese: A Guide for Americans* (Yarmouth, Maine: Intercultural Press).
Selection 1A adapted from "Japanese Style in Decision-Making" by Yoshio Terasawa, *New York Times.*

Japanese Style in Decision-Making

By YOSHIO TERASAWA

1 To talk about problem-solving or decision-making within a national environment means examining many complex cultural forces. It means trying to measure the impact of these forces on contemporary life, and also coming to grips with changes now taking place.

2 It also means using dangerous comparisons — and the need to translate certain fundamental concepts which resist translation and comparisons.

3 For example, the concept of vocational or professional identity differs markedly between the United States and Japan.

4 In the West, the emphasis is on what a man, or woman does for a living. Here in the U.S., if you ask children what their fathers do, they will say "My daddy drives a truck" or "My daddy is a stock broker" or "My daddy is an engineer."

5 But in Japan, the child will tell you "My daddy works for Mitsubishi" or "My daddy works for Nomura Securities" or for "Hitachi." But you will have no idea whether the father is president of Hitachi or a chauffeur at Hitachi.

6 In Japan, the most important thing is what organization you work for. This becomes very significant when you try to analyze the direction-taking or decision-making process. At the least, it explains the greater job stability in Japan, in contrast to the great job mobility in America.

7 While we differ in many ways, such differences are neither superior nor inferior to each other. A particular pattern of management behavior develops from a complexity of unique cultural factors — and will only work within a given culture.

8 Let me try to describe three or four characteristics of the Japanese environment that in some way affect decision-making or direction-taking and problem-solving. These characteristics are interrelated.

9 First, in any approach to a problem and in any negotiations in Japan, there is the "you to you" approach, as distinguished from the Western "I to you" approach.

10 The difference is this: in "I to you," both sides present their arguments forthrightly from their own point of view — they state what they want and what they expect to get. Thus, a confrontation situation is set up, and Westerners are very adroit in dealing with this.

11 The "you to you" approach practiced in Japan is based on each side — automatically and often unconsciously — trying to understand the other person's point of view, and for the purpose of the discussion actually declaring this understanding. Thus, the direction of the meeting is a mutual attempt at minimizing confrontation and achieving harmony.

12 A second characteristic is based on "consensus opinion" and "bottom-up direction." In Japan great consideration is given to and reliance placed on the thoughts and opinions of everyone at all levels. This is true of corporate enterprises and Government agencies.

In Japan, negotiations seek a basis of harmony rather than confrontation, as in West.

---

13 To understand this, it is important to realize that Japan is a very densely populated homogeneous country. Moreover, the people are aware and are articulate. Literacy is almost 100 per cent. Problems are shared. In Japan there is a drive for the group — whether it is family, company, or Government — to act as a unit.

14 Tremendous weight is given to the achievement of solidarity and unanimity. Unilateral decision-making or direction-taking is generally avoided, or where it does occur for very practical urgent reasons, it usually happens along with a sounding out of all concerned.

15 This brings us to the second part of this characteristic. When I use the term "bottom-up," I am referring to a style of management — perhaps what you would call keeping your finger on the pulse of the public, or the labor force, or other audiences.

16 The difference is that in Japan we record the pulse and it has real meaning, and it influences the direction finally taken at the top regarding a specific important issue. In other words, Western style decision-making proceeds predominantly from top management and often does not consult middle management or the worker while in

Japan, direction can be formulated at the lowest levels, travel upward through an organization and have an impact on the eventual decision. This is "bottom up."

17 There is also a characteristic style of communications in Japan that is different from the Western way.

18 The Japanese business person works to achieve harmony, even if the deal falls through, and will spend whatever time is necessary to determine a "you to you" approach, communicating personal views only indirectly and with great sensitivity.

19 This places time in a different perspective. In Japan the Western deadline approach is secondary to a thorough job. Japanese are thorough in their meetings as well as in their production. Thus Americans are often exasperated by the seemingly endless sequences of meetings in many Japanese businesses.

20 But where the American is pressing for a specific decision, the Japanese is trying to formulate a rather broad direction.

21 On the other hand, once agreement is established, it is the Japanese who sometimes wonder at the leisurely pace of execution of Westerners. The Japanese are eager for execution and Westerners, perhaps, like to take the time for in-depth planning.

22 Now, while Japan's industry and technology are highly developed, they have not replaced the fundamental force of human energy and motivation. By that I mean that the Japanese take great pride in doing a job well and getting it done no matter how much time is required.

23 There is a dedication and sense of responsibility which have not been replaced by the machine age. Perhaps we are not so sophisticated yet.

24 In my field — finance and securities — I am often asked by West-

erners how Nomura Securities has managed to escape the paper log-jam that American brokerage firms have faced. We, too have had that problem.

25 The Tokyo Stock Exchange often has a turnover of between 200 and 300 million shares a day. This volume is many times more than that of the New York Stock Exchange. How can we possibly handle this load?

26 First, we have very advanced computerization. Second, and most important, the personnel responsible for processing all these transactions stay and stay till all hours until the job is done. And their families understand that this is something that they must do, for the survival and progress of the company and for their own mutual security as well.

27 Perhaps in 20 years — or sooner — they will be more Westernized and insist on going home at five o'clock. But today, still, most insist on staying until the job is done. There is concern for quality.

28 This willingness to pitch in is an important aspect of Japanese problem-solving, and you find it at every level.

29 Some years ago, the Matsushita company was having a very bad time. Among the many measures taken, Mr. Matsushita, the founder and then chairman, became the manager of the sales department.

30 Also, when we at Nomura converted to computers about five years ago, the new system eliminated the jobs of 700 bookkeepers and accountants who were using abacuses. We got rid of the abacuses but we did not get rid of the people. We converted our bookkeepers and accountants to securities sales people and some of these today are our leading sales people.

31 Where there is willingness and intelligence, there is a place within the company to try and to succeed. In Japan, a person's capabilities are not forced into an inflexible specialty. And we feel the company owes a worker something for loyalty and commitment.

* * *

This article is adapted from a speech by Mr. Terasawa, president of Nomura Securities International, Inc., before the Commonwealth Club of San Francisco.

Comprehension

Exercise 1

Each of the statements below would be true of the business world in either the United States or Japan according to the information in the article or inferences that can be drawn from the article. Indicate whether each statement below is characteristic of Japan (J) or the United States (US) according to this article. Be prepared to use parts of the article to support your decisions.

1. _____ In business meetings, confrontations are avoided by communicating one's personal views indirectly.

2. _____ An important decision is made by the president of a company and a memo is sent to all employees informing them of the decision.

3. _____ Several weeks of meetings pass before a policy decision is made.

4. _____ Several weeks pass after agreement is reached before action is taken.

5. _____ A new machine is installed to increase production and as a result 100 workers lose their jobs.

6. _____ When asked what his father does, a child answers, "My daddy is an engineer."

7. _____ Young employees move from one company to another in order to improve their position.

8. _____ Employees often stay at work after hours, until a job is finished.

9. _____ Most companies employ workers of several different cultural and national backgrounds.

Exercise 2

The following questions will help you summarize "Japanese Style in Decision-Making."

1. According to the article, how does the concept of professional identity differ between the United States and Japan?

2. According to the article, what is the difference between the Western "I to you" approach and the Japanese "you to you" approach? What is the difference between Western-style unilateral decision-making and Japanese "consensus opinion" and "bottom-up direction"?

3. Compare the American and Japanese sense of time in business transactions.
   a. Why do Japanese seem to take longer to reach an agreement?
   b. Why do Americans seem to take longer to act after an agreement has been reached?

4. According to the author, how have the Japanese managed to "escape the paper logjam that American . . . firms have faced"?

5. Who is the author of this article? From what source has the article been adapted?

Discussion/Composition

1. The author admits that "to talk about problem-solving or decision-making within a national environment . . . means using dangerous comparisons." Are there generalizations in the article that you find unconvincing either for lack of information or because of your personal experience?

2. Do you think it's possible to transfer management methods from one culture to another? Support your position.

3. Write an article or prepare a speech similar to the one above, explaining to American business people how to do business in your community.

Vocabulary from Context

Exercise 1

Both the ideas and the vocabulary in the exercise below are taken from "Japanese Style in Decision-Making." Use the context provided to determine the meanings of the italicized words. Write a definition, synonym, or description of each of the italicized vocabulary items in the space provided.

1. _____

2. _____

When *formulating* business decisions, Japanese businesses do not depend only on the opinions of a few at the top of the company; rather, *reliance* is placed on the opinions of everyone, at all levels.

3. _____

4. _____

In the United States business people are skilled at handling strong disagreements in meetings. The Japanese, on the other hand, are *adroit* at avoiding such *confrontations*.

5. _____

6. _____

The Japanese business person tries to create a situation in which all people present feel comfortable. Only in such an atmosphere of *harmony* are decisions made. *Consensus* decision-making, a process by which action is taken only after everyone is in agreement, is an important part of Japanese business practices.

7. _____

It is important that people from different cultures come to understand each other and develop *mutual* trust. Only when people trust each other is international cooperation possible.

8. _____

9. _____

The majority of people in Japan are *literate*. Because most people are able to read newspapers and magazines, they generally have opinions on most important matters. In addition, they are quite *articulate* and therefore able to state their ideas clearly to their superiors.

10. _____   People are more likely to change jobs in the United States
                        than they are in Japan. There are several possible explanations
                        for the greater job *stability* in Japan in contrast to the great job
11. _____   *mobility* in the United States.

12. _____   The Japanese are often *exasperated* by the seriousness with
                        which Americans approach time limits. Similarly, Americans
                        are often impatient with the Japanese seeming lack of concern
13. _____   for *deadlines*.

14. _____   Because Japanese workers willingly stay after hours to finish
                        work, they are well known for their *dedication* to their
                        company.

15. _____   We thought we were in complete agreement and we expected a
                        unanimous vote. However, one person voted against the plan.

16. _____   Unlike the United States, where many different nationalities
                        make up the population, Japan's population is quite
                        homogeneous.

17. _____   A company's structure should not be so *inflexible* that it does
                        not allow people to change jobs as their abilities and the needs
                        of the company change.

18. _____   Unlike decisions that are made on the basis of mutual
                        concerns, *unilateral* decisions can be unpopular because they
                        are made by only one of the parties concerned.

19. _____   Some *firms* offer their employees company-paid health
                        insurance.

Exercise 2

This exercise should be done after you have finished reading "Japanese Style in Decision-Making." The exercise is designed to determine how well you have been able to use context clues to guess the meaning of unfamiliar vocabulary in the article. Give a definition, synonym, or description of each of the words below. The number in parentheses indicates the paragraph in which the word can be found. Your teacher may want you to do these orally or in writing.

1. (3) vocational (Find a synonym in the same paragraph.) _____

2. (10) forthrightly _____

3. (13) densely _____

4. (16) consult _____

5. (16) impact _____

6. (30) converted _____

Figurative Language and Idioms

In the paragraph indicated by the number in parentheses, find the phrase that best fits the definition given. Your teacher may want to read these aloud as you quickly scan the paragraph to find the answer.

1. (1)   What phrase means *understanding and taking appropriate action?*

2. (4)   What phrase means *as a profession; to support oneself?*

3. (14) What phrase means *trying to find out someone's opinion?*

4. (15) What phrase means *knowing the feelings of a group of people?*

5. (18) What phrase means *fails; comes to nothing?*

6. (24) What phrase means *a situation in which progress is stopped because there is too much paper work?*

7. (28) What phrase means *begin to work energetically; help do a job?*

Vocabulary Review

Exercise 1

Place the appropriate word from this list in each of the blanks below. Do not use any word more than once.

formulate	articulate	exasperated	adroit
dedicated	deadlines	transactions	reliance

There are two reasons why Lynn was made president of her company last week. First,

Lynn is very _____ at handling people. She is a(n) _____ woman who is

able to express her thoughts and desires very precisely. Her ability helps her in

business _____. When other people become _____ because they cannot find

the right words to express their thoughts, Lynn can make everyone feel comfortable by helping

them to find the right words.

Lynn's second characteristic is her ability to get work done on time, to

meet _____. She has always been a(n) _____ employee

whose _____ on hard work has earned her the respect of her superiors. In fact,

Lynn's success is due to her hard work and her ability to _____ plans that will get

work done efficiently.

Exercise 2

*The words in this list are opposite in meaning to the italicized words in the following passage.
Change the story below by substituting an* antonym *for each of the italicized words or phrases.
Each word should be used at least once.*

unilaterally	mobility	unilateral
confrontation	inflexible	heterogeneous

1. _____   In my company all decisions are made *by consensus* in an

2. _____   atmosphere of *harmony.* The employees are educationally

3. _____   *homogeneous.* Like most workers in this country, employees

4. _____   here experience great job *stability.* However, the policy for

5. _____   changing jobs within the company is quite *flexible.* Requests to

6. _____   change jobs are approved on the basis of *mutual* concerns.

Selection 1B   **Feature Article**

Before You Begin   1. Have you ever felt that salespeople in another community or country were rude?

2. In what ways was their behavior different from what you expected? What did you do?

3. Is it possible for salespeople to be too polite?

Here is another feature article on Japan that appeared in a newspaper in the United States. The article contrasts customer service in the U.S. and Japan. Read the article quickly to get a general idea of the areas of contrast. Your teacher may want you to do the Vocabulary from Context exercise on page 210 before you begin.

FOCUS/A YEN TO PLEASE

Happy Customers Matter of Honor among Japanese

By John Burgess
The Washington Post
    TOKYO

1 In an age when personal service as a significant aspect of merchandising is dying out in the United States, Japan clings tenaciously to it.

2 Service is viewed by people in Japan not as a luxury, but as an essential ingredient for the success of individual companies and the Japanese economy as a whole.

3 Americans who move to Japan never get used to the range of services and courtesies taken for granted here. To those old enough to remember how things used to be at home, life can bring on twinges of nostalgia.

4 Supermarket check-out counters have two or three people ringing up and bagging groceries. Some stores deliver, with each bag arriving neatly stapled closed. Dry ice is inserted alongside the frozen foods to ensure that they don't spoil on the way.

5 Television shops normally send a technician to install and fine-tune a newly purchased set. The technician will rush back if anything goes wrong. Car salespeople are known to bring new models around to customers' homes for test drives and loaners are available for people whose cars are in for repairs.

6 There are no limits to what is home-delivered — video movies, dry cleaning, health foods, rented tailcoats (this last one requires two visits from the sales staff, first for a fitting, second for delivery of the altered and freshly pressed garment). Office deliveries are common, too, especially of lunch.

7 Japanese barbers often give back massages as part of an ordinary haircut. If they remove a customer's eyeglasses, they may polish the lenses before returning them.

Self-service gasoline has yet to make its appearance here in any significant way. At the minimum, attendants fill the tank and wipe the windshield. They often empty ashtrays and stop traffic to let the motorist back on the road.

8 Department stores seem to have twice, if not three times the floor staff of American ones. Many stores wrap everything they sell. Upscale customers don't have to come in at all — the goods are taken to their homes for display and selection.

9 Feudal Japan evolved tight rituals of personal service. Many survive in the traditional inns called *ryokan*. Proprietors bow when guests arrive and straighten the shoes they

step out of. Welcoming tea and elaborate meals are brought to the rooms. Bedding is laid out and cleared away in the morning. On departure, the bows may be held until a guest's car is out of sight.

10 But even in modern businesses, the culture's attention to detail and doing things the "correct" way fit well into the service mentality. While Americans may find it demeaning to fuss over a customer, Japanese worry — with reason — that their shop will be laughed at if they don't.

11 Perhaps the darkest spot on personal service in Japan is how remarkably impersonal it can be. Everyone is treated exactly

From the *Washington Post*.

alike. Employee's cheery greetings and directions, in fact, are often memorized from a company manual. After a month's stay in a hotel, guests may find the staff still has no idea who they are.

12   Still, the Japanese view service as the glue that holds commercial relationships together. If the correct personal contact and follow-up come with the first sale, a second is sure to come. Market share and loyal customers are the first goal, not short-term profit. Service may cost but it helps ensure these more important objectives.

13   While Americans in need of something think of stores, Japanese often think of dealers, individuals who supply and advise over the years on product lines like sake, clothing and electronic equipment.

14   Memories of service may help a company weather hard times. If a computer firm drops behind in product quality or price, its customers will not abandon it en masse. They would feel treacherous doing so. After all, didn't the company send a technician to the office a dozen times to answer questions on that little desk-top model? Expand that to national scale and you have a more stable, predictable economy and job market in the Japanese view.

15   Japanese officials often say one reason why many American companies do poorly in Japan is because people can't believe they will give good service. Even if an American machine tops a Japanese one in price and quality, the buyer will be suspicious. Will I have to phone Houston every time

something goes wrong? he may wonder.

16   Service is plugged as being "free," but of course, is not. Each woman who wraps and each man who lugs groceries is part of why prices are so high in Japan. They are also part of why unemployment is so low. Some economists, in fact, view some of these jobs as disguised welfare programs, financed through high prices rather than taxes.

17   Invariably, as Japan internationalizes, some firms are opting to follow the foreign pattern and cut service to lower prices. Supermarkets and chain stores have gained ground. Department stores have done away with the women who once bowed to every customer who stepped onto an escalator. Some shops now have a tape machine, not a person, saying

"*irashaimase*," or welcome, at the door.

18   Proliferation of American fast-food is another sign of these times. McDonald's now has 573 outlets in Japan. But characteristically, cleanliness and employee courtesy seem to be generally higher than in the United States.

19   The Japanese over the years have borrowed heavily in commercial ideas from the United States but generally look elsewhere concerning service. There are exceptions, however, such as American-style home-delivery pizza. In the last two years, motorbikes darting around with pizza have been growing in numbers on Tokyo streets. Delivery in 30 minutes is guaranteed, or the customer gets about $5 back.

Critical Reading

Exercise 1

Indicate if each of the statements below is true (T) or false (F) according to your understanding of the article.

1. _____ In a Japanese supermarket, you will find several employees at a single check-out counter.

2. _____ Japanese customers are suspicious of the quality of products manufactured in the United States.

3. _____ The author prefers the courtesy of Japanese hotels to the impersonal practices in U.S. hotels.

4. _____ Japanese customers don't pay for these personal services.

5. _____ The author believes that as Japan internationalizes, it will do away with some services that are not economical.

Exercise 2

Although this article is about Japan, it provides a good deal of information about the United States. For the reader, the contrasts mentioned can only be significant in contrast to what is considered "normal" in the U.S.

For each of the activities listed below infer how the author assumes service people behave in the United States. What is your experience of this activity in the U.S. or elsewhere? Your teacher may want you to do this in small groups or pairs.

1. shopping for food   4. buying gas for a car

2. purchasing a T.V.   5. shopping in a department store

3. getting a haircut   6. staying at a hotel

Discussion/Composition

What do you think mainstream U.S. culture could learn from your culture? Compare the two, pointing out the advantages of your native culture.

Vocabulary from Context

Both the ideas and the vocabulary in the following exercise are taken from "Happy Customers Matter of Honor among Japanese." Use the context provided to determine the meanings of the italicized words. Write a definition, synonym, or description of each of the italicized vocabulary items in the space provided.

1. _____

2. _____
3. _____

4. _____

5. _____

6. _____

7. _____

8. _____

9. _____
10. _____
11. _____

In Japan, good service is not considered a *luxury,* but a necessity. In most stores you will find more salespeople than you would in a comparable store in the United States. This larger sales *staff* allows the *proprietor* of the store to spend time greeting customers.

What is considered an unnecessary bother in the U.S., too much of a *fuss,* is considered fundamental in Japan. Owners of American shops might find giving personal attention to customers to be beneath them. But this is not considered *demeaning* in Japan. On the contrary, personal attention is considered one of the necessary *ingredients* for business success. If a company provides good service, it hopes for customer loyalty during bad times. The hope is that customers would feel *treacherous* if they left a company with which they had a personal relationship.

Thus, for the business person, being polite is as necessary for poor customers as it is for more *upscale* customers. And the *courtesies* shown customers exist throughout Japan *on a national scale.* One hopes that this will not change with the introduction and *proliferation* of American-style stores.

Reading Selection 2

Satire

Before You Begin   1. T / F   Men have more power in society.

2. T / F   A briefcase is the same as a purse.

3. T / F   Clothing is an important aspect of men's position in society.

Satire is a style of writing that pretends to be serious in order to demonstrate the humor of a particular situation. Read the following article to determine what the author is satirizing.

You may want to do the Vocabulary from Context exercise on page 214 and the Dictionary Study exercise on page 215 before you begin reading.

Pockety Women Unite?

Jane Myers

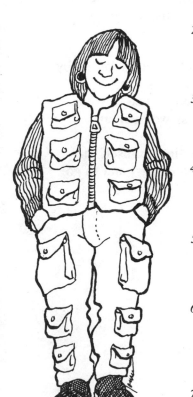

1   Pockets are what women need more of. The women's movement in the past decade has made giant strides in achieving greater social justice for females, but there's a great deal of work yet to be done. And it can't be done without pockets.

2   It has been commonly thought that men get the best jobs and make the most money and don't have to wash the dinner dishes simply because they're men, that cultural traditions and social conditioning have worked together to give them a special place in the world order.

3   While there is undoubtedly some truth to this, the fact remains that no one has investigated the role that pockets have played in preventing women from attaining the social status and rights that could and should be theirs.

4   Consider your average successful executive. How many pockets does he wear to work? Two in the sides of his trousers, two in the back, one on the front of his shirt, three on his suit coat, and one on the inside of the suit coat. Total: nine.

5   Consider your average woman dressed for office work. If she is wearing a dress or skirt and blouse, she is probably wearing zero pockets, or one or two at the most. The pantsuit, that supposedly liberating outfit, is usually equally pocketless.

6   Now, while it is always dangerous to generalize, it seems quite safe to say that, on the whole, the men of the world, at any given time, are carrying about a much greater number of pockets than are the women of the world. And it is also quite clear that, on the whole, the men enjoy more power, prestige, and wealth than women do.

7   Everything seems to point to a positive correlation between pockets, power, prestige, and wealth. Can this be?

Adapted from "Pockety Women Unite?" by Jane Myers, Staff Reporter, *Ann Arbor News*.

8   An examination of the function of the pocket seems necessary. Pockets are for carrying money, credit cards, identification (including access to those prestigious clubs where people presumably sit around sharing powerful secrets about how to run the world), important messages, pens, keys, combs, and impressive-looking handkerchiefs.

9   All the equipment essential to running the world. And held close to the body. Easily availablle. Neatly classified. Pen in the inside coat pocket. Keys in the back left trouser pocket. Efficiency. Order. Confidence.

10   What does a woman have to match this organization? A purse.

The most hurried examination will show that a purse, however large or important-looking, is no match for a suitful of pockets. If the woman carrying a purse is so lucky as to get an important phone number or market tip from the executive with whom she is lunching, can she write it down? Can she find her pen? Perhaps she can, but it will probably be buried under three old grocery lists, two combs, a checkbook, and a wad of Kleenex. All of which she will have to pile on top of the lunch table before she can find the pen.

11   Will she ever get another tip from this person of power? Not likely. Now she has lost any psychological advantage she may have had. He may have been impressed with her intelligent discussion of the current economic scene before she opened her handbag, but four minutes later, when she is still digging, like a busy little prairie dog, for that pen, he is no longer impressed.

12   He knows he could have whipped his pen in and out of his pocket and written fourteen important messages on the table napkin in the time she is still searching.

What can a pocketless woman do?

Two solutions seem apparent. The women can form a pocket lobby (Pocket Power?) and march on the New York garment district.*

13   Or, in the event that effort fails (and well it might, since it would, by necessity, have to be run by a bunch of pocketless women) an alternate approach remains.

14   Every man in the country for his next birthday finds himself the lucky recipient of one of those very stylish men's handbags, and to go with it, one of those no-pocket body shirts.

---

*A major center of fashion design in the United States

Comprehension

Exercise 1

Answer the following questions. Your teacher may want you to do this exercise orally, in writing, or by underlining appropriate parts of the text.

1. What are reasons commonly given to explain why men hold better positions in society than women? _____

   _____

2. How many pockets does the average successful male executive wear to work? _____

3. How many pockets does the average woman wear for office work? _____

4. According to the author, what is the correlation between power and pockets?

   _____

5. According to the author, why do people need pockets? _____

   _____

6. According to the author, what are the disadvantages of women's purses? _____

   _____

7. What two solutions does the author propose for women's pocket problems? _____

   _____

Exercise 2

In your opinion which of the following groups of people does the author find humorous (make fun of)? Be prepared to defend your choices with portions of the text.

1. _____ people who are well organized

2. _____ people who judge the efficiency of others on the basis of the way they dress

3. _____ people who feel that women can improve their situation in life by being more like men

4. _____ women

5. _____ businessmen

6. _____ people who make correlations between unrelated events

7. _____ people who describe human behavior by counting things

Discussion/Composition

1. Give examples of the ways in which clothing contributes to people's success.

2. Approaching the issue of the unequal position of women and men satirically, why do you think men have more power? For example, how do men's shoes contribute to their position in society?

Vocabulary from Context

Both the ideas and the vocabulary in this exercise are taken from "Pockety Women Unite?" Use the context provided to determine the meanings of the italicized words. Write a definition, synonym, or description of each of the italicized vocabulary items in the space provided.

1. _____   It is always dangerous to generalize; however, it seems obvious that, on the whole, men hold a higher position in society than women. Because of this *status*, men enjoy more power than women.

2. _____   People's *prestige* often depends on their title or profession. For example, in many countries, doctors and lawyers are greatly admired.

3. _____   There seems to be a *correlation* between one's sex and one's status in society. On the whole, men enjoy higher status than women.

4. _____   Most women's clothing is made without pockets. As a result, women are forced to carry their belongings in a *purse*.

5. _____   Despite the fact that women often make valuable contributions, they have not been able to *attain* the same social and economic status as men.

Dictionary Study

Many words have more than one meaning. When you use the dictionary to discover the meaning of an unfamiliar word, you need to use the context to determine which definition is appropriate. Use the portions of the dictionary provided to select the best definition for each of the italicized words below.

1. As long as women insist on using purses, they will never be as organized as men. A purse, however large or important-looking, is no *match* for a suitful of pockets.

2. If a woman with a purse is lucky enough to get a business *tip* from the executive with whom she is lunching, she will not be able to find a pen with which to write it down.

3. Women should become *lobbyists* and try to influence the garment industry.

lob·by (lŏb′i), *n.* [*pl.* LOBBIES (-iz)], [ML. *lobium, lobia;* see LODGE], 1. a hall or large anteroom; waiting room or vestibule, as of an apartment house, hotel, theater, etc. 2. a large hall adjacent to the assembly hall of a legislature and open to the public. 3. a group of lobbyists representing the same special interest: as, a cotton *lobby.* *v.i.* [LOBBIED (-id), LOBBYING], to act as a lobbyist. *v.t.* to get or try to get legislators to vote for (a measure) by acting as a lobbyist (often with *through*).
lob·by·ism (lŏb′i-iz′m), *n.* the practice of lobbying.
lob·by·ist (lŏb′i-ist), *n.* [*lobby* + *-ist*], a person who tries to get legislators to introduce or vote for measures favorable to a special interest that he represents.

match (mach), *n.* [ME. *macche;* OFr. *mesche* (Fr. *mèche*), wick of a candle, match; prob. < L. *myxa,* wick of a candle; Gr. *myxa,* nozzle of a lamp], 1. originally, a wick or cord prepared to burn at a uniform rate, used for firing guns or explosives. 2. a slender piece of wood, cardboard, waxed cord, etc. tipped with a composition that catches fire by friction, sometimes only on a specially prepared surface. 3. [Obs.], a slip of paper, splinter of wood, etc. dipped in sulfur so that it can be ignited with a spark, for lighting candles, lamps, etc.
match (mach), *n.* [ME. *macche;* AS. *gemæcca,* one suited to another, mate < base of *macian,* to make, form (see MAKE, *v. & n.*); sense development: what is put to-gether—what is suitable (for putting together), etc.], 1. any person or thing equal or similar to another in some way; specifically, *a)* a person, group, or thing able to cope with or oppose another as an equal in power, size, etc.; peer. *b)* a counterpart or facsimile. *c)* either of two corresponding things or persons; one of a pair. 2. two or more persons or things that go together in appearance, size, or other quality; pair: as, her purse and shoes were a good *match.* 3. a contest or game involving two or more contestants. 4. *a)* an agreement to marry or mate. *b)* a marriage or mating: as, she made a good *match.* 5. a person regarded as a suitable or possible mate. *v.t.* 1. to join in marriage; get a (suitable) match for; mate. 2. *a)* formerly, to meet as an antagonist; hence, *b)* to compete with suc-cessfully. 3. to put in opposition (*with*); pit (*against*). 4. to be equal, similar, suitable, or corresponding to in some way: as, his looks *match* his character. 5. to make, show, produce, or get a competitor, counterpart, or equivalent to: as, I want to *match* this cloth. 6. to suit or fit (one thing) to another. 7. to fit (things) together; make similar or corresponding. 8. to com-pare. 9. *a)* to flip or reveal (coins) as a form of gam-bling or to decide something contested, the winner being determined by the combination of faces thus exposed. *b)* to match coins with (another person), usually betting that the same faces will be exposed. *v.i.* 1. to get married; mate. 2. to be equal, similar, suitable, or corresponding in some way.

tip (tip), *n.* [ME. *tippe;* prob. < MD. or MLG. *tip,* point, top; akin to G. *zipf-* in *zipfel,* an end, tip; prob. IE. base *dā(i)-,* to part, divide up (cf. TIDE, TIME)], 1. the pointed, tapering, or rounded end or top of something long and slim. 2. something attached to the end, as a cap, ferrule, etc. 3. a top or apex, as of a mountain. *v.t.* [TIPPED (tipt), TIPPING], 1. to make a tip on. 2. to cover the tip or tips of (*with* something). 3. to serve as the tip of.
tip (tip), *v.t.* [TIPPED (tipt), TIPPING], [prob. < ME. *tippe,* a tip, or its base], 1. to strike lightly and sharply; tap. 2. to give a small present of money to (a waiter, porter, etc.) for some service. 3. [Colloq.], to give secret information to in an attempt to be helpful: often with *off.* 4. in *baseball,* etc., to hit (the ball) a glancing blow. *v.i.* to give a tip or tips. *n.* 1. a light, sharp blow; tap. 2. a piece of information given secretly or confidentially in an attempt to be helpful: as, he gave me a *tip* on the race. 3. a sugges-tion, hint, warning, etc. 4. a small present of money given to a waiter, porter, etc. for services; gratuity.
tip (tip), *v.t.* [TIPPED (tipt), TIPPING], [ME. *tipen* (short vowel prob. < p.t. *tipte*); Northern word, prob. < ON.], 1. to overturn or upset: often with *over.* 2. to cause to tilt or slant. 3. to raise slightly or touch the brim of (one's hat) in salutation. *v.i.* 1. to tilt or slant. 2. to overturn or topple: often with *over.* *n.* a tipping or being tipped; tilt; slant.

From *Webster's New World Dictionary,* College Edition (World Publishing Company).

Reading Selection 3
Poetry

In Units 1, 3, and 7 you read poems to determine the main ideas, to discover what the poems were about. But poetry can be enjoyed on many levels, and read in many ways. You can read a poem once, simply to enjoy the language or the main message of the poem. Or you can decide to experience a poem more fully, by reading it several times for different purposes or meanings. The two poems that follow describe this process of intense discovery.

How to Eat a Poem

1   Don't be polite.
    Bite in.
    Pick it up with your fingers and lick the juice that
       may run down your chin.
5   It is ready and ripe now, whenever you are.

6   You do not need a knife or fork or spoon
    or plate or napkin or tablecloth.

8   For there is no core
    or stem
    or rind
    or pit
12 or seed
    or skin
    to throw away.

Eve Merriam

Unfolding Bud

1   One is amazed
    By a water-lily bud
    Unfolding
    With each passing day,
    Taking on a richer color
6   And new dimensions.

"How to Eat a Poem" by Eve Merriam, from *Jamboree: Rhymes for All Times* (New York: Dell); "Unfolding Bud" by Naoshi Koriyama, *Christian Science Monitor.*

7   One is not amazed,
    At a first glance,
    By a poem,
    Which is as tight-closed
11 As a tiny bud.

12 Yet one is surprised
    To see the poem
    Gradually unfolding,
15 Revealing its rich inner self,
    As one reads it
    Again
18 And over again.

Naoshi Koriyama

Comprehension

Answer the following questions. Your teacher may want you to discuss these questions as a class, in small groups, or in pairs.

1. Eve Merriam, the author of "How to Eat a Poem," compares the process of reading a poem to eating a fruit. What does she mean?

   a. In what ways is reading a poem like eating?

   b. What does the author mean when she advises us, "Don't be polite"?

   c. Why don't you need a plate or a napkin in order to eat a poem?

   d. Why do you think the author chose eating a fruit instead of a piece of bread for her analogy?

   e. The author gives us a model for reading poetry. Are there other things that you read in this way?

2. Naoshi Koriyama compares poetry to an unfolding bud. What does she mean?

   a. In what ways is a poem like a water-lily bud?

   b. According to Koriyama, what is a difference between our reaction to a water-lily and to a poem?

   c. What are the similarities and differences in these two poets' views of reading poetry?

The three selections that follow will give you an opportunity to eat poems, to watch them unfold. Read each poem once. Then work with your classmates to answer the questions that follow. Because so much of poetry depends upon individual response, there is no single correct answer to many of these questions. Your teacher may want you to discuss these questions as a class, in small groups, or in pairs.

This is Just to Say

1 I have eaten
   the plums
   that were in
   the icebox

5 and which
   you were probably
   saving
   for breakfast

9 Forgive me
   they were delicious
   so sweet
   and so cold.

William Carlos Williams

Comprehension

1. Some people think this is a wonderful poem, others don't think it is a poem at all. What do you think accounts for these different reactions?

2. The poem seems to be in the form of a note. Why do you think it was written? Did this note need to be written? Do you think the writer believes that the reader will be angry with him? Is this really an apology?

3. What do you think is the relationship between the writer and the addressee of the note? Do they live together? Are they close? What is their relationship?

4. Why do you think this poem/note was written?

5. Do you think this is a poem? If you had found it in your kitchen, would you experience it as a poem?

"This is Just to Say" by William Carlos Williams, from *Collected Poems, Volume I: 1909–1939* (New York: New Directions); "in Just-" by e.e. cummings, from *Tulips & Chimneys* (New York: Liveright); "Spring and Fall: To a Young Child" by Gerald Manley Hopkins, from *Poetry: From Statement to Meaning* (New York: Oxford University Press).

The poet e. e. cummings is noted for the unusual placement of words on the page and his lack of capital letters. Your teacher will read the following poem aloud to show the effects achieved by this unusual spacing.

_____

in Just-

1   in Just-
     spring   when the world is mud-
     luscious the little
     lame balloonman

5   whistles far and wee

     and eddieandbill come
     running from marbles and
     piracies and it's
     spring

10   when the world is puddle-wonderful

     the queer
     old balloonman whistles
     far and wee
     and bettyandisbel come dancing

15   from hop-scotch and jump-rope and

     it's
     spring
     and
       the

20   goat-footed

     balloonMan whistles
     far
     and
     wee

              e. e. cummings

Comprehension

1. This poem describes spring. What aspects of springtime does it mention?

2. What are the names of the children?

3. Cummings is also noted for inventing words. In this poem, the words *mud-luscious* and *puddle-wonderful* have been created by combining common English words. What do you think each of these means? Do you find cummings's unusual spacing and invented words effective?

4. What is e. e. cummings's attitude toward spring? Toward the balloonman? What is the spirit or mood of the poem? Is it happy? sad? threatening? Use evidence from the poem to support your position.

5. Both Williams and cummings use the word *just*. Is this *just* spring; was Williams's poem *just* an apology?

Spring and Fall:
To a Young Child

1   Margaret, are you grieving
    Over Goldengrove unleaving?
    Leaves, like the things of man, you
    With your fresh thoughts care for, can you?
5   Ah! as the heart grows older
    It will come to such sights colder
    By and by, nor spare a sigh
    Though worlds of wanwood leafmeal lie;
    And yet you will weep and know why.
10 Now no matter child, the name:
    Sorrow's springs are the same.
    Nor mouth had, no nor mind, expressed
    What heart heard of, ghost guessed:
    It is the blight man was born for,
15 It is Margaret you mourn for.

Gerard Manley Hopkins

Comprehension

1. This poem begins with a question: Why is Margaret grieving? The poem unfolds in a way that answers this question. To discover the answer, first we must untangle some unusual syntax.

   a. Rearrange the words in lines 3 and 4 so that the word order is closer to standard English.

   _____

   _____

   b. Change lines 12 and 13 so that they too are closer to standard English. In this case you may want to change or add words, for example *neither* usually precedes *nor*.

   _____

   _____

2. In this poem, Hopkins has invented a number of new words. These have been created by combining words or word forms. What do you think is the meaning of each of the following? Feel free to use your dictionary to look up the meanings of parts of these compound words.

   Goldengrove (line 2) _____

   unleaving (line 2) _____

   wanwood (line 8) _____

   leafmeal (line 8) _____

3. Now that you have looked more closely at the language of the poem, read it through once again. Why is Margaret grieving?

Reading Selection 4

Short Story

Before You Begin   There is a saying in English, "Be careful, or your wishes will come true."

1. What does this mean?

2. Do you believe there is wisdom in this saying?

Alan Austen is a troubled young man. Luckily, he finds a strange old man who can help him. There's just one problem. . . .

Read the selection, then do the exercises that follow. Your teacher may want to do Vocabulary from Context exercise 1 on page 226 before you begin reading.

The Chaser

John Collier

1   Alan Austen, as nervous as a kitten, went up certain dark and creaky stairs in the neighborhood of Pell Street, and peered about for a long time on the dim hallway before he found the name he wanted written obscurely on one of the doors.

2   He pushed open this door, as he had been told to do, and found himself in a tiny room, which contained no furniture but a plain kitchen table, a rocking-chair, and an ordinary chair. On one of the dirty buff-coloured walls were a couple of shelves, containing in all perhaps a dozen bottles and jars.

3   An old man sat in the rocking-chair, reading a newspaper. Alan, without a word, handed him the card he had been given. "Sit down, Mr. Austen," said the old man very politely. "I am glad to make your acquaintance."

4   "Is it true," asked Alan, "that you have a certain mixture that has-er-quite extraordinary effects?"

"My dear sir," replied the old man, "my stock in trade is not very large—I don't deal in laxatives and teething mixtures—but such as it is, it is varied. I think nothing I sell has effects which could be precisely described as ordinary."

"Well, the fact is . . ." began Alan.

5   "Here, for example," interrupted the old man, reaching for a bottle from the shelf. "Here is a liquid as colourless as water, almost tasteless, quite imperceptible in coffee, wine, or any other beverage. It is also quite imperceptible to any known method of autopsy."*

"The Chaser" by John Collier. Originally published in the *New Yorker.*
*autopsy: the examination of a dead body to determine the cause of death

6   "Do you mean it is a poison?" cried Alan, very much horrified.

"Call it a glove-cleaner if you like," said the old man indifferently. "Maybe it will clean gloves. I have never tried. One might call it a life-cleaner. Lives need cleaning sometimes."

7   "I want nothing of that sort," said Alan.

"Probably it is just as well," said the old man. "Do you know the price of this? For one teaspoonful, which is sufficient, I ask five thousand dollars. Never less. Not a penny less."

"I hope all your mixtures are not as expensive," said Alan apprehensively.

8   "Oh dear, no," said the old man. "It would be no good charging that sort of price for a love potion, for example. Young people who need a love potion very seldom have five thousand dollars. Otherwise they would not need a love potion."

"I am glad to hear that," said Alan.

9   "I look at it like this," said the old man. "Please a customer with one article, and he will come back when he needs another. Even if it is more costly. He will save up for it, if necessary."

"So," said Alan, "you really do sell love potions?"

10   "If I did not sell love potions," said the old man, reaching for another bottle, "I should not have mentioned the other matter to you. It is only when one is in a position to oblige that one can afford to be so confidential."

"And these potions," said Alan. "They are not just-just-er-"

11   "Oh, no," said the old man. "Their effects are permanent, and extend far beyond the mere casual impulse. But they include it. Oh, yes, they include it. Bountifully, insistently. Everlastingly."

"Dear me!" said Alan, attempting a look of scientific detachment. "How *very* interesting!"

12   "But consider the spiritual side," said the old man.

"I do, indeed," said Alan.

"For indifference," said the old man, "they substitute devotion. For scorn, adoration. Give one tiny measure of this to the young lady—its flavour is imperceptible in orange juice, soup, or cocktails—and however gay and giddy she is, she will change altogether. She will want nothing but solitude and you."

13   "I can hardly believe it," said Alan. "She is so fond of parties."

"She will not like them *any* more," said the old man. "She will be afraid of the pretty girls you may meet."

"She will actually be jealous?" cried Alan in a rapture. "Of me?"

"Yes, she will want to be everything to you."

"She is, already. Only she doesn't care about it."

14   "She will, when she has taken this. She will care intensely. You will be her sole interest in life."

"Wonderful!" cried Alan.

"She will want to know *all* you do," said the old man. "*All* that has happened to you during the day. *Every* word of it. She will want to know what you are thinking about, why you smile suddenly, why you are looking sad."

"That is love!" cried Alan.

15   "Yes," said the old man. "How carefully she will look after you! She will never allow you to be tired, to sit in a draught, to neglect your food. If you are an hour late, she will be terrified. She will think you are killed, or that some siren has caught you."

"I can hardly imagine Diana like that!" cried Alan, overwhelmed with joy.

16   "You will not have to use your imagination," said the old man. "And, by the way, since there are always sirens, if by any chance you *should,* later on, slip a little, you need not worry. She will forgive you, in the end. She will be terribly hurt, of course, but she will forgive you—in the end."

"That will not happen," said Alan fervently.

17   "Of course not," said the old man. "But, if it did, you need not worry. She would never divorce you. Oh, no! And, of course, she will never give you the least, the very least, grounds for—uneasiness."

"And how much," said Alan, "is this wonderful mixture?"

"It is not as dear," said the old man, "as the glove-cleaner, or life-cleaner, as I sometimes call it. No. That is five thousand dollars, never a penny less. One has to be older than you are, to indulge in that sort of thing. One has to save up for it."

18   "But the love potion?" said Alan.

"Oh, that," said the old man, opening the drawer in the kitchen table, and taking out a tiny, rather dirty-looking phial. "That is just a dollar."

"I can't tell you how grateful I am," said Alan, watching him fill it.

19   "I like to oblige," said the old man. "Then customers come back, later in life, when they are better off, and want more expensive things. Here you are. You will find it very effective."

"Thank you again," said Alan. "Good-bye."

"*Au revoir,*"* said the old man.

Comprehension

Answer the following questions. Your teacher may want you to do this exercise orally, in writing, or by underlining appropriate parts of the text. True/False items are indicated by a T / F preceding a statement.

1. T / F   Alan Austen accidentally discovered the old man's room.

2. T / F   The old man sold a large number of mixtures commonly found in pharmacies.

3. What did the old man call the $5,000 mixture? _____

4. What was the $5,000 mixture? _____

5. T / F   Alan Austen loved Diana more than she loved him.

---

au revoir: (French) goodbye; until we meet again

6. How would you describe Diana? _____

_____

7. According to the old man, what effect would the love potion have on Diana? _____

_____

8. T / F   Alan felt that he could never love anyone but Diana.

9. A chaser is a drink taken to cover the unpleasant taste of a preceding drink. What is the first drink in this story? What is its unpleasant "taste"? What is the chaser?

_____

10. How could the old man make enough money to live if he sold his love potion for only one dollar?

_____

_____

Drawing Inferences

In part, what makes "The Chaser" an interesting story is the fact that the author and the reader share a secret: they know something that Alan Austen doesn't know. Each reader will discover the meaning of the title, "The Chaser," at a different moment in the story. However, even if you finished the story before you realized the real meaning of the old man's words, you were probably able to go back and find double meanings in many of the passages in the story.

The following quotations are taken from "The Chaser." Read each one, then give two possible meanings: (1) the meaning Alan Austen understands, and (2) what you consider to be the real meaning. The number in parentheses indicates the paragraph where the quotation can be found. Your teacher may want you to do this exercise orally or in writing.

1. (14) "She will want to know *all* you do," said the old man. "*All* that has happened to you during the day. *Every* word of it. She will want to know what you are thinking about, why you smile suddenly, why you are looking sad."

2. (17) ". . . you need not worry. She would never divorce you."

3. (19) "I like to oblige," said the old man. "Then customers come back, later in life, when they are better off, and want more expensive things."

4. (19) "Thank you again," said Alan. "Goodbye."
    "*Au revoir,*" said the old man.

Discussion/Composition

1. This short story suggests that love potions require an antidote. By this logic, are there other desires that, if fulfilled, require an antidote? What are some of these?

2. Write a scene between Alan and the old man or Alan and Diana that takes place in the future.

Vocabulary from Context

Exercise 1

Use the context provided to determine the meanings of the italicized words. Write a definition, synonym, or description of each of the italicized vocabulary items in the space provided.

1. _____ The doctor said that if a person ate even one leaf of the hemlock plant, he would die, because the plant is a deadly *poison.*

2. _____ The murderer had developed a poison which could not be tasted or smelled when mixed with food. Because it was *imperceptible,* he was able to murder a number of people without being caught.

3. _____ "When making this mixture," the man said, "you don't need two teaspoons of salt, because one teaspoon is *sufficient.*"

4. _____ "Since you are my best friend, and because I can trust you, I know I can be *confidential* with you. Listen carefully, because what I am going to tell you is a secret," said Henry.

5. _____ "I am able to *oblige* you sir; I can give you the item you wanted so badly."

6. _____ There are times when one wants to be surrounded by people, and there are times when one needs *solitude.*

7. _____ The man was so *jealous* of his wife that he would not allow her to talk to other men.

Exercise 2

This exercise is designed to give you additional clues to determine the meanings of unfamiliar vocabulary items in context. In the paragraph indicated by the number in parentheses, find the word that best fits the meaning given. Your teacher may want to read these aloud as you quickly scan the paragraph to find the answer.

1. (1)   Which word means *poorly lighted; dark?*

2. (4)   Which word means *objects for sale; items kept for sale?*

3. (7)   Which word means *worriedly; with alarm or concern?*

4. (10) Which word means *to perform a service; to please or help someone?*

5. (16) Which word means *women who attract, seduce, lure men?*

6. (17) Which word means *reason; basis; foundation?*

Exercise 3

This exercise should be done after you have finished reading "The Chaser." The exercise is designed to determine how well you have been able to use context clues to guess the meaning of unfamiliar vocabulary. Give a definition, synonym, or description of each of the words or phrases below. The number in parentheses indicates the paragraph in which the word can be found. Your teacher may want you to do these orally or in writing.

1. (1)   peered _____

2. (8)   potion _____

3. (16) slip a little _____

4. (17) dear _____

5. (19) better off _____

11

Nonprose Reading

Road Map

If you travel by car in an English-speaking country, you will need to read road maps in English. This exercise is designed to give you practice in many aspects of map reading.*

Before You Begin   Reflect on road travel in your country:

1. If you are traveling to an unfamiliar area, how do you find out about the route? Do you ever rely on road maps?

2. Why do you think road maps are important to travel in the United States?

Introduction

Exercise 1

Examine the parts of the map you will need to use in order to answer the questions below.

1. On page 232 is a section of a *map* of Tennessee (Tenn.) and Kentucky (Ky.), two states of the United States.

   Find the Kentucky-Tennessee border.

2. On page 231 is a section of the *Tennessee City and Town Index*. This lists the larger cities and towns in Tennessee with coordinates to help you find the names of these cities and towns on the map.

   a. What are the coordinates of Clarksville, Tenn.? _____

   b. Locate Clarksville on the map on page 232.

_____

*For an explanation of nonprose reading, see Unit 1.

3. On page 233 is an *inset* (a larger, more detailed reproduction) of Nashville, Tenn. You will need to use the inset of Nashville to find information about major roads and landmarks within Nashville.

    Riverside Hospital (on the north side of the city) is located near the intersection of which two streets?

    _____

4. On page 234 is a *legend,* that is, a list of symbols to help you interpret the map on page 232. On the legend is the *distance scale,* which tells you the relationship of both miles and kilometers to inches on the map. Examine the legend carefully to see if you have any questions.

    a. Using the distance scale, estimate the distance in both miles and kilometers from Bowling Green, Ky. (coordinates: J-13), to the Ky.-Tenn. border.

       _____

    b. What is the difference between the two roads, route 31W and route 65, that connect Bowling Green and Nashville?

       _____

       _____

5. Finally, on page 234 you will find a *driving distance map.* This map will tell you the exact distance in miles between many of the large cities in Kentucky, Tennessee, and surrounding states. It also estimates the driving time from city to city.

    What is the distance between Bowling Green, Ky., and Nashville, Tenn.? _____

Exercise 2

This exercise is designed to give you practice in deciding where to look for specific pieces of information. Below are questions you might ask if you needed to find information from a map. Read each question, then decide if you would look for the answer on the map itself, in the Tennessee City and Town Index, on the inset of Nashville, on the legend, or on the driving distance map. Put the appropriate letter in the blank provided.

   a. map
   b. city and town index
   c. inset
   d. legend
   e. driving distance map

Where should you look to find:

1. _____ the distance between Bowling Green, Ky., and Cincinnati, Ohio?

2. ____ the coordinates of McMinnville, Tenn.?

3. ____ the best route from Ashland City, Tenn., to Murfreesboro, Tenn.?

4. ____ the location in Nashville of the Country Music Hall of Fame?

5. ____ what the symbol **𝗫** means?

6. ____ how to get to Vanderbilt University in Nashville from Interstate highway 65?

Map Reading

Use all the information provided on pages 231–34 to do the exercises that follow.

Exercise 1

Indicate if each statement below is true (T) or false (F). Work as quickly as you can.

1. ____ There is a direct route going northwest between Nashville and Clarksville, Tenn.

2. ____ Franklin, located north of Nashville, is in Tennessee.

3. ____ Cincinnati, Ohio, is about 300 miles driving distance from Nashville, Tenn.

4. ____ In southwest Nashville, route 70S will take you directly to the Tennessee Botanical Gardens and Fine Arts Center.

5. ____ There is a passenger service airport near Nashville, Tenn.

6. ____ Going toward downtown Nashville from the southeast, you can get onto route 40 from route 24.

7. ____ Northwest of Nashville, a state highway connects Ashland City and Clarksville.

8. ____ Bellwood, Tenn., is west of Bellsburg, Tenn.

9. ____ Ashland City, Tenn., northwest of Nashville, is less than 15 miles/24 kilometers from Bellsburg.

10. ____ Nashville is the capital of Tennessee.

11. ____ Coming into downtown Nashville from the north on route 431 (Whites Creek Pike), you can exit directly onto route 65.

Exercise 2

If you were to take a trip by car through Kentucky and Tennessee, you would have to solve problems such as the ones posed by the questions in this exercise. Answer each question as completely as possible. Often there is more than one correct answer. Your teacher may ask you to do these orally or in writing.

1. Could you leave Chattanooga, Tenn., at 8:00 A.M. and get to Bowling Green, Ky., in time for a 12:00 lunch? How fast would you have to drive?

   _____

2. Which route would you take going northeast from Bowling Green to Mammoth Cave National Park?

   _____

   Can you spend the night at Mammoth Cave National Park? _____

3. Which route would you take from McMinnville, Tenn., to Nashville, Tenn., if you wanted to see the Edgar Evins State Park (northeast of McMinnville) and Cedars of Lebanon State Park (north of Murfreesboro)?

   _____

TENNESSEE CITY AND TOWN INDEX

Acton....R-7	Auburntown....O-15	Buckeye....M-21	Centertown....O-15	Collierville....R-3
Adair....O-6	Austin Sprs....M-27	Bucksnort....O-10	Centerville....O-10	Collinwood....Q-9
Adams....L-12	Avoca....L-28	Buena Vista....N-8	Chalk Level....M-25	Columbia....P-12
Adamsville....Q-7	Bailey....R-3	Buffalo....O-9	Chapel Hill....P-13	Comfort....R-16
Aetna....P-10	Baileyton....M-26	Buffalo Springs....M-23	Chapmansboro....M-12	Como....M-7
Alamo....O-5	Bairds Mill....N-14	Buffalo Valley....N-16	Charleys Branch....N-21	Conasauga....R-20
Alcoa....O-22	Bakerville....N-9	Buladeen....L-28	Charleston....Q-19	Concord....O-13
Alexandria....N-14	Bakewell....Q-18	Bulls Gap....M-25	Charlotte....N-11	Cookeville....N-17
Algood....N-17	Banner Hill....N-27	Bumpus Mill....L-9	Chattanooga....R-42	Coopertown....M-12
Allardt....M-19	Banner Springs....M-19	Burke....O-18	Cherry....O-3	Copperhill....R-20
Allens....P-5	Barefield....O-14	Burlison....P-3	Cherry Valley....N-15	Corbin Hill....N-20
Allisona....O-13	Bargerton....O-7	Burns....N-11	Chesney....M-23	Cordova....Q-3
Allons....M-17	Barkertown....Q-17	Burrville....M-19	Chesterfield....P-8	Cornersville....Q-14
Allred....M-18	Barnesville....Q-11	Burwood....O-12	Chestnut Mound....N-16	Corryton....N-23
Almaville....O-13	Barren Plains....L-12	Butler....M-28	Chewalla....R-6	Cosby....O-24
Alnwick....O-22	Bartlett....Q-3	Bybee....N-24	Chic....N-3	Cottage Grove....M-7
Alpha....N-24	Bath Springs....Q-8	Byrdstown....L-18	Christiana....O-14	Cottontown....M-13
Alpine....L-18	Baxter....N-16	Cainsville....N-15	Christmasville....N-7	Cottonwood Grove....M-4
Altamont....Q-16	Beacon....P-8	Calderwood....P-22	Chuckey....M-26	Coulterville....P-18
Alto....P-15	Beans Creek....R-15	Calhoun....Q-19	Church Hill....L-26	Counce....R-8
Anderson....R-15	Bean Station....M-24	Camden....N-8	Churchton....N-5	Cove Creek
Andersonville....N-23	Beardstown....O-9	Camelot....L-25	Clairfield....L-22	Cascades....O-23
Annadel....N-19	Bear Spring....L-10	Campbellsville....Q-11	Clarkrange....N-18	Covington....P-3
Apison....R-19	Beech Bluff....P-6	Camp Creek....N-26	Clarksburg....O-7	Cowan....R-15
Archer....Q-13	Beechgrove....P-15	Caney Branch....N-25	Clarksville....L-10	Crab Orchard....O-19
Archville....R-20	Beersheba Sprgs....P-16	Caneyspring....P-13	Clayton....L-5	Crabtree....M-27
Ardmore....R-12	Belfast....Q-13	Capleville....R-3	Cleveland....R-19	Craggie Hope....N-11
Arlington....Q-3	Bell Buckle....P-14	Carlisle....M-9	Clevenger....N-24	....
Armathwaite....M-19	Belle Mead....N-44	Carter....M-28	Clifton....Q-9	McMinnville....O-16
Arp....O-3	Belleville....Q-13	Carthage....M-16	Clifty....O-18	....
Arrington....O-13	Bells....O-5	Caryville....M-21	Clinton....N-21	Murfreesboro....O-14
Arthur....L-23	Bellsburg....M-11	Cash Point....R-12	Cloverport....Q-5	
Ashland City....M-12	Bell Town....N-11	Castalian Springs....M-14	Coalfield....N-20	
Ashport....O-3	Bellwood....M-15	Catlettsburg....O-23	Coalmont....Q-16	
Aspen Hill....R-12	Belvidere....R-15	Cavvia....O-8	Coble....O-10	
Athens....P-20	Benton....R-20	Cedar Creek....O-25	Coghill....Q-20	
Atoka....P-3	....	Cedar Grove....O-7	Coldwater....R-13	
Atwood....N-7	Buchanan....M-8	Cedar Hill....L-12	Colesburg....N-11	
		Celina....L-17	College Grove....O-13	

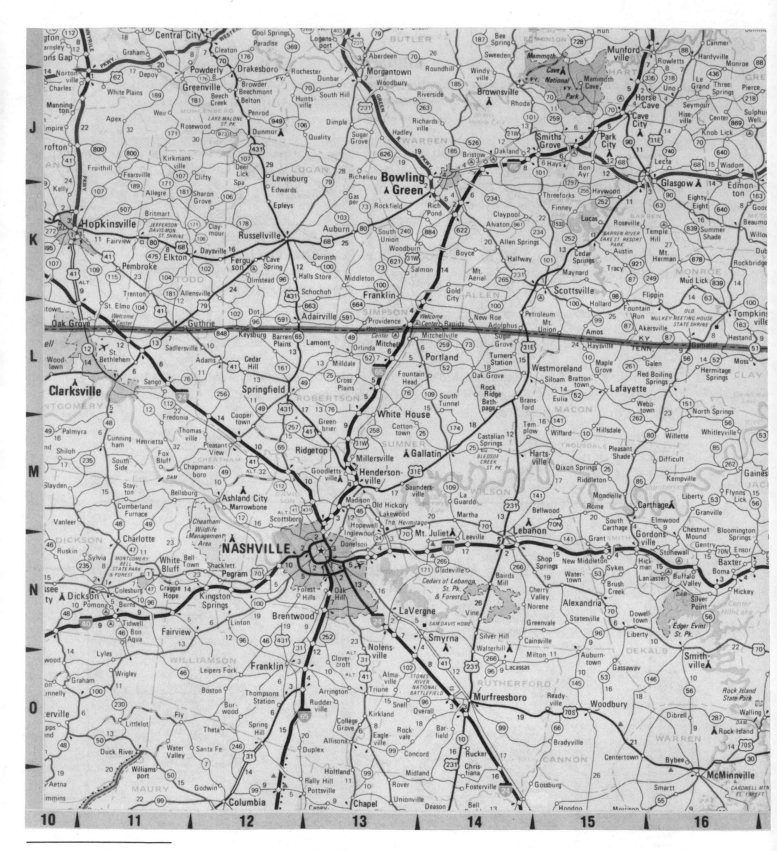

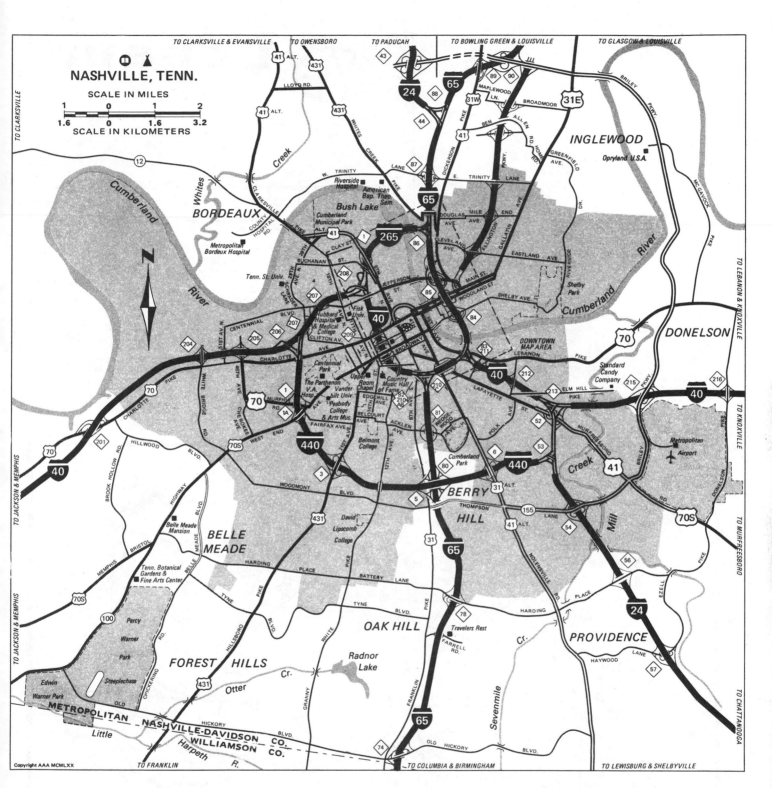

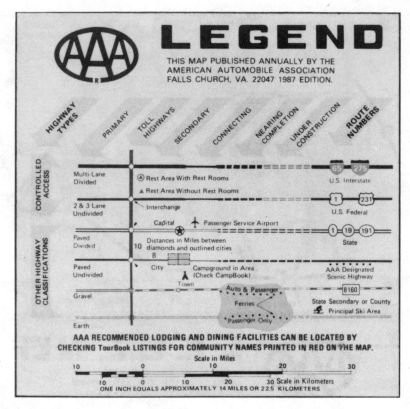

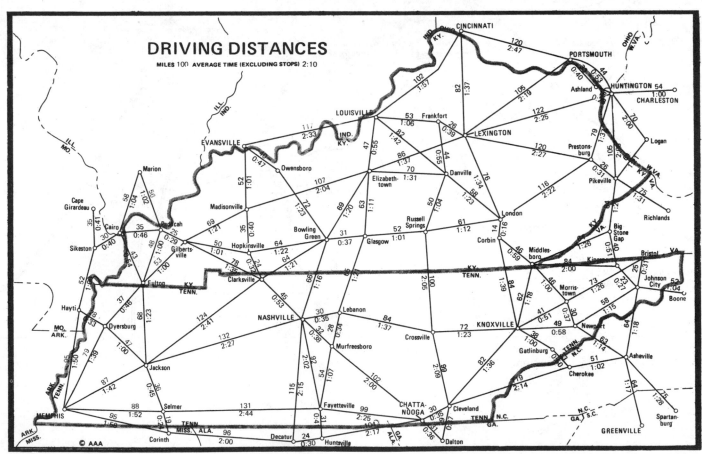

© AAA—Reproduced by permission.

Word Study

Context Clues

――――

Exercise 1

In the following exercise, do NOT try to learn the italicized words. Concentrate on developing your ability to guess the meaning of unfamiliar words using context clues. Read each sentence carefully, and write a definition, synonym, or description of the italicized word on the line provided.

1. _____   As he reached for the rock above him, his rope broke and he hung *precariously* by one hand as the rescuers ran toward him.

2. _____   The tired soldiers *trudged* through knee-deep mud for hours before they found a dry place to sleep.

3. _____   In the past, the world seemed to run in an orderly way. Now, however, everything seems to be in a state of *turmoil.*

4. _____   Monkeys are well known for their *grooming* habits; they spend hours carefully cleaning bits of dirt and straw from their coats.

5. _____   *Matrimony* doesn't seem to agree with Liz—she's been unhappy ever since she got married.

6. _____   Using a long, slender instrument called a *probe,* doctors are able to locate and remove pieces of metal from a patient's wounds.

7. _____   The following Monday, when the president *convened* the second meeting of the committee, we all sat down quietly and waited for him to begin.

8. _____   We think of plants in general as absorbing water and food; of animals as *ingesting* or "eating it."

9. _____   Robben is considered an *autocratic* administrator because he makes decisions without seeking the opinions of others.

10. _____   There is an element of word magic here: entomology and *limnology* sound more important than merely insect biology and fresh water biology.

Exercise 2

This exercise is designed to give you practice using context clues from a passage. Use your general knowledge along with information from the entire text below to write a definition, synonym, or description of the italicized word on the line provided. Read through the entire passage before making a decision. Note that some of the words appear more than once; by the end of the passage you should have a good idea of their meaning. Do not worry if your definition is not exact; a general idea of the meaning will often allow you to understand the meaning of a written text.

Major Personality Study Finds That Traits Are Mostly Inherited

Daniel Goleman

The *genetic* makeup of a child is a stronger influence on personality than child *rearing,* according to the first study to examine identical twins *reared* in different families. The *findings shatter* a widespread belief among experts and laypeople alike in the *primacy* of family influence and are sure to lead to fierce debate.

The *findings* are the first major results to emerge from a longterm project at the University of Minnesota in which more than 350 pairs of twins have gone through six days of extensive testing that has included analysis of blood, brain waves, intelligence, and allergies.

For most of the traits measured, more than half the variation was found to be due to *heredity,* leaving less than half determined by the influence of parents, home environment and other experiences in life.

The Minnesota *findings* stand in sharp contradiction to standard wisdom on nature vs. *nurture* in forming adult personality. Virtually all major theories since Freud have given far more importance to environment, or *nurture,* than to *genes* or nature.

genetic/genes _____

rearing/reared _____

findings _____

shatter _____

primacy _____

heredity _____

nurture _____

From the *New York Times.*

Sentence Study

Restatement and Inference

This exercise is similar to the one found in Unit 7.* Each sentence below is followed by five statements. The statements are of four types:
1. Some of the statements are restatements of the original sentence. They give the same information in a different way.
2. Some of the statements are inferences (conclusions) that can be drawn from the information given in the original sentence.
3. Some of the statements are false based on the information given.
4. Some of the statements cannot be judged true or false based on the information given in the original sentence.

Put a check (✓) next to all restatements and inferences (types 1 and 2). Note: do not check a statement that is true of itself but cannot be inferred from the sentence given.

1. A favorite definition of joking has long been the ability to find similarity between dissimilar things—that is, hidden similarities.

    _____ a. Joking is the ability to find similarity in dissimilar things.

    _____ b. It takes a long time to develop the ability to tell good jokes.

    _____ c. This definition of joking is a new one in literary theory.

    _____ d. Many people define joking as the ability to find similarity in dissimilar things.

    _____ e. The author agrees with this definition.

2. Since the Romantic period, most modern theory has dealt with the peculiar act of the poet rather than his product or its effect on the audience.

    _____ a. Most modern theory does not deal with the poem itself or its effect on the audience.

    _____ b. Most modern theory of poetry deals with the act of the poet.

    _____ c. Since the Romantic period, literary theory has dealt with the effect of poetry on the reader.

    _____ d. The author believes that literary theory should only deal with the peculiar act of the poet.

    _____ e. Modern theory is considered to begin at the Romantic period.

---

*For an introduction to sentence study, see Unit 1.

3. Although housewives still make up the majority of volunteer groups, male participation is reported on the rise nationwide as traditional distinctions between men's work and women's work begin to fade.

_____ a. As traditional societal roles change, more men are becoming members of volunteer groups.

_____ b. Most members of volunteer groups are women.

_____ c. In the past, volunteer work was done mainly by women.

_____ d. Male participation in volunteer groups is increasing in all cities.

_____ e. The author believes there is a relationship between the changing societal roles and the increasing willingness of men to do work previously done by females.

4. The overall picture of this very early settled Peruvian population is that of a simple, peaceful people living in a small cultivable oasis by the sea, fishing, raising a few food crops, living in small, simple, nonmasonry houses and making the objects necessary for their economic and household life, with slight attention to art.

_____ a. This early Peruvian population had all the basic necessities of life available to it.

_____ b. We can assume that art only exists in very advanced societies.

_____ c. This society moved many times during the year.

_____ d. Because the people worked so hard they had no time for art.

_____ e. The author believes this society provides nothing of interest for historians.

5. Only a small number of scholars can be named who have entered at all deeply into the problems of jokes.

_____ a. Only a few scholars have studied jokes.

_____ b. The area of jokes is so complex that only a small number of people have been able to study it.

_____ c. Few scholars have studied the problem of jokes at all deeply.

_____ d. The author cannot remember the names of scholars who have studied jokes.

_____ e. It is not possible to name all those who have studied jokes at all deeply.

6. There is a question about the extent to which any one of us can be free of a prejudiced view in the area of religion.

_____ a. Probably everyone is prejudiced in his views on religion.

_____ b. Any one of us can be free of prejudice in the area of religion.

_____ c. To some extent we can never be free of prejudice in the area of religion.

_____ d. A prejudiced view in the area of religion is undesirable.

_____ e. Because we can't be free of prejudice in the area of religion, we should not practice a religion.

7. Although the November election may significantly change the face of the county Board of Commissioners, the group will still have to confront the same old problems.

_____ a. The November election may give the Board of Commissioners a new building.

_____ b. The Board of Commissioners consists of several members.

_____ c. The November election may change the membership of the Board of Commissioners.

_____ d. Although board members may change, the problems will remain the same.

_____ e. The author does not believe that this election will change the difficulties facing the commissioners.

8. If this book begins with a familiar theme—the Indian experience of the last 120 years—the author brings to it great power and deep understanding.

_____ a. This book was written 120 years ago.

_____ b. The Indian experience of the last 120 years is a familiar experience, and nothing new can be written about it.

_____ c. The book lacks understanding of the Indian experience.

_____ d. The book begins with a familiar theme.

_____ e. The author of this sentence likes the book.

9. In this part of the world, the political and social changes of the past 20 years have by no means eliminated the old upper class of royalty and friends and advisors of royalty, the holders of state monopolies, the great landlords and lords of commercial fiefs, tribal sheikhs, and village leaders.

_____ a. In this part of the world, political and social changes have eliminated great landlords, lords of commercial fiefs, and village leaders.

_____ b. In this part of the world, the upper class and their friends and advisors have not been eliminated by political and social change.

_____ c. No means can eliminate the old upper class of royalty in this part of the world.

_____ d. The upper class of royalty has not changed in the past 20 years in this part of the world.

_____ e. In this part of the world, village leaders hold as much power as the advisors of royalty.

10. People should and do choose their elected representatives partly on the basis of how well they believe these representatives, once in office, can convince them to do or support whatever needs to be done.

_____ a. It is the author's belief that people should choose representatives whom they believe will convince them to take action.

_____ b. People choose representatives on the basis of whether or not they believe the representatives can be convinced to do what needs to be done.

_____ c. Although people should choose representatives whom they believe will convince them to take action, often they do not.

_____ d. People choose representatives whom they believe will convince them to take action.

_____ e. Representatives are elected only on the basis of their ability to take action.

Paragraph Analysis

Reading for Full Understanding

This exercise is similar to the one found in Unit 7. Read each paragraph carefully. Try to determine the author's main idea while attempting to remember important details. For each of the questions below, select the best answer. You may refer to the passage to answer the questions.

Paragraph 1

1. Summers with father were always enjoyable. Swimming, hiking,
2. boating, fishing—the days were not long enough to contain all of our
3. activities. There never seemed to be enough time to go to church,
4. which disturbed some friends and relations. Accused of neglecting this
5. part of our education, my father instituted a summer school for my
6. brother and me. However, his summer course included ancient history,
7. which Papa felt our schools neglected, and navigation, in which we first
8. had a formal examination in the dining room, part of which consisted
9. of tying several knots in a given time limit. Then we were each
10. separately sent on what was grandly referred to as a cruise in my
11. father's 18-foot knockabout, spending the night on board, and loaded
12. down, according to my mother, with enough food for a week. I
13. remember that on my cruise I was required to formally plot our
14. course, using the tide table, even though our goal was an island I could
15. see quite clearly across the water in the distance.

1. What was the original reason for holding the summer school?
   _____ a. Friends and relatives thought the children should learn religion.
   _____ b. The father wanted the children to learn more about religion.
   _____ c. The children got poor grades in their regular school.
   _____ d. The regular school teachers neglected the children.

2. The purpose of the cruise mentioned in the passage was to _____

   _____ a. have fun.
   _____ b. test the author's sailing ability.
   _____ c. reward the author for completing summer school.
   _____ d. get to the island.

3. Why did the author have to plot the course of her cruise?

   _____ a. She had to demonstrate her ability to do so.
   _____ b. She was afraid of getting lost.
   _____ c. The coast was dangerous.
   _____ d. The tides were strong.

From Sylvia Wright, Introduction to *Islandia*, by Austin Tappan Wright (New York: Rinehart and Co.).

4. How long did the author's cruise last?

_____ a. all summer   _____ c. overnight
_____ b. a week   _____ d. one day, morning till night

5. Apparently a knockabout is _____

_____ a. an island.   _____ c. a boat.
_____ b. a cruise.   _____ d. a seaman's knot.

Paragraph 2

1   The cicada exemplifies an insect species which uses a
2   combinatorial communication system. In their life cycle,
3   communication is very important, for only through the exchange of
4   sounds do cicadas know where to meet and when to mate. Three
5   different calls are employed for this purpose. Because of their limited
6   sound producing mechanisms, cicadas can make only ticks and buzzes.
7   The only way they can distinguish between congregation and courtship
8   calls is by varying the rate with which they make ticks and buzzes. The
9   congregation call consists of 12 to 40 ticks, delivered rapidly, followed
10 by a two-second buzz. It is given by males but attracts cicadas of both
11 sexes. Once they are all together, the males use courtship calls. The
12 preliminary call, a prolonged, slow ticking, is given when the male
13 notices a female near him. The advanced call, a prolonged series of
14 short buzzes at the same slow rate, is given when a female is almost
15 within grasp. The preliminary call almost invariably occurs before the
16 advanced call, although the latter is given without the preliminary call
17 occurring first if a female is suddenly discovered very near by. During
18 typical courtship, though, the two calls together result in ticking
19 followed by a buzzing—the same pattern which comprises the
20 congregation call but delivered at a slower rate. In this way, cicadas
21 show efficient use of their minimal sound producing ability, organizing
22 two sounds delivered at a high rate as one call and the same sounds
23 delivered at a slow rate as two more calls.

---

1. The cicada congregation call _____

_____ a. attracts only males.   _____ c. is given only by males.
_____ b. is given by both sexes.   _____ d. attracts only females.

2. During typical courtship, when a male first notices a female near him, he gives _____

_____ a. the two courtship calls together.   _____ c. 12 to 40 rapid ticks.
_____ b. a series of slow ticks.   _____ d. a two-second buzz.

From David McNeill, *The Acquisition of Language* (New York: Harper and Row).

3. How does the congregation call differ from the two courtship calls together?

____ a. It is delivered at a slower rate.   ____ c. The ticks precede the buzzes.
____ b. It is delivered at a faster rate.   ____ d. The buzzes precede the ticks.

4. According to this passage, why is communication so important for cicadas?

____ a. It helps them defend themselves against other insect species.
____ b. It warns them of approaching danger.
____ c. It separates the males from the females.
____ d. It is necessary for the continuation of the species.

Paragraph 3

1   Robert Spring, a 19th century forger, was so good at his profession
2 that he was able to make his living for 15 years by selling false
3 signatures of famous Americans. Spring was born in England in 1813
4 and arrived in Philadelphia in 1858 to open a bookstore. At first he
5 prospered by selling his small but genuine collection of early U.S.
6 autographs. Discovering his ability at copying handwriting, he began
7 imitating signatures of George Washington and Ben Franklin and
8 writing them on the title pages of old books. To lessen the chance of
9 detection, he sent his forgeries to England and Canada for sale and
10 circulation.
11   Forgers have a hard time selling their products. A forger can't
12 approach a respectable buyer but must deal with people who don't
13 have much knowledge in the field. Forgers have many ways to make
14 their work look real. For example, they buy old books to use the aged
15 paper of the title page, and they can treat paper and ink with
16 chemicals.
17   In Spring's time, right after the Civil War, Britain was still fond of
18 the Southern states, so Spring invented a respectable maiden lady
19 known as Miss Fanny Jackson, the only daughter of General
20 "Stonewall" Jackson. For several years Miss Fanny's financial
21 problems forced her to sell a great number of letters and manuscripts
22 belonging to her famous father. Spring had to work very hard to satisfy
23 the demand. All this activity did not prevent Spring from dying in
24 poverty, leaving sharp-eyed experts the difficult task of separating his
25 forgeries from the originals.

1. Why did Spring sell his false autographs in England and Canada?

____ a. There was a greater demand there than in America.
____ b. There was less chance of being detected there.
____ c. Britain was Spring's birthplace.
____ d. The prices were higher in England and Canada.

From the *Michigan Daily.*

2. After the Civil War, there was a great demand in Britain for ____

    ____ a. Southern money.   ____ c. Southern manuscripts and letters.
    ____ b. signatures of George Washington   ____ d. Civil War battle plans.
           and Ben Franklin.

3. Robert Spring spent 15 years ____

    ____ a. running a bookstore in Philadelphia.   ____ c. as a forger.
    ____ b. corresponding with Miss Fanny Jackson.   ____ d. as a respectable dealer.

4. According to the passage, forgeries are usually sold to ____

    ____ a. sharp-eyed experts.   ____ c. book dealers.
    ____ b. persons who aren't experts.   ____ d. owners of old books.

5. Who was Miss Fanny Jackson?

    ____ a. the only daughter of General "Stonewall" Jackson
    ____ b. a little-known girl who sold her father's papers to Robert Spring
    ____ c. Robert Spring's daughter
    ____ d. an imaginary person created by Spring

Paragraph 4

1   In science the meaning of the word "explain" suffers with
2 civilization's every step in search of reality. Science cannot really
3 explain electricity, magnetism, and gravitation; their effects can be
4 measured and predicted, but of their nature no more is known to the
5 modern scientist than to Thales who first speculated on the
6 electrification of amber. Most contemporary physicists reject the notion
7 that human beings can ever discover what these mysterious forces
8 "really" are. Electricity, Bertrand Russell says, "is not a thing, like St.
9 Paul's Cathedral; it is a way in which things behave. When we have
10 told how things behave when they are electrified, and under what
11 circumstances they are electrified, we have told all there is to tell."
12 Until recently scientists would have disapproved of such an idea.
13 Aristotle, for example, whose natural science dominated Western
14 thought for two thousand years, believed that human beings could
15 arrive at an understanding of reality by reasoning from self-evident
16 principles. He felt, for example, that it is a self-evident principle that
17 everything in the universe has its proper place, hence one can deduce
18 that objects fall to the ground because that's where they belong, and
19 smoke goes up because that's where it belongs. The goal of Aristotelian
20 science was to explain *why* things happen. Modern science was born
21 when Galileo began trying to explain *how* things happen and thus
22 originated the method of controlled experiment which now forms the
23 basis of scientific investigation.

---

1. The aim of controlled scientific experiments is _____

   _____ a. to explain why things happen.
   _____ b. to explain how things happen.
   _____ c. to describe self-evident principles.
   _____ d. to support Aristotelian science.

2. What principles most influenced scientific thought for two thousand years?

   _____ a. the speculations of Thales
   _____ b. the forces of electricity, magnetism, and gravity
   _____ c. Aristotle's natural science
   _____ d. Galileo's discoveries

3. Bertrand Russell's notion about electricity is _____

   _____ a. disapproved of by most modern scientists.
   _____ b. in agreement with Aristotle's theory of self-evident principles.
   _____ c. in agreement with scientific investigation directed toward "how" things happen.
   _____ d. in agreement with scientific investigation directed toward "why" things happen.

4. The passage says that until recently scientists disagreed with the idea _____

   _____ a. that there are mysterious forces in the universe.
   _____ b. that man cannot discover what forces "really" are.
   _____ c. that there are self-evident principles.
   _____ d. that we can discover why things behave as they do.

Paragraph 5

1   Dice, the plural of die, are small cubes used in games. They are
2 usually made of ivory, bone, wood, bakelite, or similar materials. The
3 six sides are numbered by dots from 1 to 6, so placed that the sum of
4 the dots on a side and the opposite side equals 7.
5   A simple form of play with dice is for each player to throw, or
6 shoot, for the highest sum. However, the most popular dice game in
7 the United States is called craps. It is played with 2 dice and the
8 underlying principle of the game is the fact that the most probable
9 throw is a 7. On the first throw, if a player shoots a 7 or 11 (called a
10 natural), he wins and begins again, but if he shoots 2, 3, or 12 (called
11 craps) on the first throw, he loses. If on the first throw he shoots 4, 5,
12 6, 8, 9, or 10, that number becomes his point. He continues to throw
13 until he shoots that number again (makes his point), in which case he
14 wins and begins again. However, if he shoots a 7 before he makes his
15 point, he loses and relinquishes the dice to the next player. Usually all
16 others in the game bet against the thrower, and in gambling halls bets
17 are made against the house.

From *Columbia Encyclopedia,* 2d ed. (New York: Columbia University Press).

1. In craps, a throw of 11 _____

   _____ a. always wins.
   _____ b. sometimes loses.
   _____ c. sometimes wins.
   _____ d. becomes the point.

2. If one side of a die has three dots on it, the opposite side has _____

   _____ a. 6.
   _____ b. 4.
   _____ c. 3.
   _____ d. 7.

3. To shoot the dice means to _____

   _____ a. throw them.
   _____ b. lose.
   _____ c. make a natural.
   _____ d. make one's point.

4. In a game of craps, if a player throws a 5 and then a 3, he _____

   _____ a. wins.
   _____ b. loses.
   _____ c. shoots again.
   _____ d. makes his point.

5. In a game of craps, if a player throws a 6, 3, 4, 4, 6, 11, in that order, he has _____

   _____ a. won twice.
   _____ b. made his point twice.
   _____ c. made two naturals.
   _____ d. shot craps.

6. In a game of craps, if the player throws a 12 on his first throw, _____

   _____ a. he has the highest sum, so he wins.
   _____ b. that number is his point.
   _____ c. he has shot craps.
   _____ d. he has made a natural.

7. What number is most probable on a throw of the dice?

   _____ a. 7 and 11 have equal probabilities
   _____ b. 7
   _____ c. 11
   _____ d. craps

Discourse Focus

Prediction

This exercise is similar to the one found in Unit 7. It is designed to give you practice in consciously developing and confirming expectations.

   Below is part of an article about the family. Read the article, stopping to respond to the questions that appear at several points throughout. Remember, you cannot always predict precisely what an author will do, but you can use knowledge of the text and your general knowledge to make good guesses. Work with your classmates on these items, defending your predictions with parts of the text. Do not worry about unfamiliar vocabulary.

The Changing Family

by Maris Vinovskis

1. Based on the title, what aspect of the family do you think this article will be about? List several possibilities.

_____

_____

_____

Now read the opening paragraph to see what the focus of the article will be.

There is widespread fear among policymakers and the public today that the family is falling apart. Much of that worry stems from a basic misunderstanding of the nature of the family in the past and a lack of appreciation for its strength in response to broad social and economic changes. The general view of the family is that it has been a stable and relatively unchanging institution through history and is only now undergoing changes; in fact, change has always been characteristic of it.

The Family and Household in the Past

2. This article seems to be about the changing nature of the family throughout history. Is this what you expected?

3. The introduction is not very specific, so you can only guess what changing aspects of the family will be mentioned in the next section. Using information from the introduction and your general knowledge, check (✓) those topics from the list on page 248 that you think will be mentioned:

From *LSA* magazine.

_____ a. family size
_____ b. relations within the family
_____ c. the definition of a family
_____ d. the role of the family in society
_____ e. different family customs

_____ f. the family throughout the world
_____ g. the economic role of the family
_____ h. sex differences in family roles
_____ i. the role of children
_____ j. sexual relations

Now read the next section, noting which of your predictions is confirmed.

> In the last twenty years, historians have been re-examining the nature of the family and have concluded that we must revise our notions of the family as an institution, as well as our assumptions about how children were perceived and treated in past centuries. A survey of diverse studies of the family in the West, particularly in seventeenth- eighteenth- and nineteenth-century England and America shows something of the changing role of the family in society and the evolution of our ideas of parenting and child development. (Although many definitions of *family* are available, in this article I will use it to refer to kin living under one roof.)

4. Which aspects of the family listed above were mentioned in this section? _____

_____

_____

5. Which other ones do you predict will be mentioned further on in the article? _____

_____

6. What aspects of the text and your general knowledge help you to create this prediction?

_____

_____

7. Below is the topic sentence of the next paragraph. What kind of supporting data do you expect to find in the rest of the paragraph? How do you think the paragraph will continue?

_____

_____

_____

> Although we have tended to believe that in the past children grew up in "extended households" including grandparents, parents, and children, recent historical research has cast considerable doubt on the idea that as countries became increasingly urban and industrial, the Western family evolved from extended to nuclear [i.e., parents and children only].

The rest of the paragraph is reprinted below. Read on to see if your expectations are confirmed.

Historians have found evidence that households in pre-industrial Western Europe were already nuclear and could not have been greatly transformed by economic changes. Rather than finding definite declines in household size, we find surprisingly small variations, which turn out to be a result of the presence or absence of servants, boarders, and lodgers, rather than relatives. In revising our nostalgic picture of children growing up in large families, Peter Laslett, one of the foremost analysts of the pre-industrial family, contends that most households in the past were actually quite small (mean household size was about 4.75). Of course, patterns may have varied somewhat from one area to another, but it seems unlikely that in the past few centuries many families in England or America had grandparents living with them.

8. Were your predictions confirmed?

9. Here is the list of topics you saw in question 3. Now *skim* the rest of the article; check (✓) the topics that the author actually discusses

_____ a. family size
_____ b. relations within the family
_____ c. the definition of a family
_____ d. the role of the family in society
_____ e. different family customs

_____ f. the family throughout the world
_____ g. the economic role of the family
_____ h. sex differences in family roles
_____ i. the role of children
_____ j. sexual relations

However, as Philip Aries has argued in his well-known *Centuries of Childhood*, the medieval family was nevertheless quite different from its modern counterpart, largely because the boundary between the household and the larger society was less rigidly drawn, and the roles of parents, servants, or neighbors in the socialization of children were more blurred. Relationships within the nuclear family were not much closer, it seems, than those with neighbors, relatives, or other friends.

Another difference, according to Lawrence Stone, was that within property-owning classes, as in sixteenth-century England, for example, marriage was a collective decision, involving not only the immediate family, but also other kin. Protection of long-term interests of lineage and consideration for the needs of the larger kinship group were more important than individual desires for happiness or romantic love. In addition, because the strong sense of individual or family privacy had not yet de-veloped, access to the household by local neighbors was relatively easy. But this type of family gave way in the late sixteenth century to a "restricted patriarchical nuclear family," which predominated from 1580 to 1640, when concern for lineage and loyalty to the local community declined, and allegiances to the State and Church and to kin within the household increased. The authority of the father, as head of the household, was enhanced and bolstered by State and Church support. This drive toward parental dominance over children was particularly characteristic of the Puritans and was not limited to the child's early years; upper-class parents, especially, sought to extend their control to their children's choices of both career and spouse.

By the mid-seventeenth century, the family was increasingly organized around the principle of personal autonomy and was bound together by strong ties of love and affection. The separation, both physical and emotional, between members of a nuclear family and their servants or boarders widened, as did the distance between the household and the rest of society. Physical privacy became more important, and it became more acceptable for individual family members to pursue their own happiness.

Throughout most of the pre-industrial period, the household was the central productive unit of society. Children either were trained for their future occupations in their own homes or were employed in someone else's household. As the economic functions of the household moved to the shop or factory in the late-eighteenth and nineteenth centuries, the household, no longer an economic focal point or an undifferentiated part of neighborhood activities, increasingly became a haven or escape from the outside world. Children growing up in fifteenth-century England were expected and encouraged to interact closely with many adults besides their parents, but by the eighteenth and nine-teenth centuries, they had come to rely more and more upon each other and their parents for their emotional needs.

The families that migrated to the New World, especially the Puritans, brought with them the ideal of a close and loving family, and although the economic functions of the American household were altered in the nineteenth century, the overall change was less dramatic than it had been in Western Europe. Thus, although the relationship between parents and children has not remained constant in America during the past three hundred years, the extent of the changes is probably less than it was in Western Europe.

Changing perceptions and treatment of children

We usually assume that an innate characteristic of human beings is the close and immediate attachment between the newborn child and its parents, especially its mother. Because abandonment or abuse of children seems to defy such beliefs, we are baffled by reports of widespread parental abuse of children. A look at the past may provide a different perspective on the present.

According to some scholars, maternal indifference to infants may have been typical of the Middle Ages. Aries says there is evidence that in the sixteenth and seventeenth centuries parents showed little affection for their children, and Edward Shorter argues that this indifference was probably typical among the ordinary people of Western Europe, even in the eighteenth and nineteenth centuries. The death of young children seems to have been accepted casually, and although overt infanticide was frowned upon, allowing children to die was sometimes encouraged, or at least tolerated. For example, in Western Europe it was common for mothers to leave infants at foundling hospitals or with rural wet nurses, both

---

Efforts to prevent cruelty to animals preceded those to accomplish the same ends for children by nearly a half century.

---

of which resulted in very high mortality rates. Whether these practices were typically the result of economic desperation, the difficulty of raising an out-of-wedlock child, or lack of attachment to an infant is not clear, but the fact that many well-to-do married women casually chose to give their infants to wet nurses, despite the higher mortality risks, suggests that the reasons were not always economic difficulty or fear of social stigma.

While the practice of overt infanticide and child abandonment may have been relatively widespread in parts of Western Europe, it does not seem to have been prevalent in either England or America. Indeed, authorities in both those countries in the sixteenth and seventeenth centuries prosecuted infanticide cases more vigorously than other forms of murder, and the practice of leaving infants with wet nurses went out of fashion in England by the end of the eighteenth century.

By the eighteenth century in Western Europe, parents were expressing more interest in their children and more affection for them, and by the nineteenth century, observers were beginning to criticize parents for being too child-centered. Nevertheless, parents were still not prevented from abusing their own children, as long as it did not result in death. Because the parent-child relationship was regarded as sacred and beyond State intervention, it was not until the late nineteenth century that reformers in England were able to persuade lawmakers to pass legislation to protect children from abusive parents. Ironically, efforts to prevent cruelty to animals preceded those to accomplish the same ends for children by nearly a half century.

Some of the earliest studies of colonial America suggested that at that time childhood was not viewed as a distinct stage: children, these historians said, were expected to think and behave pretty much as adults from an early age. Although a few recent scholars of the colonial American family have supported this view, others have questioned it, pointing out that New England Puritans were well aware that children had different abilities and temperaments and believed that childrearing should be molded to those individual differences.

While young children in colonial America probably were not seen as miniature adults, they *were* thought to be more capable intellectually at a young age than their counterparts generally are today. The Puritans believed that because it was essential for salvation, children should be taught to read the Bible as soon as possible. Indeed, the notion that children could and should learn to read as soon as they could talk was so commonly accepted by educators that they did not think it necessary to justify it in their writings. The infant school movement of the late 1820s reinforced this assumption until it was challenged by Amariah Brigham, a prominent physician who claimed that early intellectual training seriously and permanently weakened growing minds and could lead to insanity later in life.

When the kindergarten movement became popular in the United States, in the 1860s and 70s, intellectual activities such as reading were deliberately avoided. Such examples are a clear indication of how the socialization of children is dependent on our perceptions of children, and one might even speculate that as we become in-

Given the recent concern about the "epidemic" of adolescent pregnancies, we might expect more attention to be given to the attitudes of our forebears towards teenage parents.

creasingly willing to incorporate the latest scientific and medical findings into our care of the young, shifts in childrearing practices will increase in frequency.

Youth

Not only young children were perceived and treated differently in the past. Although there is little agreement among scholars either about when "adolescence" came to be viewed as a distinct stage or about the importance of education in the lives of nineteenth-century youths, many family historians have offered their perspectives on these topics. Surprisingly little, however, has been done to explore changes in teenage sexuality, pregnancy, and childbearing. Given the recent concern about the "epidemic" of adolescent pregnancies, we might expect more attention to be given to the attitudes of our forebears towards teenage parents.

Because of the stringent seventeenth-century prohibitions against premarital sexual relations and the low percentage of early teenage marriages, teenage pregnancy seems not to have been a problem in colonial New England. Early Americans were more concerned about pre-marital sexual relations, in general, than about whether teenage or adult women were involved. Not until the late nineteenth and early twentieth centuries did society clearly differentiate between teenage and adult sexual behavior, with a more negative attitude towards the former.

Only in the post-World War II period has the issue of teenage pregnancy and childbearing become a major public concern. But although the rates of teenage pregnancy and childbearing peaked in the late 1950s, the greatest attention to this phenomenon has come during the late 1970s and early 80s. The controversy over abortion, the great increase in out-of-wedlock births to adolescents, and the growing concern about the long-term disadvantages of early childbearing to the young mother and her child have made this issue more important today than thirty years ago.

Parent-child relations

Historically, the primary responsibility for the rearing of young children belonged almost exclusively to the parents, especially the father. It was not until the late nineteenth and early twentieth centuries that the State was willing to remove a young child from direct supervision of negligent or abusive parents. Even so, in order to reduce welfare costs to the rest of the community, a destitute family in early America, incapable of supporting its own members, was sometimes broken up and the children placed in other households.

During the eighteenth and nineteenth centuries the mother's role in the upbringing of children was enhanced: women became the primary providers of care and affection; and as men's church membership declined, women also became responsible for the catechizing and educating of young children, even though they often were less literate than men. While childrearing manuals continued to acknowledge the importance of the father, they also recognized that the mother had become the major figure in the care of the young.

Throughout much of Western history, as long as children remained in the home, parents exercised considerable control over them, even to the extent of arranging their marriages and influencing their career choices. Children were expected to be obedient and to contribute to the well-being of the family. And, perhaps more in Western Europe than in America, children were often expected to turn over almost all of their earnings directly to the parents — sometimes even after they had left home.

By the late eighteenth or early nineteenth century some of this control had eroded, and the rights of children as individuals were increasingly recognized and acknowledged. Interestingly, the development of children's rights has proceeded so rapidly and so far that we may now be in the midst of a backlash, as efforts are being made to re-establish parental responsibility in areas such as the reproductive behavior of minor children.

Clearly there have been major changes in the way our society treats children; but it would be very difficult for many of us to agree on the costs and benefits of these trends — whether from the viewpoint of the child, the parents, or society. While many applaud the increasing individualism and freedom of children within the family, others lament the loss of family responsibility and discipline. A historical analysis of parents and children cannot settle such disputes, but it can provide us with a better appreciation of the flexibility and resilience of the family as an institution for raising the young.

This essay was adapted from a longer version, "Historical Perspectives on the Development of the Family and Parent-Child Interactions," in *Parenting Across the Life Span: Biosocial Dimensions*, Jane B. Lancaster, Jeanne Altmann, Alice S. Rossi, and Lonie Sherrod, eds. (New York: Aldine 1987).

12

Reading Selection 1

Textbook

Before You Begin   Following is an article from the field of anthropology. What is the task of an anthropologist?

"The Sacred 'Rac'" is adapted from an introductory social anthropology textbook written for students in the United States. The article describes the customs of a tribe of people studied by the Indian anthropologist Chandra Thapar. Read the passage and answer the questions that follow. You may want to do the Vocabulary from Context exercise on page 255 before you begin.

The Sacred "Rac"

Patricia Hughes

1   An Indian anthropologist, Chandra Thapar, made a study of foreign cultures which had customs similar to those of his native land. One culture in particular fascinated him because it reveres one animal as sacred, much as the people in India revere the cow. The things he discovered might interest you since you will be studying India as part of this course.

2   The tribe Dr. Thapar studied is called the Asu and is found on the American continent north of the Tarahumara of Mexico. Though it seems to be a highly developed society of its type, it has an overwhelming preoccupation with the care and feeding of the rac—an animal much like a bull in size, strength and temperament. In the Asu tribe, it is almost a social obligation to own at least one if not more racs. People not possessing at least one are held in low esteem by the community because they are too poor to maintain one of these beasts properly. Some members of the tribe, to display their wealth and social prestige, even own herds of racs.

3   Unfortunately the rac breed is not very healthy and usually does not live more than five to seven years. Each family invests large sums of money each year to keep its rac healthy and shod, for it has a tendency to throw its shoes often. There are rac specialists in each

"The Sacred 'Rac'" by Patricia Hughes, in *Focusing on Global Poverty and Development* by Jayne C. Millar (Washington, D.C.: Overseas Development Council).

community, perhaps more than one if the community is particularly wealthy. These specialists, however, due to the long period of ritual training they must undergo and to the difficulty of obtaining the right selection of charms to treat the rac, demand costly offerings whenever a family must treat an ailing rac.

4   At the age of sixteen in many Asu communities, many youths undergo a puberty rite in which the rac figures prominently. Youths must petition a high priest in a grand temple. They are then initiated into the ceremonies that surround the care of the rac and are permitted to keep a rac.

5   Although the rac may be used as a beast of burden, it has many habits which would be considered by other cultures as detrimental to the life of the society. In the first place the rac breed is increasing at a very rapid rate and the Asu tribe has given no thought to curbing the rac population. As a consequence the Asu must build more and more paths for the rac to travel on since its delicate health and its love of racing other racs at high speeds necessitates that special areas be set aside for its use. The cost of smoothing the earth is too costly for any one individual to undertake; so it has become a community project and each member of the tribe must pay an annual tax to build new paths and maintain the old. There are so many paths needed that some people move their homes because the rac paths must be as straight as possible to keep the animal from injuring itself. Dr. Thapar also noted that unlike the cow, which many people in his country hold sacred, the excrement of the rac cannot be used as either fuel or fertilizer. On the contrary, its excrement is exceptionally foul and totally useless. Worst of all, the rac is prone to rampages in which it runs down anything in its path, much like stampeding cattle. Estimates are that the rac kills thousands of the Asu in a year.

6   Despite the high cost of its upkeep, the damage it does to the land, and its habit of destructive rampages, the Asu still regard it as being essential to the survival of their culture.

Comprehension

Answer the following questions. Your teacher may want you to answer the questions orally, in writing, or by underlining appropriate parts of the text. True/False items are indicated by a T / F preceding a statement.

1. What society reveres the rac? _____ Asu _____

_____

2. Where is the tribe located? _____ Nort American. _____

3. (T)/ F   People who don't own racs are not respected in the Asu community.

4. Why does it cost so much to have a rac specialist treat an ailing rac? _____

_____

curb = control

5. (T)/ F   An Asu must pass through a special ceremony before being permitted to keep a rac.

6. How is the rac helpful to the Asu? _____ carry _____

_____

7. What effects does the size of the rac population have on the life of the Asu? _____

_____

8. T /(F)   Rac excrement can be used as fuel or as fertilizer.

9. According to the author, what is the worst characteristic of the rac? _____

10. (T)/ F   The Asu feel that their culture cannot survive without the rac.

11. What is *rac* spelled backward? _____ Car. _____

Drawing Inferences

What is the author's attitude toward the rac? Why does she choose to present her opinion using this story about the Asu society?

Discussion/Composition

1. Is the rac essential to the survival of the Asu society? Of your society? What effects is the rac having on your society? Do people in your society revere the rac as much as the Asu do?

2. Describe some aspect of your culture from the point of view of an anthropologist.

Vocabulary from Context

Use the context provided and your knowledge of stems and affixes to determine the meanings of the italicized words. Write a definition, synonym, or description of the italicized vocabulary items in the space provided.

1. _____   Alex has had trouble studying for the final examination because he has been too *preoccupied* with happy thoughts of his summer vacation.

2. _____   Alice's dog is gentle and friendly; unfortunately, my dog doesn't have such a pleasant *temperament*.

3. _____   Peter wants to be a doctor because he feels it is a very *prestigious* occupation, and he has always wanted to hold a high position in society.

4. _____   Do you know a doctor who has experience *treating* children?

5. _____   Instead of complaining to me that you're *ailing,* you should see a doctor to find out what's wrong with you.

6. _____   Many people believe that only primitive societies have a special ceremony to celebrate the time when a child becomes an adult; however, anthropologists say that advanced cultures also have *puberty rites*.

7. _____   The criminal was to be killed at dawn; but he *petitioned* the king to save him and his request was granted.

8. _____   Doctors believe that smoking cigarettes is *detrimental* to your
9. _____   health. They also *regard* drinking as harmful.

Reading Selection 2
Essay

An essay is a literary composition on a single subject that usually presents the author's personal opinion. The following essay, written by John V. Lindsay when he was mayor of New York City, is taken from his book, *The City*.

Before You Begin   1. What is your attitude toward cities? Do you enjoy them, or do you find them unpleasant?

2. Do you think there is a general attitude toward cities held by most people in your country or community?

Read the passage, then do the exercises that follow. You may want to do Vocabulary from Context exercise 1 on page 261 before you begin reading.

The City

John V. Lindsay

1   In one sense, we can trace all the problems of the American city back to a single starting point: we Americans don't like our cities very much.

2   That is, on the face of it, absurd. After all, more than three-fourths of us now live in cities, and more are flocking to them every year. We are told that the problems of our cities are receiving more attention in Washington, and scholarship has discovered a whole new field in urban studies.

3   Nonetheless, it is historically true: in the American psychology, the city has been a basically suspect institution, filled with the corruption of Europe, totally lacking that sense of spaciousness and innocence of the frontier and the rural landscape.

4   I don't pretend to be a scholar on the history of the city in American life. But my thirteen years in public office, first as an officer of the U.S. Department of Justice, next in Congress, and finally as Mayor of the biggest city in America, have taught me all too well the fact that a strong anti-urban attitude runs consistently through the mainstream of American thinking. Much of the drive behind the settlement of America was in reaction to the conditions in European industrial centers—and much of the theory supporting the basis of freedom in America was linked directly to the availability of land and the perfectibility of human beings outside the corrupt influences of the city.

5   What has this to do with the predicament of the modern city? I think it has much to do with it. For the fact is that the United States,

---

Adapted from *The City* by John V. Lindsay (New York: W. W. Norton and Company).

particularly the federal government, which has historically established our national priorities, has simply never thought that the American city was "worthy" of improvement—at least not to the extent of expending any basic resources on it.

6   Antipathy to the city predates the American experience. When industrialization drove the European working man into the major cities of the continent, books and pamphlets appeared attacking the city as a source of crime, corruption, filth, disease, vice, licentiousness, subversion, and high prices. The theme of some of the earliest English novels—*Moll Flanders* for example—is that of the innocent country youth coming to the big city and being subjected to all forms of horror until justice—and a return to the pastoral life—follow.

7   The proper opinion of Europe seemed to support the Frenchman who wrote: "In the country, a man's mind is free and easy . . . ; but in the city, the persons of friends and acquaintances, one's own and other people's business, foolish quarrels, ceremonies, visits, impertinent discourses, and a thousand other fopperies and diversions steal away the greatest part of our time and leave no leisure for better and necessary employment. Great towns are but a larger sort of prison to the soul, like cages to birds or pounds to beasts."

8   This was not, of course, the only opinion on city life. Others maintained that the city was "the fireplace of civilization, whence light and heat radiated out into the cold dark world." And William Penn planned Philadelphia as the "holy city," carefully laid out so that each house would have the appearance of a country cottage to avoid the density and overcrowding that so characterized European cities.

9   Without question, however, the first major thinker to express a clear antipathy to the urban way of life was Thomas Jefferson. For Jefferson, the political despotism of Europe and the economic despotism of great concentrations of wealth, on the one hand, and poverty on the other, were symbolized by the cities of London and Paris, which he visited frequently during his years as a diplomatic representative of the new nation. In the new world, with its opportunities for widespread landholding, there was the chance for a flowering of authentic freedom, with each citizen, freed from economic dependence, both able and eager to participate in charting the course of his own future. America, in a real sense, was an escape from all the injustice that had flourished in Europe—injustice that was characterized by the big city.

10   This Jeffersonian theme was to remain an integral part of the American tradition. Throughout the nineteenth century, as the explorations of America pushed farther outward, the new settlers sounded most like each other in their common celebration of freedom from city chains.

11   The point is that all this opinion goes beyond ill feelings; it suggests a strong national sense that encouragement and development of the city was to be in no sense a national priority—that our manifest destiny* lay in the untouched lands to the west, in constant movement

---

*The nineteenth-century doctrine that the United States had the right and duty to expand throughout the North American continent

westward, and in maximum dispersion of land to as many people as possible.

12   Thus, the Northwest Ordinance of 1787—perhaps the first important declaration of national policy—explicitly encouraged migration into the Northwest Territory and provided grants of land and free public lands for schools. New York City, by contrast, did not begin a public-education system until 1842—and received, of course, no federal help at all. Similarly, the Homestead Act of 1862* was based on an assumption—supported by generations of American theory—that in the West could be found genuine opportunity and that the eastern-seaboard cities of the United States were simply hopeless collections of vice and deprivation.

13   This belief accelerated after the Civil War, for a variety of reasons. For one thing, the first waves of immigration were being felt around the country as immigrants arrived in urban areas. The poverty of the immigrants, largely from Ireland and Northern Europe, caused many people in rural America to equate poverty with personal inferiority—a point of view that has not yet disappeared from our national thinking. Attacks on the un-American and criminal tendencies of the Irish, the Slavs, and every other ethnic group that arrived on America's shore were a steady part of national thinking, as were persistent efforts to bar any further migration of "undesirables" to our country.

14   With the coming of rapid industrialization, all the results of investigations into city poverty and despair that we think of as recent findings were being reported—and each report served to confirm the beliefs of the Founding Fathers that the city was no place for a respectable American.

15   Is all this relevant only to past attitudes and past legislative history? I don't think so. The fact is that until today, this same basic belief—that our cities ought to be left to fend for themselves—is still a powerful element in our national tradition.

16   Consider more modern history. The most important housing act in the last fifty years was not the law that provided for public housing; it as the law that permitted the FHA† to grant subsidized low-interest mortgages to Americans who want to purchase homes. More than anything else, this has made the suburban dream a reality. It has brought the vision of grass and trees and a place for the kids to play within the reach of millions of working Americans, and the consequences be damned. The impact of such legislation on the cities was not even considered—nor was the concept of making subsidized money available for neighborhood renovation in the city so that it might compete with the suburbs. Instead, in little more than a decade 800,000 middle income New Yorkers fled the city for the suburbs and were replaced by largely unskilled workers who in many instances represented a further cost rather than an economic asset.

17   And recently a suggested law giving a small amount of federal money for rat control was literally laughed off the floor of the House of

---

*A law that gave a 160-acre piece of land to anyone who lived on it for five years
†Federal Housing Administration

Representatives amid much joking about discrimination against country
rats in favor of city rats.

18   What happened, I think, was not the direct result of a "the city is
evil and therefore we will not help it" concept. It was more indirect,
more subtle, the result of the kind of thinking that enabled us to spend
billions of dollars in subsidies to preserve the family farm while doing
nothing about an effective program for jobs in the city; to create
government agencies concerned with the interests of agriculture,
veterans, small business, labor, commerce, and the American Indian
but to create no Department of Urban Development until 1965; to so
restrict money that meaningful federal aid is still not possible.

19   In other words, the world of urban America as a dark and desolate
place undeserving of support or help has become fixed in the American
consciousness. And we are paying for that attitude in our cities today.

Comprehension

Exercise 1

*Check (✓) those statements that the author believes accurately reflect Americans' attitudes toward
their cities.*

1. _____ Americans don't like their cities very much.

2. _____ Americans have not thought their cities worthy of receiving financial support from the
federal government.

3. _____ Americans were suspicious of cities because cities reminded them of the corruption
of Europe.

4. _____ Most Americans believe that cities are centers of civilization.

5. _____ Americans believed that the federal government should provide support for
establishing public school systems in urban areas.

6. _____ The United States government thought it was more important to develop the
American West than to develop the cities.

7. _____ Rural Americans have been sympathetic to the problems of newly arrived immigrants
in the city.

8. _____ No one considered the effect on cities of laws to help people build homes in the
suburbs.

9. _____ The American attitude toward cities is changing.

10. _____ The American attitude toward cities has been harmful to the United States.

Exercise 2

As you read you should be able to differentiate between facts and opinions. Facts are statements of information that can be shown to be true. Opinions are beliefs, conclusions, or judgments not confirmed by positive knowledge or proof.

In this essay some of the opinions presented are those of the author; some are those of other people. Read the following sentences carefully. Indicate if each statement is a fact (F) (it could be demonstrated to be true) or an opinion (O) (not everyone would agree with the statement; it probably could not be convincingly proved to be true or false). If the statement is an opinion, indicate whose opinion it is. The number in parentheses indicates the paragraph in which each idea may be found.

Examples

F _____ New York City is the largest city in the United States. (4)

O   Founding Fathers   Good Americans should not live in cities. (14)

1. ___ _____ More than three-fourths of the American people now live in cities. (2)

2. ___ _____ There is a strong anti-urban attitude in America. (4)

3. ___ _____ When industrialization began, many Europeans went to work in cities. (6)

4. ___ _____ Cities are like prisons. (7)

5. ___ _____ Cities are centers of civilization. (8)

6. ___ _____ Although Thomas Jefferson often visited London and Paris, he did not like these cities. (9)

7. ___ _____ Because of the widespread opportunity to own land, America represented an escape from the injustices of Europe. (9)

8. ___ _____ The Northwest Ordinance gave free land to people. (12)

9. ___ _____ When New York City began its public school system, the federal government did not help. (12)

10. ___ _____ The cities on the east coast of the United States were corrupt. (12)

11. ___ _____ Many of the immigrants who came to America after the Civil War were poor. (13)

12. ___ _____ Poor immigrants are inferior to hard-working Americans. (13)

Discussion/Composition

This article describes John Lindsay's opinion about cities. What is yours?

Vocabulary from Context

Exercise 1

Use the context provided to determine the meanings of the italicized words. Write a definition, synonym, or description of each of the italicized vocabulary items in the space provided.

1. _____ The American people have never trusted the city; it has always appeared in literature and history as a *suspect* institution.

2. _____ A high *priority* should be given to providing public transportation; money for highways is less important.

3. _____ It is *absurd* to spend more money on highways. The wise solution for overcrowded roads is public transportation.

4. _____ The government gave money to people to help buy homes outside of the cities. This system of *subsidized* housing caused many people to leave urban areas.

5. _____ Lack of public transportation in the suburbs has caused a terrible *predicament* for poor people who live there; they must either buy a car or depend on friends for transportation.

6. _____ Hotels and restaurants are an *integral* part of the city; without them, the city's tourist industry could not exist.

7. _____ When Governor Holmes was first elected, he was probably an honest man. However, since then, he has become as *corrupt* as all of the dishonest people around him. Now he is as bad as the rest of the state officials.

8. _____ Although Richard Weeks has accomplished many good things during his terms as mayor, the fact that he totally controls the city makes him a *despot,* and he should be forced to give up some of his power.

Exercise 2

This exercise is designed to give you additional clues to determine the meaning of unfamiliar vocabulary items from context. In the paragraph indicated by the number in parentheses, find the word that best fits the meaning given. Your teacher may want to read these aloud as you quickly scan the paragraph to find the answer.

1. (11) Which word means *distribution*?

2. (15) Which word means *provide for; take care of*?

3. (16) Which word means *improvement by repairing*?

Exercise 3

This exercise should be done after you have finished reading "The City." The exercise is designed to determine how well you have been able to use context clues to guess the meaning of unfamiliar vocabulary in the essay. Give a definition, synonym, or description of each of the words below. The number in parentheses indicates the paragraph in which the word can be found. Your teacher may want you to do these orally or in writing.

1. (1)   trace _____

2. (2)   flocking _____

3. (6)   antipathy _____

4. (6)   pastoral _____

5. (9)   charting _____

6. (13) waves _____

7. (13) ethnic _____

8. (13) bar _____

9. (16) fled _____

10. (18) subtle _____

Reading Selections 3A–3B
Family Narratives

The two selections that follow present humorous accounts of family life written retrospectively by adults. "Attack on the Family" describes a British family in Greece between the World Wars; "Cheaper by the Dozen" describes an unusual American family growing up in the first quarter of the twentieth century.

Selection 3A   **Family Narrative**

Before You Begin   1. What is it like to be the youngest child in a family?

2. Below is a picture of a scorpion. What would be the reaction of your family if a child were to bring one home as a pet?

The following selection is taken from Gerald Durrell's book *My Family and Other Animals,* written from the point of view of the youngest child. The book is an account of the year, during Durrell's childhood, that his family spent on the Greek island of Corfu. As the title indicates, the book is not an ordinary autobiography. In this selection the author's habit of collecting strange and wonderful animal life throws the house into complete confusion.

Read the selection to get a general understanding of the story, then do the exercises that follow. You may want to do Vocabulary from Context exercise 1 on pages 267–68 before you begin reading.

An Attack on the Family

Gerald Durrell

I grew very fond of the scorpions in the garden wall. I found them to be pleasant, unassuming creatures with, on the whole, the most charming habits. Provided you did nothing silly or clumsy (like putting your hand on one) the scorpions treated you with respect, their one desire being to get away and hide as quickly as possible. They must have found me rather a trial, for I was always ripping sections of the plaster away so that I could watch them, or capturing them and making them walk about in jam-jars so that I could see the way their feet moved. By means of my sudden and unexpected assaults on the wall I discovered quite a bit about the scorpions.

2   By crouching under the wall at night with a torch, I managed to catch some brief glimpses of the scorpions' wonderful courtship dances. I saw them standing, claws joined, their bodies raised to the skies, their tails lovingly intertwined; I saw them waltzing slowly in circles, claw in claw. But my view of these performances was all too

Adapted from *My Family and Other Animals* by Gerald Durrell (New York: Viking).

short, for almost as soon as I switched on the torch the partners would stop, pause for a moment, and then, seeing that I was not going to extinguish the light, they would turn round and walk firmly away, claw in claw, side by side. They were definitely beasts that believed in keeping themselves *to* themselves. If I could have kept a colony in captivity I would probably have been able to see the whole of the courtship, but the family had forbidden scorpions in the house, despite my arguments in favour of them.

3   Then one day I found a fat female scorpion in the wall, wearing what at first glance appeared to be a pale brown fur coat. Closer inspection proved that this strange garment was made up of a mass of tiny babies clinging to the mother's back. I was enraptured by this family, and I made up my mind to smuggle them into the house and up to my bedroom so that I might keep them and watch them grow up. With infinite care I manoeuvred the mother and family into a matchbox, and then hurried to the villa. It was rather unfortunate that just as I entered the door lunch should be served; however, I placed the matchbox carefully on the mantelpiece in the drawing-room, so that the scorpions could get plenty of air, and made my way to the dining-room and joined the family for the meal. Dawdling over my food, feeding Roger under the table and listening to the family arguing, I completely forgot about my exciting new captures. At last Larry, having finished, brought the cigarettes from the drawing-room, and lying back in his chair he put one in his mouth and picked up the matchbox he had brought. Unaware of my impending doom I watched him interestedly as, still talking glibly, he opened the matchbox.

4   Now, I maintain to this day that the female scorpion meant no harm. She was agitated and annoyed at being shut up in a matchbox for so long, and so she seized the first opportunity to escape. She hoisted herself out of the box with great rapidity, her babies clinging on desperately, and scuttled on to the back of Larry's hand. There, not quite certain what to do next, she paused, her sting curved up at the ready. Larry, feeling the movement of her claws, glanced down to see what it was, and from that moment things got increasingly confused.

5   He uttered a roar of fright that made Lugaretzia drop a plate and brought Roger out from beneath the table, barking wildly. With a flick of his hand he sent the unfortunate scorpion flying down the table, and she landed midway between Margo and Leslie, scattering babies like confetti as she thumped on the cloth. Thoroughly enraged at this treatment, the creature sped towards Leslie, her sting quivering with anger. Leslie leapt to his feet, overturning his chair, and flicked out desperately with his napkin, sending the scorpion rolling across the cloth towards Margo, who promptly let out a scream that any railway engine would have been proud to produce. Mother, completely bewildered by this sudden and rapid change from peace to chaos, put on her glasses and peered down the table to see what was causing the pandemonium, and at that moment Margo, in a vain attempt to stop the scorpion's advance, hurled a glass of water at it. The shower missed the animal completely, but successfully drenched Mother, who, not being able to stand cold water, promptly lost her breath and sat gasping at the end of the table, unable even to protest. The scorpion had now

gone to ground under Leslie's plate, while her babies swarmed wildly all over the table. Roger, mystified by the panic, but determined to do his share, ran round and round the room, barking hysterically.

6 "It's that bloody boy again . . ." bellowed Larry.

"Look out! Look out! They're coming!" screamed Margo.

"All we need is a book," roared Leslie; "don't panic, hit 'em with a book."

"What on earth's the *matter* with you all?" Mother kept asking, wiping her glasses.

"It's that bloody boy . . . he'll kill the lot of us . . . Look at the table . . . kneedeep in scorpions . . ."

"Quick . . . quick . . . do something . . . Look out, look out!"

"Stop screeching and get a book, for God's sake . . . You're worse than the dog . . . Shut *up,* Roger."

"By the Grace of God I wasn't bitten . . ."

"Look out . . . there's another one . . . Quick . . . quick . . ."

"Oh, shut up and get me a book or something . . ."

"But *how* did the scorpions get on the table, dear?"

"That bloody boy . . . Every matchbox in the house is a deathtrap . . ."

"Look out, it's coming towards me . . . Quick, quick, do something . . ."

"Hit it with your knife . . . *your knife* . . . Go on, hit it . . ."

7 Since no one had bothered to explain things to him, Roger was under the mistaken impression that the family were being attacked, and that it was his duty to defend them. As Lugaretzia was the only stranger in the room, he came to the logical conclusion that she must be the responsible party, so he bit her in the ankle. This did not help matters very much.

8 By the time a certain amount of order had been restored, all the baby scorpions had hidden themselves under various plates and bits of cutlery. Eventually, after impassioned pleas on my part, backed up by Mother, Leslie's suggestion that the whole lot be killed was defeated. While the family, still simmering with rage and fright, retired to the drawing-room, I spent half an hour collecting the babies, picking them up in a teaspoon, and returning them to their mother's back. Then I carried them outside on a saucer and, with the utmost reluctance, released them on the garden wall. Roger and I went and spent the afternoon on the hillside, for I felt it would be wise to allow the family to have a siesta before seeing them again.

Comprehension

Exercise 1

Answer the following questions. Your teacher may want you to answer the questions orally, in writing, or by underlining appropriate parts of the text. True/False items are indicated by a T / F preceding a statement. In many cases you will have to use your own judgment because the answer is not specifically given in the passage.

1. T / F   Scorpions are not dangerous.

2. T / F   The author likes scorpions.

3. Why wasn't the author able to observe the whole courtship dance? _____

_____

4. T / F   The author knew that his family would not allow scorpions in the house.

5. How did the mother scorpion carry her babies? _____

6. T / F   The author caught the scorpion family in a jam-jar.

7. When was the scorpion family discovered? _____

_____

8. Why did Margo throw water on Mother? _____

_____

9. T / F   The author tried to kill the scorpions with a book.

10. T / F   The author felt that the scorpions were attacking his family.

11. T / F   Mother supported the writer in his attempt to save the scorpions.

12. How were the scorpions removed from the house? _____

_____

13. T / F   The author stayed outside for the rest of the day because he didn't want to see the
family until everyone had rested.

──────────

Exercise 2

*To answer the following questions you will have to make decisions about the story based on
careful reading. Many questions do not have clear-cut answers; you will have to decide what you
think the best answer is. Be prepared to defend your choices with portions of the text.*

1. Who is Roger? _____

2. Who is Lugaretzia? _____

3. How many people are in the Durrell family? _____ Name them, and indicate

if they are male or female. _____

_____

4. Who keeps yelling for a book? _____

5. Who says that every matchbox in the house is a death-trap? _____

6. Who is "screeching"? _____

7. Who says, "But *how* did the scorpions get on the table, dear?" _____

8. Who is the youngest member of the family? _____

9. In your opinion, who seems the most confused? _____

Discussion/Composition

Can you describe an incident from your childhood in which one of the children in your family threw the household into confusion?

Vocabulary from Context

Exercise 1

Use the context provided to determine the meanings of the italicized words. Write a definition, synonym, or description of each of the italicized vocabulary items in the space provided.

1. _____   Because the light frightened the scorpions away, I wasn't able to observe them for very long. However, by appearing suddenly with my electric torch, I was able to get brief *glimpses* of their behavior.

2. _____   I was completely *enraptured* with the scorpion family. My happiness at finding them was so great that I decided I would keep them in my room for closer study.

3. _____   The members of the family were so angry that I decided to stay away from the house until dinner. Their *rage* truly frightened me.

4. _____   Because she had not seen the scorpions, Mother was completely *bewildered* by the sudden confusion.

5. _____   I begged the family not to kill the scorpions, and they finally listened to my *pleas*.

6. _____   Mr. and Mrs. Firth had a long *courtship*. They dated for nine years before they got married.

7. _____   He *crouched* down to look under the table for his shoes.

8. _____ After the scorpion affair the whole family tried *in vain* to get me to stop collecting animals and insects. They should have known that I wouldn't stop collecting just because of one little scare.

Exercise 2

This exercise is designed to give you additional clues to determine the meanings of unfamiliar vocabulary items in context. In the paragraph indicated by the number in parentheses, find the word or phrase that best fits the meaning given. Your teacher may want to read these aloud as you quickly scan the paragraph to find the answer.

1. (1) Which word means *a bother; an annoyance; a problem*?

2. (3) Which word in the third sentence means *to bring in secretly*?

3. (3) Which word at the end of the paragraph means *fate; future problems*?

4. (5) Which two words in the middle of the paragraph mean *confusion*?

5. (8) Which word in the first sentence means *peace and quiet; organization*?

Exercise 3

This exercise should be done after you have finished reading "An Attack on the Family." The exercise is designed to determine how well you have been able to use context clues to guess the meaning of unfamiliar vocabulary in "An Attack on the Family." Give a definition, synonym, or description of each of the words or phrases below. This exercise can be done orally or in writing.

1. assaults (last sentence, paragraph 1) _____

2. clinging (second sentence, paragraph 3) _____

3. manoeuvred (middle, paragraph 3) _____

4. maintain (paragraph 4) _____

5. hoisted (paragraph 4) _____

6. scuttled (paragraph 4) _____

7. peered (middle, paragraph 5) _____

8. hurled (bottom, paragraph 5) _____

9. drenched (bottom, paragraph 5) _____

10. swarmed (bottom, paragraph 5) _____

11. screeching (middle, paragraph 6) _____

12. reluctance (bottom, paragraph 8) _____

Selection 3B

Before You Begin   Would you consider a family unusual if:

—all the shopping was done by the children in committees?
—phonographs played constantly in the bathrooms so that everyone
    could learn foreign languages as they brushed their teeth?
—the mother was a psychologist who became as famous as her engineer
    husband in the field of scientific management?

All of these statements—and many more just as unusual—apply to the family of John and Lillian
Gilbreth. These two remarkable people raised a family in the first quarter of the twentieth century,
at a time when the United States was rapidly industrializing, and when large families were
becoming less common. Through their research into scientific management, the Gilbreths showed
many large companies how to increase profits by saving time and labor. They believed that the
principles of good industrial management could also apply to the management of families, and
they set out to prove it with their twelve children.

   The following selection is taken from *Cheaper by the Dozen,* a book written by two of the
Gilbreth children. Read the passage quickly to appreciate the humor, then do the exercises that
follow. You may want to do Vocabulary from Context exercise 1 on page 276 and the Dictionary
Study exercise on page 278 before you begin reading.

Adaptation from
Cheaper by the Dozen

Frank B. Gilbreth, Jr., and Ernestine Gilbreth Carey

1   It was an off year that didn't bring a new Gilbreth baby. Both Dad and Mother
wanted a large family. And if it was Dad who set the actual goal of an even dozen, Mother
as readily agreed.
   Dad mentioned the dozen figure for the first time on their wedding day.
   "We're going to have a wonderful life, Lillie. A wonderful life and a wonderful
family. A great big family."
   "We'll have children all over the house," Mother smiled. "From the basement to the
attic."
   "From the floorboards to the chandelier."
   "How many would you say we should have, just an estimate?" Mother asked.
   "Just as an estimate, many."
   "Lots and lots."
2   "We'll settle for an even dozen," said Dad. "No less. What do you say to that?"
   "I say," said Mother, "a dozen would be just right. No less."
   "That's the minimum."
   "Boys or girls?"
   "Well, boys would be fine," Dad whispered. "A dozen boys would be just right.

Adapted from *Cheaper by the Dozen* by Frank B. Gilbreth, Jr., and Ernestine Gilbreth Carey (New York: Thomas Y.
Crowell).

But . . . well, girls would be all right too. Sure, I guess."

3   "I'd like to have half boys and half girls. Do you think it would be all right to have half girls?"

"If that's what you want," Dad said, "we'll plan it that way. Excuse me a minute while I make a note of it." He took out his memorandum book and solemnly wrote: "Don't forget to have six boys and six girls."

They had a dozen children, six boys and six girls, in seventeen years. Somewhat to Dad's disappointment, there were no twins or other multiple births. There was no doubt in his mind that the most efficient way to raise a large family would be to have one huge litter and get the whole business over with at one time.

4   One reason Dad had so many children was that he was convinced anything he and Mother teamed up on was sure to be a success.

Dad always practiced what he preached, and it was just about impossible to tell where his scientific management company ended and his family life began.

Our house at Montclair, New Jersey, was a sort of school for scientific management and the elimination of wasted motions—or "motion study," as Dad and Mother named it.

5   Dad took moving pictures of us children washing dishes, so that he could determine how we could reduce our motions and thus hurry through the task. Irregular jobs, such as painting the back porch or removing a tree stump from the front lawn, were awarded on a low-bid basis. Each child who wanted extra pocket money submitted an offer saying what he would do the job for. The lowest bidder got the contract.

6   Dad put process and work charts in the bathrooms. Every child old enough to write— and Dad expected his offspring to start writing at a tender age—was required to initial the charts in the morning after he had brushed his teeth, taken a bath, combed his hair, and made his bed. At night, each child had to weigh himself, plot the figure on a graph, and initial the process charts again after he had done his homework, washed his hands and face, and brushed his teeth. Mother wanted to have a place on the charts for saying prayers, but Dad said as far as he was concerned prayers were voluntary.

7   It was regimentation, all right. But bear in mind the trouble most parents have in getting just one child off to school, and multiply it by twelve. Some regimentation was necessary to prevent bedlam.

8   Yes, at home or on the job, Dad was always the efficiency expert. He buttoned his vest from the bottom up, instead of from the top down, because the bottom-to-top process took him only three seconds, while the top-to-bottom took seven. He even used two shaving brushes to lather his face, because he found that by so doing he could cut seventeen seconds off his shaving time. For a while he tried shaving with two razors, but he finally gave that up.

9   "I can save forty-four seconds," he grumbled, "but I wasted two minutes this morning putting this bandage on my throat."

It wasn't the slashed throat that really bothered him. It was the two minutes.

10   Mother the psychologist and Dad the motion study man and general contractor decided to look into the new field of the psychology of management, and the old field of psychologically managing a houseful of children. They believed that what would work in the home would work in the factory, and what would work in the factory would work in the home.

Dad put the theory to a test shortly after we moved to Montclair. The house was too big for Tom Grieves, the handyman, and Mrs. Cunningham, the cook, to keep in order. Dad decided we were going to have to help them, and he wanted us to offer the help willingly. He had found that the best way to get cooperation out of employees in a factory was to set up a joint employer-employee board, which would make work assignments on a basis of personal choice and aptitude. He and Mother set up a Family Council, patterned after an employer-employee board. The Council met every Sunday afternoon, immediately after dinner.

11   Like most of Dad's and Mother's ideas, the Family Council was basically a good one and, although it verged sometimes on the hysterical, brought results. Family purchasing committees, duly elected, bought the food, clothes, furniture, and athletic equipment. A utilities committee levied one-cent fines on wasters of water and electricity. A projects committee saw that work was completed as scheduled. The amount of money the children were to receive for allowances was decided by the Council, which also determined appropriate rewards and punishments.

12   One purchasing committee found a large department store which gave us wholesale rates on everything from underwear to baseball gloves. Another bought canned goods directly from a manufacturer, in truckload lots.

13   One Sunday, when Dad convened the meeting of the Council, we sat self-consciously around the table, waiting for the right moment. The chairman knew something was in the air, and it tickled him. He had trouble keeping a straight face when he called for new business.

Martha, who had been carefully instructed in private, arose.

"It has come to the attention of the membership," she began, "that the assistant chairman intends to buy a new rug for the dining room. Since the entire membership will be required to look upon, and sit in chairs resting upon, the rug, I move* that the Council be consulted before any rug is purchased."

"Second the motion," said Anne.

Dad didn't know what to make of this one. "Any discussion?" he asked, in a move designed to kill time while he planned his counter attack.

14   "Mr. Chairman," said Lillian. "We have to sweep it. We should be able to choose it."

"We want one with flowers on it," Martha put in. "When you have flowers, the crumbs don't show so easily, and you save motions by not having to sweep so often."

"We want to know what sort of a rug the assistant chairman intends to buy," said Ernestine.

"We want to make sure the budget can afford it," Fred announced.

"I recognize the assistant chairman," said Dad. "This whole Council business was your idea anyway, Lillie. What do we do now?"

15   "Well," Mother said doubtfully, "I had planned to get a plain violet-colored rug, and I had planned to spend a hundred dollars. But if the children think that's too much, and if they want flowers, I'm willing to let the majority rule."

"I move," said Frank, "that not more than ninety-five dollars be spent."

Dad shrugged his shoulders. If Mother didn't care, he certainly didn't.

"So many as favor the motion to spend only ninety-five dollars, signify by saying aye."

The motion carried unanimously.

"Any more new business?"

16   "I move," said Bill, "that we spend the five dollars we have saved to buy a collie puppy."

"Hey, wait a minute," said Dad. The rug had been somewhat of a joke, but the dog question was serious. We had wanted a dog for years. Dad thought that any pet which didn't lay eggs was an extravagance that a man with twelve children could ill afford. He felt that if he surrendered on the dog question, there was no telling what the Council might vote next. He had a sickening mental picture of a barn full of ponies, a car for Anne, motorcycles, a swimming pool, and, ultimately, the poor house or a debtors' prison, if they still had such things.

---

*"I move," "Second the motion," and "I recognize" are phrases taken from parliamentary procedure. They are generally used only in formal meetings in which each person's participation is rigidly controlled.

17   "Second the motion," said Lillian, yanking Dad out of his dreams.

"A dog," said Jack, "would be a pet. Everyone in the family could pat him, and I would be his master."

"A dog," said Dan, "would be a friend. He could eat scraps of food. He would save us waste and would save motions for the garbage man."

"A dog," said Fred, "would keep burglars away. He would sleep on the foot of my bed, and I would wash him whenever he was dirty."

"A dog," Dad mimicked, "would be an accursed nuisance. He would be our master. He would eat me out of house and home. He would spread fleas from the attic to the garage. He would be positive to sleep on the foot of *my* bed. Nobody would wash his filthy, dirty, flea-bitten carcass."

18   He looked pleadingly at Mother.

"Lillie, Lillie, open your eyes," he begged. "Don't you see where this is leading us? Ponies, cars, trips to Hawaii, silk stockings, rouge, and bobbed hair."

"I think, dear," said Mother, "that we must rely on the good sense of the children. A five-dollar dog is not a trip to Hawaii."

We voted; there was only one negative ballot—Dad's. Mother abstained. In after years, as the collie grew older, shed hair on the furniture, bit the mailman, and did in fact try to appropriate the foot of Dad's bed, the chairman was heard to remark on occasion to the assistant chairman:

19   "I give nightly praise to my Maker that I never cast a ballot to bring that lazy, ill-tempered beast into what was once my home. I'm glad I had the courage to go on record as opposing that illegitimate, shameless fleabag that now shares my bed and board. You abstainer, you!"

---

20   Mother took an active part in church and community work. She didn't teach a class, but she served on a number of committees. Once she called on a woman who had just moved to town, to ask her to serve on a fund-raising committee.

"I'd be glad to if I had the time," the woman said. "But I have three young sons and they keep me on the run. I'm sure if you have a boy of your own, you'll understand how much trouble three can be."

"Of course," said Mother. "That's quite all right. And I do understand."

"Have you any children, Mrs. Gilbreth?"

"Oh, yes."

"Any boys?"

"Yes, indeed."

"May I ask how many?"

"Certainly. I have six boys."

"Six boys!" gulped the woman. "Imagine a family of six!"

"Oh, there're more in the family than that. I have six girls, too."

"I surrender," whispered the newcomer. "When is the next meeting of the committee? I'll be there, Mrs. Gilbreth. I'll be there."

21   One teacher in the Sunday school, a Mrs. Bruce, had the next-to-largest family in Montclair. She had eight children, most of whom were older than we. Her husband was very successful in business, and they lived in a large house about two miles from us. Mother and Mrs. Bruce became great friends.

About a year later, a New York woman connected with some sort of national birth control organization came to Montclair to form a local chapter. Her name was Mrs. Alice Mebane, or something like that. She inquired among her acquaintances as to who in

Montclair might be sympathetic to the birth control movement. As a joke, someone referred her to Mrs. Bruce.

"I'd be delighted to cooperate," Mother's friend told Mrs. Mebane, "but you see I have several children myself."

22   "Oh, I had no idea," said Mrs. Mebane. "How many?"

"Several," Mrs. Bruce replied vaguely. "So I don't think I would be the one to head up any birth control movement in Montclair."

"I must say, I'm forced to agree. We should know where we're going, and practice what we preach."

"But I do know just the person for you," Mrs. Bruce continued. "And she has a big house that would be simply ideal for holding meetings."

"Just what we want," purred Mrs. Mebane. "What is her name?"

"Mrs. Frank Gilbreth. She's community-minded, and she's a career woman."

23   "Exactly what we want. Civic minded, career woman, and—most important of all—a large house. One other thing—I suppose it's too much to hope for—but is she by any chance an organizer? You know, one who can take things over and militantly drive ahead?"

"The description," gloated Mrs. Bruce, "fits her like a glove."

"It's almost too good to be true," said Mrs. Mebane, wringing her hands in ecstasy. "May I use your name and tell Mrs. Gilbreth you sent me?"

"By all means," said Mother's friend. "Please do. I shall be disappointed if you don't."

"And don't think that I disapprove of your having children," laughed Mrs. Mebane. "After all, many people do, you know."

24   "Careless of them," remarked Mrs. Bruce.

The afternoon that Mrs. Mebane arrived at our house, all of us children were, as usual, either upstairs in our rooms or playing in the back yard. Mrs. Mebane introduced herself to Mother.

"It's about birth control," she told Mother.

"What about it?" Mother asked, blushing.

"I was told you'd be interested."

"Me?"

"I've just talked to your friend, Mrs. Bruce, and she was certainly interested."

"Isn't it a little late for her to be interested?" Mother asked.

"I see what you mean, Mrs. Gilbreth. But better late than never, don't you think?"

"But she has eight children," said Mother.

Mrs. Mebane blanched, and clutched her head.

"My God," she said. Not really."

Mother nodded.

25   "How perfectly frightful. She impressed me as quite normal. Not at all like an eight-child woman."

"She's kept her youth well," Mother agreed.

"Ah, there's work to be done, all right," Mrs. Mebane said. "Think of it, living right here within eighteen miles of our national birth control headquarters in New York City, and her having eight children. Yes, there's work to be done, Mrs. Gilbreth, and that's why I'm here."

"What sort of work?"

"We'd like you to be the moving spirit behind a Montclair birth control chapter."

26   Mother decided at this point that the situation was too ludicrous for Dad to miss, and that he'd never forgive her if she didn't deal him in.

"I'll have to ask my husband," she said. "Excuse me while I call him."

Mother stepped out and found Dad. She gave him a brief explanation and then led him into the parlor and introduced him.

27   "It's a pleasure to meet a woman in such a noble cause," said Dad.

"Thank you. And it's a pleasure to find a man who thinks of it as noble. In general, I find the husbands much less sympathetic with our aims than the wives. You'd be surprised at some of the terrible things men have said to me."

"I love surprises," Dad leered. "What do you say back to them?"

"If you had seen, as I have," said Mrs. Mebane, "relatively young women grown old before their time by the arrival of unwanted young ones. And population figures show . . . Why Mr. Gilbreth, what are you doing?"

28   What Dad was doing was whistling assembly. On the first note, feet could be heard pounding on the floors above. Doors slammed, there was a landslide on the stairs, and we started skidding into the parlor.

"Nine seconds," said Dad pocketing his stopwatch. "Three short of the all-time record."

"God's teeth," said Mrs. Mebane. "What is it? Tell me quickly. Is it a school? No. Or is it . . .? For Lord's sakes. It is!"

"It is what?" asked Dad.

"It's your family. Don't try to deny it. They're the spit and image of you, and your wife, too!"

"I was about to introduce you," said Dad. "Mrs. Mebane, let me introduce you to the family—or most of it. Seems to me like there should be some more of them around here someplace."

29   "God help us all."

"How many head of children do we have now, Lillie, would you say off hand?"

"Last time I counted, seems to me there was an even dozen of them," said Mother. "I might have missed one or two of them, but not many."

"I'd say twelve would be a pretty fair guess," Dad said.

"Shame on you! And within eighteen miles of national headquarters."

30   "Let's have tea," said Mother.

But Mrs. Mebane was putting on her coat. "You poor dear," she clucked to Mother. "You poor child." Then turning to Dad. "It seems to me that the people of this town have pulled my leg on two different occasions today."

"How revolting," said Dad. "And within eighteen miles of national headquarters, too."

Comprehension

Indicate if each statement is true (T) or false (F) according to your understanding of the passage. Use information in the passage and inferences that can be drawn from the passage to make your decisions.

1. _____ Mr. Gilbreth had difficulty convincing his wife to have twelve children.

2. _____ Mr. Gilbreth would have liked to have a family of twelve boys.

3. _____ Mr. Gilbreth made every effort to separate his professional life from his family life.

4. _____ The Gilbreth Company showed other businesses how to save time.

5. ____ At the Gilbreth home, jobs that were performed regularly were studied so that they could be performed without wasted motion.

6. ____ Irregular jobs were assigned to the child who had the necessary amount of knowledge and free time.

7. ____ Each Gilbreth child was expected to perform certain duties before leaving for school.

8. ____ Mr. Gilbreth set up the Family Council to make sure that the household chores would be distributed among the family members.

9. ____ Apparently, the Gilbreth family had been run for a number of years without the Family Council.

10. ____ A cow is the type of pet Mr. Gilbreth would have liked.

11. ____ The Council voted 12 to 2 in favor of getting a dog.

12. ____ Although the Council was set up as a democracy, Mr. Gilbreth had complete control, and would defeat decisions he did not like.

13. ____ The children hoped that they would soon be able to buy ponies and cars.

14. ____ Mr. Gilbreth finally began to like the dog.

15. ____ Because of her large family, Mrs. Gilbreth was not able to participate in community affairs.

16. ____ Birth control organizations are in favor of small families.

17. ____ Mrs. Bruce and Mrs. Gilbreth were recommended to Mrs. Mebane because both women were very active in the community.

18. ____ Mrs. Bruce was correct when she recommended Mrs. Gilbreth as a good organizer.

19. ____ Mr. Gilbreth whistled to assemble the family.

20. ____ Mrs. Mebane apparently felt that the closer one got to the national birth control headquarters, the smaller families should be.

Discussion/Composition

Do you find the Gilbreth family odd? Describe a day in the life of your family. You may be serious or humorous.

Vocabulary from Context

Exercise 1

Use the context provided to determine the meanings of the italicized words. Write a definition, synonym, or description of each word in the space provided.

1. _____ Although dogs and cats often have large families, rabbits are famous for the size of their *litters,* which sometimes number more than twelve bunnies at one time.

2. _____ By putting his fingers in his mouth and blowing hard through his teeth and fingers, Mr. Gilbreth produced a loud *whistle.*

3. _____ Richard organized his staff with a rigid schedule of jobs and responsibilites which often occupied them twelve hours a day, seven days a week. Many people, unable to tolerate this *regimentation,* quit their jobs after the first week.

4. _____ In order to discover who had a natural ability to learn languages, the students were given tests to determine their language *aptitude.*

5. _____ His behavior became more and more unusual until, just as his family was on the *verge* of sending him to a mental hospital, he recovered.

6. _____ Mark became *hysterical* when his basketball team won, and he did not calm down for several days.

7. _____ Pets are a *nuisance*; if you have one, you can't go anywhere or do anything without making arrangements for them to stay behind or accompany you.

8. _____ That horse won't work without some reward, but it is remarkable how much he can accomplish with a carrot as an *incentive.*

9. _____ Some of the jobs around the house were required, while others were done on a *voluntary* basis.

10. _____ With mud from head to toe, flowers still clutched in his hand, John looked so *ludicrous* that we couldn't help laughing.

Exercise 2

This exercise should be done after you have finished reading the selection from Cheaper *by the* Dozen. *The exercise is designed to determine how well you have been able to use context clues to guess the meaning of unfamiliar vocabulary in the story. Give a definition, synonym, or description of each of the words below. The number in parentheses indicates the paragraph in which the word can be found. Your teacher may want you to do these orally or in writing.*

1. (6)   offspring _____

2. (6)   tender _____

3. (9)   slashed _____

4. (14) sweep _____

5. (17) mimicked _____

6. (18) abstained _____

Figurative Language and Idioms

In the paragraph indicated by the number in parentheses, find the phrase that best fits the meaning given. Your teacher may want to read these aloud as you quickly scan the paragraph to find the answer.

1. (4)   What phrase in the second sentence means *do what he says others should do*?

2. (16) What phrase means *impossible to predict*?

3. (17) What phrase means *cost a great deal to support; cost too much to support*?

4. (23) What phrase means *fits exactly; is exactly correct or appropriate*?

5. (26) What phrase in the first sentence means *include him*?

6. (30) What phrase means *played a joke on*?

Dictionary Study

Many words have more than one meaning. When you use the dictionary to discover the meaning of an unfamiliar word, you need to use the context to determine which definition is appropriate. Use the portions of the dictionary provided on page 279 to select the best definition for each of the italicized words below.

1. "It was an *off* year that didn't bring a new Gilbreth baby."

   _____

2. "Some regimentation was necessary to prevent *bedlam*."

   _____

3. The Family Council determined the amount of the children's *allowances*.

   _____

4. Mr. Gilbreth knew that the children had planned a surprise and it *tickled* him.

   _____

5. He had trouble keeping a *straight face* when he asked for suggestions.

   _____

6. "They're all your children. Don't try to deny it. They're the *spit and image* of you, and

   your wife, too!" _____

7. "How many head of children do we have now, Lillie, would you say *off hand*?"

   _____

al·low·ance (ə-lou′əns), *n.* 1. an allowing. 2. something allowed. 3. an amount of money, food, etc. given regularly to a child, dependent, soldier, etc. 4. a reduction in the price of something in consideration of a large order or of turning in a used article, etc. 5. the amount by which something is allowed to be more or less than stated, as to compensate for the weight of the container, inaccuracy of machining, etc. *v.t.* [ALLOW-ANCED (-ənst), ALLOWANCING], 1. to put on an allowance or a ration. 2. to apportion economically.
  make allowance (or **allowances**), to take circumstances, limitations, etc. into consideration.
  make allowance (or **allowances**) **for,** 1. to forgive or excuse because of mitigating factors. 2. to leave room, time, etc. for: allow for.

bed·lam (bed′ləm), *n.* [ME. *Bedlem, Bethlem* < the London hospital of St. Mary of *Bethlehem*], 1. [B-], a famous old London hospital for the mentally ill. 2. any similar hospital. 3. any noisy, confused place or situation. 4. noise and confusion; uproar. *adj.* full of noise and confusion.

off (ôf), *adv.* [a Late ME. variant spelling of *of*, later generalized for all occurrences of *of* in stressed positions; *off* is thus merely *of* stressed], 1. so as to be away, at a distance, to a side, etc.: as, he moved *off* toward the door. 2. so as to be no longer on, attached, united, in contact, etc.: as, he took *off* his coat, he tore a sheet *off*. 3. (a specified distance) away: *a*) in space: as, the road is 200 yards *off*. *b*) in time: as, my vacation is only two weeks *off*. 4. *a*) so as to be no longer in operation, function, continuance, etc.: as, he turned the motor *off*. *b*) to the point of completion or exhaustion: as, drink it *off*. 5. so as to be less, smaller, fewer, etc.: as, the number of customers dropped *off*. 6. away from one's work or usual activity: as, let's take the week *off*. *prep.* 1. (so as to be) no longer (or not) on, attached, united, etc.: as, it rolled *off* the table, the car is *off* the road. 2. from the substance of; on: as, he lived *off* the fat of the land. 3. coming or branching out from: as, an alley *off* Main Street. 4. free or relieved from: as, *off* duty. 5. not up to the usual level, standard, etc. of: as, badly *off* one's game. 6. [Colloq.], no longer using, engaging in, supporting, etc.; abstaining from: as, he's *off* liquor for life. 7. in *nautical usage*, away from (shore): as, a mile *off* shore. *adj.* 1. not on, attached, united, etc.: as, his hat is *off*. 2. not in operation, function, continuance, etc.: as, the motor is *off*. 3. gone away; on the way: as, the children are *off* to school. 4. less, smaller, fewer, etc.: as, profits are *off* this year. 5. away from work, etc.; absent: as, the office force is *off* today. 6. not up to the usual level, standard, etc.: as, an *off* season. 7. more remote; further: as, on the *off* chance, *off* side. 8. on the right: said of a horse in double harness, etc. 9. in (specified) circumstances: as, they are well *off*. 10. wrong; in error: as, you are *off* in your calculations. 11. in *cricket*, designating the side of the field facing the batsman. 12. in *nautical usage*, toward the sea; seaward. *n.* 1. the fact or condition of being off: as, I've had my *off*s and ons. 2. in *cricket*, the off side. *interj.* go away! stay away! *Off* is also used in various idiomatic expressions, many of which are entered in this dictionary under the key words. Abbreviated **o.**
  be (or **take**) **off,** to go away; depart.
   off and on, now and then; intermittently.
   off with, put off! take off! remove!
   off with you! go away! depart!
off., 1. office. 2. officer. 3. official. 4. officinal.
off·cast, off-cast (ôf′kast′, ôf′käst′), *adj. & n.* castoff.
off-chance (ôf′chans′, ôf′chäns′), *n.* a slight chance.
off-col·or (ôf′kul′ẽr), *adj.* 1. varying from the usual, standard, or required color. 2. not quite proper; in rather poor taste; risqué: as, an *off-color* joke.
off·hand (ôf′hand′), *adv.* without prior preparation or study; at once; extemporaneously. *adj.* 1. said or done offhand; extemporary; unpremeditated; hence, 2. casual, curt, informal, brusque, etc.
off·hand·ed (ôf′han′did), *adj.* offhand.

spit (spit), *n.* [ME. *spite;* AS. *spitu;* akin to OHG. *spizzi,* a point; IE. base **spei-,* a point (cf. SPIRE)], 1. a thin, pointed rod or bar on which meat is impaled and held to be broiled or roasted over a fire. 2. a narrow point of land extending into a body of water. 3. a long, narrow reef, shoal, or sandbank extending from the shore. *v.t.* [SPITTED (-id), SPITTING], to thrust a pointed rod through; fix or impale on or as on a spit.

spit (spit), *v.t.* [SPAT (spat) or SPIT, SPITTING], [ME. *spitten;* AS. *spittan;* akin to Dan. *spytte;* IE. echoic base **sp(h)jēu-,* etc., as also in L. *sputum,* Eng. *spew*], 1. to eject from within the mouth. 2. to eject, throw out, emit, or utter explosively: as, the man *spat* an oath. 3. to light (a fuse). *v.i.* 1. to eject saliva from the mouth; expectorate. 2. to rain or snow lightly or briefly. 3. to make an explosive hissing noise, as an angry cat. *n.* 1. the act of spitting. 2. saliva. 3. something like saliva, as the frothy secretion of certain insects. 4. a light, brief shower of rain or fall of snow. 5. [Colloq.], the likeness or counterpart, as of a person.
  spit and image, [Colloq.], perfect likeness; exact image.
  spit on (or **at**), to express contempt for, hatred of, etc. by or as if by ejecting saliva on or at.

straight (strāt), *adj.* [ME. *streght* (pp. of *strecchen,* to stretch, used as *adj.*); AS. *streht,* pp. of *streccan,* to stretch; cf. STRETCH], 1. having the same direction throughout its length; having no curvature or angularity: as, a *straight* line. 2. not crooked, bent, bowed, wavy, curly, etc.; upright; erect: as, a *straight* back, *straight* hair. 3. with all cylinders in a direct line: said of some internal-combustion engines. 4. direct; undeviating; continuous; uninterrupted, etc.: as, a *straight* course. 5. following strictly the principles, slate of candidates, etc. of a political party: as, he votes a *straight* ticket. 6. following a direct or systematic course of reasoning, etc.; methodical; accurate. 7. in order; properly arranged, etc.: as, put your room *straight*. 8. *a*) honest; sincere; upright. *b*) [Colloq.], reliable, as information. 9. outspoken; frank. 10. unmixed; undiluted: as, *straight* whisky. 11. unqualified; unmodified: as, a *straight* answer. 12. at a fixed price per unit regardless of the quantity bought or sold: as, the apples are ten cents *straight*. 13. in *card games*, consisting of cards in sequence: as, a *straight* flush. *adv.* 1. in a straight line; unswervingly. 2. upright; erectly. 3. without deviation, detour, circumlocution, etc.; directly. *n.* 1. the quality or condition of being straight. 2. something straight; specifically, *a*) the straight part of a racecourse between the last turn and the winning post. *b*) in *poker*, a series of five cards in sequence.
  straight away (or **off**), at once; without delay.
straight angle, an angle of 180 degrees.
straight-arm (strāt′ärm′), *v.t.* in *football*, to push away (a tackler) with the arm outstretched. *n.* the act of straight-arming.
straight·a·way (strāt′ə-wā′), *adj.* extending in a straight line. *n.* a track, or part of a track, that extends in a straight line.
straight·edge (strāt′ej′), *n.* a piece or strip of wood, etc. having a perfectly straight edge used in drawing straight lines, testing plane surfaces, etc.
straight·en (strāt′'n), *v.t. & v.i.* to make or become straight.
straight-faced (strāt′fāst′), *adj.* showing no amusement or other emotion.
straight·for·ward (strāt′fôr′wẽrd), *adj.* 1. moving or leading straight ahead; direct. 2. honest; frank; open. *adv.* in a straightforward manner; directly.
straight·for·wards (strāt′fôr′wẽrdz), *adv.* straightforward.
straight-line (strāt′līn′), *adj.* 1. composed of straight lines. 2. having the parts arranged in a straight line or lines. 3. designating a linkage or similar device (*straight-line motion*) used to produce or copy motion in straight lines.
straight man, in the *theater*, an actor who serves as a foil for a comedian.
straight-out (strāt′out′), *adj.* [Colloq.], 1. straightforward; direct. 2. unrestrained; outright. 3. thoroughgoing; unqualified.
straight·way (strāt′wā′), *adv.* at once; without delay.

tick·le (tik′'l), *v.t.* [TICKLED (-'ld), TICKLING], [ME. *tikelen;* akin to G. dial. *zickeln;* for the base see TICK (insect)], 1. to please; gratify: as, this dessert will *tickle* the palate. 2. to amuse; delight: as, the story *tickled* him. 3. to excite the surface nerves of by touching or stroking lightly with the finger, a feather, etc. so as to cause involuntary twitching, laughter, etc. 4. to rouse, stir, move, get, etc. by or as by touching lightly. *v.i.* 1. to have an itching or tingling sensation: as, my palm *tickles*. 2. to be affected by excitation of the surface nerves; be ticklish. *n.* 1. a tickling or being tickled. 2. a tickling sensation.
  tickle one pink, [Slang], to please one greatly.
tick·ler (tik′lẽr), *n.* 1. a person or thing that tickles. 2. a memorandum pad, file, or other device for aiding the memory. 3. an irritating problem; puzzle. 4. an account book showing notes due and the dates of these.
tick·lish (tik′lish), *adj.* 1. sensitive to tickling. 2. easily upset; unstable; unsteady; touchy; fickle. 3. needing careful handling; precarious; delicate.

From *Webster's New World Dictionary,* College Edition (New York: World Publishing Company).

13

Longer Reading

Psychology

This unit addresses issues of obedience to authority. Before you begin the longer reading in this unit, you will need to complete the Attitude Questionnaire and discuss The Question of Obedience. These selections will provide an introduction to the longer reading, "The Milgram Experiment."

Attitude Questionnaire

In the following questionnaire you are asked to predict your behavior in particular situations and to predict the behaviors of others. Specifically, you are asked to indicate three things:
1. What you, yourself, would do in the situations. Indicate your opinion on the scale marked *S* (for self).
2. What you think would be the reactions of people from your native culture. Indicate this opinion on the scale marked *C* (for native culture).
3. What you think would be the reactions of people in the United States. Indicate this opinion on the scale marked *U* (for U.S. native).

Example

The following item was marked by a college student from Japan.

You are a department head in a company that has very strict rules concerning punctuality. One of your most talented and productive employees is habitually late for work in the mornings. Company policy is to reduce latecomers' wages. Do you obey the company rule?

	Definitely Yes	⟷			Definitely No
S	___ ___ ✔ ___ ___ ___
C	✔ ___ ___ ___ ___ ___
U	___ ___ ___ ___ ___ ✔

Explanation

The checks on the scale indicate that the student believes that there is some difference between her and her fellow citizens, and substantial difference between her and U.S. natives. She indicates that she would probably follow the company rule, while she thinks that most of the people from her native culture would definitely follow the rule, and that most U.S. natives would definitely not follow the rule.

In the questionnaire that follows you will be asked to respond to a number of items such as the one preceding. Remember, there are no right answers. What matters is your honest opinion.

After you have responded to all of the items, your teacher may want you to discuss your answers in small groups.

1. You travel on business a great deal with all expenses paid by your company. On one trip a waiter offers to leave the space blank on your receipt so that you can fill in whatever amount you wish. Do you accept his offer?

	Definitely Yes ⟷ Definitely No
S	___ ___ ___ ___ ___ ___
C	___ ___ ___ ___ ___ ___
U	___ ___ ___ ___ ___ ___

2. You have been attending a course regularly. An acquaintance, who rarely comes to class, asks for help with the take-home exam. Do you agree to help?

	Definitely Yes ⟷ Definitely No
S	___ ___ ___ ___ ___ ___
C	___ ___ ___ ___ ___ ___
U	___ ___ ___ ___ ___ ___

3. The police ask you for information about a friend who has strong political views. Do you give it to them?

	Definitely Yes ⟷ Definitely No
S	___ ___ ___ ___ ___ ___
C	___ ___ ___ ___ ___ ___
U	___ ___ ___ ___ ___ ___

4. You are in love with a person who is a devout follower of a different religion. What do you do?

	Continue to see the person, hoping your differences in religion will not matter.	Change your religion.	Attempt to change the religion of your lover.	End the relationship.
S	___	___	___	___
C	___	___	___	___
U	___	___	___	___

5. You are the manager of a grocery store. You notice a woman stealing food. She is an acquaintance whom you know to be the unemployed single mother of three small children. What do you do?

	Report her to the police.	Speak to her privately; allow her to replace the food.	Ignore the situation.	Secretly pay for the food she took.
S	___	___	___	___
C	___	___	___	___
U	___	___	___	___

6. In a high-level meeting with all of the bosses in your company, a superior takes credit for work of a colleague who is not present. Do you correct the information?

	Definitely Yes ⟷ Definitely No
S	___ ___ ___ ___ ___ ___
C	___ ___ ___ ___ ___ ___
U	___ ___ ___ ___ ___ ___

7. The police have captured a man who they say is a dangerous criminal and whom they hope to convict of a series of violent crimes. You have been brought in to see if he is the same person who robbed you recently in the park. He is not the man who robbed you, but the police are pressing you to testify against him. Do you identify him as the robber?

	Definitely Yes ⟷ Definitely No
S	___ ___ ___ ___ ___ ___
C	___ ___ ___ ___ ___ ___
U	___ ___ ___ ___ ___ ___

8. Your boss is about to fire a woman for a mistake which you know she did not make. You think the woman is not a very good employee. Do you correct your boss?

Definitely Yes ◄——————► Definitely No

S ___ ___ ___ ___ ___ ___

C ___ ___ ___ ___ ___ ___

U ___ ___ ___ ___ ___ ___

9. You discover that your brother is selling important information to a foreign power. What do you do?

	Report him to the police.	Try to convince him to stop.	Ignore the situation.
S	___	___	___
C	___	___	___
U	___	___	___

10. Your company is about to sign an extremely important contract. Your boss asks you to not mention a production problem you have been trying to solve because knowlege of the problem might cause the client to go to a different company. In a meeting with the client you are asked if there are any production problems. Do you tell the truth?

Definitely Yes ◄——————► Definitely No

S ___ ___ ___ ___ ___ ___

C ___ ___ ___ ___ ___ ___

U ___ ___ ___ ___ ___ ___

11. Your boss is having marital difficulties with her husband. She decides to take a weekend vacation with another man. She instructs you to tell her husband that she is at a business meeting. Do you follow her instructions?

Definitely Yes ◄——————► Definitely No

S ___ ___ ___ ___ ___ ___

C ___ ___ ___ ___ ___ ___

U ___ ___ ___ ___ ___ ___

12. You work for a large firm that owns many apartment buildings. You have been instructed to evict all tenants who are behind in their rent. Mr. and Mrs. Jones are hardworking people who have always paid on time. They have five children to support. They have both just lost their jobs and are unable to pay the rent. Do you evict them?

Definitely Yes ◄——————► Definitely No

S ___ ___ ___ ___ ___ ___

C ___ ___ ___ ___ ___ ___

U ___ ___ ___ ___ ___ ___

13. You are taking a college psychology class. The professor asks you to participate in an experiment that requires you to lie to your friends. Do you do as you are told?

Definitely Yes ◄——————► Definitely No

S ___ ___ ___ ___ ___ ___

C ___ ___ ___ ___ ___ ___

U ___ ___ ___ ___ ___ ___

Examine your answers to the questionnaire. Did you tend to see yourself as agreeing more with citizens of your country or with citizens of the U.S.? Do you see yourself as a "member of the group" or as an "individualist"? Did your answers differ markedly from those of other members of your class? What kinds of evidence did people give to support their points of view?

The Question of Obedience

The preceding questionnaire and the longer reading in the next section raise the question of obedience to authority. There are times when we must follow the orders of people in authority and times when we must follow our own conscience. Use the items below to guide your discussion of this conflict between authority and conscience.

1. The following individuals are authority figures in most cultures. Indicate the extent to which they should be obeyed. Compare your responses to those of others in your class.

Most Obedience ◄——► Least Obedience

a. employer   ___ ___ ___ ___ ___ ___

b. police officer ___ ___ ___ ___ ___ ___

c. friend   ___ ___ ___ ___ ___ ___

d. grandmother   ___ ___ ___ ___ ___ ___

e. mother   ___ ___ ___ ___ ___ ___

f. teacher   ___ ___ ___ ___ ___ ___

g. judge   ___ ___ ___ ___ ___ ___

h. father   ___ ___ ___ ___ ___ ___

i. military officer ___ ___ ___ ___ ___ ___

j. religious leader ___ ___ ___ ___ ___ ___

k. grandfather   ___ ___ ___ ___ ___ ___

2. T /F Authority figures should be obeyed even when they order you to do something you disagree with.

3. What do you mean when you use the word obedience?

   a. Are there situations when one should unquestioningly obey an authority? List occasions when this is true.

   _____

   _____

   b. Can you obey someone without doing *exactly* what that person tells you to do? _____

   c. Are there times when children should not obey their elders? _____

   _____

The Milgram Experiment

During the 1960s Yale psychologist Stanley Milgram conducted a study to determine the extent to which ordinary people would obey clearly immoral orders. The results were disturbing and led Milgram to conclude that "ordinary people, simply doing their jobs, and without any hostility on their part, can become agents in a terrible destructive process."

The article that follows summarizes the experiment conducted by Milgram. Your teacher may want you to do Vocabulary from Context exercise 1 on pages 291–92 before you begin reading. Read the first eight paragraphs to understand the design of the experiment, then answer the questions that follow. Your teacher may want you to discuss your answers before continuing with the reading.

THE MILGRAM EXPERIMENT
Ronald E. Smith, Irwin G. Sarason, and Barbara Sarason

1   After World War II the Nuremberg war trials were conducted in order to try Nazi war criminals for the atrocities they had committed. In many instances the defense offered by those on trial was that they had "only followed orders." During the Vietnam War American soldiers accused of committing atrocities in Vietnam gave basically the same explanation for their actions.

2   Most of us reject justifications based on "obedience to authority" as mere rationalizations, secure in our convictions that we, if placed in the same situation, would behave differently. However, the results of a series of ingenious and controversial investigations performed in the 1960s by psychologist Stanley Milgram suggest that perhaps we should not be so sure of ourselves.

3   Milgram wanted to determine the extent to which people would obey an experimenter's commands to administer painful electric shocks to another person. Pretend for a moment that you are a subject in one of his studies. Here is what would happen. On arriving at a university laboratory in response to a classified ad offering volunteers $4 for one hour's participation in an experiment on memory, you meet another subject, a pleasant, middle-aged man with whom you chat while awaiting the arrival of the experimenter. When the experimenter arrives, dressed in a laboratory coat, he pays you and then informs you and the other person that one of you will be the subject in the experiment and that the other will serve as his assistant. You are chosen by lot to be the assistant, but in reality you are the subject.

4   The experimenter explains that the study is concerned with the effects of punishment on learning. Accompanied by you, the "subject" is conducted into a room and strapped into a chair, and a large electrode is attached to his wrist. He is told that he is to learn a list of word pairs and that whenever he makes an error he will receive electric shocks of increasing intensity. On hearing this, the "subject" responds, "When I was at the West Haven V.A. Hospital a few years

---

Ronald E. Smith, Irwin G. Sarason, and Barbara R. Sarason, "Blind Obedience to Authority" (pp. 19–22 sans table, figure, and quotes by Milgram) from *Psychology: The Frontiers of Behavior* by Ronald E. Smith, Irwin G. Sarason, and Barbara R. Sarason (New York: Harper and Row).

ago, they detected a slight heart condition. Nothing serious, but are these shocks dangerous?" The experimenter replies in an unconcerned manner that although the shocks may be painful, they will cause no permanent tissue damage.

5   You and the experimenter then proceed to an adjoining room connected by an intercom so that the "subject's" responses can be heard. You are seated in front of an apparatus with 30 toggle switches ranging from 15 volts to 450 volts. (See Figure 1.) Your task is to administer the learning task to the "subject." Whenever he gives an incorrect answer, you must give him an electric shock, starting at the lowest level (15 volts) and increasing the level by 15 volts each time. You are given a sample shock of 45 volts and find it moderately painful.

6   What you are unaware of at this point is that you are in a carefully contrived situation. The learner is actually an actor who receives no shock at all, and the responses you hear over the intercom are tape-recorded so that they will be exactly the same for each "assistant." The experimenter's actions are also carefully programmed.

7   As the experiment proceeds, the learner makes error after error. You increase the shock level steadily until he is clearly experiencing pain. The tape-recorded responses are programmed to correspond to the shock intensities as follows:

75 volts	Ugh!
90 volts	Ugh!
105 volts	Ugh! (louder)
120 volts	Ugh! Hey, this really hurts.
135 volts	Ugh!!
150 volts	Ugh!!! Experimenter! That's all. Get me out of here. I told you I had heart trouble. My heart's starting to bother me now. Get me out of here. I told you I had heart trouble. My heart's starting to bother me. I refuse to go on. Let me out.
165 volts	Ugh! Let me out. (shouting)
180 volts	Ugh! I can't stand the pain. Let me out of here! (shouting)
195 volts	Ugh! Let me out of here. Let me out of here. My heart's bothering me. Let me out of here! You have no right to keep me here! Let me out! Let me out of here! My heart's bothering me. Let me out! Let me out!
210 volts	Ugh!! Experimenter! Get me out of here. I've had enough. I won't be in the experiment any more.
225 volts	Ugh!
240 volts	Ugh!
255 volts	Ugh! Get me out of here.
270 volts	(Agonized scream). Let me out of here. Let me out of here. Let me out of here. Let me out. Do you hear? Let me out of here.
285 volts	(Agonized scream).
300 volts	(Agonized scream). I absolutely refuse to answer any more. Get me out of here. You can't hold me here. Get me out. Get me out of here.
315 volts	(Intensely agonized scream). I told you I refuse to answer. I'm no longer part of this experiment.

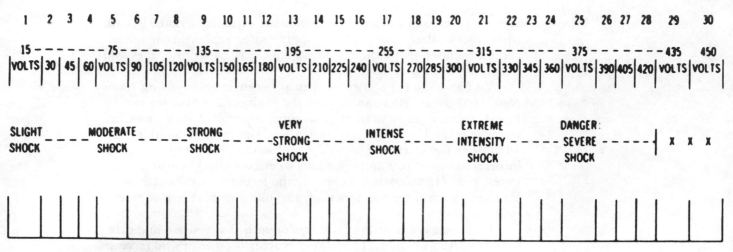

Figure 1 The control panel of the shocking apparatus used in the Milgram research. Copyright © 1974 by Stanley Milgram. Reprinted by permission of Harper & Row, Publishers, Inc.

330 volts   (*Intense and prolonged agonized scream*). Let me out of here. Let me out of here. My heart's bothering me. Let me out, I tell you. (*Hysterically*) Let me out of here. Let me out of here. You have no right to hold me here. Let me out! Let me out! Let me out of here! Let me out! Let me out!

345 volts   (*At 345 volts and thereafter, there was only silence.*)[1]

8   But supposing you express unwillingness at some point to continue shocking the learner? In that event the experimenter, sitting at a nearby desk, would respond in one of the following ways:

"Please continue" or "Please go on."
"The experiment requires that you continue."
"It is absolutely essential that you continue."
"You have no other choice. You must go on."

[1]Stanley Milgram, *Obedience to Authority* (New York: Harper and Row, 1975).

Comprehension

Exercise 1

Pretend you have volunteered to participate in Milgram's experiment as you answer the following questions. True/False items are indicated by a T / F preceding the item.

1. T / F̶   The person you first meet at the laboratory is the experimenter.

2. T / F̶   You have an equal chance of being the person giving the shocks (the assistant) or the person receiving the shocks (the learner).

3. T̶ / F   You are told you will be the assistant.

4. T / F The experimenter does not tell you the true purpose of the experiment.

5. T / F In reality, the experiment studies the effects of punishment in learning.

6. T / F The shocks are not dangerous.

7. T / F When you pull a switch, the learner receives a shock.

8. T / F Some learners make more mistakes than others.

9. T / F If you say that you do not want to continue, the experimenter stops the experiment.

10. Why is *subject* in quotation marks in paragraphs 4 and 5? _____ *not really the subject* _____

_____

11. If you were a participant in this experiment, at what point would you stop administering

"shocks"? _____

_____

12. What results would you predict for the experiment?

   a. Do you think most people would continue pulling the switches? How long do you think
      most people would continue?

      _____

   b. Do you think there would be different results depending on the subject's age, education,
      nationality, sex?

      _____

Now, read the rest of the article and answer the questions that follow.

9   Having now experienced the Milgram situation at least in your
imagination, how long do you think you would continue to <u>administer</u>
shocks? Most of our students maintain that they would not go beyond
105 volts before <u>refusing</u> to continue the experiment. A panel of
<u>psychiatrists</u> predicted before the experiment that perhaps only 1
percent of the subjects would proceed to the 450-volt level.

10   In fact, however, the "shock" produced by the results of this
study was much more startling than the <u>simulated</u> shocks in the experiment. Forty men ranging in age from 20 to 50 and representing a
cross section of the population, participated in the <u>investigation</u>. The
maximum shock levels they <u>administered</u> are shown in Table 1.
Nearly two-thirds of them <u>administered</u> the 450-volt maximum
shock, and the average maximum shock they <u>administered</u> was 368
volts.

Table 1 Maximum shock levels administered by subjects in the Milgram experiment.

Shock level	Verbal designation and voltage level	Number of subjects giving each maximum shock level
	Slight Shock	
1	15	
2	30	
3	45	
4	60	
	Moderate Shock	
5	75	
6	90	1
7	105	
8	120	
	Strong Shock	
9	135	
10	150	6
11	165	
12	180	1
	Very Strong Shock	
13	195	
14	210	
15	225	
16	240	
	Intense Shock	
17	255	
18	270	2
19	285	
20	300	1
	Extreme-Intensity Shock	
21	315	1
22	330	1
23	345	
24	360	
	Danger: Severe Shock	
25	375	1
26	390	
27	405	
28	420	
	XXX	
29	435	
30	450	26
	Average maximum shock level	368 volts
	Percentage of obedient subjects	65.0%

11   Virtually all the people who administered high levels of shock exhibited extreme discomfort, anxiety, and distress. Most verbally refused to continue on one or more occasions. But continue they did when ordered to do so by the experimenter, who assured them that what happened in the experiment was his responsibility.

12   By contriving a situation with many real-life elements, Milgram succeeded in demonstrating that a high percentage of "normal" people will obey an authority figure even when the destructive effects of

their obedience are obvious. The conclusions that he draws from his work are chilling indeed:

13   A commonly offered explanation is that those who shocked the victim at the most severe level were monsters, the sadistic fringe of society. But if one considers that almost two-thirds of the participants fall into the category of "obedient" subjects, and that they represented ordinary people drawn from working, managerial, and professional classes, the argument becomes very shaky. . . . After witnessing hundreds of ordinary people submit to the authority in our own experiments, I must conclude that [Hannah] Arendt's conception of the *banality of evil* comes closer to the truth than one might dare imagine. The ordinary person who shocked the victim did so out of a sense of obligation — a conception of his duties as a subject — and not from any peculiarly aggressive tendencies.

14   This is, perhaps, the most fundamental lesson of our study: ordinary people, simply doing their jobs, and without any particular hostility on their part, can become agents in a terrible destructive process. Moreover, even when the destructive effects of their work become patently clear, and they are asked to carry out actions incompatible with fundamental standards of morality, relatively few people have the resources needed to resist authority. A variety of inhibitions against disobeying authority come into play and successfully keep the person in his place. (Milgram, 1974, pp. 5–6) [2]

15 Milgram's method of investigation also generated shock waves among psychologists. Many questioned whether it was ethical to expose subjects without warning to experiments that were likely to generate considerable stress and that might conceivably have lasting negative effects on them. But supporters of Milgram's work argue that adequate precautions were taken to protect participants. There was an extensive debriefing at the conclusion of the experiment, and participants were informed that they had not actually shocked anyone. They had a friendly meeting with the unharmed "subject." The purpose of the experiment was explained to them, and they were assured that their behavior in the situation was perfectly normal. Further, supporters argue, the great societal importance of the problem being investigated justified the methods the experimenters used. Finally, they cite follow-up questionnaire data collected by Milgram from his subjects after they received a complete report of the purposes and results. Eighty-four percent of the subjects stated that they were glad to have been in the experiment (and several spontaneously noted that their participation had made them more tolerant of others or otherwise changed them in desirable ways). Fifteen percent expressed neutral feelings, and only 1.3 percent stated that they were sorry to have participated.

16 The controversy over the ethics of Milgram's research has raged for decades. In combination with other controversial issues, it has prompted a deep and abiding concern for protecting the welfare of subjects in psychological research. Because of such concerns, it is most unlikely that Milgram's research could be conducted today.

---

[2]Stanley Milgram, *Obedience to Authority* (New York: Harper and Row, 1975).

Exercise 2

Answer the following questions. Your teacher may want you to do this exercise orally, in writing, or by underlining appropriate parts of the text. True/False items are indicated by a T / F preceding a statement.

1. What was the purpose of Milgram's experiment? _____

   _____

2. T / F   Most of the subjects continued to shock the learners when the shock level reached the danger level.

3. T / F   The subjects appeared to enjoy the opportunity to hurt other people.

4. T / F   The people who shocked the learners at the most severe level were mentally disturbed or in other ways antisocial.

5. T / F   Today we are far more sophisticated than we were in the 1960s and therefore we do not have to worry about people submitting to an immoral authority.

6. T / F   Most professionals, school teachers for example, are incapable of inflicting pain on others while following a superior's orders.

7. The authors state that the subjects were visibly shaken by the experience, and that many refused to continue. Why *did* they continue if it was so painful for the learner and so upsetting for them? Why didn't they just refuse to go on?

   _____

   _____

8. Follow-up studies indicated that the subjects' opinions of the experiment were generally positive.

   a. T / F   These positive evaluations could be attributed to the subjects' respect for the experimenter, and their obedience to his authority.

   b. T / F   The results of the experiment should cause us to doubt the validity of the follow-up study.

9. T / F   If Stanley Milgram participated in such an experiment, he would probably agree to push the shocks above the comfort level.

Vocabulary from Context

Use the context provided to determine the meanings of the italicized words. Write a definition, synonym, or description of each of the italicized items in the space provided.

1. _____   Many people, when forced to justify poor behavior, come up with *rationalizations* that seem convincing but are really just excuses.

2. _____   The experiment was cleverly organized to appear as if it were real, but in fact it was merely a *simulation* in which all of the participants were actors.

3. _____   Extraordinary evil is very frightening, but when it appears as if evil has a common, everyday quality about it, its *banality* is even more frightening.

4. _____   Scientists cannot agree on the value of the Milgram study. Heated debate and angry disagreement have surrounded the *controversial* research ever since the first experiment was completed.

5. _____   We are all comforted by the thought that society is governed by a system of moral principles and human values. It is, in fact, our confidence in the *ethical* nature of the common person that gives us peace of mind.

Exercise 2

This exercise is designed to give you additional clues to determine the meanings of unfamiliar words in context. In the paragraph indicated by the number in parentheses, find the word that best fits the meaning given. Your teacher may want to read these aloud as you quickly scan the paragraph to find the answer.

1. (1)   Which word means *extremely wicked or cruel acts*?

2. (2)   Which word means *very clever*?

3. (3)   Which word means *give*?

4. (3)   Which word means *person studied in an experiment*?

5. (6)   Which word means *constructed, designed*?

6. (11) Which word means *almost*?

7. (13) Which word means *cruel; experiencing pleasure from others' suffering*?

8. (15) Which word means *a session provided to give information to an experimental subject after the experiment*?

Figurative Language and Idioms

In the paragraph indicated by the number in parentheses, find the phrase that best fits the meaning given. Your teacher may want to read these aloud as you quickly scan the paragraph to find the answer.

1. (3)   What phrase means *by chance, at random*?

2. (10) What phrase means *a wide variety*?

3. (12) What word means *frightening*?

4. (13) What phrase means *the edges of normal society*?

5. (16) What phrase means *has occurred energetically and violently*?

Discussion/Composition

1. What is the correct balance between individual conscience and one's obedience to authority? How do we protect ourselves against evil leaders and immoral authority figures?

2. Some scientists argue that experiments such as this violate basic human rights of the subjects because they deceive the participants. Others claim that the deception is justified because of the importance of the findings. What do you think?

   a. In what ways are the subjects deceived?

   b. What might be the negative effects upon the subjects of having participated in the study?

   c. What is the importance of this sort of study? What do you know now about society that you did not know before reading the article?

14

Longer Reading

Suspense

Before You Begin   1. Is it possible to rob a bank and not commit a crime?

                                          2. Why would someone want to rob a bank? Money of course. But is that the only reason?

Read "The Dusty Drawer" carefully. It is a special kind of mystery story that raises some interesting questions about human nature and about the difference between breaking the law and doing something that is wrong.

    You may want to do the Vocabulary from Context exercise on pages 305–6 and the Dictionary Study on page 307 before you begin reading. In addition, after you have read the first eleven paragraphs, you may want to do the first four items of the Figurative Language and Idioms exercise on page 306.

The Dusty Drawer

Harry Miles Muheim

1   Norman Logan paid for his apple pie and coffee, then carried his tray toward the front of the cafeteria. From a distance, he recognized the back of William Tritt's large head. The tables near Tritt were empty, and Logan had no desire to eat with him, but they had some unfinished business that Logan wanted to clear up. He stopped at Tritt's table and asked, "Do you mind if I join you?"

2   Tritt looked up as he always looked up from inside his teller's cage in the bank across the street. He acted like a servant—like a fat, precise butler that Logan used to see in movies—but behind the film of obsequiousness was an attitude of vast superiority that always set Logan on edge.

3   "Why, yes, Mr. Logan. Do sit down. Only please, I must ask you not to mention that two hundred dollars again."

    "Well, we'll see about that," said Logan, pulling out a chair and seating himself. "Rather late for lunch, isn't it?"

    "Oh, I've had lunch," Tritt said. "This is just a snack." He cut a large piece of roast

"The Dusty Drawer" by Harry Miles Muheim, from *Alfred Hitchcock Presents a Month of Mystery* (New York: Random House).

beef from the slab in front of him and thrust it into his mouth. "I don't believe I've seen you all summer," he added, chewing the meat.

4   "I took a job upstate," Logan said. "We were trying to stop some kind of blight in the apple orchards."

"Is that so?" Tritt looked like a concerned bloodhound.

"I wanted to do some research out West," Logan went on, "but I couldn't get any money from the university."

"You'll be back for the new term, won't you?"

5   "Oh, yes," Logan said with a sigh, "we begin again tomorrow." He thought for a moment of the freshman faces that would be looking up at him in the lecture room. A bunch of high-strung, mechanical New York City kids, pushed by their parents into his botany class. They were brick-bound people who had no interest in growing things, and Logan sometimes felt sad that in five years of teaching he had communicated to only a few of them his own delight with his subject.

6   "My, one certainly gets a long vacation in the teaching profession," Tritt said. "June through September."

"I suppose," Logan said. "Only trouble is that you don't make enough to do anything in all the spare time."

Tritt laughed a little, controlled laugh and continued chewing. Logan began to eat the pie. It had the drab, neutral flavor of all cafeteria pies.

"Mr. Tritt," he said after a long silence.

"Yes?"

"When are you going to give me back my two hundred dollars?"

7   "Oh, come now, Mr. Logan. We had this all out ten months ago. We went over it with Mr. Pinkson and the bank examiners and everyone. I did *not* steal two hundred dollars from you."

"You did, and you know it."

"Frankly, I'd rather not hear any more about it."

"Mr. Tritt, I had three hundred and twenty-four dollars in my hand that day. I'd just cashed some bonds. I know how much I had."

"The matter has been all cleared up," Tritt said coldly.

8   "Not for me, it hasn't. When you entered the amount in my checking account, it was for one hundred and twenty-four, not three hundred twenty-four."

9   Tritt put down his fork and carefully folded his hands. "I've heard you tell that story a thousand times, sir. My cash balanced when you came back and complained."

"Sure it balanced," Logan exploded. "You saw your mistake when Pinkson asked you to check the cash. So you took my two hundred out of the drawer. No wonder it balanced!"

Tritt laid a restraining hand on Logan's arm. "Mr. Logan, I'm going a long, long way in the bank. I simply can't afford to make mistakes."

10   "You also can't afford to admit it when you do make one!"

"Oh, come now," said Tritt, as though he were speaking to a child. "Do you think I'd jeopardize my entire career for two hundred dollars?"

"You didn't jeopardize your career," Logan snapped. "You knew you could get away with it. And you took my money to cover your error."

11   Tritt sat calmly and smiled a fat smile at Logan. "Well, that's your version, Mr. Logan. But I do wish you'd quit annoying me with your fairy tale." Leaving half his meat untouched, Tritt stood up and put on his hat. Then he came around the table and stood looming over Logan. "I will say, however, from a purely hypothetical point of view, that if I *had* stolen your money and then staked my reputation on the lie that I hadn't, the worst thing I could possibly do would be to return the money to you. I think you'd agree with that."

"I'll get you, Tritt," said Logan, sitting back in the chair. "I can't stand to be had."

"I know, I know. You've been saying that for ten months, too. Good-by, now."

12   Tritt walked out of the cafeteria. Norman Logan sat there motionless watching the big teller cross the street and enter the bank. He felt no rage—only an increased sense of futility. Slowly, he finished his coffee.

A few minutes later, Logan entered the bank. Down in the safe-deposit vaults, he raised the lid of his long metal box and took out three twenty-five dollar bonds. With a sigh, he began to fill them out for cashing. They would cover his government insurance premium for the year. In July, too, he'd taken three bonds from the box, when his father had overspent his pension money. And earlier in the summer, Logan had cashed some more of them, after slamming into a truck and damaging his Plymouth. Almost every month there was some reason to cash bonds, and Logan reflected that he hadn't bought one since his Navy days. There just wasn't enough money in botany.

13   With the bonds in his hand, he climbed the narrow flight of stairs to the street floor, then walked past the long row of tellers' cages to the rear of the bank. Here he opened an iron gate in a low marble fence and entered the green-carpeted area of the manager and assistant manager. The manager's desk was right inside the gate, and Mr. Pinkson looked up as Logan came in. He smiled, looking over the top of the glasses pinched on his nose.

14   "Good afternoon, Mr. Logan." Pinkson's quick eyes went to the bonds; and then, with the professional neutrality of a branch manager, right back up to Logan's thin face. "If you'll just sit down, I'll buzz Mr. Tritt."

"Mr. Tritt?" said Logan, surprised.

"Yes. He's been moved up to the first cage now."

Pinkson indicated a large, heavy table set far over against the side wall in back of his desk, and Logan sat in a chair next to it.

"Have a good summer?" The little man had revolved in his squeaky executive's chair to face Logan.

"Not bad, thanks."

"Did you get out of the city?"

"Yes, I had a job upstate. I always work during my vacations."

15   Mr. Pinkson let out a controlled chuckle, a suitable reply when he wasn't sure whether or not the customer was trying to be funny. Then he revolved again; his chubby cue-ball head bobbed down, and he was back at his figures.

Logan put the bonds on the clean desk blotter and looked over at Tritt's cage. It was at the end of the row of cages, with a door opening directly into the manager's area. Tritt was talking on the telephone inside, and for a long, unpleasant minute Logan watched the fat, self-assured face through the greenish glass. I'll get him yet, Logan thought. But he didn't see how. Tritt had been standing firmly shielded behind his lie for nearly a year now, and Norman Logan didn't seem to know enough about vengeance to get him.

16   Restive, Logan sat back and tipped the chair onto its hind legs. He picked ineffectually at a gravy stain on his coat; then his eye was attracted to a drawer, hidden under the overhang of the tabletop. It was a difficult thing to see, for it had no handle, and its face was outlined by only a thin black crack in the darkstained wood. Logan could see faintly the two putty-filled holes that marked the place where the handle had once been. Curious, he rocked forward a little and slipped his fingernails into the crack along the bottom of the drawer. He pulled gently, and the drawer slid smoothly and silently from the table.

17   The inside was a dirty, cluttered mess. Little mounds of grayish mold had formed on the furniture glue along the joints. A film of dust on the bottom covered the bits of faded yellow paper and rusted paper clips that were scattered about. Logan rocked the chair back farther, and the drawer came far out to reveal a delicate spider web. The spider was

dead and flaky, resting on an old page from a desk calendar. The single calendar sheet read October 2, 1936. Logan pushed the drawer softly back into the table, wondering if it had actually remained closed since Alf Landon was running against Roosevelt.

18   The door of Tritt's cage clicked open, and he came out, carrying a large yellow form. William Tritt moved smoothly across the carpet, holding his fat young body erect and making a clear effort to keep his stomach in.

"Why, hello, Mr. Logan," he said. "I'm sorry for the delay. The main office called me. I can't hang up on them, you know."

"I know," Logan said.

The teller smiled as he lowered himself into the chair opposite Logan. Logan slid the bonds across the table.

19   "It's nice to see you again," Tritt said pleasantly as he opened his fountain pen. "Preparing for the new semester, I suppose?" There was no indication of their meeting across the street. Logan said nothing in reply, so Tritt went to work, referring rapidly to the form for the amount to be paid on each bond. "Well, that comes to sixty-seven dollars and twenty-five cents," he said, finishing the addition quickly.

Logan filled out a deposit slip. "Will you put it in my checking account, please?" He handed his passbook across the table. "And will you please enter the right amount?"

20   "Certainly, Mr. Logan," Tritt said, smiling indulgently. Logan watched carefully as Tritt made the entry. Then the teller walked rapidly back to his cage, while Logan, feeling somehow compelled to do so, took another glance into the dusty drawer. He kept thinking about the drawer as he got on a bus and rode up to the university. It had surprised him to stumble upon a dirty, forgotten place like that in a bank that was always so tidy.

21   Back in the biology department, Logan sat down at his desk, planning to prepare some roll sheets for his new classes. He stayed there for a long time without moving. The September sun went low behind the New Jersey Palisades, but he did not prepare the sheets, for the unused drawer stayed unaccountably in his mind.

Suddenly he sat forward in his chair. In a surprising flash of creative thought, he had seen how he could make use of the drawer. He wasn't conscious of having tried to develop a plan. The entire plan simply burst upon him all at once, and with such clarity and precision that he hardly felt any responsibility for it. He would rob the bank and pin the robbery on Tritt. That would take care of Tritt . . .

22   In the weeks that followed, Norman Logan remained surprisingly calm about his plan. Each time he went step by step over the mechanics of the robbery, it seemed more gemlike and more workable. He made his first move the day he got his November pay check.

Down on Fifty-first Street, Logan went into a novelty-and-trick store and bought a cigarette case. It was made of a dark, steel-blue plastic, and it looked like a trim thirty-eight automatic. When the trigger was pressed, a section of the top of the gun flipped upon a hinge, revealing the cigarettes inside the handle.

23   With this in his pocket, Logan took a bus way down to the lower part of Second Avenue and entered a grimy little shop displaying pistols and rifles in the window. The small shopkeeper shuffled forward, and Logan asked to see a thirty-eight.

"Can't sell you a thing until I see your permit," the man said. "The Sullivan Law."

"Oh, I don't want to buy a weapon," Logan explained. He took out his plastic gun. "I just want to see if the real thing looks like mine here."

24   The little man laughed a cackle laugh and brought up a thirty-eight from beneath the counter, placing it next to Logan's. "So you'll just be fooling around, eh?"

"That's right," said Logan, looking at the guns. They were almost identical.

"Oh, they look enough alike," said the man. "But lemme give you a tip. Put some Scotch tape over that lid to keep it down. Friend of mine was using one of those things, mister. He'd just polished off a stick-up when he pulled the trigger and the lid flopped open. Well, he tried to offer the victim a cigarette, but the victim hauled off and beat the hell out of him."

"Thanks," Logan said with a smile. "I'll remember that."

"Here, you can put some Scotch tape on right now."

25   Logan walked over to the Lexington Avenue line and rode uptown on the subway. It was five minutes to three when he got to the bank. The old, gray-uniformed guard touched his cap as Logan came through the door. The stand-up desks were crowded, so it was natural enough for Logan to go through the little iron gate and cross to the table with the drawer. Mr. Pinkson and the new assistant manager had already left; their desks were clear. As Logan sat down, Tritt stuck his head out the door of his cage.

"More bonds, Mr. Logan?" he asked.

"No," said Logan. "Just a deposit."

26   Tritt closed the door and bent over his work. Logan took out his wallet, removed the pay check, then looked carefully the length of the bank. No one was looking in his direction. As he put the wallet back into his inside coat pocket, he withdrew the slim plastic gun and eased open the drawer. He dropped the gun in, shut the drawer, deposited the check, and went home to his apartment. In spite of the Sullivan Law, he was on his way.

27   Twice during November he used the table with the drawer. Each time he checked on the gun. It had not been moved. By the time he deposited his December check, Logan was completely certain that nobody ever looked in there. On the nineteenth of the month, he decided to take the big step.

28   Next morning, after his ten-o'clock class, Logan walked six blocks through the snow down the hill to the bank. He took four bonds out of his safe-deposit box and filled them out for cashing. The soothing sound of recorded Christmas carols floated down from the main floor.

29   Upstairs, he seated himself at the heavy table to wait for Tritt. Pinkson had nodded and returned to his figuring; the nervous assistant manager was not around. The carols were quite loud here, and Logan smiled at this unexpected advantage. He placed the bonds squarely on the blotter. Then he slipped open the drawer, took out the gun with his left hand, and held it below the table.

30   Tritt was coming toward him, carrying his bond chart. They said hello, and Tritt sat down and went to work. He totaled the sum twice and said carefully, still looking at the figures, "Well, Mr. Logan, that comes to eighty-three fifty."

"I'll want something in addition to the eighty-three fifty," said Logan, leaning forward and speaking in an even voice.

"What's that?" asked Tritt.

"Ten thousand dollars in twenty-dollar bills."

Tritt's pink face smiled. He started to look up into Logan's face, but his eyes froze on the muzzle of the gun poking over the edge of the table. He did not notice the Scotch tape.

"Now just go to your cage and get the money." Logan said.

31   It was William Tritt's first experience with anything like this. "Mr. Logan. Come now, Mr. Logan . . ." He swallowed and tried to start again, but his self-assurance had deserted him. He turned toward Pinkson's back.

"Look at me," snapped Logan.

Tritt turned back. "Mr. Logan, you don't know what you're doing."

"Keep still."

"Couldn't we give you a loan or perhaps a—"

32   "Listen to me, Tritt." Logan's voice was just strong enough to carry above "The

First Noel." He was amazed at how authoritative he sounded. "Bring the money in a bag. Place it on the table here."

Tritt started to object, but Logan raised the gun slightly, and the last resistance drained from Tritt's fat body.

"All right, all right. I'll get it." As Tritt moved erratically toward his cage, Logan dropped the gun back into the drawer and closed it. Tritt shut the door of the cage, and his head disappeared below the frosted part of the glass. Immediately, Mr. Pinkson's telephone buzzed, and he picked it up. Logan watched his back, and after a few seconds, Pinkson's body stiffened. Logan sighed, knowing then that he would not get the money on this try.

33   Nothing happened for several seconds; then suddenly the little old guard came rushing around the corner of the cages, his big pistol drawn and wobbling as he tried to hold it on Logan.

"Okay, Okay. Stay there! Put your hands up, now!"

Logan raised his hands, and the guard turned to Pinkson with a half-surprised face. "Okay, Mr. Pinkson. Okay, I've got him covered now."

34   Pinkson got up as Tritt came out of the cage. Behind the one gun, the three men came slowly toward Logan.

"Careful, Louie, he's armed," Tritt warned the guard.

"May I ask what this is all about?" Logan said, his hands held high.

"Mr. Logan," said Pinkson, "I'm sorry about this, but Mr. Tritt here tells me that—that—"

"That you tried to rob me of ten thousand dollars," said Tritt, his voice choppy.

"I—I *what?*"

"You just attempted an armed robbery of this bank," Tritt said slowly. "Don't try to deny it."

35   Logan's face became the face of a man so completely incredulous that he cannot speak. He remembered not to overplay it, though. First he simply laughed at Tritt. Then he lowered his hands, regardless of the guard's gun, and stood up, the calm, indignant faculty member.

"All I can say, Mr. Tritt, is that I do deny it."

"Goodness," said Pinkson.

"Better take his gun, Louie," Tritt ordered the guard.

The guard stepped gingerly forward to Logan and frisked him, movie style. "Hasn't got a gun, Mr. Tritt," he said.

36   "Of course he's got a gun," snapped Tritt. He pushed the guard aside. "It's right in his coat." Tritt jammed his thick hand into Logan's left coat pocket and flailed it about. "It's not in that pocket," he said after a moment.

"It's not in any pocket," Logan said. "I don't have one."

37   "You do. You *do* have a gun. I saw it," Tritt answered, beginning to sound like a child in an argument. He spun Logan around and pulled the coat off him with a jerk. The sleeves turned inside out. Eagerly, the teller pulled the side pockets out, checked the inside pocket and the breast pocket, then ran his hands over the entire garment, crumpling it. "The—the gun's not in his coat," he said finally.

"It's not in his pants," the guard added.

38   Tritt stepped over to the table quickly. "It's around here somewhere," he said. "We were sitting right here." He stood directly in front of the closed drawer, and his hands began to move meaninglessly over the tabletop. He picked up the neat stack of deposit slips, put them down again, then looked under the desk blotter, as though it could have concealed a gun.

39   Logan knew he had to stop this. "Is there any place I can remove the rest of my

clothes?" he asked loudly, slipping the suspenders from his shoulders. Several depositors had gathered on the other side of the marble fence to watch, and Mr. Pinkson had had enough.

40   "Oh, no, no," he said, almost shouting. "That won't be necessary, Mr. Logan. Louie said you were unarmed. Now, Louie, put *your* gun away, and for goodness' sake, request the customers to please move on."

"But Mr. Pinkson, you must believe me," Tritt said, coming over to the manager. "This man held a gun on me and—"

"It's hard to know what to believe," said Pinkson. "But no money was stolen, and I don't see how we can embarrass Mr. Logan further with this matter. Please, Mr. Logan, do pull up your suspenders."

41   It was a shattering moment for the teller—the first time his word had ever been doubted at the bank.

"But sir, I insist that this man—"

"I must ask you to return to your cage now, Mr. Tritt," Pinkson said, badly agitated. Tritt obeyed.

The manager helped Logan put on his coat, then steered him over to his desk. "This is all a terrible mistake, Mr. Logan. Please do sit down now, please." The friendly little man was breathing heavily. "Now, I just want you to know that if you should press this complaint, it—it would go awfully bad for us down in the main office downtown, and I—"

42   "Please don't get excited, Mr. Pinkson," Logan said with a smile. "I'm not going to make any complaint." Logan passed the whole thing off casually. Mr. Tritt imagined he saw a gun, that's all. It was simply one of those aberrations that perfectly normal people get occasionally. Now, could Mr. Pinkson finish cashing his bonds? The manager paid him the eighty-three fifty, continuing to apologize.

Logan left the bank and walked through the soft snowfall, whistling a Christmas carol. He'd handled himself perfectly.

43   In the weeks that followed, Logan continued to do business with Tritt, just as though nothing had happened. The teller tried to remain aloof and calm, but added sums incorrectly, and his hands shook. One day late in January, Tritt stood up halfway through a transaction, his great body trembling, "Excuse me, Mr. Logan," he murmured, and rushed off into the corridor behind the cages. Pinkson followed him, and Logan took advantage of the moment to check on the gun. It lay untouched in the drawer. Then Pinkson came back alone. "I'm awfully sorry to delay you again, sir," he said. "Mr. Tritt doesn't feel too well."

44   "Did he imagine he saw another gun?" Logan asked quietly.

"No. He just upsets easily now. Ever since that incident with you last month, he's been like a cat on a hot stove."

"I've noticed he's changed."

"He's lost that old, calm banking touch, Mr. Logan. And of course, he's in constant fear of a new hallucination."

"I'm sorry to hear that," Logan said, looking genuinely concerned. "It's very sad when a person loses his grip."

45   "It's particularly disappointing to me," the manager said sadly. "I brought Tritt into the bank myself, you see. Had him earmarked for a big spot downtown someday. Fine man. Intelligent, steady, accurate—why he's been right down the line on everything. But now—now he's—well, I *do* hope he gets over this."

46   "I can understand how you feel," Logan said sympathetically. He smiled inside at the precision of his planning. Fat William Tritt had been undermined just enough—not only in Pinkson's mind but in his own.

47   On the tenth of March, Norman Logan acted again. When Tritt was seated across from him, Logan said, "Well, here we go again, Mr. Tritt." Tritt's head came up, and once

more he was looking into the barrel of the toy automatic. He did not try to speak. "Now go get the ten thousand," ordered Logan. "And this time, do it."

48   Without objecting, the teller moved quickly to his cage. Logan slipped the gun back into the drawer; then he picked up his brief case and stood it near the edge of the table. Pinkson's telephone didn't buzz, and the guard remained out of sight. After a few minutes, Tritt came out of the cage, carrying a small cloth bag.

49   "All right, continue with the bonds," Logan said. "The bag goes on the table between us." Logan shifted forward and opened the bag, keeping the money out of sight behind the brief case. The clean new bills were wrapped in thousand-dollar units, each package bound with a bright yellow strip of paper. Logan counted through one package, and, with Tritt looking right at him, he placed the package of money carefully in the brief case.

50   "There," he said. "Now finish with the bonds." Tritt finished filling out the form and got Logan's signature. He was not as flustered as Logan had thought he'd be. "Now listen, Tritt," Logan went on, "My getaway is all set, of course, but if you give any signal before I'm out of the bank, I'll put a bullet into you—right here." Logan pointed to the bridge of his own nose. "Please don't think I'd hesitate to do it. Now get back to your cage."

51   Tritt returned to the cage. While his back was turned, Logan slipped the bag of money from his brief case and dropped it into the drawer, next to the gun. He eased the drawer into the table, took the brief case, and walked out of the bank.

Outside, he stood directly in front of the entrance, as though he were waiting for a bus. After just a few seconds, the burglar alarm went off with a tremendous electrical shriek, and the old guard came running out of the door after him.

He was followed immediately by Pinkson, the assistant manager, and Tritt.

52   "Well, gentlemen," said Logan, his hands raised again in front of the guard's gun, "here we are again, eh?"

A crowd was gathering, and Pinkson sent the assistant to turn off the alarm. "Come, let's all go inside," he said. "I don't want any fuss out here."

It was the same kind of scene they'd played before, only now Logan—the twice-wronged citizen—was irate, and now ten thousand dollars was missing from William Tritt's cage. Tritt was calm, though.

53   "I was ready for him this time," he said proudly to Pinkson. "I marked ten thousand worth of twenties. My initial is on the band. The money's in his brief case."

"Oh, for Heaven's sake, Tritt," Logan shouted suddenly, "who ever heard of making a getaway by waiting for a bus. I don't know what your game is, but—"

"Never mind my game," said Tritt. "Let's just take a look in your brief case."

54   He wrenched it from Logan's hand, clicked the lock, and turned the brief case upside down. A group of corrected examination books fell out. That was all.

"See?" said Logan. "Not a cent."

The guard put away his gun as Pinkson began to pick up the scattered books.

55   Tritt wheeled, threw the brief case against the wall, and grabbed Logan by the lapels. "But I gave you the money. I did. I did!" His face was pasty gray, and his voice was high. "You put it in the brief case. I saw you. I *saw* you do it! He began to shake Logan in a kind of final attempt to shake the ten thousand dollars out of him.

Pinkson straightened up with the exam books and said, "For goodness' sake, Mr. Tritt. Stop it. Stop it."

Tritt stopped shaking Logan, then turned wildly to Pinkson. "You don't believe me!" he shouted. "You don't believe me!"

"It's not a question of—"

56   "I'll find that money. I'll show you who's lying." He rushed over to the big table and swept it completely clear with one wave of his heavy arm. The slips fluttered to the floor, and the inkwell broke, splattering black ink over the carpet. Tritt pulled the table in a

wild, crashing arc across the green carpet, smashing it into Pinkson's desk. Logan saw the dusty drawer come open about a half-inch.

57   The big man dropped clumsily to his knees and began to pound on the carpet with his flattened hands as he kept muttering, "It's around here someplace—a cloth bag." He grabbed a corner of the carpet and flipped it back with a grunt. It made a puff of dust and revealed only a large triangle of empty, dirty floor. A dozen people had gathered outside the marble fence by now, and all the tellers were peering through the glass panes of the cages at Tritt.

58   "I'll find it! I'll find it!" he shouted. A film of sweat was on his forehead as he stood up, turned, and advanced again toward the table. The slightly opened drawer was in plain sight in front of him, but everyone's eyes were fixed on Tritt, and Tritt did not see the drawer under the overhang of the table.

Logan turned quickly to Pinkson and whispered, "He may be dangerous, Mr. Pinkson. You've got to calm him." He grabbed Pinkson by the arm and pushed him backward several feet, so that the manager came to rest on the edge of the table, directly over the drawer. The exam books were still in his hand.

59   "Mr. Tritt, you *must* stop this!" Mr. Pinkson said.

"Get out of my way, Pinkson," said Tritt, coming right at him, breathing like a bull. "You believe him, but I'll show you. I'll find it!" He placed his hands on Pinkson's shoulders. "Now get away, you fool."

"I won't take that from anyone," snapped Pinkson. He slapped Tritt's face with a loud, stinging blow. The teller stopped, stunned, and suddenly began to cry.

"Mr. Pinkson. Mr. Pinkson, you've *got* to trust me."

Pinkson was immediately ashamed of what he had done. "I'm sorry my boy. I shouldn't have done that."

60   "I tell you he held a gun on me again. A real gun—it's not my imagination."

"But why didn't you call Louie?" Pinkson said. "That's the rule, you know."

"I wanted to catch him myself. He—he made such a fool of me last time."

"But that business last time was hallucination," said Pinkson, looking over at Logan. Logan nodded.

"It's no hallucination when ten thousand dollars is missing," Tritt shouted.

"That's precisely where the confusion arises in my mind," Mr. Pinkson said slowly. "We'll get it straight, but in the meantime, I must order your arrest, Mr. Tritt."

61   Logan came and stood next to Pinkson, and they both looked sympathetically at the teller as he walked slowly, still sobbing, back to the cage.

"I'm just sick about it," Pinkson said.

"I think you'll find he's not legally competent," said Logan, putting a comforting thought into Pinkson's head.

"Perhaps not."

62   Logan showed his concern by helping to clean up the mess that Tritt had made. He and the assistant manager placed the table back into its position against the far wall, Logan shoving the dusty drawer firmly closed with his fingertips as they lifted it.

Norman Logan returned to the bank late the next day. He sat at the table to make a deposit, and he felt a pleasantly victorious sensation surge through him as he slipped the gun and the ten thousand dollars out of the drawer and into his overcoat pocket. As he walked out the front door past the guard, he met Mr. Pinkson, who was rushing in.

63   "Terrible. Terrible," the little man said without even pausing to say hello.

"What's that?" Logan asked calmly.

"I've just been talking to the doctors at Bellevue about Tritt," Pinkson said. "He seems all right, and they've released him. Unfortunately, he can answer every question except 'Where's the money?' " Logan held firmly to the money in his pocket and continued to extend his sympathies.

Back at his apartment, Logan borrowed a portable typewriter from the man upstairs. Then he sat down and wrote a note:

> *Dear Mr. Pinkson:*
>
> *I'm returning the money. I'm so sorry. I guess I didn't know what I was doing. I guess I haven't known for some time.*

After looking up Tritt's initials on an old deposit slip, he forged a small tidy *W.T.* to the note.

64   Logan wiped his fingerprints from the bills and wrapped them, along with the note, in a neat package. For one delicious moment he considered how nice it would be to hang on to the money. He could resign from the university, go out West, and continue his research on his own. But that wasn't part of the plan, and the plan was working too well to tamper with it now. Logan drove to the post office nearest Tritt's apartment and mailed the money to Pinkson at the bank.

65   In the morning, Mr. Pinkson telephoned Logan at the university. "Well, it's all cleared up," he said, relieved but sad. "Tritt returned the money, so the bank is not going to press the charges. Needless to say, we're dropping Tritt. He not only denies having taken the money, he also denies having returned it."

"I guess he just doesn't know what he's doing," Logan said.

66   "Yes. That's what he said in the note. Anyway, Mr. Logan, I—I just wanted to call and apologize for the trouble we've caused you."

"Oh, it was no trouble for me," Logan replied, smiling.

"And you've been very helpful, too," Pinkson added.

"I was glad to be of help," Logan said quietly. "Delighted, in fact."

They said good-by then, and Logan walked across the hall to begin his ten o'clock botany lecture.

Comprehension

1. Before you can appreciate a suspense story, you must understand the characters involved. Below is a list of physical and personality characteristics. Put a *T* next to those that describe Tritt and an *L* next to those that describe Logan. Some adjectives may describe both men. Be prepared to defend your choices with portions of the text.

   _____ a. fat   _____ d. ambitious   _____ g. greedy   _____ j. clever
   _____ b. stubborn   _____ e. thin   _____ h. careless
   _____ c. dishonest   _____ f. careful   _____ i. self-assured

2. The most important factor in enjoying a suspense story is a complete understanding of the plot. The following sentences will tell the story of "The Dusty Drawer" when they are arranged in the correct sequence. Read all of the sentences quickly, then number the sentences according to the order in which the events occur.

   _____ a. Logan writes a note to the bank and forges Tritt's initials, then returns the money by mail.

   _____ b. Tritt steals $200 from Logan to cover a mistake he had made while depositing money in Logan's account.

   _____ c. Logan learns that Tritt has been fired from his position at the bank.

   _____ d. Logan buys a toy gun and hides it in the dusty drawer.

   _____ e. Logan gets $10,000 from Tritt and hides it in the drawer.

   _____ f. Logan's first attempt to rob the bank causes Tritt to lose his banker's touch.

3. What was Tritt's position in the bank? _____

4. What was Logan's profession? _____

5. T / F   Tritt was considered a valuable employee who would make great progress in the bank if he made no mistakes.

6. Logan believed that Tritt stole the $200 because _____

   _____ a. he needed the money.
   _____ b. he had made an error and didn't want to admit it.
   _____ c. he hated Logan and wanted a safe way to hurt him.
   _____ d. he knew he would not be caught.

7. Logan suspected that $200 had been stolen when _____

   _____ a. he noticed that the wrong amount of money had been deposited in his account by Tritt.
   _____ b. he didn't receive the right amount of cash when his bonds were cashed by Tritt.
   _____ c. he checked his wallet after talking to Tritt.
   _____ d. he returned from his summer vacation and the money wasn't in his account.

8. T / F   As they were talking in the cafeteria, Tritt admitted to Logan that he had taken the money.

9. Although Tritt denied taking the $200, he did say that _____

   _____ a. Mr. Pinkson might have made a mistake when he counted the money.
   _____ b. he would have told Logan if he had stolen it.
   _____ c. he thought he knew who did.
   _____ d. he certainly wouldn't return the money if he had stolen it.

10. Logan wanted to get even with Tritt because _____

   _____ a. he had difficulty living without that $200.
   _____ b. he hated Tritt.
   _____ c. he did not like to be cheated.
   _____ d. he wanted to prevent Tritt from cheating other people.

11. T / F   Logan made regular trips to the bank.

12. Logan's plan to pin the robbery on Tritt _____

   _____ a. had been carefully developed over a period of ten months.
   _____ b. developed because he learned that Tritt had been promoted to the first cage.
   _____ c. was suggested to him by something that a shop owner told him.
   _____ d. came to him suddenly after he found an unused drawer in the bank.

13. T / F   Tritt had received a promotion while Logan was away on summer vacation.

14. T / F   The Sullivan Law prevents the sale of guns unless the customer has a permit.

15. T / F   In order to convince Tritt that the robbery was genuine, Logan bought a .38 caliber pistol.

16. T / F   The shopkeeper of the gun store assumed that Logan was going to attempt a robbery.

17. Logan became convinced the old drawer was never used because _____

_____ a. the handles had been removed before the desk was painted.
_____ b. the rest of the bank was so clean and efficient.
_____ c. the gun was not moved during the time that he watched it.
_____ d. neither Mr. Pinkson nor Mr. Tritt ever mentioned it.

18. The first time Logan tried to rob the bank _____

_____ a. Tritt placed the money in a cloth bag after initialing the packets of bills.
_____ b. Tritt said he would not bring the money from his cage.
_____ c. Tritt signaled Mr. Pinkson from his cage.
_____ d. Tritt thought it was all a joke.

19. T / F   Logan offered to remove all his clothes because he was afraid that Tritt might accidentally find the drawer.

20. In the months following the first robbery attempt, Tritt _____

_____ a. questioned Logan carefully about the robbery whenever he entered the bank.
_____ b. tried to prove that Logan had had a gun.
_____ c. became nervous and easily upset.
_____ d. lost his position in the first cage because of his frequent errors.

21. T / F   The second time Logan attempted the robbery, Tritt brought the money.

22. T / F   When no one was looking, Logan moved the money from the brief case to the drawer.

23. Logan didn't keep the $10,000 because _____

_____ a. the plan was working so well that he didn't want to change it.
_____ b. he was too honest.
_____ c. he was afraid that someone would find the drawer.
_____ d. he knew that crime never benefits anyone.

Discussion/Composition

1. Do you believe that Tritt stole $200 from Logan? On what do you base your opinion? (How did you learn that the money was missing?)

2. What is the nature of the crimes committed in "The Dusty Drawer"? What is the difference between the consequences of Tritt's actions as compared to Logan's? Is there any moral difference between the two men? Is one better than the other?

3. Was Logan justified in doing what he did? How would you defend him? Has he committed a crime? Are there other considerations that should be used to judge his actions besides the question of whether or not he has broken the law?

4. Has justice been served in "The Dusty Drawer"?

Vocabulary from Context

Both the ideas and the vocabulary in the following sentences are taken from "The Dusty Drawer." Use the context provided to determine the meanings of each italicized word. Your teacher may want you to do this exercise orally or in writing.

1. _____   The man's *obsequious* behavior made everyone nervous. Like a servant, he was always rushing to open doors and perform other small tasks, apologizing unnecessarily for any inconvenience that he might have caused.

2. _____   Although he really did not want to open the mysterious drawer again, his curiosity *compelled* him to take one last look.

3. _____   The shop was dusty and dirty. Everything seemed to be covered with grease. He was very happy to escape that *grimy* place.

4. _____   Logan wanted to hit Tritt in the nose, but he *restrained* himself because he knew that violence would not help him get his money back.

5. _____   Tritt never allowed himself to become angry with customers. Like a parent with spoiled children, he always listened *indulgently* to their complaints.

6. _____   Both men had convincing stories to tell concerning the missing money, but Mr. Logan's *version* of what happened was by far more believable.

7. _____   Logan felt that the situation was hopeless, and the *futility* of his efforts bothered him a great deal.

8. _____   Logan finally decided that, although he might not recover the money that had been stolen from him, he would have the pleasure of seeing the thief punished. Soon, Logan could think of little else but *vengeance*.

9. _____   The floor of the grimy little store was covered with paper, boxes, pieces of metal and wood, empty paint cans and used brushes. The floor was so *cluttered* that Carl had difficulty walking to the door.

10. _____   Tritt was sure that he had seen a pistol, but everyone else felt that the robbery was just a product of Tritt's imagination—the *hallucination* of an overworked man.

11. _____   The banker was *incredulous* when the money did not fall out of the thief's brief case; he couldn't believe that it wasn't there because he had seen him put the bills inside just before leaving the bank.

12. _____   Logan certainly had reason to be *indignant;* twice he had been unjustly accused of trying to rob the bank.

13. _____   After the first time someone tried to rob him, the banker became *flustered* easily, and in his confusion he would make many careless errors.

14. _____   Although he often had the opportunity, Mr. Tritt never stole money from a customer. This would have endangered his position at the bank, and he did not want to *jeopardize* his future.

Figurative Language and Idioms

In the second half of the section indicated by the number in parentheses, find the word or phrase that best fits the meaning given. Your teacher may want to read these aloud as you quickly scan the paragraph to find the answer.

1. (9)   What phrase means *advancing greatly in one's career*?

2. (10) What phrase means *escape without punishment*?

3. (11) What phrase is used to promise vengeance?

4. (11) What phrase means *not able to tolerate being cheated*?

5. (21) What phrase means *put the blame on someone for something*?

6. (24) What phrase means *completed*?

7. (24) Which word means *a robbery*?

Dictionary Study

Many words have more than one meaning. When you use the dictionary to discover the meaning of an unfamiliar word or phrase, you need to use the context to determine which definition is appropriate. Use the portions of the dictionary provided to select the best definition for each of the italicized words below.

1. Logan *reflected* that all had gone well for him in the bank so far.

2. As he sat waiting for the cashier, Logan *stumbled* across the old drawer.

3. After the first robbery attempt, the cashier began to lose his *grip* on reality.

4. Tritt knew that if he were caught stealing money from the bank, he would lose his position and go to prison, but he *staked* his future on the hope that the manager would believe his version of the robbery.

grip (grip), *n.* [ME.; AS. *gripe,* a clutch, *gripa,* handful < var. of the base of AS. *gripan* (see GRIPE) with a reduced vowel; akin to G. *griff;* some senses < the *v.*], 1. the act of taking firmly and holding fast with the hand, teeth, an instrument, etc.; secure grasp; firm hold. 2. the manner in which this is done. 3. any special manner of clasping hands by which members of a secret or fraternal society identify each other as such. 4. the power of grasping firmly: as, his hand has lost its *grip.* 5. the power of understanding; mental grasp. 6. firm control; mastery: as, in the *grip* of disease, get a *grip* on yourself. 7. a mechanical contrivance for clutching or grasping. 8. the part by which a tool weapon, etc. is grasped in the hand; handle. 9. [prob. < or after D.], a small bag for holding clothes, etc. in traveling; valise. 10. a sudden, intense pain. 11. [Slang], in a motion-picture studio, a stagehand. 12. in *sports,* the manner of holding a bat, club, racket, etc. *v.t.* [GRIPPED or GRIPT (gript), GRIPPING], 1. to take firmly and hold fast with the hand, teeth, an instrument, etc. 2. to give a grip (sense 3) to. 3. to fasten or join firmly (*to*). 4. to get and hold the attention of. 5. to take hold upon; control (the attention, emotions, etc.). *v.i.* to get a grip.
   come to grips, 1. to engage in hand-to-hand fighting. 2. to struggle; try to cope (*with*).

re·flect (ri-flekt′), *v.t.* [ME. *reflecten;* OFr. *reflecter;* L. *reflectere; re-,* back + *flectere,* to bend], 1. to bend or throw back, as light, heat, or sound. 2. to give back an image of; mirror or reproduce. 3. to cast or bring back as a consequence (with *on*): as, his deeds *reflect* honor on the nation. 4. [Rare], to fold or turn back. *v.i.* 1. to be bent or thrown back: as, the light *reflected* from the water into his eyes. 2. to bend or throw back light, heat, sound, etc. 3. *a*) to give back an image or likeness. *b*) to be mirrored. 4. to think seriously; contemplate; ponder (with *on* or *upon*). 5. to cast blame or discredit (with *on* or *upon*). —*SYN.* see **consider, think.**

stake (stāk), *n.* [ME.; AS. *staca;* akin to D. *staak;* base as in *stick*], 1. a length of wood or metal pointed at one end for driving into the ground. 2. the post to which a person is tied for execution by burning. 3. execution by burning. 4. a pole or post fitted upright into a socket, as at the edge of a railway flatcar, truck bed, etc., to help hold a load. 5. a truck having a stake body. 6. *often pl.* something, especially money, risked or hazarded, as in a wager, game, or contest: as, the gamblers were playing for high *stakes.* 7. *often pl.* a reward given a winner, as in a race; prize. 8. a race in which a prize is offered. 9. a share or interest, especially a financial one, in property, a person, a business venture, or the like. 10. [Colloq.], a grubstake. *v.t.* [STAKED (stākt), STAKING], 1. to mark the location or boundaries of with or as with stakes, specifically so as to establish a claim (with *out,* etc.). 2. to fasten or support with a stake or stakes. 3. to hitch or tether to a stake. 4. to close (*up* or *in*), shut (*out*), etc. by stakes in the form of a fence or barrier. 5. [influenced by MD. *staken,* to fix, place], to risk or hazard; gamble; bet: as, he *staked* his winnings on the next hand. 6. [Colloq.], to furnish with money or resources, as for a business venture. 7. [Colloq.], to grubstake.
   at stake, being risked or hazarded, or dependent upon the outcome (of something specified or implied).
   pull up stakes, [Colloq.], to change one's place of residence, business, etc.
stake body, a flat truck body having sockets into which stakes may be fitted, as to support railings.
stake·hold·er (stāk′hōl′dẽr), *n.* one who holds money, etc. bet by others and pays it to the winner.

stum·ble (stum′b'l), *v.i.* [STUMBLED (-b'ld), STUMBLING], [ME. *stomblen, stomelen;* prob. < ON. **stumla* (cf. Norw. *stumla,* to stumble in the dark, etc.) < the base seen in *stammer*], 1. to trip or miss one's step in walking, running, etc. 2. to walk or go in an unsteady or awkward manner, as from age, weakness, etc. 3. to speak, act, or proceed in a confused, blundering manner: as, he *stumbled* through his recitation. 4. to fall into sin or error; do wrong. 5. to come by chance; happen: as, I *stumbled* across a clue. *v.t.* to cause to stumble. *n.* 1. the act of stumbling. 2. a blunder, error, or sin.
stumbling block, something that causes stumbling; obstacle, hindrance, or difficulty.

From *Websters New World Dictionary,* College Edition (New York: World Publishing Company).

Vocabulary Review

Exercise 1

Place the appropriate word or phrase from the following list in each of the blanks below. Do not use any word more than once.

indulgent	indignantly	grime	clutter
get away with it	go a long way	compelled	restraint
futile	hallucinations	incredulous	grip
obsequiousness	vengeance	flustered	
reflect	jeopardize	version	

1. Although it is true that a good employee should be respectful and helpful, Harry's extreme

    _____ makes everyone uncomfortable.

2. John is intelligent, hardworking, and honest. He should _____ in his profession.

3. Douglas is well known for his self-_____; it is said that, no matter how angry he becomes, he never allows himself to show it.

4. John becomes _____ easily these days. Merely by asking him a simple question you can confuse him.

5. My aunt Vera suffers from frequent _____; just last night she thought she saw a pink elephant in a tree.

6. If you don't clean your kitchen regularly, the _____ on the wall above the stove will become too thick to remove with soap and water alone.

7. Dick knew that the bank officials regularly examined his records. He should have known

    that he couldn't steal any money and _____.

8. After he was robbed, Robert ran around madly shouting "I'll get him, I'll get him!" It was

    obvious that he could think of nothing but _____.

9. Arthur's behavior became stranger every day until he seemed to completely lose

    his _____ on reality.

10. The judge told us not to be impatient; after the other man told his story, we could tell our

    _____ of what had happened.

11. I have tried for a number of years to get my grandfather to buy a new car, but my attempts

    have been _____; he just won't part with his old Ford.

12. Although I didn't particularly want to accompany the children to the zoo, my sense of

    responsibility _____ me to go with them.

13. No matter how often we reminded the children, they never cleaned their room; the

    _____ in the room became so bad that we couldn't even open the door.

14. Before I make an important decision, I need some time to just sit and _____.

15. As Uncle Andy described the size of the fish he had caught, I became more and more

    _____. (You just never know when he is telling the truth.)

16. Grandparents are always more _____ of children than parents. For that
    reason, we always enjoyed our vacations on our grandparents' farm.

17. Angry and insulted because he had been accused of stealing the money, Dean calmly but

    _____ demanded to see his lawyer.

18. Corey had been working so hard that he decided to take a vacation, even though he knew

    he might _____ his chances of doing well on the upcoming examination.

Exercise 2

Complete the sentences below with the correct form of the word provided on the left.

1. obsequiousness   Quite apart from any question of the man's honesty, I would

                     not hire him because I dislike his _____ manner.

2. incredulity   The policeman watched _____ as the family
                     proceeded to do their laundry in the public swimming pool.

3. futility   "If wishes were horses, beggars would ride," is an old saying

                     that emphasizes the _____ of dreaming about

                     unrealistic good fortune.

4. vengeful   The man promised the judge that he would not seek

                     _____ against the person who had robbed him.

5. indulgence   Some people believe that modern parents are far too

                     _____ of their children.

6. grimy   No matter how hard we try, we will not be able to remove the

                     _____ from public monuments.

7. jeopardy   Most of us would not _____ our lives without a
                     good reason, but firemen are in almost constant danger.

15

Anthropology

The author of this selection, Jane van Lawick-Goodall, spent six years observing chimpanzees at the Gombe Stream Chimpanzee Reserve on the shores of Lake Tanganyika in Tanzania before she wrote *In the Shadow of Man.* In this selection, a chapter from that book, she compares chimpanzees and people in five areas: brain development, tool-using and toolmaking, communicatory gestures, speech, and awareness of self. As you read, look for the similarities and differences.

You may want to do the Vocabulary from Context exercise on pages 316–17 before you begin reading.

In the Shadow of Man

Jane van Lawick-Goodall

1   The amazing success of humans as a species is the result of the evolutionary development of our brains which has led, among other things, to tool-using, toolmaking, the ability to solve problems by logical reasoning, thoughtful cooperation, and language. One of the most striking ways in which chimpanzees biologically resemble humans lies in the structure of their brains. The chimpanzee, with the capacity for primitive reasoning, exhibits a type of intelligence more like that of humans than does any other mammal living today. The brain of the modern chimpanzee is probably not too dissimilar to the brain that so many millions of years ago directed the behavior of the first ape man.

2   For a long time, the fact that prehistoric people made tools was considered to be one of the major criteria distinguishing them from other creatures. As I pointed out earlier, I have watched chimpanzees modify grass stems in order to use them to probe for termites. It is true that the chimpanzee does not fashion tools to "a regular and set pattern"—but then, prehistoric people, before their development of stone tools, undoubtedly poked around with sticks and straws, at which stage it seems unlikely that they made tools to a set pattern either.

3   It is because of the close association in most people's minds of tools with humans that special attention has always been focused upon any animal able to use an object as a tool; but it is important to realize that this ability, on its own, does not necessarily indicate any special intelligence in the creature concerned. The fact that the Galápagos woodpecker finch uses a cactus spine or twig to probe insects from crevices in the bark is indeed a

Adapted from *In the Shadow of Man* by Jane van Lawick-Goodall (Boston: Houghton Mifflin Company).

fascinating phenomenon, but it does not make the bird more intelligent than a genuine woodpecker that uses its long beak and tongue for the same purpose.

4   The point at which tool-using and toolmaking, as such, acquire evolutionary significance is surely when an animal can adapt its ability to manipulate objects to a wide variety of purposes, and when it can use an object spontaneously to solve a brand-new problem that without the use of a tool would prove insoluble.

5   At the Gombe Stream alone we have seen chimpanzees use objects for many different purposes. They use stems and sticks to capture and eat insects, and, if the material picked is not suitable, then it is modified. They use leaves to sop up water they cannot reach with their lips—and first they chew on the leaves and thus increase their absorbency. We have seen them use handfuls of leaves to wipe dirt from their bodies or to dab at wounds.

6   In captivity chimpanzees often use objects as tools quite spontaneously. One group that was studied intensively by Wolfgang Köhler used sticks to try to pry open box lids and dig in the ground for roots. They wiped themselves with leaves or straw, scratched themselves with stones and poked straws into columns of ants in order to eat the insects much like the Gombe Stream chimpanzees probe for termites. They often used sticks and stones as weapons during aggressive encounters. Extensive tests have been carried out in laboratory settings in order to find out more about the tool*making* ability of chimpanzees. Results show that they can pile up to five boxes one on top of the other in order to climb to hanging food, that they can fit up to three tubes together to reach food placed outside the bars of their cages, and that they can unwind part of a length of wire for the same purpose. So far, however, no chimpanzee has succeeded in using one tool to make another. Even with teaching, one chimpanzee, the subject of exhaustive tests, was not able to use a stone hand ax to break a piece of wood into splinters suitable for obtaining food from a narrow pipe. She could do this when the material was suitable for her to break off pieces with her teeth but, although she was shown how to use the hand ax on tougher wood many times, she never even attempted to make use of it when trying to solve the problem. However, many other chimpanzees must be tested before we say that the chimpanzee as a species is unable to perform this act. Some humans are mathematicians—others are not.

7   When the performance of chimpanzees in the field is compared with their actual abilities in test situations, it would seem that, in time, they might develop a more sophisticated tool-culture. After all, primitive people continued to use their early stone tools for thousands of years, virtually without change. Then we find a more sophisticated type of stone tool-culture suddenly appearing widespread across the continents. Possibly a stone-age genius invented the new culture and others, who undoubtedly learned from and imitated each other, copied the new technique.

8   If chimpanzees are allowed to continue living they, too, might suddenly produce a race of chimp superbrains and evolve an entirely new tool-culture. For it seems almost certain that, although the ability to manipulate objects is innate in a chimpanzee, the actual tool-using patterns practiced by the Gombe Stream chimpanzees are learned by the infants from their elders. We saw one very good example of this. It happened when a female had diarrhea: she picked a large handful of leaves and wiped her messy bottom. Her two-year-old infant watched her closely and then twice picked leaves and wiped his own clean bottom.

9   To Hugo and me, and assuredly to many scientists interested in human behavior and evolution, one significant aspect of chimpanzee behavior lies in the close similarity of many of their communicatory gestures and postures to those of humans. Not only are the actual positions and movements similar to our own but also the contexts in which they often occur.

10   When a chimpanzee is suddenly frightened it frequently reaches to touch or embrace a chimpanzee nearby, much like a child watching a horror film may seize a companion's

hand. Both chimpanzees and humans seem reassured in stressful situations by physical contact with another individual. Once David Graybeard caught sight of his reflection in a mirror. Terrified, he seized Fifi, then only three years old. Even such contact with a very small chimp appeared to reassure him; gradually he relaxed and the grin of fear left his face. Humans may sometimes feel reassured by holding or stroking a dog or some other pet in moments of emotional crisis.

11   This comfort, which chimpanzees and humans alike appear to derive from physical contact with each other, probably originates during the years of infancy, when for so long the touch of the mother, or the contact with her body, serves to calm the frights and soothe the anxieties of both ape and human infants. So, when the child grows older and its mother is not always close at hand, it seeks the next best thing—close physical contact with another individual. If its mother is around, however, it may deliberately pick her out as its comforter. Once when Figan was about eight years old he was threatened by Mike. He screamed loudly and hurried past six or seven other chimps nearby until he reached Flo; then he held his hand toward her and she held it with hers. Calmed, Figan stopped screaming almost at once. Young human beings, too, continue to unburden their hearts to their mothers long after the days of childhood have passed—provided, of course, that an affectionate relationship exists between them.

12   When chimpanzees are overjoyed by the sight of a large pile of bananas they pat and kiss and embrace one another as two friends might embrace when they hear good news, or as a child may leap to hug its mother when told of a special treat. We all know those feelings of intense excitement or happiness which cause people to shout and leap around, or to burst into tears. It is not surprising that chimpanzees, if they feel anything like this, should seek to calm themselves by embracing their companions.

13   Chimpanzees, after being threatened or attacked by a superior, may follow the aggressor, screaming and crouching to the ground or holding out their hands. They are, in fact, begging a reassuring touch from the other. Sometimes they will not relax until they have been touched or patted, kissed or embraced. Figan several times flew into a tantrum when such contact was withheld, hurling himself about on the ground, his screams cramping in his throat until the aggressor finally calmed him with a touch. I have seen a human child behaving in the same sort of way, following his mother around the house after she has told him off, crying, holding on to her skirt, until finally she picked him up and kissed and cuddled him in forgiveness. A kiss or embrace or some other gesture of endearment is an almost inevitable outcome once a matrimonial disagreement has been resolved, and in many cultures the clasping of hands occurs to demonstrate renewal of friendship and forgiveness after a quarrel.

14   When one human begs forgiveness from or gives forgiveness to another there are, however, moral issues involved; it is when we consider these that we get into difficulties in trying to draw parallels between chimpanzees and human behavior. In chimpanzee society the principle involved when a subordinate seeks reassurance from a superior, or when a high-ranking individual calms another, is in no way concerned with the right or wrong of an aggressive act. A female who is attacked for no reason other than she happens to be standing too close to a charging male is quite as likely to approach the male and beg a reassuring touch as is the female who is bowled over by a male while she attempts to take a fruit from his pile of bananas.

15   Again, while we may make a direct comparison between the effect on an anxious chimpanzee or human of a touch or embrace of reassurance, the issue becomes complicated if we probe into the motivation that directs the gesture of the ape or the human who is doing the reassuring. Human beings are capable of acting from purely unselfish motives; we can be genuinely sorry for others and try to share in their troubles in an effort to offer comfort. It is unlikely that a chimpanzee acts from feelings quite like these; I doubt whether even members of one family, united as they are by strong mutual

affections, are ever motivated by pure altruism in their dealings with one another.

16   On the other hand, there may be parallels in some instances. Most of us have experienced sensations of extreme discomfort and unease in the presence of an abject, weeping person. We may feel compelled to try to calm the person, not because we feel compassion in the altruistic sense, but because the behavior disturbs our own feeling of well-being. Perhaps the sight—and especially the sound—of a crouching, screaming subordinate similarly makes a chimpanzee uneasy; the most efficient way of changing the situation is to calm the other with a touch.

17   Another area of similarity between chimpanzees and humans is greeting behavior. When two chimpanzees greet each other after a separation, their behavior often looks amazingly like that shown by two humans in the same context. Chimpanzees may bow or crouch to the ground, hold hands, kiss, embrace, touch, or pat each other on almost any part of the body, especially the head and face. A male may chuck a female or an infant under the chin. Humans in many cultures, show one or more of these gestures.

18   In human societies much greeting behavior has become ritualized. People who smile when greeting a friend, or who incline their heads when passing an acquaintance in the street, are not necessarily acknowledging that the other has a superior social status. Yet the nod undoubtedly derives from submissive bowing or prostration and the smile from a nervous grin. Often, though, human greetings still do serve to clarify the relative social status of the individuals concerned, particularly on formal occasions.

19   A greeting between two chimpanzees nearly always serves such a purpose—it reestablishes the dominance status of the one relative to the other. When nervous Olly greets Mike she may hold out her hand toward him, or bow to the ground, crouching submissively with downbent head. She is, in effect, acknowledging Mike's superior rank. Mike may touch or pat or hold her hand, or touch her head, in response to her submission. A greeting between two chimps is usually more demonstrative when the individuals concerned are close friends, particularly when they have been separated for days rather than hours. Goliath often used to fling his arms around David, and the two would press their lips to each other's faces or necks when they met; whereas a greeting between Goliath and Mr. Worzle seldom involved more than a casual touch even when the two had not seen each other for some time.

20   If we survey the whole range of the communication signals of chimpanzees on the one hand and humans on the other, we find striking similarities in many instances. It would appear, then, that human and chimp either have evolved gestures and postures along a most remarkable parallel or that we share with the chimpanzees an ancestor in the dim and very distant past; an ancestor, moreover, who communicated by means of kissing and embracing, touching and patting and holding hands.

21   One of the major differences between humans and our closest living relative is, of course, that the chimpanzee has not developed the power of speech. Even the most intensive efforts to teach young chimps to talk have met with almost no success. Verbal language represents a truly gigantic step forward in human evolution.

22   Chimpanzees do have a wide range of calls, and these certainly serve to convey some types of information. When a chimp finds good food it utters loud barks; other chimps in the vicinity instantly become aware of the food source and hurry to join in. An attacked chimpanzee screams and this may alert its mother or a friend, either of whom may hurry to its aid. A chimpanzee confronted with an alarming and potentially dangerous situation utters a spine-chilling *wraaaa*—again, other chimps may hurry to the spot to see what is happening. A male chimpanzee, about to enter a valley or charge toward a food source, utters his pant-hoots—and other individuals realize that another member of the group is arriving and can identify which one. To our human ears each chimpanzee is characterized more by its pant-hoots than by any other type of call. This is significant since the pant-hoot in particular is the call that serves to maintain contact between the separated groups

of the community. Yet the chimps themselves can certainly recognize individuals by other calls; for instance, a mother knows the scream of her offspring. Probably a chimpanzee can recognize the calls of most of its acquaintances.

23   While chimpanzee calls do serve to convey basic information about some situations and individuals, they cannot for the most part be compared to a spoken language. Humans by means of words can communicate abstract ideas; they can benefit from the experiences of others without having to be present at the time; they can make intelligent cooperative plans.

24   Recently it has been proved that the chimpanzee is capable of communicating with people in quite a sophisticated manner. There are two scientists in America, R. Allen and Beatrice Gardner, who have trained a young chimpanzee in the use of the approved sign language of the deaf. The Gardners felt that, since gesture and posture formed such a significant aspect of *chimpanzee* communication patterns, such a sign language might be more appropriate than trying to teach vocal words.

25   Washoe was brought up from infancy constantly surrounded by human companions. These people from the start communicated in sign language with Washoe and also with each other when in the chimp's presence. The only sounds they made were those approximating chimpanzee calls such as laughter, exclamations, and imitations of Washoe's own sounds.

26   Their experiment has been amazingly successful. At five years of age Washoe can understand some three hundred and fifty different symbols, many of which signify clusters of words rather than just a single word, and she can also use about one hundred and fifty of them correctly.

27   I have not seen Washoe; but I have seen some film demonstrating her level of performance and, strangely enough, I was most impressed by an error she made. She was required to name, one after the other, a series of objects as they were drawn from a sack. She signed off the correct names very fast—but even so, it could be argued that an intelligent dog would ultimately learn to associate the sight of a bowl with a correct response. And then a brush was shown to Washoe, and she made the sign for a comb. That to me was very significant. It is the sort of mistake a small child might make, calling a shoe a slipper or a plate a saucer—but never calling a shoe a plate.

28   Perhaps one of the Gardners' most fascinating observations concerns the occasion when for the first time Washoe was asked (in sign language) "Who is that?" as she was looking into a mirror. Washoe, who was very familiar with mirrors by that time, signaled back, "Me, Washoe."

29   This is, in a way, a scientific proof of a fact we have long known—that, in some way, the chimpanzee has a primitive awareness of Self. Undoubtedly there are people who would prefer not to believe this, since even more firmly rooted than the old idea that humans alone are the only toolmaking beings is the concept that humans alone in the animal kingdom are Self-conscious. Yet, this should not be disturbing. It has come to me, quite recently, that it is only through a real understanding of the ways in which chimpanzees and humans show similarities in behavior that we can reflect with meaning on the ways in which humans and chimpanzees *differ*. And only then can we really begin to appreciate, in a biological and spiritual manner, the full extent of our uniqueness.

30   Yes, human beings definitely overshadow the chimpanzee. The chimpanzee is, nevertheless, a creature of immense significance to the understanding of humans. Just as they are overshadowed by us, so the chimpanzees overshadow all other animals. They have the ability to solve quite complex problems, they can use and make tools for a variety of purposes, their social structure and methods of communication with each other are elaborate, and they show the beginnings of Self-awareness. Who knows what the chimpanzees will be like forty million years hence? It should be of concern to us all that we permit them to live, that we at least give them the chance to evolve.

Comprehension

Exercise 1

Indicate if each statement below is true (T) or false (F) according to your understanding of the passage. Use information in the passage and inferences that can be drawn from the passage to make your decisions.

1. ____ The brain structure of the chimpanzee probably resembles that of early humans.

2. ____ Toolmaking distinguishes humans from all other animals.

3. ____ Using a familiar tool to solve an unfamiliar problem is common among animals.

4. ____ No chimp can learn to use one tool to make another tool.

5. ____ In the future there might be chimpanzee geniuses.

6. ____ Baby chimpanzees learn how to use tools by watching older chimpanzees.

7. ____ Hugo, mentioned in paragraph 9, is apparently one of the Gombe Stream chimpanzees.

8. ____ Chimpanzee gestures are very different from human gestures.

9. ____ A touch or embrace is reassuring to both anxious chimpanzees and anxious humans.

10. ____ Both apes and humans comfort an upset individual for unselfish reasons.

11. ____ The greeting behavior of chimpanzees serves to distinguish social position.

12. ____ Chimpanzees can recognize each other by their calls.

13. ____ Washoe has learned to speak.

14. ____ Washoe's mistakes in using language seem to indicate that chimp language learning proceeds similarly to the language learning of the human child.

Exercise 2

Check (✓) those statements with which you think the author would agree.

1. ____ Prehistoric people were similar to the modern chimpanzee in several ways.

2. ____ Chimpanzees, like humans, may have varying abilities.

3. ____ Chimpanzee society has different social ranks.

4. _____ Issues of morality seem to enter into chimpanzee behavior.

5. _____ Physical contact plays an important part in the security of chimpanzees throughout their lives.

6. _____ Humans are the only animals with self-awareness.

7. _____ Chimps have reached the height of their development.

8. _____ The similarities between humans and chimpanzees prove that humans are not unique.

Vocabulary from Context

Both the ideas and the vocabulary in the sentences below are taken from "In the Shadow of Man." Use the context provided to determine the meanings of the italicized words. Give a definition, synonym, or description of each italicized vocabulary item.

1. _____   Chimpanzees in the wild use simple objects as tools, but in laboratory situations they can use more *sophisticated* items.

2. _____   A chimpanzee is born with the ability to handle objects, but the actual tool-using patterns are not *innate;* the infants learn them by observing their elders.

3. _____   Some people believe that one's *posture* tells us a lot about one's self-confidence. They claim that people who stand up straight are generally more self-confident than people who stand bent over.

4. _____   The baby chimp *hurled* himself to the ground, screaming and crying, until his mother picked him up.

5. _____   Humans may sometimes feel reassured by touching and *stroking* a dog or some other pet in moments of emotional crisis.

6. _____   When chimps are angry, they may raise their arms rapidly and wave them wildly. These *gestures* are similar to those of an angry human.

7. _____   Most troubles can be avoided, but death and taxes are *inevitable*.

8. _____   Whereas humans are able to offer help unselfishly, chimpanzees do not seem to help each other for purely *altruistic* reasons.

9. _____   A chimp gets reassurance from touching another chimp just as a person *derives* comfort from touching another person.

10. _____ Some chimps are very independent and appear to be the superior members of a group; others seem to be ruled by the leaders and are quite *submissive*.

11. _____ For chimpanzees, the use of tools is learned behavior that is limited to familiar tasks. They have not demonstrated an ability to use tools *spontaneously* to solve new problems.

12. _____ Hungry chimpanzees have demonstrated their intelligence by using sticks to *probe* for insects in narrow spaces.

Stems and Affixes

The words in the left column are taken from "In the Shadow of Man." Using your knowledge of stems and affixes, match each word on the left with its synonym or definition on the right. The number in parentheses indicates the paragraph in which the word can be found.

1. _____ dissimilar (1)   a. unable to be solved

2. _____ prehistoric (2)   b. in a lower or inferior class

3. _____ manipulate (4)   c. unlike; different

4. _____ insoluble (4)   d. to free or relieve from trouble

5. _____ reassure (10)   e. occurring before written history

6. _____ unburden (11)   f. to control by skilled use of the hands

7. _____ overjoyed (12)   g. to give confidence or assurance again

8. _____ endearment (13)   h. delighted; filled with joy

9. _____ uneasy (16)   i. restless; without ease or comfort

10. _____ subordinate (16)   j. a loving word; an expression of affection

Figurative Language and Idioms

In the paragraph indicated by the number in parentheses find the word or phrase that best fits the meaning given. Your teacher may want to read these aloud as you quickly scan the paragraph to find the answer.

1. (4)   Which word means *without an external cause; arising out of the individual?*

2. (12)   What phrase means *to begin to cry suddenly?*

3. (13)   What phrase in sentence four means *became violently angry?*

4. (13)   What phrase in sentence five means *scolded; spoke angrily with?*

5. (14)   What phrase in sentence one means *to find similarities?*

6. (14)   What phrase means *is knocked down?*

Discussion/Composition

Each of the quotations below is taken from "In the Shadow of Man." They are intended to focus your attention on specific aspects of the author's point of view.

Quotation 1

> It would appear, then, that human and chimp either have evolved gestures and postures along a most remarkable parallel or that we share with the chimpanzees an ancestor in the dim and very distant past; an ancestor, moreover, who communicated by means of kissing and embracing, touching and patting and holding hands.

What are the two possibilities suggested to explain the similarities between human and chimpanzee behavior? Do you agree with either of these explanations? Why or why not?

Quotation 2

> Yes, human beings definitely overshadow the chimpanzee. The chimpanzee is, nevertheless, a creature of immense significance to the understanding of humans.

Do you think that we can reach an understanding of the human race by studying animals?

Quotation 3

> Recently it has been proved that the chimpanzee is capable of communicating with people in quite a sophisticated manner.

Is it important that humans attempt to communicate with animals? Why? What animals other than chimpanzees can humans communicate with? What kind of information can animals convey to people?

Quotation 4

In human societies much greeting behavior has become ritualized. People who smile when greeting a friend, or who incline their heads when passing an acquaintance in the street, are not necessarily acknowledging that the other has a superior social status. . . . Often, though, human greetings still do serve to clarify the relative social status of the individuals concerned, particularly on formal occasions.

What greetings are you familiar with that indicate social rank? What differences are there in the way you greet your teacher, your parents, and your best friend? What special greetings are used on formal occasions?

Quotation 5

The author concludes her essay with the following thought:

Just as they are overshadowed by us, so the chimpanzees overshadow all other animals. They have the ability to solve quite complex problems, they can use and make tools for a variety of purposes, their social structure and methods of communication with each other are elaborate, and they show the beginnings of Self-awareness. Who knows what the chimpanzees will be like forty million years hence?

What does the author suggest about the chimpanzee's potential for development? Do you believe that chimpanzees will continue to develop? Do you think that chimpanzees will ever have the same abilities as humans?

Vocabulary Review

Place the appropriate word or phrase from the following list in each of the blanks below. Do not use any word or phrase more than once.

flew into a tantrum	submissive	altruism
draw parallels	sophisticated	inevitable
burst into tears	posture	hurled
spontaneously	gestured	derived
innate	probes	stroking

1. Unlike the simple machines of the early 1900s, today's automobiles are quite

_____ .

2. "Have a seat," said the professor kindly as she _____ toward a chair.

3. People today are fond of saying that only two things are _____: death and taxes.

4. Some scientists believe that the ability to learn a language is _____ rather than learned.

5. The little girl picked up a stone and _____ it at the letter carrier.

6. The children were so saddened by the death of their pet that they _____ .

7. _____ is encouraged by many religions. Some even suggest that a certain percentage of one's income be given to the poor.

8. My mother always advised me, "Be firm but not aggressive; be polite but not _____ ."

9. When the little boy was told to go to bed, he _____ . His mother had to carry him, kicking and screaming, into the house.

10. A good scientist _____ into all aspects of a problem in order to find solutions.

11. Children are often told to stand up straight so that when they grow up they will have good

_____ .

12. A person who is truly kind does thoughtful things for others _____ , without having to be asked or reminded.

13. The political situation is so different in the two countries that it is foolish to try to

_____ between them.

14. The children loved their pet dog and would spend hours _____ it and talking to it.

15. The ritualized greetings used today are probably _____ from the primitive gestures of prehistoric human beings.

Appendix

Below is a list of the stems and affixes that appear in *Reader's Choice*. The number in parentheses indicates the unit in which an item appears.

Prefixes

(5) **a-, an-**   without, lacking, not

(3) **ante-**   before

(5) **bene-**   good

(5) **bi-**   two

(9) **by-**   aside or apart from the common, secondary

(3) **circum-**   around

(1) **com-, con-, col-, cor-, co-**   together, with

(3) **contra-, anti-**   against

(9) **de-**   down from, away

(9) **dia-**   through, across

(9) **epi-**   upon, over, outer

(9) **hyper-**   above, beyond, excessive

(9) **hypo-**   under, beneath, down

(1) **in-, im-, il-, ir-**   in, into, on

(1) **in-, im-, il-, ir-**   not

(3) **inter-**   between

(3) **intro-, intra-**   within

(1) **micro-**   small

(5) **mis-**   wrong

(5) **mono-**   one, alone

(7) **multi-**   many

(7) **peri-**   around

(5) **poly-**   many

(3) **post-**   after

(1) **pre-**   before

(1) **re-, retro-**   back, again

(7) **semi-**   half, partly

(3) **sub-, suc-, suf-, sug-, sup-, sus-**   under

(3) **super-**   above, greater, better

(5) **syn-, sym-, syl-**   with, together

(3) **trans-**   across

(7) **tri-**   three

(7) **ultra-**   beyond, excessive, extreme

(7) **uni-**   one

Stems

(5) **-anthro-, -anthropo-**   human

(5) **-arch-**   first, chief, leader

(7) **-aster-, -astro-, -stellar-**   star

(1) **-audi-, -audit-**   hear

(7) **-auto-**   self

(7) **-bio-**   life

(9) **-capit-**   head, chief

(3) **-ced-**   go, move, yield

(1) **-chron-**   time

(9) **-corp-**   body

(7) **-cycle-**   circle

(9) **-derm-**   skin

(1) **-dic-, -dict-**   say, speak

(3) **-duc-**   lead

(5) **-fact-, fect-**   make, do

(3) **-flect-**   bend

(5) **-gam-**   marriage

(9) **-geo-**   earth

(1) **-graph-, -gram-**   write, writing

(5) **-hetero-**   different, other

(5) **-homo-**   same

(9) **-hydr-, -hydro-**   water

(1) **-log-, -ology-**   speech, word, study

(5) **-man-, -manu-**   hand

(7) **-mega-**   great, large

(3) **-mit-, -miss-**   send

(5) **-morph-**   form, structure

(7) **-mort-**   death

(5) **-onym-, -nomen-**   name

(9) **-ortho-**   straight, correct

(5) **-pathy-**   feeling, disease

(7) **-phil-**   love

(1) **-phon-**   sound

(9) **-pod-, -ped-**   foot

(3) **-pon-, -pos-**   put, place

(7) **-polis-**   city

(3) **-port-**   carry

(7) **-psych-**   mind

(1) **-scrib-, -script-**   write

(3) **-sequ-, -secut-**   follow

(9) **-son-**   sound

(1) **-spect-**   look at

(3) **-spir-**   breathe

(7) **-soph-**   wise

(3) **-tele-**   far

(5) **-theo-, -the-**   god

(9) **-therm-, -thermo-**   heat

(3) **-ven-, -vene-**   come

(9) **-ver-**   true

(1) **-vid-, -vis-**   see

(3) **-voc, -vok-**   call

Suffixes

(3) **-able, -ible, -ble**   capable of, fit for

(9) **-ate**   to make

(1) **-er, -or**   one who

(9) **-fy**   to make

(5) **-ic, -al**   relating to, having the nature of

(5) **-ism**   action or practice, theory or doctrine

(1) **-ist**   one who

(7) **-ity**   condition, quality, state of being

(9) **-ize**   to make

(7) **-ness**   condition, quality, state of being

(5) **-oid**   like, resembling

(3) **-ous, -ious, -ose**   full of, having the qualities of

(1) **-tion, -ation**   condition, the act of

Answer Key

The processes involved in arriving at an answer are often more important than the answer itself. It is expected that students will not use the Answer Key until they have completed the exercises and are prepared to defend their answers. If a student's answer does not agree with the Key, it is important for the student to return to the exercise to discover the source of the error. No answer is provided in instances where the students have been asked to express their own opinions or when there is no one best answer.

Unit 1

Nonprose Reading: Menu

Exercise 1 (pages 1–2)
1. Cocktails
2. Beverages
3. Desserts
4. Weight Watchers' Special
5. Answers are listed by section.
   For Your Late Breakfast Pleasure: fried ham, bacon, sausage
   Omelettes: ham (and cheese) omelettes
   Steaks and Chops: pork chops
   Plain Sandwiches: grilled bacon and cheese; crisp bacon, lettuce, tomato; grilled ham and cheese; Canadian bacon; bacon burger
   Special Sandwiches: ham and cheese delight
   Special Daily Dinners: pork chop sandwich
   Salads: Julienne salad bowl (Julienne salads usually contain ham)
   Side orders: Small Julienne (Julienne salads usually contain ham)
6. No
7. $7.00 (plus tax)
8. Side Orders
9. For Your Late Breakfast Pleasure, Omelettes
10. $4.50 (plus tax)
11. Yes; tipping is permitted unless otherwise stated.

Exercise 2 (page 2)
1. F (a fish sandwich costs $4.65)   3. T   5. F
2. F   4. F   6. F
7. T (pork chop sandwich, $6.25; ice cream, $1.25; and tip of between 15% and 20%)

Word Study: Context Clues

Exercise 1 (page 5)
1. to pounce: to jump
2. to adapt: to adjust to new circumstances
3. egret: a type of bird
4. to inveigh against: to talk loudly against; to attack verbally; to protest
5. to slither: to move like a snake; to slide
6. to pelt: to hit
7. kinesics: the study of body motion
8. gregarious: sociable; friendly
9. ravenous: extremely hungry
10. to salvage: to save

Word Study: Dictionary Use

Exercise 2 (page 8)
1. no   7. gloweringly
2. five   8. glossography
3. glu*tam*ic   9. Benjamin Peter Gloxin
4. paw, for   10. French and Greek
5. glottiss   11. no
6. glued   12. four; although synonyms,

their meanings are not exactly the same
13. 1714   14. 26,000
15. Answers include such things as the following: definitions; synonyms; parts of speech; pronunciation (syllabification and stress); alternate pronunciations; spelling and alternate spellings; if verb—principal parts; if noun—plural form; usage labels (archaic, obsolete, regional, etc.); origin of word (etymology); derived words; information about famous people; information about geographical places.

Word Study: Stems and Affixes

Exercise 1 (page 10)
1. a. 1   b. 2   c. 3
2. insane, inactive, invisible
3. For example, coworker, coauthor, copilot
4. For example, rework, replay, rewind, relive

Exercise 2 (pages 11–12)
1. inhale: breathe in
2. import: bring in from outside the country; buy from other countries
3. collaborated: worked together
4. informal: casual (not formal)
5. prediction: statement foretelling the future; statement saying what will happen in the future
6. inscriptions: writings, drawings, or marks written on or into some surface
7. preregister: register before classes start
8. reflection: image; likeness
9. dictated: spoke or read (the letter) aloud so that it could be written down
10. graphologist: person who studies handwriting
11. microbiology: the branch of biology that deals with animal or vegetable organisms that can be seen only with a microscope
12. phonograph recordings: records (from: write [record] sound)
13. prescription: written order for medicine
14. chronic: long-lasting; constant; continuous
15. reapplied: applied again
16. recall: remember
17. in retrospect: looking back
18. audiovisual: involving both hearing and sight (such as movies)
19. immoral: not moral; against ethical principles; wrong
20. prenatal: before birth

Exercise 3 (page 12)
1. g   3. c   5. h   7. a
2. d   4. f   6. e   8. b

Paragraph Reading: Main Idea (pages 15–21)

Paragraph 1: b   Paragraph 3: b
Paragraph 2: b   Paragraph 4: d

Paragraph 5: c
Paragraph 6: Contrary to popular opinion, change has
   always characterized the family.
Paragraph 7: Our ideas about the ancient Mayas are
   changing; we once thought them to be peaceful but
   now believe them to have been warlike.
Poem: We seem to appreciate the accomplishments of
   science more than the miracles of nature.

Discourse Focus: Scanning

Exercise 1 (page 22)
 1. Religious Information, pp. 339–349
 2. Population, U.S., pp. 217–274 or Population, World,
    pp. 634–635
 3. Calendars, pp. 342–344, 724–735, 738–742
 4. Maps (color), pp. 462–472

Exercise 2 (page 24)
 1. Angel 3,212 ft.
 2. Highest fall, Angel 2,648 ft.
 3. 40 ft. (Urubupunga in Brazil)
 4. 984 ft., Cusiana R.
 5. 1
 6. 0
 7. 1

Exercise 3 (page 26)
 1. Theater, Children's Theater, Community Theater
 2. Nightlife, Discotheque
 3. Sunday, Wednesday, Friday
 4. yes; Hyatt Regency
 5. James Tatum Trio
 6. Detroit Symphony, Oakway Symphony
 7. We don't know.

Exercise 4 (page 28)
 1. A TOEFL score of 500 or the equivalent. (Two re-
    quire lower scores; one requires a higher score.)
 2. Largest international student enrollment: Lane Com-
    munity College (105).
    Largest percentage of international student enroll-
    ment: Concordia College (20%).
 3. Chemeketa Community College, Concordia College
 4. No costs listed for Concordia College, but you can
    call the Admissions Office at (503) 288-9371.
 5. Eastern Oregon State College
 6. Central Oregon Community College, Clackamas
    Community College, Clatsop Community College,
    Concordia College, Eastern Oregon State College
 7. We don't know you, so we couldn't say what you
    would prefer, but Concordia would be our choice.

Unit 2

Selection 1A: Essay
"Culture Shock and the Problem of Adjustment in New Cultural Environments"

Comprehension (page 33)

 1. Culture shock is caused by the anxiety resulting
    from losing the familiar signs and signals of every-
    day life.
 2. *Step 1:* People are fascinated by the new culture.
    They enjoy nationals who can speak their language.
    Step 2: People become hostile toward the new cul-
    ture. During this stage people tend to band together
    with others from the home culture and criticize the
    host country with stereotypes.
    Step 3: Some knowledge of the language begins to
    open the way to the new culture. People take a

superior attitude toward the host culture, but
aggression is replaced by humor.
Step 4: Visitors accept the customs of the new
culture. They can operate without anxiety although
they still experience moments of social strain.
 3. F   4. F

Vocabulary from Context

Exercise 1 (page 34)
 1. occupational disease: illness caused by a particular
    job
 2. precipitated by: caused by
 3. props: supports; things that you depend on and that
    strengthen you
 4. cues: signals that guide behavior; information that
    indicates what to do
 5. to orient: to indicate location; to adjust or adapt to
    a particular situation
 6. to cope with: to adjust to, to deal with
 7. to tip: to give a small gift of money to a waiter, for
    example, for some service
 8. irrational: not logical; unreasonable
 9. pampered: treated very carefully as one would a
    child
10. petted: treated very gently
11. to grouse: to complain
12. nationals: people who belong to a certain nation by
    birth or nationalization; citizens
13. caricatures: exaggerated images that make fun of
    the thing being represented
14. indolence: laziness
15. fountainhead: source

Exercise 2 (page 35)
 1. transplanted: moved; relocated
 2. intercourse: interaction; interchange
 3. mentality: point of view; a characteristic way of
    looking at the world

Figurative Language and Idioms (page 35)

 1. "like a fish out of water"
 2. "band together"

Selection 1B: Essay
"Your Actions Speak Louder..."

Comprehension (page 39)

 1. F
 2. F
 3. F
 4. T
 5. T
 6. b: chronemics   d: kinesics   c: proxemics
    e: haptics   a: oculesics
 7. The doctor pointed her finger at the patient and
    beckoned him to come. She should have extended
    her arm and hand and beckoned by holding the
    hand out, palm down, opening and closing the hand
    repeatedly. To gesture an adult for silence in Ethio-
    pia, you put four fingers on the lips; in the U.S.
    you would bring only one finger to the lips.
 8. Move the side of index finger along the neck in a
    cutting motion.

Vocabulary from Context (page 40)

 1. prolonged   3. interface   5. channels
 2. arbitrary   4. to map out

Reading Selection 2: Mystery "The Midnight Visitor"

Comprehension Clues (page 43)

1. T   2. F   3. T   4. T   5. T

Max will not return because he jumped onto a balcony that did not exist.

Reading Selection 3: Conversation "Toledo: A Problem of Menus"

Comprehension (pages 47–48)

1. T
2. The tourist menu offers a good meal at a low price.
3. T   4. T
5. Michener was refused the tourist menu because he had not asked for it when he sat down.
6. T   7. T   8. T
9. a. The tourist menu did not include partridge.
   b. It only offered three dishes.
   c. It did not include the special wine.
10. F
11. following in order without interruption; consecutively; successively
    synonyms: running; straight
12. T
13. The man wore a tweed suit.
14. raunchy: offending; gamy; rotten
15. It was spoiled, rotten.
16. Well-hung partridge is partridge that has been left to hang without refrigeration before being cooked.
17. F
18. He didn't want the man to make a fool of himself.
19. inedible: unable to be eaten
20. This question is intended for discussion.

Vocabulary from Context (page 49)

1. à la carte: with a separate price for each item on the menu
2. surcharge: an additional charge
3. adamant: firm, inflexible, determined; unwilling to change one's mind
4. rotten: spoiled; decomposed; tainted; bad
5. abuses: insulting or coarse language
   also: mistreatment, injuries
6. to reprimand: to criticize formally or severely; to scold
7. gravely: seriously
8. objectionable: offending; disagreeable
9. enticing: pleasing; tempting
10. gamy: having a strong smell like that of cooked game; slightly tainted
11. raunchy: ugly, unpleasant; rotten
12. to console: to comfort; to cheer (a person) up after a disappointment
13. gingerly: carefully; cautiously; timidly; delicately

Unit 3

Nonprose Reading: Newspaper Advertisements (pages 50–52)

1. Lost and Found
2. Business Services
3. Wanted to Rent
4. Roommates
5. 800-4300
6. December 1
7. 2 ads under For Rent (Luxury A/C Studio, Efficiency); 1 ad under Sublet (To Sublet)

8. Early Hour Wake-Up Service
9. Jon or Pat
10. 800-6157, 800-6906
11. Bob
12. Babysitter—My home
13. 800-9846, 800-7487
14. 800-0557; Friday
15. No
16. There is a one-bedroom, modern, furnished apartment for rent. It costs $600.00 per months and has air conditioning. It is available after Christmas.
17. Moving: Must sell before Jan. 31. TV; A/C, misc. clothing, used refrig., artif. Xmas tree, elec. typewriter (avail. after Jan. 20). Call Bob, 800-7351 bef. 9 P.M.

Word Study: Stems and Affixes

Exercise 1 (pages 53–55)

1. c   2. a   3. b   4. c   5. c
6. telephone: an instrument that reproduces sound that comes from far away (*tele:* far; *phon:* sound)
   telegram: a written message sent far away (*tele:* far; *gram:* written)
   television: an instrument that produces a picture of something that is far away (*tele:* far)
7. when he or she wants to take a picture of something far away
8. support: to hold up physically or emotionally (*sup:* under; *port:* carry)
9. Interstate commerce is business between different states. Intrastate commerce is business within one state.
10. aqueduct: a structure built to carry (lead) water from one place to another
11. He is going bald; his hairline is moving back.
12. *post meridiem*
13. *Sub* means under or below. *Scribe* means write.
    a. When people subscribe to a magazine, they sign an agreement to buy the magazine for a certain period of time. They *write* their name at the *bottom* of a contractual agreement.
    b. To subscribe to a theory means to believe it or support it (figuratively, you sign your name in support of that theory).

Exercise 2 (pages 55–56)

1. to the contrary: against (this belief)
2. postpone: delay; put forward to a later time
3. supervisor: boss
4. remit: send back
5. superscript: symbol that is immediately above and to the right of another symbol
6. antibiotics: chemical substances that kill bacteria and other small organisms
7. transported: carried (from one place to another)
8. inexcusable: not acceptable; very bad; unpardonable
9. interaction: actions between two or more people
10. transmit: send
11. reconvene: meet (come together) again
12. revoked: called back
13. flexible: able to bend without breaking
14. portable: lightweight; capable of being carried
15. circumnavigate: sail around
16. imposed: placed (the tax) upon

Exercise 3 (page 56)

1. b	3. a	5. e	7. d	9. a	11. c
2. d	4. c	6. b	8. e	10. f	

Word Study: Dictionary Use (pages 57–58)

1. a. 1. adjective
      2. weak; exhausted
   b. 1. noun
      2. break
2. consecutively
3. a and c
4. b
5. a
6. a
7. a
8. a. runner: 8
   b. runway: 6
   c. runes: 1
9. b
10. b
11. ruralist
12. a. 2
    b. 1

Sentence Study: Comprehension (pages 62–63)

1. c   3. b   5. a   7. c   9. c
2. b   4. d   6. d   8. a

Paragraph Reading: Main Idea (pages 64–69)

Paragraph 1: c   Paragraph 3: d   Paragraph 5: c
Paragraph 2: d   Paragraph 4: a

Paragraph 6: A summit is a meeting between leaders of enemy Great Powers trying to reach agreements in order to avoid future conflict.

Paragraph 7: The ideals that children hold have important implications for their school experiences. Belief in the value of hard work, the importance of personal responsibility, and the importance of education itself contributes to greater success in school.

Poem: Our photo albums show our lives as we want to believe they were.

Discourse Focus: Skimming (pages 71–73)

1. no   2. yes   3. no   4. yes   5. yes

Unit 4

Selection 1B: Newspaper Article
"Parents Seeking Cool Classroom for Son"

Comprehension (pages 77–79)

1. He is unable to walk due to an auto accident in infancy.
2. His body is unable to control its temperature.
3. Above 78 degrees.
4. The district provided a transparent air-conditioned cubicle for Raul. The box was placed within the classroom.
5. F
6. F
7. His parents believe that the cubicle is too restrictive. Raul is unable to interact normally with his classmates and teacher.
8. This item is intended for discussion.
9. F (We know from paragraph 13 that the school district has already air-conditioned its high schools.)
10. T or F. You might answer true if you believe the statements of school district personnel. You might answer false if you believe that the school board could find funds if it wished to do so.
11. Based on the information in paragrah 13, the cost might be about $5,700.
12. T or F. You might answer true if you believe that the school board made the decision to air-condition high school classrooms based on the ability of the younger students to handle heat. You might answer false if you believe the decision was made for other reasons.

13. We could not think of any alternatives. Can you?
14–17. These questions are intended for discussion.

Vocabulary from Context

Exercise 1 (pages 79–80)
1. resume: start again
2. transparent: clear; capable of being seen through
3. alternatives: different choices; different possibilities
4. persuade: convince
5. restrictive: limiting; confining

Exercise 2 (page 80)
1. swelter   4. paraplegic   7. jealousy
2. peering   5. environment   8. discrimination
3. cubicle   6. dismayed

Reading Selection 2: Newspaper Questionnaire
"How Do You Handle Everyday Stress?"

Vocabulary (page 83)

attempt

Reading Selection 3: Magazine Article
"Graveyard of the Atlantic"

Comprehension

Exercise 1 (pages 86–87)
1. T   3. F   5. T   7. F
2. F   4. F   6. F

Exercise 2 (page 87)
1. 1,000
2. "curious glowing streaks of 'white water'"
3. 1973
4. ghost ship: a ship with no people aboard
5. Unique features include the swift Gulf Stream Current, underwater canyons, violent weather patterns, and the fact that compass needles point true north rather than magnetic north in the triangle.
6. Since all maps and charts are based on magnetic north, sailors who forget that in the triangle compass needles point true north, will find themselves off course.
7. This question is intended for discussion.
8. This question is intended for discussion.

Vocabulary from Context (pages 88–89)

1. unique: exceptional; odd; unusual; one of a kind
2. treacherous: unreliable; unpredictable; changeable; dangerous
3. freak: unusual; oddly different from what is normal; queer; abnormal
4. impassable: not able to be traveled through; not navigable
5. to vanish: to disappear
6. cargo: the load of articles carried by a ship; freight
7. malfunction: failure to function, perform, or work as it should
8. evidence: signs; indications; information
9. to attribute: to think of as produced by or resulting from
10. extraterrestrial: from outer space; not of this universe or planet
11. weird: strange; unusual; odd; queer; mysterious; eerie
12. eerie: weird; frightening; strange; unusual

Unit 5

Word Study: Context Clues

Exercise 1 (page 92)
1. hazy: not clear
2. to anticipate: to guess in advance; to think of ahead of time; to foresee
3. massive: large; heavy; clumsy
4. vague: not specific; not clear; imprecise
5. to appease: to satisfy
6. to provoke: to cause
7. to manifest: to show; to demonstrate
8. toll: total; count; extent of loss
9. wretched: poor; terrible; miserable
10. mammoth: large

Exercise 2 (page 93)
site: location; a place where something was located
occupation: habitation; settlement
NATURE: the title of a magazine
to resolve: to solve; to remove doubt about; to decide; to settle
disputes: disagreements; debates
firmly: definitely; positively; strongly; well

Word Study: Stems and Affixes

Exercise 1 (pages 94–96)
1. a	3. c	5. d	7. d	9. c	11. d
2. d	4. a	6. b	8. b	10. c	

12. Originally, *manufacture* meant to make by hand (*manu:* hand; *fact:* make). Now, products that are manufactured are often made by machine. Originally, *manuscripts* were books written by hand (*manu:* hand; *script:* write). Today, a manuscript is a document that is either handwritten or typed, but not printed; it is a document in prepublication form.

Exercise 2 (page 96)
1. beneficial: good (for)
2. mislaying: misplacing; putting in a place that is later forgotten
3. bilingual: speaks two languages
4. misbehave: behave badly; act the wrong way
5. anonymous: nameless; not named; without giving their name

Exercise 3 (pages 96–97)
1. e	3. c	5. d	7. b	9. d	11. e
2. f	4. b	6. a	8. f	10. c	12. a

Sentence Study: Comprehension (pages 98–99)

1. d	3. c	5. b	7. a	9. a
2. c	4. d	6. c	8. b	

Paragraph Reading: Restatement and Inference (pages 101–3)

Paragraph 1: b, d, e	Paragraph 4: b, d, e
Paragraph 2: b, d, e	Paragraph 5: a, b, e
Paragraph 3: a, c	

Discourse Focus: Careful Reading/Drawing Inferences (pages 104–6)

1. "Class Day": The museum authorities knew the communication was not an authentic one because of the manner of expressing the dates of the Pharaoh's reign. All B.C. dates are expressed in the reverse manner from A.D. dates. Thus, for example, Moses lived from 1571 to 1451 B.C. and Tutankhamen reigned from 1358 to 1350 B.C.

2. "Ruth's Birthday": Her bill smelled of the perfume she'd spilled on her purse.
3. "The Ex-Wife Murder": Rogers could not have known that his ex-wife had been shot unless he had guilty knowledge of the crime. The maid did not say why she had been taken to the hospital, yet Roger's first words on entering it were "Who shot her?"
4. "Case #463": Fordney knew that the dog had not bitten Miss Marshall because he found no teeth marks in the dress. She later confessed to inflicting the wound herself with a fork in the hope of collecting damages from Mrs. McGuire.

Unit 6

Selection 1A: Magazine Editorial
"A Burning Issue on the Job and Off"

Comprehension (page 108)

1. F
2. F (We assume that all educated adults know that smoking is a health hazard.)
3. F   4. F   5. T

Vocabulary from Context

Exercise 1 (page 110)
1. sirens: attractive, seductive women
2. brawny: strong, muscular
3. cowpokes: cowboys
4. seductive: strongly attractive; tempting, particularly in a sexual way
5. vice: moral failing; serious fault of character
6. linked to: related to
7. to sap: to use up; to weaken, exhaust, devitalize
8. to obscure: to hide from view; to make less intelligible
9. target: object; victim
10. obscene: immoral; indecent; disgusting
11. perverse: not right or acceptable; wicked
12. pernicious: evil; destructive; dangerous
13. incentive: reason; encouragement; reward that makes one work or achieve; motive; stimulus
14. condition of employment: requirement necessary to get and keep a job
15. personnel: employees
16. to fritter away: to waste; to use carelessly
17. to chatter: to talk about unimportant things
18. to flick: to use a light, quick motion [The definition of this term is best demonstrated nonverbally.]
19. butts: remaining ends; remaining parts of partially smoked cigarettes

Exercise 2 (page 111)
1. formulated: formed; made; developed; invented
2. withdrawal: the discomfort suffered when one attempts to end (draws away from) an addiction
3. dictate: control; say what people must do
4. premature: early; happening before maturity, before full development
5. counterproductive: not useful; the opposite of productive; producing effects opposite to those desired
6. maltreatment: mistreatment; unkindness; abuse
7. impose: force (place onto)

Figurative Language and Idioms (page 111)

1. "hard line"
2. "went cold turkey"
3. "the butt stops here"
4. "raising its ugly head again"
5. "going a giant step"

Selection 1B: Newspaper Advertisement
"Smoking in Public: Live and Let Live"

Recognizing a Point of View (page 113)

1. a, b, d (Note: you might also have checked *c*. It can be argued that in their attempt to portray smokers as just like everyone else, the advertiser wants us to like smokers.)
2. a, d
3. a, b, c, d

Evaluating a Point of View (page 114)

1. b, c

Selection 1C: Magazine Graphic
"Smoke Alert: Who's Puffing 5 Trillion Cigarettes"

Overview (page 115)

1. how much adults in different countries smoke; what total world cigarette consumption is; how cigarette consumption is changing in various countries; which countries are major cigarette exporters
2. 1,000 cigarettes consumed per capita (adults only)
3. They are leading tobacco exporters.
4. increasing

Comprehension (page 115)

1. 5.37 trillion
2. increased
3. increase; there will be increasing population growth in developing countries, which are being targeted by cigarette exporting nations, whose own people are smoking less.
4. U.S.
5. Cyprus
6. Egypt
7. Zimbabwe
8. because figures are shown only for major exporters and/or consumers and countries with a rise or fall in the rate of cigarette consumption of more than 50% between 1970 and 1985

Critical Reading (page 116)

1. by dividing the total number of cigarettes sold in a country by the total number of adults (people over 18?) in the country
2. The authors of *Reader's Choice* were surprised, for example, that "adult cigarette consumption per capita" in the U.S. is shown as much higher than in many other countries. We wondered if the U.S. figure was obtained by dividing the total number of cigarettes produced by the U.S. (instead of the number sold in the U.S.) by the number of adults in the U.S.

   Among possible explanations for surprising contrasts are the following. For countries with surprisingly high "adult consumption" rates: Perhaps there are large numbers of children smoking in these countries, but it is assumed that cigarettes are sold only to adults.

   For countries with surprisingly low "adult consumption" rates, we thought of two possible explanations. First, perhaps these are countries in which few women smoke. Therefore, even if adult male cigarette consumption were high, overall adult consumption would appear low. Second, perhaps these are countries in which many smokers roll their own cigarettes while the figures on the map reflect only the number of manufactured cigarettes consumed.

   It is also possible that our impressions of cigarette consumption rates in these countries are incorrect and that the map is correct.

Selection 1D: Magazine Exposé
"America's New Merchants of Death"

Comprehension (page 121)

1. T
2. T
3. They replace those who have quit smoking or have died. Also, if people are unlikely to begin smoking if they don't start when they are young.
4. T
5. Africa, Asia, Europe, South America, North America.
6. F
7. advertising nontobacco products and services named after cigarette brands
8. T
9. It associates smoking with fitness (health).
10. F
11. Young people around the world are interested in what is supposed to be a glamorous and wealthy U.S. lifestyle. If U.S. cigarettes can be associated with this lifestyle, the cigarette companies hope that young people will want to smoke their cigarettes.
12. F
13. The biggest market, with the most money to be made by cigarette companies, is China. It is a dream come true.
14. F
15. The U.S. government has threatened to impose tariffs against imports from countries that place restrictions on U.S. cigarettes.
16. Write to the President of the United States.

Vocabulary from Context

Exercise 1 (pages 122–24)

1. merchants: salespeople; buyers and sellers of things for profit; traders
2. promote: encourage; advertise; push
3. overseas: in other countries; outside the U.S.
4. appeal: attract; make attractive to
5. lured: strongly attracted; drawn
6. habit: a behavior you can't stop; addiction
7. addiction: habit; uncontrollable use of a harmful substance
8. succumb: give in to; are attracted by; yield to
9. deny: declare untrue; say it is false
10. devastating: destructive; ruining; very terrible
11. stockholders: those who own part of (stock in) a corporation
12. abroad: overseas; in other countries; outside the U.S.
13. ban: stop; get rid of completely; disallow the use of; prohibit; forbid; exclude
14. curtail: make less; reduce; curb
15. curbed: curtailed; controlled; reduced
16. violate: go against; fail go show respect for; break; disregard
17. spirit: meaning; purpose; idea; significance; sense; intent
18. insidious: harmful, but not obviously so; harmful, but

appealing; harmful, but taking a long time to show it's effects; sneaky
19. sponsor: pay for the cost of in return for advertising time/space; support
20. brands: company names; kinds
21. logo: a picture or design associated with a product, such as a camel for Camel cigarettes
22. pervasive: all around; everywhere; throughout every part; common
23. outrage: act causing injury; act that violates accepted behavior; mistreatment; therefore, acts that cause anger
24. barriers: actions that stop movement or action; actions that keep people and things out
25. retaliated: taken counter action; responded; given in return; countered; reciprocated
26. tariffs: charges; price charge; money charged by governments on imported products; duties
27. punitive: punishing; retaliatory
28. soaring: increasing at a great rate
29. booming: very high; developing rapidly; very strong; prospering; thriving; flourishing

Exercise 2 (page 124)
1. leaflet
2. original
3. classic
4. disregard
5. ally
6. prospects
7. fitness
8. theme

Exercise 3 (page 125)
1. passersby: people who are passing/walking by
2. giveaways: free gifts
3. frequented: regularly visited
4. domestic: national; within the country (U.S.)
5. growth industry: an industry that is expected to continue growing rapidly
6. timetable: schedule showing when things will be done

Figurative Language and Idioms (page 125)
1. kick their habit
2. begin as cobwebs end up as steel cables
3. sea of denim
4. joined forces
5. at the end of the rainbow
6. pave the way

Stems and Affixes (page 126)
1. c
2. d
3. e
4. a
5. f
6. b

Dictionary Study (page 126)
1. vt 1a or d
2. vt 3a
3. vt 3a
4. n 10

Vocabulary Review (page 127)
1. exported

2. sophisticated
3. invasion
4. addiction
5. devastating
6. machines
7. insidious

Reading Selection 2: Magazine Article "Conjugal Prep"

Comprehension (page 129)
1. F
2. T
3. housing, insurance, and child care
4. T
5. nine weeks; ten years
6. renting an apartment, having a baby, paying medical and other bills
7. a mother-in-law moves in, death, imprisonment
8. Some have found the experience "chastening to their real-life marital plans."
9. This question is intended for discussion.
10. This question is intended for discussion.

Vocabulary from Context (page 131)
1. mock: not real; imitation; false
2. to drown out: to cover (up) a sound
3. to giggle: to laugh nervously
4. adjustment: a change (made in order to fit a new situation)
5. to expose: to allow to be seen or experienced
6. nitty-gritty: basic; fundamental
7. trials and tribulations: problems
8. to strain: to weaken by force; to put pressure on
9. alimony: money paid to a former wife or husband
10. unsettling: disturbing
11. to endorse: to give support or approval

Reading Selection 3: Magazine Article "Sonar for the Blind"

Comprehension

Exercise 1 (pages 135–36)
1. They are unable to see and they are likely to be slow in intellectual development.
2. F
3. Dennis used clicking sounds to create echoes.
4. F   6. F   8. T
5. T   7. F
9. They help him distinguish objects on the right from those on the left.
10. a   11. c   12. c
13. The child covers his eyes to make another "disappear"; then he uncovers his eyes and shouts, "peek-a-boo!"
14. T

Exercise 2 (pages 136–37)
1, 3, 4

Vocabulary from Context (page 137)
1. handicap: disadvantage; hindrance; a difficulty that holds one back
2. to lag: to fall behind
3. echo: the repetition of a sound produced by reflection of sound waves off a surface
4. to orient: to locate
5. pitch: the frequency (number of repetitions in a

period of time) of vibrations of sound waves; higher frequency = higher pitch
6. to cope: to fight successfully; to be a match for; to manage; to handle

Unit 7

Nonprose Reading: Poetry

Comprehension Clues (page 141)

"Living Tenderly": a turtle
1. rounded   4. T
2. a short snake   5. F
3. F

"Southbound on the Freeway": a highway with motorists and a police car
1. The tourist is parked in the air.
2. They are made of metal and glass.
   a. Their feet are round.
   b. They have four eyes; the two in back are red.
3. the road on which they travel
4. a. They have a fifth turning red eye on top.
   b. The others go slowly when it is around.
5. a large roadway

"By Morning": snow
1. fresh, daintily, airily
2. transparent
3. a covering
4. They become like fumbling sheep.
5. snow

Word Study: Context Clues

Exercise 1 (page 142)
1. attributes: qualities; talents; abilities
2. to confer: to grant; to give to
3. plump: fat; chubby
4. pedantic: bookish; boring; giving attention to small, unimportant, scholarly details
5. aloof: above; apart from
6. to refrain: to hold back; to control oneself
7. ineffectual: not effective; not producing the intended effect
8. marigolds: a (type of) flower
9. drab: uninteresting; dull; cheerless; lacking in color or brightness
10. skin/cortex/membrane: outside cover of a body or organ; boundary

Exercise 2 (page 143)
babbling: meaningless sounds that babies make before they learn to talk
sequence: related group; series; the coming of one thing after another
hearing impaired: deaf; having problems hearing
myth: untruth; an untrue story or belief

Word Study: Stems and Affixes

Exercise 1 (pages 144–45)
1. b   3. d   5. b   7. c
2. c   4. d   6. b   8. a
9. An astronaut is a person who sails (travels) to the stars (outer space). (astro: star)
10. All the clothes look the same.
11. birth rate

Exercise 2 (page 146)
1. biographies: life histories
2. triplets: three children born at a single birth
3. multimillionaire: person who is worth many millions of dollars

4. metropolitan: a population area consisting of a central city and smaller surrounding communities
5. semiprivate: partly, but not completely private; a room with more than one person
6. multivolume: several-volume; consisting of more than one book
7. peripheral: (vision) away from the center, at the sides; having good peripheral vision means having the ability to see things on either side
8. semiprecious: of lesser value; semiprecious stones have lower value than "precious stones"
9. mortal wound: injury that causes death
10. periodontist: dentist concerned with diseases of the bone and tissue around the teeth
11. popularity: the state or quality of being popular; being liked by the general population

Exercise 3 (page 147)
1. f	4. d	7. c	10. e	13. a	16. b
2. e	5. c	8. a	11. d	14. f	17. e
3. a	6. b	9. f	12. b	15. d	18. c

Sentence Study: Restatement and Inference (pages 149–51)

1. c, e	3. b, e	5. b, d	7. b, c	9. a, c, d
2. b, c, e	4. b, c	6. d	8. b, d, e	10. b, e

Paragraph Analysis: Reading for Full Understanding (pages 155–60)

Paragraph 1
1. a	4. c	5. b	7. a
2. d	5. a	6. b	8. a
3. a	6. d		

Paragraph 2
1. c	3. b
2. c	4. c

Paragraph 3
1. d	3. a
2. d	4. c

Paragraph 4
1. c	5. c
2. b	6. a
3. c	7. c
4. a	

Paragraph 5
1. d	3. d
2. a	4. a

Discourse Focus: Prediction (pages 162–64)

There are no single correct responses to the items in this exercise. Students should work interactively: interacting with each other and the text in order to form predictions, then reading to see if these are confirmed. The answers, therefore, are available by further reading.

3. While there is no single correct answer, *a* and *d* are the most likely. The inset suggests that the author will *begin* by reviewing the current troubled state of calculus instruction.

4–5. These questions require a personal response.

6. This paragraph presents calculus instruction in a negative light: calculus is described as a *barrier;* students have *no choice* but to take it; calculus brings back *painful memories.* This very *general* introductory description might lead us to expect that the author will go on to describe *specific* aspects of the current state of calculus instruction.

7. This question is intended for discussion.

8. The final, transition sentence of the previous paragraph states that "participants brought worthwhile suggestions." One might expect that suggestions for change will follow.

9. This question requires a personal response.

10. This question is intended for discussion.

11. This question requires a personal response.

12. The rest of the article discusses suggestions for change and issues involved in implementing that change. Suggestions for change include utilizing the potential of handheld calculators to eliminate routine problems, thus concentrating on the central ideas of calculus. Other suggestions are to reinforce the important role of approximation and to streamline courses by eliminating much specialized material. In terms of implementation, issues discussed are the need for change in high school math curricula, for new textbooks, and for smaller university calculus classes.

Unit 8

Selection 1A: Magazine Article
"Crowded Earth—Billions More Coming"

Comprehension (pages 165–66)

1. F	4. T	7. T	10. F	13. T	16. F
2. T	5. T	8. T	11. T	14. F	17. T
3. F	6. F	9. F	12. T	15. F	18. F

19. decline in infant mortality; increased life spans
20. greater likelihood of violence and upheaval
21. It is based on the 1972 rate of increase. Factors include medical advances, birth control education, natural disasters, etc.

Selection 1B: Magazine Article
"World Population Growth Rate Slows"

Comprehension (page 168)

1. F	6. 2, 1, 3
2. T	7. T
3. T	8. F
4. F	9. T
5. F	10. T

Reading Selection 2: Magazine Article
"Why We Laugh"

Comprehension

Exercise 1 (pages 171–73)

1. T	4. T	7. F	10. T	13. T
2. T	5. F	8. T	11. T	14. F
3. T	6. F	9. T	12. F	

Exercise 2 (page 173)

1. 3 (4)   2. 4   3. 12   4. 8   5. 1   6. 2
(Other answers are possible for these questions.)

Critical Reading

Exercise 1 (pages 173–74)

1. Bergson: essayist
2. Grotjahn: psychiatrist
3. Levine: professor of psychology
4. Plato: philosopher

Exercise 2 (page 174)

1. Freud	3. author	5. author
2. author	4. Grotjahn	6. author

Vocabulary from Context

Exercise 1 (pages 175–76)

1. anxiety: uneasiness; worry; nervousness, tension
2. to resent: to feel displeasure; to feel injured or offended
3. conscious: aware; knowing what one is doing and why

4. tension: nervousness; anxiety; mental or physical strain
5. to disguise: to hide; to cover up; to make unrecognizable
6. aggressive: attacking; bold; energetic; active
7. butt: the object of joking or criticism; target
8. target: the object of verbal attack or criticism; butt
9. to master: to control; to conquer; to overcome
10. factor: any circumstance or condition that brings about a result; a cause; an element
11. crucial: of extreme importance; decisive; critical; main
12. to suppress: to keep from appearing or being known; to hide; to repress
13. to repress: to prevent unconscious ideas from reaching the level of consciousness; to suppress
14. drive: basic impulse or urge; desire; pressure
15. to discharge: to release; to get rid of; to emit; to relieve oneself of a burden
16. to trigger: to initiate an action; to cause a psychological process to begin
17. cue: a stimulus that triggers a behavior; a trigger
18. crisis: an emergency; a crucial or decisive situation whose outcome decides whether possible bad consequences will follow
19. guilty: having done wrong; feeling responsible for wrongdoing
20. integral: essential; basic; necessary for completeness

Exercise 2 (pages 176–77)

1. to intersperse: to put among things; to interrupt
   to avert: to avoid; to miss; to prevent
2. to inhibit: to suppress; to hide
3. foible: weakness; fault; minor flaw in character
4. to ogle: to keep looking at with fondness or desire
   dowdy: not neat or fashionable

Vocabulary Review (page 177)

1. cue	3. resent	5. aggression
2. trigger	4. conscious	

Reading Selection 3: Short Story
"The Lottery"

Comprehension

Exercise 1 (pages 181–82)

1. T	3. F	5. F	7. T	9. T
2. F	4. T	6. F	8. F	

Exercise 2 (page 182)

1. T	3. T	5. T	7. F
2. F	4. T	6. F	

Drawing Inferences (page 182)

1. Answers might include such things as the following:
   People were nervous.
   Tessie didn't want to win the lottery.
2. Answers might include such things as the following:
   Normal Lottery
   a. The whole village was present.
   b. Tessie's arrival was good-humored.
   c. Mr. Summers conducted square dances, teen clubs, and the lottery.
   d. The slips of paper and the initial ritual of the lottery seemed typical.
   Strange Lottery
   a. Piles of rocks were prepared.
   b. People hesitated to volunteer to hold the box.
   c. Some villages had already stopped having a lottery.

d. Mr. Warner considered such villages barbaric.
e. A girl whispered, "I hope it's not Nancy."
f. Tessie didn't want to win; she wanted to include her married children in the second drawing.

Double Meaning
a. There was no place to leave the box during the year.
b. The Watson boy blinked his eyes "nervously."
c. There were continual references to tension, nervousness, and humorless grins.
d. Mrs. Dunbar said to "get ready to run tell Dad."

3. They had to take part so that everyone would be responsible, so that everyone would have to take part next year.
4. Mr. Warner felt that giving up the lottery would bring bad luck and would be uncivilized. He represents the older, more conservative members of a society who resist change.
5. Tessie wanted more people to be included in the final drawing so that her chances of "winning" would be reduced.
6. *Changes in the Lottery*
a. The original paraphernalia had been lost.
b. The box had changed.
c. Slips of paper had replaced wooden chips.
d. There used to be a recital and ritual salute.

Unchanged Elements of the Lottery
a. The list of names was checked in the same way.
b. The black box was made with wood from the original box.
c. There were two drawings and the result of the lottery had remained the same.

Vocabulary from Context

Exercise 1 (page 183)
1. ritual: any formal, customary observance or procedure; ceremony; rite
2. paraphernalia: equipment; any collection of things used in some activity
3. drawing: a lottery; the act of choosing a winner in a lottery
4. gravely: seriously; soberly; somberly; solemnly
5. soberly: seriously; gravely; solemnly; sedately
6. murmur: a low, indistinct, continuous sound
7. to discard: to throw away, abandon, or get rid of something that is no longer useful
8. to disengage: to release oneself; to get loose; to leave

Exercise 2 (page 184)
1. boisterous 3. gossip 5. interminably
2. reprimands 4. fussing

Exercise 3 (page 184)
1. to devote: to give
2. stirred up: moved; shook; displaced
3. to fade off: to slowly disappear or end; to die out
4. shabbier: older; more broken down; worn out; showing more wear
5. to lapse: to fall away; to slip from memory; to return to former ways
6. craned: raised or moved
7. tapped: hit lightly
8. consulted: looked at; checked; referred to; sought information from

Unit 9

Nonprose Reading: Bus Schedule

Exercise 1 (page 186)
1. 20th Avenue
2. The schedule does not list the university; however, if you knew that the university was in downtown Denver, you would know that the bus goes near the university. The bus does go by the museum.
3. "Peak hours" are when the most traffic is on the road: 6–9 A.M. and 4–6 P.M. weekdays. Because the traffic moves more slowly, your ability to get to work on time may depend on this knowledge. Also, it costs more to ride the bus during peak hours.
4. $2.80 (round-trip: 70 cents per adult each way; children 5 or under may ride free)
5. Yes, you must have exact change or use tokens.
6. 573-2288
7. 778-6000 or 753-9405 (for hearing impaired)
8. Five cents

Exercise 2 (page 187)
1. Yes 2. Yes 3. F
4. During selected trips only (on days of Bronco football games)
5. Yes (on selected trips only)

Exercise 3 (page 187)
1. T
2. All 20th Avenue buses are accessible to wheelchairs.
3. The 8:55 A.M. bus will get you there 40 minutes early. The 9:57 bus will get you there 22 minutes late. You decide which bus to take.
4. The 6:07 P.M. bus
5. None
6. F
7. F
8. T or F. You might answer true if you believe that the amount of Spanish written on this schedule is sufficient to enable a speaker of Spanish to use it. You would answer false if you believe the amount of Spanish is insufficient.

Word Study: Stems and Affixes

Exercise 1 (pages 190–91)
1. hydroelectric (plant): a plant that uses water power to produce electricity
2. thermometer: an instrument that measures heat and indicates temperature
3. hyperactive: overactive; too active; abnormally active
4. to verify: to make sure it is true; to confirm
5. pedals: the parts of the bicycle moved by the feet to make the wheels turn
6. dehydration: loss of water from the body
7. tripod: a three-legged stand used to hold a camera
8. hypersensitive: overly sensitive; too easily hurt
9. hypodermic: a needle used to inject substances under the skin
10. orthodontics: a type of dentistry concerned with straightening teeth
11. deported: made (him) leave the country
12. per capita: individual; for each person
13. dermatologist: a doctor who treats skin diseases
14. geothermal: heat of the earth
15. bipedal: walked on two feet
16. veracity: truth
17. supersonic: faster than (above) the speed of sound

Exercise 2 (pages 191–92)

1. d	6. e	12. c	18. a
2. a	7. f	13. a	19. c
3. e	8. d	14. d	20. e
4. c	9. b	15. f	21. d
5. b	10. a	16. b	22. b
	11. c	17. e	

Sentence Study: Comprehension (pages 193–94)

1. d	3. a	5. c	7. b	9. b
2. b	4. c	6. a	8. d	

Paragraph Reading: Restatement and Inference (pages 195–97)

Paragraph 1: e   Paragraph 4: a (c)
Paragraph 2: a, b, c, d   Paragraph 5: a, d
Paragraph 3: b

Discourse Focus: Careful Reading/Drawing Inferences (pages 198–200)

1. "Murder on Board": Nathan Cohen was held because it would have been impossible for him to have written in small, precise handwriting during a violent storm.
2. "Death in the Mountains": It was a dark, starless, moonless night. No animal's eyes shine unless there is a light that can be reflected from them. A human's eyes NEVER shine under any circumstances.
   Wylie could not possibly have seen eyes shining at him in the dark. It was clearly murder.
3. "Case #194": If the newspaper account was correct, Mayer was lying. He could not possibly have been in the water, walked half a mile through ten below zero weather, and then shaken water from his clothes. Had the tragedy happened as he described it, the water on his clothes would have been frozen.
4. "The Break": Before ascertaining the killer's identity we will find out who is the mob leader.
   The leader is not Louis Segal (2). And he is not Anton Kroll or Sam Chapin (3), therefore the leader is Dan Morgan. Dan Morgan (the leader) is not the killer (4). The killer is not Louis Segal (2 and 4) and in (5) we learn Anton Kroll is not the murderer. Hence the man who killed Trooper Burton is Sam Chapin.

Unit 10

Selection 1A: Feature Article
"Japanese Style in Decision-Making"

Comprehension

Exercise 1 (page 203)

1. J	3. J	5. US	7. US	9. US
2. US	4. US	6. US	8. J	

Exercise 2 (page 203)

1. In Japan the most important thing is what organization you work for; in the United States one's position in a company defines one's professional identity.
2. See paragraphs 10 and 11, page 191, for explanations of the "I to you" and "you to you" approaches.
   See paragraph 16, page 191, for an explanation of Western versus Japanese decision-making.
3. a. The Japanese try to formulate a rather broad direction.

b. Westerners like to take time for in-depth planning.
4. Employees stay at work after hours, until the job is completed.
5. The author is Yoshio Terasawa, President of Nomura Securities International, Inc. The article was adapted from a speech before the Commonwealth Club of San Francisco.

Vocabulary from Context

Exercise 1 (pages 204–5)

1. to formulate: to form; to express in a systematic way
2. reliance: dependence
3. adroit: skillful; clever
4. confrontation: a face-to-face meeting, as of antagonists, competitors, or enemies
5. harmony: agreement of feeling, action, ideas, interests, etc.; peaceful or friendly relations
6. consensus: agreement in opinion; agreement among all parties
7. mutual: done, felt, etc., by two or more people for each other; reciprocal
8. literate: able to read and write; educated
9. articulate: able to express oneself clearly
10. stability: resistance to change; permanence
11. mobility: movement; change
12. exasperated: angered; irritated; frustrated; annoyed
13. deadline: a time limit
14. dedication: seriousness; loyalty; faithfulness; devotion to some duty
15. unanimous: showing complete agreement; united in opinion
16. homogeneous: composed of similar elements or parts; similar; identical; uniform
17. inflexible: not flexible; rigid; not adjustable to change; not capable of modification
18. unilateral: done or undertaken by one side only; not reciprocal
19. firm: company; business

Exercise 2 (page 205)

1. vocational: professional; relating to one's job
2. forthrightly: directly
3. densely: with many people in a small area; with the parts crowded together
4. consult: to seek information
5. impact: effect; influence
6. converted: changed

Figurative Language and Idioms (page 206)

1. "coming to grips with"
2. "for a living"
3. "sounding out"
4. "keeping (your) finger on the pulse"
5. "falls through"
6. "paper logjam"
7. "pitch in"

Vocabulary Review

Exercise 1 (pages 206–7)

1. adroit	4. exasperated	7. reliance
2. articulate	5. deadlines	8. formulate
3. transactions	6. dedicated	

Exercise 2 (page 207)

1. unilaterally	3. heterogeneous	5. inflexible
2. confrontation	4. mobility	6. unilateral

Selection 1B: Feature Article
"Happy Customers Matter of Honor among Japanese"

Critical Reading

Exercise 1 (page 209)
1. T   2. T   3. F   4. F   5. T

Exercise 2 (pages 209–10)
Apparently the author assumes the following to be typical of the United States:
1. *shopping for food:* Check-out counters typically have only one or two people ringing up and bagging food; stores do not deliver food to your home.
2. *purchasing a T.V.:* Customers install their own T.V. sets; technicians do not come to your home.
3. *getting a haircut:* In the U.S. barbers only give haircuts; they do not give massages or clean glasses.
4. *buying gas for a car:* In the U.S., the popular self-service gas stations do not provide the services available in Japan: putting gasoline in the car, wiping the windshield, emptying ash trays, stopping traffic to let the motorist back on the road.
5. *shopping in a department store:* Apparently the author finds fewer salespeople in department stores, and finds it unusual for purchases to be wrapped and for shopping to be done at home.
6. *staying at a hotel:* The author finds more personalized service in U.S. hotels: he expects to be personally greeted and, after a long stay, he expects the staff to know who he is.

Vocabulary from Context (page 210)
1. luxury: something adding to pleasure or comfort but not absolutely necessary
2. staff: group of workers; force
3. proprietor: owner
4. fuss: unnecessary bother
5. demeaning: degrading; making your status lower
6. ingredients: parts; constituents; things that a mixture is made of
7. treacherous: disloyal; untrustworthy
8. upscale: rich
9. courtesies: polite acts
10. on a national scale: nationally; throughout the country
11. proliferation: rapid growth; rapid increase in the number

Reading Selection 2: Satire
"Pockety Women Unite?"

Comprehension

Exercise 1 (page 213)
1. They hold better positions because they are men; cultural traditions and social conditioning have worked together to give them a special place in the world order.
2. 9
3. none
4. There is a positive correlation between pockets and power.
5. Pockets hold all the equipment necessary for running the world; they are necessary for efficiency, order, confidence.
6. It is difficult to organize one's belongings in a purse; a purse makes one appear to be disorganized.
7. Women should form a pocket lobby and march on the New York garment district. Women should give men gifts of pocketless shirts and men's handbags.

Exercise 2 (pages 213–14)
This exercise is intended to encourage discussion and to force students to come to a better understanding of the purpose of the article. Students can potentially defend all seven items.

Vocabulary from Context (page 214)
1. status: position; rank; standing
2. prestige: power to command admiration; distinction based on achievement; reputation; standing in the community
3. correlation: a close or natural relation; a correspondence
4. purse: a handbag, pocketbook; a bag in which money and personal belongings are carried
5. to attain: to gain through effort; to achieve; to come to, arrive at; to reach; to get

Dictionary Study (page 215)
1. match: (*n.* 1*a.*) a person, group, or thing able to cope with or oppose another as an equal in power, size, etc.
2. tip: (second entry, *n.* 2.) a piece of information given secretly or confidentially in an attempt to be helpful: as, he gave me a *tip* on the race. also: (*n.* 3.) a suggestion, hint, warning, etc.
3. lobbyist: (*n.*) a person who tries to get legislators to introduce or vote for measures favorable to a special interest that he represents. [a person who attempts to change a group's opinions]

Reading Selection 3: Poetry

Comprehension: "How to Eat a Poem" / "Unfolding Bud" (page 217)
1. a. Reading a poem is like eating because, to enjoy a poem, you bite into it; you make a poem part of you and it nourishes you. You "ingest" the poem: you pick it up, examine it closely, enjoy it, and put it inside you. You can enjoy every part of it; every part provides nourishment.
   b. The author is urging us to "get our hands dirty," to really experience and ingest the poem, to touch all parts of it.
   c. There is nothing to throw away; no part of a poem is left uneaten.
   d. Eating fruit is messier than eating bread, but it can be sweeter. Similarly, reading poetry can require taking more chances, making more guesses, but it too can be very satisfying.
   e. This question is intended for discussion.
2. a. Like a water-lily bud, a poem can appear at first to be closed. As we read, we open the bud, revealing the many wonderful things inside.
   b. We expect a bud to reveal a rich inner self; we forget that poems, too, reveal different colors and dimensions upon rereading.
   c. Both points of view suggest that one needs to examine poems closely, to fully appreciate them. Many differences might be mentioned. Among them is the fact that Merriam stresses the sensuous joy of consuming poetry, while Koriyama stresses the contemplation of beauty.

Comprehension: "This is Just to Say" (page 218)

1. People who don't like the poem mention such things as the fact that it lacks poetic rhyme and rhythm, is not on a lofty topic, and it contains everyday language. People who like the poem tend to enjoy its haiku-like format, its references to nature, and the simplicity of the presentation.
2. Although the note says, "forgive me," this is not primarily an apology. The writer does not seem to fear serious punishment.
3. Most readers agree that there is a degree of intimacy between the writer and the receiver of this note. They appear to live together. Students have suggested the following relationships between the two: spouses, lovers, child and parent, siblings. This may be considered a love letter.
4. The note may have been written to ask forgiveness, but the expression of intimacy and caring seems to be its primary purpose.
5. This question is intended for discussion.

Comprehension: "in Just-" (page 220)

1. The poem mentions spring weather (mud puddles), children's games (pirates, hop-scotch, jump-rope, marbles), and seasonal salespeople (the balloonman).
2. Eddie, Bill, Betty, and Isabel
3. mudluscious: the wonderful feeling of playing in the mud
puddle-wonderful: the fun of playing in puddles; for children, the wonder of a newly wet world
4. You can argue either that the poem evokes a happy springtime or suggests a sadder or more sinister theme. To argue for a joyful poem you can point to the use of words like *mudluscious* and *puddle-wonderful,* and to the joyful games of the children. A sadder theme is suggested by the description of the physical handicap of the balloonman who is referred to as *old* and *lame.* The balloonman is also described as *queer* and *goat-footed* (like the devil). If we change the title from "in Just-" to *injust,* it suggests that some injustice has or will occur. Is our view of the balloonman unjust, or will he perpetrate an injustice upon the children?
5. This question is intended for discussion.

Comprehension: "Spring and Fall: To a Young Child" (page 221)

1. a. Can you with your fresh thoughts care for leaves like the things of man?
   b. Neither the mouth nor the heart had expressed what heart heard of, ghost guessed.
2. *Goldengrove:* The initial capital letter indicates that this is the name of an imaginary place where a group of trees have turned golden during the fall season.
unleaving: The trees are losing their leaves.
wanwood: Wan is a colorless, sick color. The term suggests colorless, dead stems and branches.
leafmeal: In this context, meal refers to any substance with a powdered, grainy quality, e.g., corn meal. Leafmeal suggests a ground substance made of leaves. The leafmeal also apparently contains colorless, dead stems and branches.
3. Margaret is grieving for herself: like all living things she, too, will one day die.

Reading Selection 4: Short Story "The Chaser"

Comprehension: (pages 224–25)

1. F
2. F
3. a glove-cleaner or a life-cleaner
4. poison
5. T
6. She is sociable, fond of parties, and not interested in Alan.
7. Diana will want nothing but solitude and Alan; she will be jealous; Alan will be her sole interest in life; she will want to know all that he does; she will forgive him anything but will never divorce him.
8. T
9. The first drink is the love potion; the unpleasant "taste" is the fact that Diana will be so possessive; the chaser will be the poison (the glove-cleaner).
10. People who bought the love potion always came back for the $5,000 mixture.

Drawing Inferences (page 225)

1. Alan thinks the old man is describing love. The old man knows he is describing a terrible situation.
2. Alan thinks it is wonderful that his wife will never divorce him. The old man knows that some day Alan may want his wife to give him a divorce and she will refuse.
3. Alan thinks customers come back, as they do to any store, because they have found something there before that they needed; they come back of their own free will. The old man knows that if he "obliges" his customers with the love potion, they *must* come back.
4. Alan thinks the old man means goodbye. The old man means, "until I see you again"; he knows that Alan will return.

Vocabulary from Context

Exercise 1 (page 226)
1. poison: a substance, usually a drug, causing death or severe injury
2. imperceptible: not able to be perceived; unnoticeable
3. sufficient: enough
4. confidential: trusting; entrusted with private or secret matters
5. to oblige: to satisfy, please, help someone; to do a favor for; to perform a service
6. solitude: to be alone; isolation
7. jealous: demanding exclusive loyalty; resentfully suspicious of competitors; envious; distrustful; suspicious

Exercise 2 (page 227)
1. dim
2. stock
3. apprehensively
4. oblige
5. sirens
6. grounds

Exercise 3 (page 227)
1. peered: looked at closely and searchingly in order to see more clearly
2. potion: a drink, especially a medicine or poison
3. slip a little: make a mistake; fall into error; be unfaithful to his wife
4. dear: expensive
5. better off: wealthier; richer

Unit 11

Nonprose Reading: Road Map

Introduction

Exercise 1 (pages 228–29)
2. a. L-10
3. W. Trinity Lane and Whites Creek Pike
4. a. Bowling Green is about 25 miles/40 kilometers from the Ky.-Tenn. border.
   b. Route 31W is a Federal highway while route 65 is an Interstate highway.
      [*All* Interstate highways are multilane, divided, controlled access roads. In contrast, Federal highways have widely varying characteristics. For instance, although some Federal highways are divided, 31W is not.]
5. 66 miles (106 kilometers)

Exercise 2 (pages 229–30)
1. e   3. a   5. d
2. b   4. c   6. c

Map Reading

Exercise 1 (page 230)
1. T   3. T   5. T   7. T   9. T   11. F
2. F   4. F   6. T   8. F   10. T

Exercise 2 (page 231)
1. yes; 50 miles per hour/80 kilometers per hour
2. Answers might include such routes as the following:
   31W or 65 → 101 → 259 → 70
   or (31W) → 65 → 70
   You can spend the night at the Park.
3. Answers might include such routes as the following:
   56 (E. E. State Park) →40————→
                        →70 → 96 → 266 ↗

   231 (C. L. State Park) ————→ 40 or 41 (Nashville)

Word Study: Context Clues

Exercise 1 (page 235)
1. precariously: dangerously; uncertainly
2. to trudge: to walk tiredly, slowly
3. turmoil: confusion
4. grooming: personal cleaning; the act of making neat and tidy
5. matrimony: marriage
6. probe: a long slender instrument used for delicate exploration
7. to convene: to call together; to start
8. to ingest; to eat; to take inside
9. autocratic: dictatorial; undemocratic; tyrannical; domineering
10. limnology: fresh water biology

Exercise 2 (page 236)
genetic/genes: referring to biological inheritance; the elements by which parents biologically transmit characteristics to their children
rearing/reared: referring to the process of raising children, bringing them up. In this article nurture (child rearing) is contrasted to nature (genetics).
findings: discoveries; conclusions
shatter: disprove; destroy
primacy: being first in importance; supremacy
heredity: the biological process of passing on characteristics from parent to child
nurture: the act of raising, rearing; all the environmental factors that affect individuals as distinguished from their nature or heredity

Sentence Study: Restatement and Inference (pages 237–40)

1. d   5. c   9. b
2. a, b   6. a, c   10. a, d
3. a, b, c, e   7. b, c, d, e
4. a   8. d, e

Paragraph Analysis: Reading for Full Understanding (pages 241–46)

Paragraph 1
1. a   4. c
2. b   5. c
3. a

Paragraph 2
1. c   3. b
2. b   4. d

Paragraph 3
1. b   4. b
2. c   5. d
3. c

Paragraph 4
1. b   3. c
2. c   4. b

Paragraph 5
1. c   5. a
2. b   6. c
3. a   7. b
4. c

Discourse Focus: Prediction (pages 247–49)

There are no single correct responses to the items in this exercise. Students should work interactively: interacting with each other and the text in order to form predictions, then reading to see if these are confirmed. The answers, therefore, are available by further reading.
   1. This article is about changes in the family. You might expect to read about changes in such things as the size of families, the roles of family members, the role of families in society, or even the definition of the family. There are many other possible responses.
2–3. These questions require a personal response.
   4. b, d, i
5–6. There are many possible answers. Based on the mention of family members and the reference to definition, you might have listed such things as the roles of family members, the definition of the family, perhaps the size of the family.
   7. Because the opening sentence discusses changes in the historical view of family size and definition, you might expect to find historical data that speaks to these issues.
   8. This question requires a personal response.
   9. b, d, e, g, h, i, j

Unit 12

Reading Selection 1: Textbook
"The Sacred 'Rac'"

Comprehension (pages 253–54)

1. the Asu
2. They live on the American continent north of the Tarahumara of Mexico.
3. T
4. The cost is so high because of the long period of training the specialist must undergo and the difficulty of obtaining the right selection of magic charms.
5. T
6. It may be used as a beast of burden.
7. The Asu must build more paths for the rac; the Asu must pay high taxes; some Asu must move their homes.
8. F

9. The rac kills thousands of the Asu a year.
10. T
11. car

Drawing Inferences (page 254)

She feels that individuals and societies are foolish to sacrifice so much for cars. People often notice problems of other cultures more easily than those of their own culture. The author hopes that people in the United States will be able to examine the effect of the car on their society more realistically if they do not realize immediately that they are reading about themselves.

Vocabulary from Context (page 255)

1. preoccupied: absorbed in one's thoughts; unable to concentrate
2. temperament: disposition; emotional or psychological characteristics; frame of mind
3. prestigious: admired; important; distinguished; of a high rank
4. to treat: to give medical care to
5. ailing: sick
6. puberty rites: ceremonies that mark adulthood
7. to petition: to make a formal request; to ask; to beg
8. detrimental: damaging; harmful; injurious
9. to regard: to consider or think of as being something

Reading Selection 2: Essay
"The City"

Comprehension

Exercise 1 (page 259)
1, 2, 3, 6, 8, 10

Exercise 2 (page 260)
1. F
2. O author
3. F
4. O Frenchman
5. O others
6. F
7. O Jefferson
8. F
9. F
10. O generations of American theory; those responsible for the Homestead Act
11. F
12. O rural Americans

Vocabulary from Context

Exercise 1 (page 261)
1. suspect: viewed with mistrust; believed to be bad, wrong, harmful, questionable
2. priority: value, rank; the right to come first; precedence
3. absurd: ridiculous; silly
4. to subsidize: to grant money to, as the government granting money to a private enterprise; to support
5. predicament: a troublesome or difficult situation
6. integral: essential; basic; necessary for completeness
7. corrupt: spoiled; evil; bad; morally unsound; departing from the normal standard
8. despot: oppressor; dictator; tyrant; autocrat

Exercise 2 (page 262)
1. dispersion
2. fend (for)
3. renovation

Exercise 3 (page 262)
1. to trace: to find the source of something by following its development from the latest to the earliest time

2. flocking: coming in large numbers
3. antipathy: a definite dislike
4. pastoral: rural
5. charting: planning; plotting; mapping
6. waves: arrivals of large groups of people
7. ethnic: of or pertaining to nationalities
8. to bar: to stop; to prevent
9. fled: left; ran away from
10. subtle: indirect; difficult to understand, solve, or detect; clever; skillful

Selection 3A: Family Narrative
"An Attack on the Family"

Comprehension

Exercise 1 (pages 265–66)
1. F
2. T
3. When he switched on the torch, they would walk away. Also, the family would not allow him to bring scorpions into the house to study.
4. T
5. The babies clung to the mother's back.
6. F
7. when Larry went to light a match after dinner
8. Margo was trying to throw water on the scorpions but missed.
9. F
10. F
11. T
12. The author carried them outside on a saucer.
13. T

Exercise 2 (pages 266–67)
1. Roger is a dog.
2. Lugaretzia is not a member of the family; she is probably a servant.
3. five: Mother (f), Larry (m), author (m), Leslie (m), Margo (f)
4. Leslie
5. Larry
6. Margo
7. Mother
8. the author
9. This question is intended for discussion.

Vocabulary from Context

Exercise 1 (pages 267–68)
1. glimpses: brief, quick views; passing looks
2. enraptured (with/by): fascinated; enchanted; entranced; filled with pleasure
3. rage: extreme anger
4. bewildered: confused
5. plea: a request; appeal; statement of begging
6. courtship: the process or period of time during which one person attempts to win the love of another
7. to crouch: to bow low with the arms and legs drawn close to the body; to bend low; to squat
8. in vain: without effect; fruitlessly

Exercise 2 (page 268)
1. trial
2. to smuggle
3. doom
4. chaos, pandemonium
5. order

Exercise 3 (page 268)
1. assaults: attacks; invasions
2. clinging: holding on to
3. manoeuvred: managed or planned skillfully; manipulated; moved
4. maintain: argue; affirm; declare to be true

5. hoisted: pulled; lifted
6. scuttled: ran or moved quickly, as away from danger
7. peered: looked closely and searchingly, as in order to see more clearly
8. hurled: threw
9. drenched: made wet all over; saturated with water
10. swarmed: moved around in large numbers; completely covered something
11. screeching: screaming
12. reluctance: hesitation; unwillingness; a feeling of not wanting to do something

Selection 3B: Family Narrative
Adaptation from Cheaper by the Dozen

Comprehension (pages 274–75)

1. F	5. T	9. T	13. F	17. F
2. T	6. F	10. T	14. F	18. T
3. F	7. T	11. F	15. F	19. T
4. T	8. T	12. F	16. T	20. T

Vocabulary from Context

Exercise 1 (page 276)
1. litter: the total number of animals born at one time of one mother
2. whistle: a shrill musical sound made by forcing air through the teeth
3. regimentation: rigid organization by which tasks are assigned
4. aptitude: special ability, talent; quickness to learn
5. (on the) verge: on the edge; about to do something
6. hysterical: wild; emotionally uncontrolled
7. nuisance: a bother; an act, condition, thing, or person causing trouble
8. incentive: encouragement; reward that makes one work or achieve; motive; stimulus
9. voluntary: of one's own will; without being forced to do something
10. ludicrous: extremely funny; ridiculous; silly; absurd

Exercise 2 (page 277)
1. offspring: children
2. tender: young
3. slashed: cut
4. sweep: clean (a floor with a broom)
5. mimicked: copied; imitated
6. abstained: didn't vote

Figurative Language and Idioms (page 277)

1. "practiced what he preached"
2. "no telling"
3. "eat (me) out of house and home"
4. "fits (her) like a glove"
5. "deal him in"
6. "pulled (my) leg"

Dictionary Study (page 278)

1. off: (*adj.* 6.) not up to the usual level, standard, etc.: as, an *off* season
2. bedlam: (*n.* 4.) noise and confusion; uproar also: (*n.* 3.) any noisy, confused place or situation
3. allowances: (*n.* 3.) an amount of money, food, etc. given regularly to a child, dependent, soldier, etc.
4. to tickle: (*v.t.* 2.) to amuse; delight: as, the story *tickled* him.
5. straight face: [from the adjective straight-faced] showing no amusement or emotion

6. spit and image: [Colloq.] perfect likeness; exact image
7. offhand: (*adv.*) without prior preparation or study; at once; extemporaneously

Unit 13

Longer Reading: Psychology
"The Milgram Experiment"

Comprehension

Exercise 1 (pages 286–87)

1. F	4. T	7. F
2. F	5. F	8. F
3. T	6. T	9. F

10. The quotation marks around "subject" indicate that the man strapped into the chair is not the real subject. The real subject is the person who administers the shocks.
11–12. These items are intended to provoke discussion. There is no single correct answer.

Exercise 2 (page 290)
1. Milgram wanted to determine the extent to which people would obey an experimenter's commands to administer painful electric shocks to another person.
2. T
3. F
4. F
5. This item is intended for discussion.
6. F
7. The answer depends on your view of human nature. You might agree with Milgram, who believed that few people have the resources needed to resist authority. On the other hand, you might believe that people are sadistic and that they want to hurt other people.
8. a. T or F. You might answer true if you believe that the subjects were simply obedient and gave positive evaluations. On the other hand, you might answer false if you believe that the subjects rated the experiment positive for another reason—if, for example, they felt that they learned something.
   b. T or F. Your answer might be either true or false depending on your answer to 8a. If obedient subjects merely continued to respond obediently to the follow-up study, the answers would not reflect their true feelings.
9. T or F. You might answer true if you consider Stanley Milgram to be an ordinary person subject to the same pressures as the rest of us. On the other hand, you might answer false if you consider Milgram to have special knowledge about the experiment that he authored.

Vocabulary from Context

Exercise 1 (page 291)
1. rationalizations: excuses; explanations that are based on logical reasoning, but are essentially false
2. simulation: imitation; artificial situation created to resemble a real situation.
3. banality: commonness; ordinariness
4. controversial: full of controversy; causing argument or disagreement
5. ethical: having ethics; acting according to moral principles or beliefs

Exercise 2 (pages 291–92)

1. atrocities
2. ingenious
3. administer
4. subject
5. contrived
6. virtually
7. sadistic
8. debriefing

Figurative Language and Idioms (page 292)

1. "by lot"
2. "a cross section"
3. "chilling"
4. "fringe of society"
5. "has raged"

Unit 14

Longer Reading: Suspense
"The Dusty Drawer"

Comprehension (pages 302–4)

1. The answers to this question depend on the reader's perception of people and events. Students can potentially defend Tritt and/or Logan as answers to all items except a and e (we know from paragraphs 2 and 11 that Tritt is fat).
2. b, d, f, e, a, c
3. Tritt was a teller.
4. Logan was a professor of botany at a local university.

5. T	10. c	15. F	20. c
6. b	11. T	16. T	21. T
7. a	12. d	17. c	22. T
8. F	13. T	18. c	23. a
9. d	14. T	19. T	

Vocabulary from Context (pages 305–6)

1. obsequious: being excessively willing to serve or obey; extremely submissive; acting like a servant
2. to compel: to force
3. grimy: extremely dirty and greasy
4. to restrain: to hold back; to control
5. indulgently: patiently; kindly
6. version: an account showing a particular point of view; a particular form or variation of something
7. futility: uselessness; hopelessness
8. vengeance: injuring someone in return for an injury he has caused you; the return of one injury for another
9. cluttered: messy; confused, disorganized; filled with junk
10. hallucination: a product of the imagination; the apparent perception of sights, sounds, etc., that are not actually present
11. incredulous: unbelieving; doubtful; unwilling or unable to believe; skeptical
12. indignant: angry; scornful, especially when one has been improperly or unjustly treated
13. flustered: upset; confused; nervous
14. to jeopardize: to endanger; to put into danger

Figurative Language and Idioms (page 306)

1. "going a long, long way"
2. "get away with it"
3. "I'll get you"
4. "I can't stand to be had"
5. "pin (the robbery) on"
6. "polished off"
7. "a stick-up"

Dictionary Study (page 307)

1. to reflect: (v.i. 4.) to think seriously; contemplate; ponder (with *on* or *upon*) Note: the answer is misleading. Many people would consider *reflect* in this sentence to be a transitive verb. However, there is not an appropriate definition in the dictionary entry under *v.t.* An example of *reflect* used in an obviously intransitive sense is the following: After hearing that he had lost his job, John just sat for several minutes and *reflected*.
2. to stumble: (v.i. 5.) to come by chance; happen: as, I *stumbled* across a clue.
3. grip: (n. 5.) the power of understanding; mental grasp
4. to stake: (v.t. 5.) to risk or hazard; gamble; bet: as, he *staked* his winnings on the next hand.

Vocabulary Review

Exercise 1 (pages 308–9)

1. obsequiousness
2. go a long way
3. restraint
4. flustered
5. hallucinations
6. grime
7. get away with it
8. vengeance
9. grip
10. version
11. futile
12. compelled
13. clutter
14. reflect
15. incredulous
16. indulgent
17. indignantly
18. jeopardize

Exercise 2 (page 309)

1. obsequious
2. incredulously
3. futility
4. vengeance
5. indulgent
6. grime
7. jeopardize

Unit 15

Longer Reading: Anthropology
"In the Shadow of Man"

Comprehension

Exercise 1 (page 315)

1. T	6. T	11. T
2. F	7. F	12. T
3. F	8. F	13. F
4. F	9. T	14. T
5. T	10. F	

Exercise 2 (pages 315–16)

1, 2, 3, 5, 6

Vocabulary from Context (pages 316–17)

1. sophisticated: complex; complicated
2. innate: possessed from birth; inborn; not learned
3. posture: the position of the body; carriage; bearing
4. to hurl: to throw with force; to move vigorously
5. to stroke: to caress; to rub lightly with the hand
6. gesture: movement of the body or part of the body to express ideas, emotions, etc.
7. inevitable: something that cannot be avoided or prevented
8. altruistic: unselfishly concerned for another person
9. to derive: to get or receive (from a source); to trace from or to a source; to originate
10. submissive: humble; compliant; yielding to others
11. spontaneously: naturally; voluntarily; freely
12. to probe: to search; to explore with an instrument; to investigate with great thoroughness

Stems and Affixes (page 317)

1. c	6. d
2. e	7. h
3. f	8. j
4. a	9. i
5. g	10. b

Figurative Language and Idioms (page 317–18)

1. "spontaneously"
2. "to burst into tears"
3. "flew into a tantrum"
4. "told (him) off"
5. "to draw parallels"
6. "bowled over"

Vocabulary Review (pages 319–20)

1. sophisticated
2. gestured
3. inevitable
4. innate
5. hurled
6. burst into tears
7. Altruism
8. submissive
9. flew into a tantrum
10. probes
11. posture
12. spontaneously
13. draw parallels
14. stroking
15. derived